PENGUIN

T0276506

ECCLESIASTICAL HISTORY OF
THE ENGLISH PEOPLE

ADVISORY EDITOR: BETTY RADICE

Bede was born in 673. He himself tells us that he became a monk at an early age and lived most of his life at Jarrow. Scholar, teacher and writer, he wrote biblical and other works. He has been described as the 'Father of English History'. His historical works include *Life of Cuthbert* and *Lives of the Abbots of Wearmouth and Jarrow*, both in *The Age of Bede* (a Penguin Classic). Bede died in 735.

Leo Sherley-Price served in the Royal Navy for twenty-seven years, his last appointment being with the Royal Naval College, Greenwich. Subsequently he has been Rural Dean and parish priest in Devon. He has translated Thomas à Kempis' *Imitation of Christ*, Walter Hilton's *The Ladder of Perfection*, *The Little Flowers of Saint Francis* and a number of other historical and theological books. He is now retired and is Honorary Assistant priest at the church of St John the Evangelist, Bovey Tracey, in Newton Abbot, Devon, and he remains in active ministry.

D. H. Farmer (B.Litt. Oxon) was Reader in History at Reading University until 1988. He is author and editor of several books on ecclesiastical and monastic history such as *Benedict's Disciples* (2nd edition, 1999), *The Age of Bede* (a Penguin Classic, 1983), *St Hugh of Lincoln* (3rd edition, 2000) and *The Oxford Dictionary of Saints* (1978; 4th edition, 1997). This has been translated into Italian, Slovakian and Roumanian. A work on Anglo-Saxon missionaries in Europe is in preparation. He has also been principal consultant for the new twelve-volume edition of *Butler's Lives of the Saints* (1995–9).

BEDE

ECCLESIASTICAL HISTORY
OF THE
ENGLISH PEOPLE

WITH

BEDE'S LETTER TO EGBERT

AND

CUTHBERT'S LETTER
ON THE DEATH OF BEDE

The History *translated by*
Leo Sherley-Price
revised by R. E. Latham
Translation of the minor works,
new Introduction and Notes
by D. H. Farmer

PENGUIN BOOKS

PENGUIN BOOKS

UK | USA | Canada | Ireland | Australia
India | New Zealand | South Africa

Penguin Books is part of the Penguin Random House group of companies
whose addresses can be found at global.penguinrandomhouse.com.

This translation first published 1995
Reprinted with revised 1965
Revised edition 1968
Revised edition 1990

054

Printed in England by Clays Ltd, Elcograf S.p.A.
Set in Linotron Bembo

ISBN-13: 978-0-14-0445657

www.greenpenguin.co.uk

MIX
Paper | Supporting
responsible forestry
FSC® C018179

Penguin Random House is committed to a
sustainable future for our business, our readers
and our planet. This book is made from Forest
Stewardship Council® certified paper.

CONTENTS

Contents

Contents

Contents

Book Two

BOOK THREE

Contents

Contents

BOOK FOUR

Contents

Contents

BOOK FIVE

Contents

Contents

BEDE'S LETTER TO EGBERT

CUTHBERT'S LETTER ON THE DEATH OF BEDE

ACKNOWLEDGEMENTS

❧

L IKE all previous editions of Bede's Ecclesiastical History this one depends on the pioneer work of Charles Plummer in *Baedae Opera Historica* (Oxford, 1896 and 1956). Grateful recognition is also made to the edition and notes of B. Colgrave and R. A. B. Mynors (Oxford, 1969) and to the historical commentary by J. M. Wallace Hadrill (Oxford, 1988), which have been invaluable in providing much material for this work. Among more recent writers James Campbell, first in his essay on Bede in *Latin Historians* (ed. T. A. Dorey, 1966) and then in *The Anglo-Saxons* (1982), has placed all scholars in this field in his debt. At a late stage of preparation David Howlett and Richard Sharpe (of the *Dictionary of Medieval Latin from British Sources*) gave generous help, especially in the preparation of the subsidiary texts and the footnotes. For any errors none of these benefactors are responsible.

LIST OF ABBREVIATIONS

AB	J. F. Webb and D. H. Farmer, *The Age of Bede* (Penguin Classics 1989)
ASE	*Anglo-Saxon England* (periodical, 1972–)
Campbell	J. Campbell, ed. *The Anglo-Saxons* (1982)
CCSL	*Corpus Christianorum Scriptorum Latinorum*
Colgrave and Mynors	B. Colgrave and R. A. B. Mynors, *Bede's Ecclesiastical History* (Oxford 1969)
EHD I	D. Whitelock, ed., *English Historical Documents*, vol. I (1968)
Famulus Christi	G. Bonner, ed., *Famulus Christi* (1976)
Kirby	D. P. Kirby, ed., *St Wilfrid at Hexham* (Newcastle 1974)
ODS	D. H. Farmer, *The Oxford Dictionary of Saints* (Oxford 1987)
ODCC	F. L. Cross and E. A. Livingstone, *The Oxford Dictionary of the Christian Church* (Oxford 1974)
PBA	*Proceedings of the British Academy*
Plummer	C. Plummer, *Bedae Opera Historica* (Oxford 1956)
WH	J. M. Wallace Hadrill, *Bede's Ecclesiastical History: a Historical Commentary* (Oxford 1988)

INTRODUCTION

Bede's *History*, the first account of Anglo-Saxon England ever written, has always been highly esteemed. Bede was a monk of Jarrow who worked on this book for several years before completing it in 731. Over the next fifty years it was copied in Northumbria and elsewhere (four eighth-century manuscripts survive), and it became widely diffused in western Europe throughout the Middle Ages. It was first printed in *c.* 1480 and nowadays it enjoys a wider distribution than ever before.*

The *History* is readable and attractive. Whether he writes of the geography of Britain (i. 1), the coming of Augustine (i. 26), the Northumbrian council concerned with the acceptance of Christianity (ii. 13) or the achievements of Abbess Hilda and the poet Caedmon (iv. 23–4), Bede's insight, empathy and concision are evident. Elsewhere his descriptions of natural phenomena such as the recovery of a horse from illness (ii. 9), the speech therapy provided for a boy (v. 2) and the supernatural experiences of the visionary Drythelm (v. 12) reveal his talent as a descriptive writer. Even more important, his power of synthesis, making a coherent whole from fragmentary elements, together with his telling use of original sources, make him a fine historian.

The few known details of his life are soon told. The last chapter of the *History* (v. 24) is our principal source, and this is completed both by Bede's *Lives of the Abbots* (*AB*, pp. 185–208) and by the monk Cuthbert's account of Bede's death (see below, pp. 357–60).

Bede tells us that he was born in 673 on land owned by the

monastery of Wearmouth. He was offered to its abbot, Benedict Biscop, seven years later for his education. A few years afterwards, he moved to the new foundation of Jarrow under the care of Abbot Ceolfrith: here he remained for the rest of his life. In his early days there, as the anonymous *Life of Ceolfrith* records, a young boy and the abbot were the only two monks capable of singing the Divine Office 'with antiphons' after the plague had swept through the monastery. It seems highly probable, if not absolutely certain, that this young boy was none other than Bede himself.*

Bede was ordained as a deacon at the age of nineteen by John, Bishop of Hexham, and priest at the age of thirty. For the rest of his life he gladly took part in the Liturgy and other exercises of the community, but was particularly drawn to study, teaching and writing. The study was concerned principally with Latin and the Bible. It may well be claimed that the principal element in his formation as a scholar was the Latin Bible. This was the central element of the monks' sacred reading. Its entire text was copied with meticulous care at least three times in Ceolfrith's abbey. One of these massive one-volume Latin bibles survives complete in the Bibliotheca Laurenziana at Florence; another fragment of a few pages is in the British Library. It is possible but not certain that Bede as a young monk worked on one or more of these volumes.*

In Bede's lifetime, not only was Jarrow a centre of excellence for study, thanks to the acquisition of books from Italy and France by Benedict Biscop and Ceolfrith, but the whole environment reflected a cultural standard achieved by few others at the time. The churches were built of stone and adorned with panel paintings brought back from the Continent, and it is now known, thanks to recent archaeological excavation, that there was a flourishing stained-glass workshop. In 716 the two abbeys of Wearmouth and Jarrow housed 600 monks. It is likely that Jarrow was the smaller monastery of the two: the restricted site (not yet fully excavated) would hardly be able to house 200 monks.*

Bede's teaching and writing were based on the resources of

the library. These included Latin grammars, books of computistics and chronology, history, hagiography and patristic commentaries on the Bible. Much of Bede's teaching must have been basic. Most monks, when they arrived at the monastery, would have been ignorant of Latin and may have been unable to read their native tongue. After some years of learning Latin they would advance to the other subjects already mentioned.

Bede regarded himself primarily as a biblical commentator: the number and size of these works far exceed his others. His sermons also reveal him as a contemplative scholar whose world was that of the mysteries of the Christian faith. Not being a speculative genius like Augustine or Aquinas, he might have been thought of (in patristic terms) as one who ruminated like the ox rather than one who soared like the eagle. His commentaries on nearly every book of the Bible have seemed unoriginal and derivative to many, but they at least provided admirable digests of patristic commentary to preachers in England and overseas in an age when books were very scarce and very expensive. Moreover Bede's use and skilful editing of his sources often makes his works more valuable than at first appears.

Most readers now think of Bede primarily as a historian. His *History* was the work of his mature years, completed when he was aged about sixty. His earlier works of chronology, computistics and hagiography prepared him, in different ways, for his masterpiece. The details of dating, including his personal contribution of popularizing 'AD' dating, carefully worked out in harmony with imperial 'indictions', formed an indispensable tool for his task. Indeed his professional interest in computing Easter dates is sometimes obsessively present in the text of his *History*. His previous experience in recording the lives of Cuthbert and of the Abbots of his own monastery also prepared him well for narrating the achievements of other worthies. In addition to these works, his main output of biblical commentaries was completed and continued by the *History*.

This was entitled, very precisely, *An Ecclesiastical History of the English People*. It was a Church history, not a political, economic or social history. Inevitably, however, some of these elements were included in the story of the progress and development of the Christian Church. Also it concerned the English people, that is, the Germanic peoples who settled in England and who are generally known as the Anglo-Saxons (see i. 15, v. 9 and notes). The Church in Anglo-Saxon England, rather than the Church in Ireland, Scotland or Wales, was Bede's subject. Bede wrote in Latin like all scholars of his time and this ensured that his work would be read in western Europe as well as in England. He dedicated the work to Ceolwulf, King of Northumbria, who presumably knew enough Latin to understand it. The style was simple, the content attractive. Clerical readers would be much more numerous than lay ones. Bede, fine Latin scholar though he was, also understood and provided for laypeople's needs by translating prayers and the Scriptures (see pp. 340, 358–9). He also emphasized the importance of Caedmon and vernacular poetry in the spread of Christianity in his day (iv. 24). This was an integral part of the progress of the Church and so it deserved mention beside the other fine contemporary achievements. Bede completed his *History* in 731. His *Letter to Egbert* shows more clearly its enduring difficulties and limitations. This was written in 734, the year before he died. Cuthbert's moving account of his death (pp. 355–60) was written soon afterwards.

Sir Frank Stenton wrote of the *History* over fifty years ago:

> The essential quality of Bede's History carries it into the small class of books which transcend all but the most fundamental conditions of time and place . . . the quality which makes his work great is not his scholarship nor the faculty of narrative which Bede shared with many contemporaries, but his astonishing power of co-ordinating the fragments of information which came to him through tradition, the relation of friends, or documentary evidence. In an age when little was attempted beyond the registration of fact, he had reached the conception of history.*

In most ways this judgement still stands, though Bedan studies have moved fast in recent years. His text has been rightly subjected to much critical scrutiny. His motives, his limitations and his omissions have all been examined in detail. More clearly than formerly have his regional bias, his academic partisanship and the paucity of his sources been revealed.

There has also been enrichment from other directions. Archaeologists have made and are still making important discoveries. Sometimes these seem to contradict Bede's statements; often they simply complete them. Recent studies of Christianity in Ireland and Wales throw further light on realities adjacent to, rather than in the centre of, Bede's outlook.* Bede did not know everything, nor did he always tell us all that he knew: sometimes he oversimplified complex realities, sometimes he concentrated on the didactic value (as he saw it) in a particular narrative.

Another valuable insight which has developed since Stenton's time is that Anglo-Saxon society is now seen to resemble Frankish society far more closely than was previously thought. The roles of the kings and the military aristocracy as well as the laws were similar on both sides of the English channel. The Frankish Church had a notable share in the development of the Church in Anglo-Saxon England. Gregory of Tours, its historian, was a bishop much involved with the Merovingian court. He explicitly narrated in considerable detail the frequent violence which took place there. Bede's treatment of court life (which he probably never experienced) gives the impression of far greater tranquillity. Was this because the realities were different, or because each writer reflected his own life-style in his narrative? It is not always easy to say, but it seems certain that Anglo-Saxon society was more violent than Bede makes out.*

Yet a further growth point is the increasing realization of the importance of Bede's biblical works as a key to understanding the *History*. These throw light on Bede's purpose in writing and help us to understand him better as a person and a scholar. Sometimes they shed light on his miracle stories, his ideas of

kingship and his concept of history in terms of the realization of
the divine plan for mankind.★

In the realization of his task Bede had to use the few sources
available and was often at a considerable chronological distance
from the events he related. It is easy to forget that he was 130
years distant from the coming of Augustine and 300 from the
arrival of the Anglo-Saxons in England. Hence Bede's first book
has been criticized more than the others. Here he inevitably
depended heavily on Gildas, whose *Liber querulus de excidione
Britanniae* is more of a homily than a history. Explicitly dependent on the biblical account of Jeremiah, it saw the downfall of
the British in terms of Israel's fall to the Assyrians. It had little
good to say about the rulers of this people, and Bede shared the
belief that the invaders, although pagan, were instruments of
God's punishment of an unworthy people.★ Later, unknown to
Bede, Gildas emerged as an important abbot and teacher who
helped to link the churches of Ireland and Wales.

Bede's famous account of the Angles, Saxons and Jutes,
however, reflected the political realities of his own time rather
than the archaeological realities to which he had no access. It is
now recognized that the Anglo-Saxon invasions were a long,
gradual settlement lasting about 200 years, that the invaders
were much more mixed in the same areas than Bede supposed,
that the kingdoms were 'made in England' and that the native
population survived, especially in the West, in a stronger and
more coherent state than was previously supposed. However,
by the time Augustine arrived (and Columba of Iona died) in
597, the invaders were in firm political control of most of what
is now England. Their settlements were numerous and were
usually outside the decayed old Roman towns. Their living
standards were reflected by the wealth of Sutton Hoo and the
grandeur of the poem *Beowulf* at royal level, but also by ground-
house settlements at Sutton Courtenay and elsewhere at a
peasant level.★

These considerations are largely supplementary to Bede's own
information. What did this consist of? What sources were
available to him? What was he trying to do? Bede gives us most

of the answers in his Preface, which was addressed to the literate King Ceolwulf, who subsequently abdicated and became a monk at Lindisfarne.

Bede listed his contemporary sources not his ancient ones. The latter had included Orosius, Pliny and Solinus as well as Gildas and the *Life of Germanus* by Constantius. In the Preface Bede was concerned with more recent and regional correspondents. These came from different areas of Anglo-Saxon England, but none were from Celtic Britain.* Abbot Albinus of Canterbury, who ruled there from 709 to 732, was not only the principal source for Kent, but also the animator of the whole project. His scholarly assistant, the London priest Nothelm, researched the papal archives at Rome for letters of Gregory the Great and later popes relating to England. These letters were inserted by Bede, it seems, into a narrative already begun. Bede may have lived long enough to learn of Nothelm's promotion to the See of Canterbury in 735; he died in 739. Other correspondents included Daniel, Bishop of Winchester (who also wrote to St Boniface), the monks of Lastingham (who provided information about Chad, Cedd and the Mercian apostolate), the otherwise unknown Esi the abbot (who covered East Anglian affairs) and above all 'countless faithful witnesses' from Northumbria. These must have included members of his own community as well as that of Lindisfarne, where Bede was well known since he had written his *Life of Cuthbert* at their request in 721. Information concerning Columba, Aidan and the final reconciliation came from Iona. Other written sources included Eddius' *Life of Wilfrid* and the anonymous lives of Gregory, Cuthbert and possibly Ceolfrith. Bede was the most eminent writer in eighth-century Northumbria, but by no means the only one.

The Preface tells us not only about sources, but also about why Bede was writing. The modern reader cannot fail to notice Bede's explicit moral purpose. Glossing Tacitus, he wrote: 'if history records good things of good men, the thoughtful reader is encouraged to imitate what is good; if it records evil of wicked men, the devout reader is encouraged to avoid all that is sinful and perverse.' Hence King Ceolwulf wanted Bede's *History* to be diffused for the good of the people over whom he ruled. The *History*, however, is not just a gallery of good and bad examples, but a coherent narrative in which these examples are introduced within the context of a fuller story. The examination both of Bede's models and of his limitations should throw further light on this topic.*

At first sight Bede had no models: his was a pioneering work without any exact precedent. In fact he owed much to earlier historians. The most important of these was Eusebius, the fourth-century Bishop of Caesarea, whose *Ecclesiastical History* recounted the story of the Christian Church from Pentecost until his own times: how it spread through the Roman Empire in spite of numerous persecutions, how the bishops succeeded one another and how they resisted the evil influence of heretics. Bede, who knew Eusebius in Rufinus' Latin translation, tried to do for the Church in Anglo-Saxon England what Eusebius had done for the Church as a whole. For each the history of the Church was simply a development of the story of the *Acts of the Apostles*. Just as Christ's apostles had worked, preached and suffered to establish the Church in obedience to Christ, so did their successors in whatever time or place. Bede wrote his commentary on *Acts* during part of the time when he was also writing the *History*. If persecution and martyrdom were lacking in the account of the Christianization of England, there was no lack of signs or miracles. Both Eusebius and Bede expected these to accompany the pioneering spread of the Gospel. Contrary to previous opinions, it is clear that both sophisticated Romans and uncultured barbarians expected religion to be accompanied by miracles of one kind or another.*

In view of this, it is unsurprising that Bede's *History* contains miracle stories. Not all have the same explanation: some were probably the result of natural forces, psychological factors or apparent coincidence. But all contained some marvellous element (*mirum*) which revealed God's power and care. Some of the stories reveal significant detail of interest to the historian. Although many of them seem to be a stumbling block to the modern reader, their absence would have been an even greater difficulty to Bede's contemporaries.

Other earlier historians to whom he owed a debt include Gregory of Tours, whose *History of the Franks* is very different, but from it Bede took the idea of a final autobiographical survey. The task which Bede set himself was extraordinarily difficult. Pre-Christian Anglo-Saxon society had virtually no documents and no books. Laws and property transactions were promulgated by the king's word. There was however a lively oral tradition of poetry. Even after the coming of Christianity, written records of all kinds were very few. Bede made the best of what there was: papal letters, episcopal lists, conciliar documents as well as the sources mentioned above. It was Bede's skill which made coherent a number of disparate and scrappy elements.

The main theme of the *History* was the progression from diversity to unity. This was an idea worked out by Gregory the Great, whom Bede admired so much both as a teacher and as the apostle of the English. Both aspects are incorporated in his admirable panegyric (ii. 1). Bede began his work with a geographical and racial survey of Britain (i. 1). He saw Christianity as the unifying force which brought together Picts, Irish, Angles, Saxons, Jutes and, hopefully, Britons. A principal sign of this unity was the common celebration by all on the same day of the principal Christian mystery, that of the Passion and Resurrection of Christ. That was why any deviation or schism caused by rival calculations of Easter was so unacceptable. Bede's concern, almost obsession, with this issue shows itself repeatedly in his judgements on Welsh and Irish Christians, even St Aidan (iii. 17). It also explains the great length of his account of the Synod of Whitby, the dramatic centre-piece of the whole work (iv. 25). The technical details of the 'Roman' calculation of the Easter date are explained at great length in Ceolfrith's letter to Nectan (v. 21). This is immediately followed by the account of Iona's conformity to this reckoning in 716. The remainder of Book V is interesting summary material, added after the main point has been made.

Whitby was an important turning point, but Bede's full treatment still left much unsaid. Bede nowhere says clearly that the bulk of the Church in Ireland had already accepted the 'Roman' calculation long before. The point which affected England was that Iona and its dependencies had not initially done so; hence the divergence in Northumbria which Bede deplored. The account in Eddius' *Life of Wilfrid* is much shorter, but substantially identical. It reports the speeches of the main protagonists, Colman and Wilfrid, at considerably less length than Bede. Bede no doubt used the historical convention, deriving from Thucydides, of 'composing' speeches to suit the convictions of the characters, but there is no need to suppose that he seriously distorted either.

A point often noted in Bede's account was that both King Oswy, the convoker, and Abbess Hilda, the hostess of the assembly, had initially favoured the Iona case. Eddius' account depicts the king accepting the decision of the Synod in favour of Rome, manifested by a choral recitation of the 'Thou art Peter' text from St Matthew's Gospel, but 'with a smile'. Some have asked if the smile was one of relief that he had warded off imminent political danger from his son Alcfrith, the patron of Wilfrid. Bede said nothing of this dimension: he rightly stressed that the Whitby decision was one for universalism against localism. This was the principal point of Wilfrid's speech rather than the pseudo-historical arguments (advanced by both sides) about the supposed apostolic origins of their own calculations of Easter.

The consequences of Whitby were important and permanent. Although it was called primarily to solve Northumbria's problems, delegates came from other kingdoms too. The dispute about the date of Easter, it must be stressed, was not one of doctrine but of discipline. Neither side was heretical, but feeling ran high on both sides. In the event, many good ecclesiastics like Cuthbert, who had been trained in the Iona-Lindisfarne tradition, changed sides and accepted the decision. In the longer term the thirty years' ascendancy of Lindisfarne was replaced by

Canterbury. The decision was made obligatory for all in England by the next Archbishop of Canterbury, Theodore; he was neither English nor Irish, Italian nor Frankish, but Greek and appointed by the papacy. This was an inspired but unexpected choice. Theodore was a monk and sixty-six years old; his long tenure of office and his numerous reforming policies made him the most important Archbishop of Canterbury between Augustine and Dunstan. Theodore was one of Bede's heroes: monk, teacher and reorganizer of the Church.

He had no contemporary biographer, but some of his theological works have recently been discovered.* His work of training the clergy through his schools at Canterbury and his policy of dividing large dioceses met with Bede's full approval (see below, pp. 214, 339–43). In the wider context of the missions of Anglo-Saxons to Frisia and Germany, Theodore's well-organized and educated Church provided the model for both Willibrord and Boniface. Like Canterbury, both Utrecht and Mainz became metropolitan Sees, which reflected and increased papal influence in the Western Church.

How did Bede succeed in his self-appointed task? In most ways remarkably well. This however does not mean that he had no limitations. Like all people of his time he had strong regional sympathies. This was inevitable in an age before there was a single king or government of all England, which came two centuries after Bede's death. Even then, regionalism was far from dead. Bede had a Northumbrian viewpoint and Northumbrian events figure more prominently than those of other regions. He did however try to transcend this limitation. He had a knowledge of both East Anglia and the Isle of Wight which must have been unique for a Northumbrian monk; thanks to his correspondents, he also knew much detail about Kent and Sussex. It is in his attitudes to the two larger kingdoms, Mercia and Wessex, that his regionalism shows. Mercia, with its king Penda, had in Bede's view been the aggressive pagan force whose alliance with Christian Gwynedd had resulted in the death in battle of Edwin, the first Christian king of Northumbria, which was followed by a year of persecution and slaughter that the chroniclers erased from the annals. His successor Oswald also died by Mercian hands. Later, after the conversion of Mercia, Bede noted with anxiety its growing power; by the time he was writing the *History* Northumbria's exceptional political predominance was on the wane.

With regard to Wessex the problem was somewhat different. Bede's sources were slight, and his omissions significant. He had little to say about King Ina and his justly famous law-code and nothing at all about Boniface, whose missionary achievements far surpassed those of any Northumbrian evangelist. From Ina and from the Boniface correspondence, to say nothing of the interesting but turgid writings of Aldhelm, we can deduce the existence of a confident and developed Christian life with flourishing monasteries, which could not be suspected from Bede's text.*

Bede's ambivalent attitude to Celtic Christians has often been noted. He admired the Irish bishops and abbots, whom he regarded as personifying the simplicity and poverty that had apparently become rare by 731. His repeated reservation about them was their attachment to an Easter calculation which seemed to him wrong. The warmth of his appreciation of Aidan and Columba was not matched by appreciation of any comparable Welsh bishop or monk. For Bede the difference was that the Welsh had persistently refused to evangelize the Anglo-Saxons from the time of Augustine and earlier. Moreover they had joined with pagan Penda of Mercia in the invasion of Northumbria and in the atrocities which had followed (ii. 20). Bede could not forget these events.

His personal sympathy for Irish apostles in Northumbria should be compared with his deeper loyalty to Rome. For him Gregory, rather than either Augustine or Aidan, was the apostle of the English (ii. 1); his own abbots, Benedict Biscop and Ceolfrith, had repeatedly visited Rome and brought back books, relics and paintings; Bede also attested with approval to the growing practice of pilgrimage to Rome by kings, bishops, monks and others (v. 7, v. 19, etc.). Bede was an outstanding

writer of Latin and a staunch supporter of the 'Roman' calculation of Easter. In contrast, his reserved attitude to Bishop
Wilfrid has often been noted (see Kirby, pp. 35–59 and *AB*,
Introduction). His selective treatment was due probably to
Bede's unwillingness to disturb his main message of the progress
to unity from diversity. Wilfrid's controversial career, although
it included elements like the Easter controversy and the introduction of the Rule of St Benedict as well as Roman music with
which Bede sympathized, was also divisive. Wilfrid's Merovingian life-style as bishop, shared by a number of his successors,
was unsympathetic to Bede (see below, pp. 339–43). Bede's
semi-official obituary of Wilfrid (v. 19), which completes valuable information given elsewhere (iv. 13, 16, 20) may best be
interpreted as an attempt to formulate an agreed statement
which would be acceptable to both sides in a controversy which
had been quietened by Wilfrid's death twenty years earlier.
None the less, Roman order and seriousness deeply appealed to
Bede, and, like most of his scholarly contemporaries, he was
conscious of the duty to preserve for posterity all that was best
in the old world. At the outer edge of civilization as it was then
known, and himself a member of a barbarian race, Bede brought
to his own primitive age much of what was best in the old
world of Roman culture, both classical and Christian. The very
existence of this volume is one indication of how well he had
succeeded.

It may be useful, especially for the first-time reader, to add a
short summary of the work. Book One is concerned with
Christianity in Roman Britain, leading up to the arrival of
Augustine from Rome as the evangelist of the Anglo-Saxons.
Book Two continues the story from the death of Gregory the
Great up to the first evangelization in Northumbria: it continues
the story of the Church in Kent, including the abortive meetings
with the Welsh. It ends with apparent failure, insofar as Northumbria's powerful Christian King Edwin was killed by Penda's army and Bishop Paulinus retired to Kent. Book Three
relates how the previous disaster was offset by the return of the

Introduction

Christian King Oswald to rule in his stead. As he had been
converted in Iona, he introduced Aidan from Iona to be bishop
of Lindisfarne. But Oswald after only eight years was also killed
in battle, to be succeeded by Oswy. In reading these two books
it is important to note that there were two ruling houses in
Northumbria, those of Bernicia (roughly Northumberland and
Durham) and of Deira (roughly modern Yorkshire). Initially
divided, Northumbria emerged as a single kingdom first under
Deiran Edwin and then under Bernician Oswald and Oswy.
Deiran Oswini, with whom Bede had much sympathy, was
assassinated at Oswy's instigation. The Church however grew
stronger, especially after disparate elements were reconciled at
Whitby. The die-hard Irish opposition left Northumbria with
Colman.

Book Four opens with the story of the consecration of
Theodore as Archbishop of Canterbury and spells out the
consequences of his visitation. During this episcopate the
Church in England comes of age, is more closely united to the
rest of the Church in Europe and produces examples of holiness
such as Etheldreda, Hilda and Cuthbert. Meanwhile the last
pagan kingdom, Sussex, is evangelized by Wilfrid.

In Book Five the succession of Northumbrian holiness is
represented by Ethelwald and by John of Hexham, the important missionary work in Frisia is pioneered by Willibrord and
others, while Northumbrian influences penetrate also to Pictland
and Iona, whose acceptance of the Roman Easter marks the end
of disunity. Not only holiness but also mystical experiences (v.
19) and pilgrimage (v. 7) were additional signs of the maturity
of the Church.

In the face of solid achievement there was also an element of
foreboding. This concerned the decline of Northumbria and the
ominous threat of the Saracens in western Europe. Bede then
added a survey of the Church and a personal conclusion.

The *Letter to Egbert* throws further light on Bede's anxieties. It
was a personal and pastoral text, whereas the *History* was public
and even official. Because of this difference in character, it

32

should not be thought of as simply an extra book of the *History*. Nevertheless it tells of a Church somewhat in decline. Bede's attack on the pseudo-monasteries explains his remark in the *History* (v. 23) that many Northumbrians 'have laid aside their weapons, preferring to receive the tonsure and take monastic vows rather than study the arts of war. What the result of this will be the future will show.' But not all was gloom and despondency in 734. There was genuine monastic life at Jarrow, Lindisfarne, Whitby and elsewhere; there was a vigorous effort to evangelize the tribes whence the Anglo-Saxons had sprung; the conversion of England was officially complete, even though there was plenty of scope for deepening the Christian life. Painting and poetry helped to communicate the content of vernacular preaching to the laity, many of whom Bede thought could receive the Eucharist daily. Fine libraries at Wearmouth, Canterbury and York, together with good teachers, augured well for the future of clerical life, as did the raising of York to metropolitan status in 735. It may be usefully recalled that in every age of the Church (including the apostolic age) there has been sin and imperfection by clergy as well as laity, and that in all probability there has never been in reality such a thing as a 'golden age' in the Church, although many have been so overcome with nostalgia that they have appeared to believe in it. It usually was considered to have occurred fifty to a hundred years before the 'present' day. Bede himself probably believed in a lost 'golden age'; he held up examples of seventh-century heroes as both encouragement and reproach to clergy of the eighth century.

Is it possible to paint a pen-portrait of Bede? I believe that it can be done, but that only assiduous reading of all his works will provide it. The following remarks are offered as only a rough sketch of a man who died over 750 years ago.

Bede, born in Northumbria not far from present-day Sunderland, was brought up in a monastery from a very tender age. Many human experiences were thus denied him. He ruefully admitted in a commentary on Saul's two wives: 'How can I

comment on this who have not even been married to one?'* He
was however interested in cooking, carpentry and the tides.*
He was musical and appreciated musicians.* He knew Old
English poetry and liked to translate into his native tongue.* In
his *Lives of the Abbots* one can sense a keen and sympathetic
observer, who deeply admired these abbots in their diversity.
He was deeply devoted to Ceolfrith, who was like a father to
him and to whom he probably owed his first education. When
Ceolfrith resigned in 716, Bede was so upset that he interrupted
his Commentary on Mark for several weeks.* If he admired
Biscop for his repeated achievement of bringing books and
works of art to the monastery, Bede found Eosterwine's humble
versatility and complete accessibility even more attractive.
Formed as a scholar principally by the Latin Bible, he spent the
best part of his life compiling commentaries from the Fathers
for the sake of the home and overseas missionary clergy. From
the text of the Bible developed his interests in chronology,
history, grammar, and the rest; Bede was versatile enough to
turn his hand to different types of writing.

The *History* was the work of his maturity and has long been
appreciated as his masterpiece. One can deduce from its pages
that their writer was patient, truthful, eloquent and a master of
the Latin language. He was generally fair and accurate, but not
entirely without prejudice. Some of his omissions are surprising
and should make us beware of a too uncritical or complete
acceptance of what he wrote. On the other hand, only those
who have researched in this period a topic not covered by Bede
can fully realize what a desert it can be. Source material always
has been and always will be scarce.

Bede seems seldom to have travelled. We know that he went
to Lindisfarne, Hexham and York, but he may have never left
Northumbria. It seems safe to assume that he had little or no
direct experience of kings and their courts, about which inevitably he formed his own opinions.* He wrote well about
bishops and their influence on kings and the consequent spread
of Christianity; but curiously he says little about the share of
monasteries in spreading and consolidating the Christian

message. Their influence however must have been very great. Bede could be selective in choosing material as worthy of inclusion; when he did include it, he sometimes used gentle irony in his descriptions.* Bede wrote limpid Latin; sometimes his apparent simplicity deceives. All in all, he was a fine scholar and an attractive personality whose very quirks and limitations make him the more interesting. He is an author to whom one can return with renewed interest over a period of many years. How he died as well as how he lived can be learnt in this volume: the contemporary account of his death is translated below (pp. 355–60).

Those who wish to learn of England in the age of Bede should first read Bede thoroughly and perceptively. It can be argued that Bede is the best commentator on Bede: his letters and hagiography, in particular, throw much light on his *History*. However we also need other sources: archaeological, artistic, theological. We need to make good, if possible, Bede's omissions and compensate for his selectivity. His age was rich in memorials: surviving manuscripts, jewels, churches and charters all tell us something which Bede did not.* Unfortunately much of the poetry and all the music from his time is lost; so too are all liturgical manuscripts. But when the different sources exist, they can happily complete our knowledge of realities on which Bede was silent. He himself would surely have approved of these efforts. The Age of Bede was a more diverse and important reality than Bede himself. He was however, in the words of Boniface, 'the candle of the Church lit by the Holy Spirit', and he is our first guide in the study of his Age.

D. H. Farmer

NOTES TO THE INTRODUCTION

※

p. 19 The unusual antiquity and reliability of the earliest surviving manuscripts at Leningrad and Cambridge and the
surprisingly large number of medieval manuscripts from
later centuries, which number 160 in all, most of them
still in western Europe, are admirably treated in Colgrave
and Mynors, Introduction.

p. 20 Anonymous *Life of Ceolfrith*, ch. 14 in Plummer I, 393;
translated in *EHD I*, 697–708. The crucial phrase 'with
antiphons' is best explained by reference to the *Rule of St
Benedict*, ch. 17.

p. 20 Prolonged practice in transcribing the biblical text *per cola
et commata* (each phrase on a new line) probably played an
important part in Bede's training as a scholar. He had
both exceptional knowledge of the text and considerable
skill in modelling his style on biblical passages; see p. 335.

p. 20 See Rosemary Cramp, 'Monkwearmouth and Jarrow: the
archaeological evidence' in *Famulus Christi*, pp. 5–18. The
land to the north of Jarrow church has not yet been
excavated.

p. 22 F. M. Stenton, *Anglo-Saxon England* (1965), p. 187.

p. 23 This is implicit in the very title of the work as well as in
i. 15, where Angles, Saxons and Jutes are described:
together these form the *Gens Anglorum*.

p. 23 See Kirby, ch. 1. Bede probably had no direct experience
of court life, but he referred to power struggles, exiles of
heirs apparent, attempted assassinations and the monastery of Gilling being founded in reparation for murder.

An ecclesiastical historian of his time could not possibly omit such elements from his narrative.

p. 24 Bede's scriptural works are being edited, mainly by D. Hurst, in the series *Corpus Christianorum Scriptorum Latinorum*.

p. 24 The theme of military disaster being a punishment for the peoples' sins is found in Bede himself (e.g. ii. 2), Gildas (*De Excidio*, passim), in Wulfstan's *Sermon of the Wolf* and in the *Anglo-Saxon Chronicle*: see *EHD I*, 775–77 and 854–59.

p. 24 See J. N. L. Myres, 'The Angles, Saxons and Jutes', *PBA* lvi (1970), 145–74 and *The English Settlements* (1986), passim. Archaeological discoveries at Winchester, Canterbury and Cirencester all reveal that Roman street-plans were *not* retained when Anglo-Saxons, primarily an agricultural people, eventually settled in the ruins of old Roman towns. They built 'ground-houses' across, not parallel to the Roman streets.

p. 25 Bede probably used an Iona source, but it is not listed here; see A. A. M. Duncan, 'Bede, Iona and the Picts' in R. H. C. Davis (ed.), *The Writing of History in the Middle Ages* (1981), pp. 1–42.

p. 26 Cf. Tacitus, *Annales* iii, 65; 'The chief function of history is to ensure the commemoration of virtuous acts, and to set forth before base utterance and deed the fear of the detestation of posterity.'

p. 26 See Peter Brown, *The Cult of the Saints* (1981), pp. 1–22; the same point is clear in Gregory the Great's *Dialogues* (ed. A. de Vogué, *Sources Chrétiennes* 254, Inroduction). Bede's use of miracle stories is discussed by P. Meyvaert and B. Ward in *Famulus Christi*, pp. 51–5 and 70–76; see also C. W. Jones, *Saints' Lives and Chronicles in Early England* (New York 1947).

p. 29 Notably by Professor Bernard Bischoff at Munich and by Dr J. Stevenson at Oxford. The so-called *Penitential of Theodore* however should not be cited as though Theodore himself had written it: it is actually due to at least two other writers who claimed Theodore's authority for their own compilation. It is impossible to say how much really represents his teaching.

p. 30 Ine's law-code of *c.* 690 (see *EHD I*, 364–72) punishes offences against Church laws, such as sabbath-breaking and the neglect of infant baptism, by civil penalties; it recognized a rudimentary right of sanctuary: all this reflects a Christianity firmly established. Lives of Boniface and some companions, together with his selected Letters are translated by C. H. Talbot, *Anglo-Saxon Missionaries in Germany* (1954).

p. 34 I owe this reference to Sr Benedicta Ward.

p. 34 P. Hunter Blair, *The Age of Bede* (1970), pp. viii, 5, 28.

p. 34 This seems clear from his interest in Ediius and Putta (iv. 2), John the Arch-Cantor (iv. 18) and Acca, Bishop of Hexham (v. 20).

p. 34 See below, p. 358.

p. 34 D. Hurst, ed., *In primam partem Samuhelis libri IIII*, preface to Book IV, *CCSL* cxix (1962), p. 12.

p. 34 Recent work on kings as Bede saw them include J. M. Wallace Hadrill, *Early Germanic Kingship* (1971), chs. III and IV; J. McClure, 'Bede's Old Testament Kings' and C. Stancliffe 'Kings who Opted Out' both in P. Wormald (ed.), *Ideal and Reality in Frankish and Anglo-Saxon Society* (1983), pp. 76–98 and 154–76.

p. 35 Examples occur in the descriptions of Wilfrid's and Aldhelm's achievements (v. 18–19).

p. 35 Bede nowhere mentions the churches of Brixworth and Escomb, the Lindisfarne Gospels or the pectoral cross of St Cuthbert. He must surely have known about the first two and actually seen the last two. All are important for today's students of the Age of Bede.

BEDE'S
ECCLESIASTICAL HISTORY
OF THE
ENGLISH PEOPLE
✤

PREFACE

✤

To the Most Glorious King Ceolwulf*
Bede the Priest and Servant
of Christ

SOME while ago, at Your Majesty's request, I gladly sent you the history of the English Church and People which I had recently completed, in order that you might read it and give it your approval. I now send it once again to be transcribed, so that Your Majesty may consider it at greater leisure. I warmly welcome the diligent zeal and sincerity with which you study the words of Holy Scripture and your eager desire to know something of the doings and sayings of men of the past, and of famous men of your own nation in particular. For if history records good things of good men, the thoughtful hearer is encouraged to imitate what is good: or if it records evil of wicked men, the devout, religious listener or reader is encouraged to avoid all that is sinful and perverse and to follow what he knows to be good and pleasing to God. Your Majesty is well aware of this; and since you feel so deeply responsible for the general good of those over whom divine Providence has set you, you wish that this history may be made better known both to yourself and to your people.

But in order to avoid any doubts in the mind of yourself, or of any who may listen to or read this history, as to the accuracy of what I have written, allow me briefly to state the authorities upon whom I chiefly depend.

My principal authority and adviser in this work has been the most reverend Abbot Albinus,* an eminent scholar educated in the church of Canterbury by Archbishop Theodore and Abbot Hadrian, both of them respected and learned men. He carefully transmitted to me verbally or in writing through Nothelm, a priest of the church of London, anything he considered worthy of mention that had been done by disciples of the blessed Pope Gregory in the province of Kent or the surrounding regions. Such facts he ascertained either from records or from the recollection of older men. Nothelm himself later visited Rome, and obtained permission from the present Pope Gregory (II) to examine the archives of the holy Roman Church. He found there letters of Pope Gregory (I) and other Popes, and when he returned, the reverend father Albinus advised him to bring them to me for inclusion in this history. So from the period at which this volume begins until the time when the English nation received the Faith of Christ, I have drawn extensively on the works of earlier writers gathered from various sources. But from that time until the present, I owe much of my information about what was done in the Church of Canterbury by the disciples of Pope Gregory and their successors, and under what kings events occurred, to the industry of the said Abbot Albinus made known to me through Nothelm. They also provided some of my information about the bishops from whom the provinces of the East and West Saxons, the East Angles and the Northumbrians received the grace of the Gospel and the kings who were then reigning. Indeed, it was mainly owing to the persuasion of Albinus that I was encouraged to begin this work. Also the most reverend Bishop Daniel of the West Saxons, who is still alive, sent to me in writing certain facts about the history of the Church in his province, in the adjoining province of the South Saxons, and in the Isle of Wight. I have learnt by careful enquiry from the brethren of Lastingham monastery how by the ministration of the holy priests Cedd and Chad, their founders, the faith of Christ came to the province of the Mercians, which had never known it, and returned to that of the East Saxons, which had let it die out, and how these holy fathers lived and died. In addition, I have traced the progress of the Church in the province of the East Angles, partly from writings or old traditions and writings, and partly from the account given by the most reverend Abbot Esi. The growth of the Christian Faith and succession of bishops in the province of Lindsey I have learned either from the letters of the most reverend Bishop Cynibert, or by word of mouth from other reliable persons. With regard to events in the various districts of the province of the Northumbrians, from the time that it received the Faith of Christ up to the present day, I am not dependent on any one author, but on countless faithful witnesses who either know or remember the facts, apart from what I know myself. In this connexion, it should be noted that whatever I have written concerning our most holy father and Bishop Cuthbert, whether in this book or in my separate account of his life and doings, I have in part taken and accurately copied from a Life already compiled by the brethren of the Church of Lindisfarne; and I have carefully added to this whatever I could learn from the reliable accounts of those who knew him. Should the reader discover any inaccuracies in what I have written, I humbly beg that he will not impute them to me, because, as a true law of history requires,* I have laboured honestly to transmit whatever I could ascertain from common report for the instruction of posterity.

I earnestly request all who may hear or read this history of our nation to ask God's mercy on my many failings of mind and body. And in return for the diligent toil that I have bestowed on the recordings of memorable events in the various provinces and places of greater note, I beg that their inhabitants may grant me the favour of frequent mention in their devout prayers.

BOOK ONE

✤

CHAPTER I: *The situation of Britain and Ireland: their earliest inhabitants**

BRITAIN, formerly known as Albion, is an island in the ocean, lying towards the north west at a considerable distance from the coasts of Germany, Gaul, and Spain, which together form the greater part of Europe. It extends 800 miles northwards, and is 200 in breadth, except where a number of promontories stretch further, so that the total coastline extends to 3600 miles. To the south lies Belgic Gaul, to whose coast the shortest crossing is from the city known as Rutubi Portus, which the English have corrupted to Reptacaestir.[1] The distance from there across the sea to Gessoriacum,[2] the nearest coast of the Morini, is fifty miles, or, as some have written, 450 furlongs. On the opposite side of Britain, which lies open to the boundless ocean, lie the isles of the Orcades.[3] Britain is rich in grain and timber; it has good pasturage for cattle and draught animals, and vines are cultivated in various localities. There are many land and sea birds of various species, and it is well known for its plentiful springs and rivers abounding in fish. Salmon and eels are especially plentiful, while seals, dolphins, and sometimes whales are caught. There are also many varieties of shell-fish, such as mussels, in which are often found excellent pearls of several colours, red, purple, violet, and green, but mainly white. Whelks are abundant, and a beautiful scarlet dye is extracted from them which remains unfaded by sunshine or

---

[1] Richborough.   [2] Boulogne.   [3] The Orkneys.

rain; indeed, the older the cloth, the more beautiful its colour. The country has both salt springs and hot springs, and the waters flowing from them provide hot baths, in which the people bathe separately according to age and sex. As Saint Basil says: 'Water receives heat when it flows across certain metals, and becomes hot, and even scalding.'* The land has rich veins of many metals, including copper, iron, lead, and silver. There is also much jet of fine quality, a black jewel which can be set on fire and, when burned, drives away snakes and, like amber, when it is warmed by friction, it holds fast whatever is applied to it. In old times, the country had twenty-eight noble cities, besides innumerable strongholds, which also were guarded by walls, towers, and barred gates.

Since Britain lies far north toward the pole, the nights are short in summer, and at midnight it is hard to tell whether the evening twilight still lingers or whether dawn is approaching, since the sun at night passes not far below the earth in its journey round the north back to the east. Consequently the days are long in summer, as are the nights in winter when the sun withdraws into African regions, as long in fact as eighteen hours, whereas the summer nights and winter days are very short, and last only six hours. In Armenia, Macedconia, and Italy, and other countries of that latitude, the longest day or night lasts only fifteen hours and the shortest nine.

At the present time there are in Britain, in harmony with the five books of the divine law, five languages and four nations – English, British, Irish,* and Picts. Each of these have their own language; but all are united in their study of God's truth by the fifth – Latin – which has become a common medium through the study of the scriptures. At first the only inhabitants of the island were the Britons, from whom it takes its name, and who, according to tradition, crossed into Britain from Armorica,[1] and occupied the southern parts. When they had spread northwards and possessed the greater part of the island, it is said that some Picts from Scythia[2] put to sea in a few longships, and were

---

[1] Brittany.   [2] Here probably Scandinavia.

driven by storms around the coasts of Britain, arriving at length
on the north coast of Ireland. Here they found the nation of the
Irish, from whom they asked permission to settle; but their
request was refused. Ireland is the largest island after Britain,
and lies to the west of it. It is shorter than Britain to the north,
but extends far beyond it to the south towards the northern
coasts of Spain, although a wide sea separates them. These
Pictish seafarers, as I have said, asked for a grant of land so that
they too could make a settlement. The Irish replied that there
was not room for them both, but said: 'We can give you good
advice. We know that there is another island not far to the east,
which we often see in the distance on clear days. If you choose
to go there, you can make it fit to live in; should you meet
resistance, we will come to your help.' So the Picts crossed into
Britain, and began to settle in the north of the island, since the
Britons were in possession of the south. Having no women
with them, these Picts asked wives of the Irish, who consented
on condition that, when any dispute arose, they should choose
a king from the female royal line rather than the male. This
custom continues among the Picts to this day. As time went on,
Britain received a third nation, that of the Irish; they migrated
from Ireland under their chieftain Reuda and by a combination
of force and treaty, obtained from the Picts the settlements that
they still hold. From the name of this chieftain, they are still
known as Dalreudians, for in their tongue *dal* means a division.

Ireland is far more favoured than Britain by latitude, and by
its mild and healthy climate. Snow rarely lies longer than three
days, so that there is no need to store hay in summer for winter
use or to build stables for beasts. There are no reptiles, and no
snake can exist there; for although often brought over from
Britain, as soon as the ship nears land, they breathe the scent of
its air, and die. In fact, almost everything in this isle confers
immunity to poison, and I have seen that folk suffering from
snake-bite have drunk water in which scrapings from the leaves
of books from Ireland have been steeped, and that this remedy
checked the spreading poison and reduced the swelling.* The
island abounds in milk and honey, and there is no lack of vines,

fish, and birds, while red deer and roe are widely hunted. It is the original home of the Irish, who, as already mentioned, later migrated and added a third nation to the Britons and Picts in Britain.

There is a very extensive arm of the sea,[1] which originally formed the boundary between the Britons and the Picts. This runs inland from the west for a great distance, where there stands to this day the strongly fortified British city of Alcluith.[2] It was to the northern shores of this firth that the Irish came and established their new homeland.

CHAPTER 2: *On Gaius Julius Caesar, the first Roman to reach Britain*

BRITAIN remained unknown and unvisited by the Romans until the time of Gaius Julius Caesar, who became Consul with Lucius Bibulus 693 years after the founding of Rome, and sixty years before the birth of our Lord.* During a campaign against the Germans and Gauls, whose common boundary was the Rhine, he entered the province of the Morini, from which is the nearest and quickest crossing into Britain. Here he assembled about eighty transports and galleys, and crossed into Britain, where his forces suffered in a fierce battle. Next, encountering a violent gale, he lost most of his fleet and many troops, including almost all his cavalry. So he returned to Gaul, dispersed his legions to winter quarters, and gave orders for the construction of 600 vessels of both types. With these he made a second attempt on Britain in the spring; but while he was advancing against the enemy with large forces, the fleet lying at anchor was struck by a storm, and the ships were either dashed against each other, or driven on the sands and destroyed. Forty ships were wrecked, and the remainder were only repaired with great difficulty. At the first encounter, Caesar's cavalry suffered a defeat at the hands of the Britons, and the tribune Labienus was

---

[1] Firth of Clyde.   [2] Dumbarton.

killed. In a second battle, which involved considerable risk, he put the Britons to flight. His next objective was the Thames, where a vast host of the enemy under Cassobellaunus was holding the far bank, and had constructed a defence system of sharpened stakes which ran along the bank, and under water across the ford. Traces of these stakes can still be seen; cased in lead and thick as a man's thigh, they were fixed immovably in the river-bed. But they were noticed and avoided by the Romans, and the barbarians, unable to resist the charge of the legions, hid themselves in the forests and harassed the Romans by frequent fierce sorties. Meanwhile the strongest city of the Trinovantes and its commander Androgius surrendered to Caesar and gave him forty hostages. Following its example, several other cities came to terms with the Romans and, acting on their information, Caesar, after a severe struggle, captured the stronghold of Cassobellaunus, which was sited between two swamps, flanked by forests and well provisioned. After this, Caesar left Britain for Gaul; but no sooner had he sent his legions into winter quarters than he was suddenly troubled and distracted by sudden wars and revolts on all sides.

CHAPTER 3: *Claudius, the second Roman to reach Britain, annexes the Isles of Orkney to the Roman Empire: under his direction Vespasian subdues the Isle of Wight*

IN the 798th year after the founding of Rome,* Claudius, fourth emperor in the succession beginning with Augustus, wishing to prove himself a benefactor to the State, applied himself to war and conquest on a grand scale, and undertook an expedition against Britain which had been roused to revolt by the Roman refusal to give up certain deserters. Before Claudius no Roman, either before or since Julius Caesar, had dared to land on the island; yet, within a few days, without battle or bloodshed, he received the surrender of the greater part of the island. He also annexed to the Empire the Isles of Orkney, which lie in the ocean beyond Britain; and returning to Rome only six months after his departure, he granted his son the title of Britannicus. He brought this campaign to a close in the fourth year of his reign, and in the forty-sixth year after the birth of our Lord. This was the year in which a very serious famine occurred in Syria, which is mentioned in the Acts of the Apostles as having been foretold by the prophet Agabus. Vespasian, who was to succeed Nero as Emperor, was sent by the same Claudius, and brought the Isle of Wight under Roman rule. This island lies off the south coast of Britain and is about thirty miles in length from east to west, and twelve from north to south. Six miles of sea separate it from the mainland at its eastern end, but only three at the west. When Nero succeeded Claudius as Emperor, he attempted no military expeditions, and in consequence, apart from countless other injuries to the Roman State, he nearly lost Britain, for during his reign two most noble towns there were taken and destroyed.

CHAPTER 4: *Lucius, a British king, writes to Pope Eleutherus and asks to be made a Christian*

IN the year of our Lord's Incarnation 156, Marcus Antoninus Verus, fourteenth from Augustus, became Emperor jointly with his brother Aurelius Commodus. During their reign, and while the holy Eleutherus ruled the Roman Church, Lucius, a British king, sent him a letter, asking to be made a Christian by his direction.* This pious request was quickly granted, and the Britons received the Faith and held it peacefully in all its purity and fullness until the time of the Emperor Diocletian.

CHAPTER 5: *Severus divides Roman Britain from the rest by an earthwork*

IN the year of our Lord 189, Severus, an African born at Leptis in the province of Tripolitania, became seventeenth Emperor from Augustus and ruled seventeen years. Harsh by nature, he was engaged in almost constant warfare, and ruled the State with courage, but with great difficulty. He was victorious in the grave civil wars that troubled his reign. He was compelled to come to Britain by the desertion of nearly all the tribes allied to Rome, and after many critical and hardfought battles he decided to separate that portion of the island under his control from the remaining unconquered peoples. He did this not with a wall, as some imagine, but with an earthwork. For a wall is built of stone, but an earthwork, such as protects a camp from enemy attack, is constructed with sods cut from the earth and raised high above ground level, fronted by the ditch from which the sods were cut and surmounted by a strong palisade of logs. Severus built a rampart and ditch of this type from sea to sea and fortified it by a series of towers.* After this he was taken ill and died in Eboracum,[1] leaving two sons, Bassianus and Geta. The latter was subsequently condemned to death as an enemy of the State, but Bassianus became Emperor with the cognomen of Antoninus.

CHAPTER 6: *The reign of Diocletian: his persecution of the Christian Church*

IN the year of our Lord 286, Diocletian, a nominee of the army, became thirty-third in the succession of Augustus.* He ruled twenty years, and chose Maximian, known as Herculius, as his co-Emperor. During their reign, Carausius, a man of humble birth but a capable and energetic soldier, was appointed to protect the sea-coasts, which were then being ravaged by

¹ York

50

Franks and Saxons. But he put his own interests before those of the Republic, and suspicion arose that he was deliberately permitting the enemy to raid the frontiers: any loot that he recovered from the pirates was not restored to its rightful owners, but retained for his own advantage. Maximian ordered his execution, but Carausius assumed the imperial purple and seized Britain, which he won and held for seven years with great daring. He lost his life through the betrayal of his colleague Allectus, who then held the island for three years, after which he was defeated by Asclepiodotus, Prefect of the Praetorian Guard, who thus restored Britain to the Empire after ten years.

Meanwhile Diocletian in the East and Herculius in the West ordered all churches to be destroyed and all Christians to be hunted out and killed. This was the tenth persecution since Nero, and was more protracted and horrible than all that had preceded it. It was carried out without any respite for ten years, with the burning of churches, the outlawing of innocent people, and the slaughter of martyrs. But at length the glory of these martyrs' devoted loyalty to God was to light even Britain.

CHAPTER 7: *The martyrdom of Saint Alban and his companions, who shed their life-blood for Christ at this time*

IN this country occurred the suffering of Saint Alban, of whom the priest Fortunatus in his *Praise of Virgins*, in which he mentions all the blessed martyrs who came to God from every part of the world, says:

> In fertile Britain's land
> Was noble Alban born.*

When these unbelieving Emperors were issuing savage edicts against all Christians, Alban, as yet a pagan, gave shelter to a Christian priest fleeing from his pursuers. And when he observed this man's unbroken activity of prayer and vigil, he was suddenly touched by the grace of God and began to follow the priest's example of faith and devotion. Gradually instructed by his teaching of salvation, Alban renounced the darkness of idolatry, and sincerely accepted Christ. But when the priest had lived in his house some days, word came to the ears of the evil ruler that Christ's confessor, whose place of martyrdom had not yet been appointed, lay hidden in Alban's house. Accordingly he gave orders to his soldiers to make a thorough search, and when they arrived at the martyr's house, holy Alban, wearing the priest's long cloak, at once surrendered himself in the place of his guest and teacher, and was led bound before the judge.

When Alban was brought in, the judge happened to be standing before an altar, offering sacrifice to devils. Seeing Alban, he was furious that he had presumed to put himself in such hazard by surrendering himself to the soldiers in place of his guest, and ordered him to be dragged before the idols where he stood. 'Since you have chosen to conceal a sacrilegious rebel,' he said, 'rather than surrender him to my soldiers to pay the well-deserved penalty for his blasphemy against our gods you shall undergo all the tortures due to him if you dare to abandon the practice of our religion.' But Saint Alban, who had freely confessed himself a Christian to the enemies of the Faith, was unmoved by these threats, and armed with spiritual strength, openly refused to obey this order. 'What is your family and race?' demanded the judge. 'How does my family concern you?' replied Alban; 'if you wish to know the truth about my religion, know that I am a Christian, and carry out Christian rites.' 'I demand to know your name,' insisted the judge, 'tell me at once.' 'My parents named me Alban,' he answered, 'and I worship and adore the living and true God, who created all things.' The judge was very angry, and said: 'If you want to enjoy eternal life, sacrifice at once to the great gods.' Alban replied: 'You are offering these sacrifices to devils, who cannot help their suppliants, nor answer their prayers and vows. On the contrary, whosoever offers sacrifice to idols is doomed to the pains of hell.'

Incensed at this reply, the judge ordered God's holy confessor Alban to be flogged by the executioners, declaring that he would shake his constancy of heart by wounds, since words had no effect. But, for Christ's sake, he bore the most horrible torments patiently and even gladly, and when the judge saw that no torture could break him or make him renounce the worship of Christ, he ordered his immediate decapitation. Led out to execution, the saint came to a river which flowed swiftly between the wall of the town and the arena where he was to die. There he saw a great crowd of men and women of all ages and conditions, who were doubtless moved by God's will to attend the death of his blessed confessor and martyr. This crowd had collected in such numbers and so blocked the bridge that he could hardly have crossed that evening, and so many people had come out from the city that the judge was left unattended. Saint Alban, who ardently desired a speedy martyrdom, approached the river, and as he raised his eyes to heaven in prayer, the river ran dry in its bed and left him a way to cross. When among others the appointed executioner himself saw this, he was so moved in spirit that he hurried to meet Alban at the place of execution, and throwing down his drawn sword, fell at his feet, begging that he might be thought worthy to die with the martyr if he could not die in his place.

While this man changed from a persecutor to a companion in the true Faith, and other executioners hesitated to pick up his sword from the ground, the most reverend confessor of God ascended a hill about five hundred paces from the arena, accompanied by the crowd. This hill, a lovely spot as befitted the occasion, was clad in a gay mantle of many kinds of flowers. Here was neither cliff nor crag, but a gentle rising slope made smooth by nature, its beauty providing a worthy place to be hallowed by a martyr's blood. As he reached the summit, holy Alban asked God to give him water, and at once a perennial spring bubbled up at his feet – a sign to all present that it was at the martyr's prayer that the river also had dried in its course. For it was not likely that the martyr who had dried up the waters of the river should lack water on a hill-top unless he willed it so. But the river, having performed its due service, gave proof of its obedience, and returned to its natural course. Here, then, the gallant martyr met his death, and received the crown of life which God has promised to those who love him. But the man whose impious hands struck off that pious head was not permitted to boast of his deed, for as the martyr's head fell, the executioner's eyes dropped out on the ground.

The soldier who had been moved by divine intuition to refuse to slay God's confessor was beheaded at the same time as Alban. And although he had not received the purification of Baptism, there was no doubt that he was cleansed by the shedding of his own blood, and rendered fit to enter the kingdom of heaven. Astonished by these many strange miracles, the judge called a halt to the persecution, and whereas he had formerly fought to crush devotion to Christ, he now began to honour the death of his saints.

Saint Alban suffered on the twenty-second day of June near the city of Verulamium, which the English now call Verlama-caestir or Vaeclingacaestir. Here, when the peace of Christian times was restored, a beautiful church worthy of his martyrdom was built, where sick folk are healed and frequent miracles take place to this day.

In the same persecution suffered Aaron and Julius, citizens of the City of Legions,[1] and many others of both sexes throughout the land. After they had endured many horrible physical tortures, death brought an end to the struggle, and their souls entered the joys of the heavenly City.

CHAPTER 8: *The Church in Britain enjoys peace from the end of this persecution until the time of the Arian heresy*

WHEN this storm of persecution came to an end, faithful Christians, who during the time of danger had taken refuge in woods, deserted places, and hidden caves, came into the open, and rebuilt the ruined churches. Shrines of the martyrs were founded and completed and openly displayed everywhere as tokens of victory. The festivals of the Church were observed,

---

[1] Possibly Caerleon-on-Usk.

and its rites performed reverently and sincerely. The Christian churches in Britain continued to enjoy this peace until the time of the Arian heresy.* This poisonous error after corrupting the whole world, at length crossed the sea and infected even this remote island; and, once the doorway had been opened, every sort of pestilential heresy at once poured into this island, whose people are ready to listen to anything novel, and never hold firmly to anything.

At this time, Constantius, a man of exceptional kindness and courtesy, who had governed Gaul and Spain during the lifetime of Diocletian, died in Britain. His son Constantine, the child of Helena his concubine, succeeded him as ruler of Gaul. Eutropius writes that Constantine, proclaimed Emperor in Britain, succeeded to his father's domains. In his time, the Arian heresy sprang up, and although it was exposed and condemned at the Council of Nicaea, the deadly poison of its false teaching nevertheless infected, as we have said, not only the continental churches, but even those of these islands.

CHAPTER 9: *During the reign of Gratian, Maximus is created Emperor in Britain, and returns to Gaul with a large army*

IN the year of our Lord 377, Gratian, fortieth in line from Augustus, ruled as Emperor for six years from the death of Valens; he had already reigned as co-Emperor with his uncle Valens and his brother Valentinian. Finding the affairs of the State in grave disorder and approaching disaster, he chose the Spaniard Theodosius to restore the Empire in its need, investing him with the royal purple at Sirmium, and creating him Emperor of Thrace and the East.

At this juncture, however, Maximus, an able and energetic man, well fitted to be Emperor had not ambition led him to break his oath of allegiance, was elected Emperor by the army in Britain almost against his will, and he crossed into Gaul at its head. Here he treacherously killed the Emperor Gratian who had been dumbfounded at his sudden attack, and was attempting to escape into Italy. His brother the Emperor Valentinian was driven out of Italy, and took refuge in the east, where Theodosius received him with fatherly affection. Within a short time, however, he regained the Empire, and trapping the despot Maximus in Aquileia, he captured him and put him to death.

CHAPTER 10: *During the reign of Arcadius, the Briton Pelagius presumptuously belittles the grace of God*

IN the year of our Lord 394, Arcadius, son of Theodosius, forty-third in line from Augustus, became joint-Emperor with his brother Honorius, and ruled for thirteen years. In his time, the Briton Pelagius* spread far and wide his noxious and abominable teaching that man had no need of God's grace, and in this he was supported by Julian of Campania, a deposed bishop eager to recover his bishopric. Saint Augustine and other orthodox fathers quoted many thousand Catholic authorities against them, but they refused to abandon their folly; on the contrary, their obstinacy was hardened by contradiction, and they refused to return to the true faith. Prosper the rhetorician has aptly expressed this in heroic verse:

> Against the great Augustine see him crawl,
> This wretched scribbler with his pen of gall!
> In what black caverns was this snakeling bred
> That from the dirt presumes to rear its head?
> Its food is grain that wave-washed Britain yields,
> Or the rank pasture of Campanian fields.

I N the year 407, Honorius, the younger son of Theodosius, was Emperor, and the forty-fourth in line from Augustus. This was two years before the invasion of Rome by Alaric, King of Goths, on which occasion the nations of the Alani, Suevi, Vandals, and many others defeated the Franks, crossed the Rhine, and devastated all Gaul. At this juncture, Gratian, a citizen of the island, set himself up as a despot and was killed. In his place Constantine, a common trooper of no merit, was chosen Emperor solely on account of his auspicious name. Once he had obtained power, he crossed into Gaul, where he was hoodwinked into many worthless treaties by the barbarians and caused great harm to the commonwealth. Before long, at the orders of Honorius, Count Constantius entered Gaul with an army, besieged Constantine in the city of Arles, captured him, and put him to death. His son Constans, a monk, whom he had created Caesar, was also put to death by Count Gerontius in Vienne.

Rome fell to the Goths in the 1164th year after its foundation. At the same time Roman rule came to an end in Britain, almost 470 years after the landing of Gaius Julius Caesar. The Romans had occupied the country south of the earthwork which, as I have said, Severus built across the island, as cities, forts,[1] bridges, and paved roads bear witness to this day: they also held nominal jurisdiction over the more remote parts of Britain and the islands beyond it.

[1] Or 'lighthouses'.

HENCEFORWARD, the part of Britain inhabited by the Britons which had been hurriedly stripped of all troops and military equipment and robbed of the flower of its young men, who had been led away by ambitious despots and were never to return, lay wholly exposed to attack, since its people were untrained in the science of war. Consequently for many years this region suffered attacks from two savage extraneous races, Irish from the north west, and Picts from the north. I term these races extraneous, not because they came from outside Britain, but because their lands were sundered from that of Britons: for two sea estuaries lay between, one of which runs broad and deep into the country from the sea to the east and the other from the west, although they do not actually meet. In the middle of the eastern estuary stands the city of Giudi,[1] while on the right bank of the western stands the city of Alcluith,[2] which in their language means 'the rock of Cluith', as it stands near a river of that name.*

When these tribes invaded them, the Britons sent messengers to Rome with moving appeals for help, promising perpetual submission if only the Romans would drive out their enemies. An armed Legion was quickly dispatched to the island, where it engaged the enemy, inflicted heavy losses on them, and drove the survivors out of the territory of Rome's allies. Having thus freed the Britons for a time from dire oppression, the Romans advised them to construct a protective wall across the island from sea to sea in order to keep their foes at bay. The victorious Legion then returned home. The islanders built this wall as they had been instructed, but having no engineers capable of so great an undertaking, they built it of turf and not of stone, so that it was of small value. However, they built it for many miles

---

[1] The island of Inchkeith.   [2] Dumbarton.

between the two above-mentioned estuaries or inlets, hoping
that where the sea provided no protection, they might use the
rampart to preserve their borders from hostile attack. Clear
traces of this wide and lofty earthwork can be seen to this day.
It begins about two miles west of the monastery of
Aebbercurnig[1] at a place which the Picts call Peanfahel and the
English Penneltun,[2] and runs westward to the vicinity of the
city of Alcluith. But as soon as the old enemies of the Britons
saw that the Roman forces had left, they made a seaborne
invasion, breaking in and destroying wholesale, slaughtering
right and left as men cut ripe corn. The Britons therefore sent
more envoys to Rome with pitiful appeals for help, without
which their unhappy land would be utterly ravaged and the
name of a once illustrious Roman province be brought into
disgrace and obliterated by barbarous tribes, who year by year
were carrying off their plunder unchecked. Once more a Legion
was dispatched, which arrived unexpectedly in autumn and
inflicted heavy casualties on the invaders, forcing all who
survived to escape by sea.

The Romans, however, now informed the Britons that they
could no longer undertake such troublesome expeditions for
their defence, and urged them to take up arms for their own
part and cultivate the will to fight, pointing out that it was
solely their lack of spirit which gave their enemies an advantage
over them. In addition, in order to assist these allies whom they
were forced to abandon, they built a strong wall of stone
directly from sea to sea in a straight line between the towns that
had been built as strong-points, where Severus had built his
earthwork. This famous and still conspicuous wall was built
from public and private resources, with the Britons lending
assistance. It is eight feet in breadth, and twelve in height; and,
as can be clearly seen to this day, ran straight from east to west.
When the wall was completed, the Romans gave firm advice to
the dispirited Britons, together with instructions on the manu-
facture of weapons. In addition, they built towers at intervals

---

[1] Abercorn.   [2] Old Kilpatrick.

overlooking the south coast where their ships lay, because there was a danger of barbarian raids even from this quarter. Then they bade farewell to their allies, with no intention of ever returning.

On the departure of the Romans, the Picts and Irish, learning that they did not mean to return, were quick to return themselves, and becoming bolder than ever, occupied all the northern and outer part of the island up to the wall, as if it belonged to them. Here a dispirited British garrison stationed on the fortifications pined in terror night and day, while from beyond the wall the enemy constantly harassed them with hooked weapons, dragging the cowardly defenders down from the wall and dashing them to the ground. At length the Britons abandoned their cities and wall and fled in disorder, pursued by their foes. The slaughter was more ghastly than ever before, and the wretched citizens were torn in pieces by their enemies, as lambs are torn by wild beasts. They were driven from their homesteads and farms, and sought to save themselves from starvation by robbery and violence against one another, their own internal anarchy adding to the miseries caused by others, until there was no food left in the whole land except whatever could be obtained by hunting.

CHAPTER 13: *During the reign of Theodosius the Younger, Palladius is sent to the Christians among the Irish. The Britons make an unsuccessful appeal to the Consul Aëtius* [A.D. 446]

IN the year of our Lord 423, Theodosius the Younger, next after Honorius and forty-fifth in succession from Augustus, ruled the Empire for twenty-six years. In the eighth year of his reign, the Roman Pontiff Celestine sent Palladius* to the Irish who believed in Christ to be their first bishop. In the twenty-third year of his reign, Aëtius, an illustrious patrician, became Consul for the third time together with Symmachus. To him the wretched remnant of the Britons sent a letter, which commences: 'To Aëtius, thrice Consul, come the groans of the

The groans of the Britons [I.14]

Britons', and in the course of the letter they describe their calamities: 'The barbarians drive us into the sea, and the sea drives us back to the barbarians. Between these, two deadly alternatives confront us, drowning or slaughter.' But even this plea could not obtain help; for at the time Aëtius was already engaged in two serious wars with Blaedla and Attila, the kings of the Huns. And although Blaedla had been assassinated the previous year through the treachery of his brother Attila, the latter remained so dangerous an enemy to the State that he devastated nearly all Europe, invading and destroying cities and strongholds alike. During this period there was a famine at Constantinople, followed closely by a plague, and much of the walls of that city and fifty-seven towers fell into ruin. Many other cities fell into disrepair, and the polluting stench of rotting corpses spread disease among men and beasts alike.

CHAPTER 14: *The Britons, made desperate by famine, drive the Barbarians out of their land. There soon follows an abundance of corn, luxury, plague, and doom on the nation*

MEANWHILE the famine which left a lasting memory of its horrors to posterity distressed the Britons more and more. Many were compelled to surrender to the invaders; others, trusting in God's help where no human hand could save them, continued their resistance. Making frequent sallies from the mountains, caves, and forests, they began at length to inflict severe losses on the enemy who had plundered their country for so many years. Thereupon the Irish pirates departed to their homes unabashed, intending to return after a short interval, while the Picts remained inactive in the northern parts of the island, save for occasional raids and forays to plunder the Britons.

When the depredations of its enemies had ceased, the land enjoyed an abundance of corn without precedent in former years; but with plenty came an increase in luxury, followed by every kind of crime, especially cruelty, hatred of truth, and love of falsehood. If anyone happened to be more kindly or truthful than his neighbours, he became a target for all weapons of malice as though he were an enemy of Britain. And not only the laity were guilty of these things, but even the lord's flock and their pastors. Giving themselves up to drunkenness, hatred, quarrels, and violence, they threw off the easy yoke of Christ. Suddenly a terrible plague struck this corrupt people, and in a short while destroyed so large a number that the living could not bury the dead. But not even the death of their friends or the fear of their own death was sufficient to recall the survivors from the spiritual death to which their crimes had doomed them. So it was that, not long afterwards, an even more terrible retribution overtook this wicked nation. For they consulted how they might obtain help to avoid or repel the frequent fierce attacks of their northern neighbours, and all agreed with the advice of their king, Vortigern, to call on the assistance of the Saxon peoples across the sea. This decision, as its results were to show, seems to have been ordained by God as a punishment on their wickedness.

CHAPTER 15: *The Angles are invited to Britain. At first they repel the enemy, but soon come to terms with them, and turn their weapons against their own allies*

IN the year of our Lord 449, Martian became Emperor with Valentinian, the forty-sixth in succession from Augustus, ruling for seven years.* In his time the Angles or Saxons came to Britain at the invitation of King Vortigern in three long-ships, and were granted lands in the eastern part of the island on condition that they protected the country: nevertheless, their real intention was to subdue it. They engaged the enemy advancing from the north, and having defeated them, sent back news of their success to their homeland, adding that the country was fertile and the Britons cowardly. Whereupon a larger fleet quickly came over with a great body of warriors, which, when joined to the original forces, constituted an invincible army.

These also received from the Britons grants of land where they could settle among them on condition that they maintained the peace and security of the island against all enemies in return for regular pay.

These new-comers were from the three most formidable races of Germany, the Saxons, Angles, and Jutes. From the Jutes are descended the people of Kent and the Isle of Wight and those in the province of the West Saxons opposite the Isle of Wight who are called Jutes to this day. From the Saxons – that is, the country now known as the land of the Old Saxons – came the East, South and West Saxons. And from the Angles – that is, the country known as Angulus, which lies between the provinces of the Jutes and Saxons and is said to remain unpopulated to this day – are descended the East and Middle Angles, the Mercians, all the Northumbrian stock (that is, those people living north of the river Humber), and the other English peoples. Their first chieftains are said to have been the brothers Hengist and Horsa. The latter was subsequently killed in battle against the Britons, and was buried in east Kent, where the monument bearing his name still stands. They were the sons of Wictgils, whose father was Witta, whose father was Wecta, son of Woden, from whose stock sprang the royal house of many provinces.

It was not long before such hordes of these alien peoples vied together to crowd into the island that the natives who had invited them began to live in terror. Then all of a sudden the Angles made an alliance with the Picts, whom by this time they had driven some distance away, and began to turn their arms against their allies. They began by demanding a greater supply of provisions; then, seeking to provoke a quarrel, threatened that unless larger supplies were forthcoming, they would terminate their treaty and ravage the whole island. Nor were they slow to carry out their threats. In short, the fires kindled by the pagans proved to be God's just punishment on the sins of the nation, just as the fires once kindled by the Chaldeans destroyed the walls and buildings of Jerusalem. For, as the just Judge ordained, these heathen conquerors devastated the surrounding

cities and countryside, extended the conflagration from the
eastern to the western shores without opposition and established
a stranglehold over nearly all the doomed island. Public and
private buildings were razed; priests were slain at the altar;
bishops and people alike, regardless of rank, were destroyed
with fire and sword, and none remained to bury those who had
suffered a cruel death. A few wretched survivors captured in the
hills were butchered wholesale, and others, desperate with
hunger, came out and surrendered to the enemy for food,
although they were doomed to lifelong slavery even if they
escaped instant massacre. Some fled overseas in their misery;
others, clinging to their homeland, eked out a wretched and
fearful existence among the mountains, forests, and crags, ever
on the alert for danger.

CHAPTER 16: *Under the leadership of Ambrosius, a Roman, the
Britons win their first victory against the Angles* [c. A.D. 493]

WHEN the victorious invaders had scattered and destroyed
the native peoples and returned to their own dwellings,
the Britons slowly began to take heart and recover their
strength, emerging from the dens where they had hidden
themselves, and joining in prayer that God might help them to
avoid complete extermination. Their leader at this time was
Ambrosius Aurelianus, a man of good character and the sole
survivor of Roman race from the catastrophe. Among the slain
had been his own parents, who were of royal birth and title.
Under his leadership the Britons took up arms, challenged their
conquerors to battle, and with God's help inflicted a defeat on
them. Thenceforward victory swung first to one side and then
to the other, until the battle of Badon Hill,* when the Britons
made a considerable slaughter of the invaders. This took place
about forty-four years after their arrival in Britain: but I shall
deal with this later.

CHAPTER 17: *Bishop Germanus sails to Britain with Lupus: with God's help he quells two storms, one of the sea, the other of the Pelagians* [A.D. 429]

A FEW years before their arrival, the Pelagian heresy introduced by Agricola, son of Severianus a Pelagian prelate, had seriously infected the faith of the British Church. Although the British rejected this perverse teaching, so blasphemous against the grace of Christ, they were unable to refute its plausible arguments by controversial methods, and wisely decided to ask help from the bishops of Gaul in this spiritual conflict. These summoned a great synod, and consulted together as to whom they should send to support the Faith. Their unanimous choice fell upon the apostolic bishops Germanus of Auxerre* and Lupus of Troyes, whom they appointed to visit the Britons and to confirm their belief in God's grace. The two bishops readily accepted the commands and decisions of Holy Church, and put to sea. They had safely sailed half-way on their voyage from Gaul with a favourable wind when they were suddenly subjected to the hostile power of devils, who were furious that such men as they should dare to recall the Britons to the way of salvation. They raised violent storms and turned day into night with black clouds. The sails were torn to shreds by the gale, the skill of the sailors was defeated, and the safety of the ship depended on prayer rather than on seamanship. Germanus their leader and bishop, spent and exhausted, had fallen asleep, when the storm reached a fresh pitch of violence, as though relieved of its opponent, and seemed about to overwhelm the vessel in the surging waves. At this juncture, Lupus and his companions roused their leader, and anxiously begged him to oppose the fury of the elements. More resolute than they in the face of imminent disaster, he called upon Christ and cast a few drops of holy water on the waves in the Name of the Sacred Trinity, encouraging his companions and directing them all to join him in prayer. God heard their cry and their adversaries were put to flight; the storm was stilled, the wind veered round to help them on their course and, after a swift and

peaceful passage, they arrived safely at their destination. Here
great crowds gathered from all quarters to greet the bishops,
whose arrival had been foretold even by the predictions of their
opponents. For when the evil spirits had been expelled by the
bishops from the persons of those whom they had possessed,
they disclosed their fears and revealed the origin of the storms
and perils they had raised, acknowledging themselves overcome
by the merits and power of the saints.

Meanwhile, the island of Britain was rapidly influenced by
the reasoning, preaching, and virtues of these apostolic bishops,
and the word of God was preached daily not only in the
churches, but in streets and fields, so that Catholics everywhere
were strengthened and heretics corrected. Theirs was the honour
and authority of apostles by their holy witness, the truth by
their learning, the miracles by their merits. So the majority of
the people readily accepted their teaching, while the authors of
false doctrines made themselves scarce, grieving like evil spirits
over the people who were snatched from their grasp. At length,
after due deliberation, they dared to challenge the saints and
appeared with rich ornaments and magnificent robes, supported
by crowds of flattering followers. For they preferred to hazard
a trial of strength rather than submit in shameful silence before
the people whom they had subverted, lest they should appear to
admit defeat. An immense gathering had assembled there with
their wives and children to watch and judge, but the contestants
were greatly dissimilar in bearing. On one side human presumption, on the other divine faith; on one side pride, on the other
piety; on one side Pelagius, on the other Christ. The holy
bishops gave their adversaries the advantage of speaking first,
which they did at great length, filling the time, and the ears of
their audience, with empty words. The venerable bishops then
fed the torrents of their eloquence from the springs of the
Apostles and evangelists, confirming their own words by the
word of God, and supporting their principal statements by
quotation from the scriptures. The conceit of the Pelagians was
pricked, their lies exposed, and unable to defend any of their
arguments, they admitted their errors. The people, who were

acting as their judges, were hardly restrained from violence, and confirmed their verdict with acclamation.

CHAPTER 18: *Germanus gives sight to the blind daughter of a tribune. He takes some relics from the tomb of Saint Alban, and deposits relics of the Apostles and other Martyrs*

IMMEDIATELY after this, a man who held the status of a tribune came forward with his wife and asked the bishops to cure his blind daughter, a child of ten. They directed him to take her to their opponents, but the latter, smitten by guilty consciences, joined their entreaties to those of the girl's parents and begged the bishops to heal her. Seeing their opponents yield, they offered a short prayer; then Germanus, being filled with the Holy Ghost, called on the Trinity, and taking into his hands a casket containing relics of the saints that hung around his neck, he applied it to the girl's eyes in the sight of them all. To the joy of the parents and the amazement of the crowd, the child's sight was emptied of darkness and filled with the light of truth. Thenceforward all erroneous arguments were expunged from the minds of the people, who eagerly accepted the teaching of the bishops.

Once this abominable heresy had been put down, its authors refuted, and the people established in the pure faith of Christ, the bishops paid a visit to the tomb of the blessed martyr Alban to return thanks to God through him. Germanus, who had with him relics of all the Apostles and several martyrs, first offered prayer, and then directed the tomb to be opened, so that he could deposit these precious gifts within it. For he thought it fitting that, as the equal merits of the saints had won them a place in heaven, so their relics should be gathered together from different lands into a common resting-place. And when he had reverently deposited these relics, Germanus took away with him a portion of earth from the place where the blessed martyr's blood had been shed. This earth was seen to have retained the martyr's blood, which had reddened the shrine where his persecutor had grown pale with fear. As a result of these events, a great number of people were converted to our Lord on the same day *

CHAPTER 19: *Germanus is detained by illness. He puts out a fire among houses by his prayer, and is healed of his sickness by a vision*

WHILE they were returning from this place, the ever-watchful Devil, having set his snares, contrived that Germanus should fall and break a leg, not knowing that his merits, like those of the blessed Job, would be enhanced by bodily affliction. While he was thus detained by illness, fire broke out in a cottage near his lodgings, and after destroying the adjoining dwellings which at that place were thatched with reeds from the marshes, it was carried by the wind to the cottage where he lay. The people ran to pick up the bishop and carry him to a place of safety; but, full of trust in God, he reproved them and would not allow them to do so. In despair, the people ran off to fight the fire; but to afford clearer evidence of God's power, whatever the crowd endeavoured to save was destroyed. Meanwhile the flames leaped over the house where the saint lay disabled and helpless; but, although they raged all around it, the place that sheltered him stood untouched amid a sea of fire. The crowd was overjoyed at the miracle and praised God for this proof of his power, while innumerable poor folk kept vigil outside his cottage day and night hoping for healing of soul or body.

It is impossible to relate all that Christ effected through his servant, and what wonders the sick saint performed. And while he refused any treatment for his own illness, he saw beside him one night a being in shining robes, who seemed to reach out his hand and raise him up, ordering him to stand on his feet. From that moment his pain ceased, his former health was restored, and when dawn came he continued on his journey undaunted.

CHAPTER 20: *The two bishops obtain God's help in battle, and return home*

M EANWHILE the Saxons and Picts joined forces and made war on the Britons, whom necessity had compelled to arm; and since the latter feared that their strength was unequal to the challenge, they called on the saintly bishops for help. They came at once as they had promised, and put such heart into the timid people that their presence was worth a large army. Under these apostolic leaders, Christ himself commanded in the camp. It also happened that the holy season of Lent was beginning, and was so reverently kept under the bishops' direction that the people came each day for instruction and flocked to receive the grace of Baptism. Most of the army sought Holy Baptism, and in readiness for the Feast of our Lord's Resurrection a church was constructed of interlaced boughs and set up in that armed camp as though it were a city. Strong in faith and fresh from the waters of Baptism, the army advanced; and whereas they had formerly despaired of human strength, all now trusted in the power of God. The preparation and disposition of the British forces was reported to the enemy, who, anticipating an easy victory over an ill-equipped army, advanced rapidly, closely observed by the British scouts.

After the Feast of Easter, when the greater part of the British forces, fresh from the font, were preparing to arm and embark on the struggle, Germanus promised to direct the battle in person.* He picked out the most active men and, having surveyed the surrounding country, observed a valley among the hills lying in the direction from which he expected the enemy to approach. Here he stationed the untried forces under his own orders. By now the main body of their remorseless enemies was approaching, watched by those whom he had placed in ambush. Suddenly Germanus, raising the standard, called upon them all to join him in a mighty shout. While the enemy advanced confidently, expecting to take the Britons unawares, the bishops three times shouted, 'Alleluia!' The whole army joined in this shout, until the surrounding hills echoed with the sound. The enemy column panicked, thinking that the very rocks and sky were falling on them, and were so terrified that they could not run fast enough. Throwing away their weapons in headlong flight, they were well content to escape naked, while many in their hasty flight were drowned in a river which they tried to cross. So the innocent British army saw its defeats avenged, and became an inactive spectator of the victory granted to it. The scattered spoils were collected, and the Christian forces rejoiced in the triumph of heaven. So the bishops overcame the enemy without bloodshed, winning a victory by faith and not by force.

Having restored peace to the island and overcome all its enemies, both visible and invisible, the bishops prepared to return home. Their own merits and the prayers of the blessed martyr Alban obtained them a peaceful voyage, and a propitious vessel restored them to their own welcoming people.

CHAPTER 21: *The Pelagian heresy revives, and Germanus returns to Britain with Severus. He heals a lame youth, and after denouncing or converting the heretics, restores the British Church to the Catholic Faith* [c. A.D. 438]

AFTER no great interval, news came from Britain that certain people were again promulgating the Pelagian heresy. Once again all the clergy requested blessed Germanus to defend God's cause as before. Promptly assenting, he took ship and made a peaceful crossing to Britain with a favouring wind, taking with him a man of great holiness named Severus. Severus had been a disciple of the most blessed Father Lupus, Bishop of Troyes; he subsequently became Bishop of Trier, and preached the Word in western Germany.

Meanwhile evil spirits throughout the land had been reluctantly compelled to foretell Germanus' coming, so that a local chieftain named Elaphius hurried to meet the saints before receiving any definite news. He brought with him his son, who in the very flower of his youth was crippled by a painful disease of the leg, whose muscles had so contracted that the limb was

entirely useless. Accompanying Elaphius was the whole population of his province. The bishops on arrival were met by the
ignorant folk, to whom they spoke and gave their blessing. And
having assured themselves that the people as a whole remained
loyal to the Faith as they had left them, and that the error was
restricted to a minority, they sought out its adherents and
rebuked them. Suddenly Elaphius threw himself at the bishops'
feet, and presented to them his son, the sight of whose infirmity
proclaimed his need louder than words. All were moved to pity
at the spectacle, especially the bishops, who earnestly prayed
God to show mercy. Blessed Germanus then asked the youth to
sit down, and drawing out the leg bent with disease, he passed
his healing hand over the afflicted area, and at his touch health
swiftly returned. The withered limb filled, the muscles regained
their power, and in the presence of them all the lad was restored
healed to his parents. The people were amazed at this miracle,
and the Catholic Faith was firmly implanted in all their hearts.
Germanus then warned them to live better and to shun all error.
And the false teachers, who by common consent had been
condemned to banishment, were brought before the bishops to
be taken to the Continent, so that the country might be rid of
them and they themselves brought to recognize their error.
Henceforward, the Faith was maintained uncorrupted in Britain
for a long time.

Having settled all these matters, the blessed bishops returned
home as successfully as they had come.

Germanus subsequently visited Ravenna to obtain peace for
the people of Armorica.[1] There he was received with honour by
the Emperor Valentinian and his mother Placidia, and while still
in this city he departed to Christ. His body was carried back
with a splendid escort to his own city and many signs of his
holiness were shown. Not long afterwards, in the fifth year of
Marcian's reign, Valentinian was murdered by supporters of the
patrician Aëtius, whom he had executed, and with him fell the
Empire of the West.

[1] Brittany.

CHAPTER 22: *The Britons enjoy a respite from foreign invasions, but exhaust themselves in civil wars and plunge into worse crimes* [c. 440–590]

MEANWHILE Britain enjoyed a rest from foreign, though not from civil, wars. Amid the wreckage of deserted cities destroyed by the enemy, the citizens who had survived the enemy now attacked each other. So long as the memory of past disaster remained fresh, kings and priests, commoners and nobles kept their proper rank. But when those who remembered died, there grew up a generation that knew nothing of these things and had experienced only the present peaceful order. Then were all restraints of truth and justice so utterly abandoned that no trace of them remained, and very few of the people even recalled their existence. Among the other unspeakable crimes, recorded with sorrow by their own historian Gildas, they added this – that they never preached the Faith to the Saxons or Angles who dwelt with them in Britain. But God in his goodness did not utterly abandon the people whom he had chosen; for he remembered them, and sent this nation more worthy preachers of truth to bring them to the Faith.*

CHAPTER 23: *The holy Pope Gregory sends Augustine and other monks to preach to the English nation, and encourages them in a letter to persevere in their mission* [A.D. 596]

IN the year of our Lord 582, Maurice, fifty-fourth in succession from Augustus, became Emperor, and ruled for twenty-one years. In the tenth year of his reign, Gregory, an eminent scholar and administrator, was elected Pontiff of the apostolic Roman see, and ruled it for thirteen years, six months, and ten days. In the fourteenth year of this Emperor, and about the one hundred and fiftieth year after the coming of the English to Britain, Gregory was inspired by God to send his servant Augustine with several other God-fearing monks to preach the word of God to the English nation.* Having undertaken this task in obedience to the Pope's command and progressed a short distance on their journey, they became afraid, and began to consider returning home. For they were appalled at the idea of going to a barbarous, fierce, and pagan nation, of whose very language they were ignorant. They unanimously agreed that this was the safest course, and sent back Augustine – who was to be consecrated bishop in the event of their being received by the English – so that he might humbly request the holy Gregory to recall them from so dangerous, arduous, and uncertain a journey. In reply, the Pope wrote them a letter of encouragement, urging them to proceed on their mission to preach God's word, and to trust themselves to his aid. This letter ran as follows:

'Gregory, servant of the servants of God, to the servants of our Lord. My very dear sons, it is better never to undertake any high enterprise than to abandon it when once begun. So with the help of God you must carry out this holy task which you have begun. Do not be deterred by the troubles of the journey or by what men say. Be constant and zealous in carrying out this enterprise which, under God's guidance, you have undertaken: and be assured that the greater the labour, the greater will be the glory of your eternal reward. When Augustine your leader returns, whom we have appointed your abbot,* obey him humbly in all things, remembering that whatever he directs you to do will always be to the good of your souls. May Almighty God protect you with His grace, and grant me to see the result of your labours in our heavenly home. And although my office prevents me from working at your side, yet because I long to do so, I hope to share in your joyful reward. God keep you safe, my dearest sons.

'Dated the twenty-third of July, in the fourteenth year of the reign of the most pious Emperor Maurice Tiberius Augustus, and the thirteenth year after his Consulship: the fourteenth indiction.'*

THE venerable Pontiff also wrote to Etherius, Archbishop of Arles, asking him to offer a kindly welcome to Augustine on his journey to Britain. This letter reads:

'To his most reverend and holy brother and fellow-bishop Etherius: Gregory, servant of the servants of God.

'Religious men should require no commendation to priests who exhibit the love that is pleasing to God; but since a suitable opportunity to write has arisen, We have written this letter to you, our brother, to certify that its bearer, God's servant Augustine, with his companions, of whose zeal we are assured, has been directed by us to proceed to save souls with the help of God. We therefore request Your Holiness to assist them with pastoral care, and to make speedy provision for their needs. And in order that you may assist them the more readily, we have particularly directed Augustine to give you full information about his mission, being sure that when you are acquainted with this, you will supply all their needs for the love of God. We also commend to your love the priest Candidus, our common son in Christ, whom we have transferred to a small patrimony in our church. God keep you safely, most reverend brother.

'Dated the twenty-third day of July, in the fourteenth year of the reign of the most pious Emperor Maurice Tiberius Augustus, and the thirteenth year after his Consulship: the fourteenth indiction.'

CHAPTER 25: *Augustine reaches Britain, and first preaches in the Isle of Thanet before King Ethelbert, who grants permission to preach in Kent* [A.D. 597]

REASSURED by the encouragement of the blessed father Gregory, Augustine and his fellow-servants of Christ resumed their work in the word of God, and arrived in Britain. At this time the most powerful king there was Ethelbert, who reigned in Kent and whose domains extended northwards to the river Humber, which forms the boundary between the north and south Angles. To the east of Kent lies the large island of Thanet, which by English reckoning is six hundred hides* in extent; it is separated from the mainland by a waterway about three furlongs broad called the Wantsum, which joins the sea at either end and is fordable only in two places. It was here that God's servant Augustine landed with companions, who are said to have been forty in number. At the direction of blessed Pope Gregory, they had brought interpreters from among the Franks, and they sent these to Ethelbert, saying that they came from Rome bearing very glad news, which certainty assured all who would receive it of eternal joy in heaven and an everlasting kingdom with the living and true God. On receiving this message, the king ordered them to remain in the island where they had landed, and gave directions that they were to be provided with all necessaries until he should decide what action to take. For he had already heard of the Christian religion, having a Christian wife of the Frankish royal house named Bertha, whom he had received from her parents on condition that she should have freedom to hold and practise her faith unhindered with Bishop Liudhard, whom they had sent as her helper in the faith.

After some days, the king came to the island and, sitting down in the open air, summoned Augustine and his companions to an audience. But he took precautions that they should not approach him in a house; for he held an ancient superstition that, if they were practisers of magical arts, they might have opportunity to deceive and master him. But the monks were endowed with power from God, not from the Devil, and approached the king carrying a silver cross as their standard and the likeness of our Lord and Saviour painted on a board. First of all they offered prayer to God, singing a litany for the eternal salvation both of themselves and of those to whom and for whose sake they had come. And when, at the king's command, they had sat down and preached the word of life to the king and his court, the king said: 'Your words and promises are fair indeed; but they are new and uncertain, and I cannot accept them and abandon the age-old beliefs that I have held together with the whole English nation. But since you have travelled far, and I can see you are sincere in your desire to impart to us what you believe to be true and excellent, we will not harm you. We will receive you hospitably and take care to supply you with all that you need; nor will we forbid you to preach and win any people you can to your religion.' The king then granted them a dwelling in the city of Canterbury, which was the chief city of all his realm, and in accordance with his promise he allowed them provisions and did not withdraw their freedom to preach.* Tradition says that as they approached the city, bearing the holy cross and the likeness of our great King and Lord Jesus Christ as was their custom, they sang in unison this litany: 'We pray Thee, O Lord, in all Thy mercy, that Thy wrath and anger may be turned away from this city and from Thy holy house, for we are sinners. Alleluia.'

CHAPTER 26: *The life and doctrine of the primitive Church are followed in Kent: Augustine establishes his episcopal see in the king's city*

As soon as they had occupied the house given to them they began to emulate the life of the apostles and the primitive Church. They were constantly at prayer; they fasted and kept vigils; they preached the word of life to whomsoever they could. They regarded wordly things as of little importance, and accepted only the necessities of life from those they taught. They practised what they preached, and were willing to endure any hardship, and even to die for the truth which they proclaimed. Before long a number of heathen, admiring the simplicity of their holy lives and the comfort of their heavenly message, believed and were baptized. On the east side of the city stood an old church, built in honour of Saint Martin during the Roman occupation of Britain, where the Christian queen of whom I have spoken went to pray. Here they first assembled to sing the psalms, to pray, to say Mass, to preach, and to baptize, until the king's own conversion to the Faith gave them greater freedom to preach and to build and restore churches everywhere.

At length the king himself, among others, edified by the pure lives of these holy men and their gladdening promises, the truth of which they confirmed by many miracles, believed and was baptized. Thenceforward, great numbers gathered each day to hear the word of God, forsaking their heathen rites and entering the unity of Christ's holy Church as believers. While the king was pleased at their faith and conversion, it is said that he would not compel anyone to accept Christianity; for he had learned from his instructors and guides to salvation that the service of Christ must be accepted freely and not under compulsion. Nevertheless, he showed greater favour to believers, because they were fellow-citizens of the kingdom of heaven. And it was not long before he granted his teachers in his capital of Canterbury a place of residence appropriate to their station, and gave them possessions of various kinds to supply their wants.

CHAPTER 27: *Augustine is consecrated bishop: he sends to inform Pope Gregory what has been achieved, and receives replies to his questions*

MEANWHILE God's servant Augustine visited Arles and, in accordance with the holy father Gregory's directions, was consecrated archbishop of the English nation by Etherius, archbishop of that city. On his return to Britain, he sent the priest Laurence and the monk Peter to Rome to inform the blessed Pope Gregory that the English had accepted the Faith of Christ, and that he himself had been consecrated bishop. At the same time, he sought advice on certain current problems. The Pope answered his enquiries without delay, and I have thought it proper to record these replies in my history.*

I. The first question of Augustine, Bishop of the Church of Canterbury: What is to be the relation between the bishop and his clergy? And how are the offerings made by the faithful at

the altar to be apportioned? And what are the functions of a
bishop in his church?

Gregory, Pope of the City of Rome, replies: Holy Scripture,
with which you are certainly well acquainted, offers us guidance
in this matter, and in particular the letters of blessed Paul to
Timothy, in which he carefully instructs him on a bishop's
duties in the house of God. But it is the custom of the Apostolic
See to instruct all newly consecrated bishops that all money
received is to be allocated under four heads: one for the bishop
and his household, for hospitality and other commitments;
another for the clergy; a third for the poor; and a fourth for the
upkeep of churches. In your case, my brother, having been
trained under monastic rule, you should not live apart from
your clergy in the church of the English, which by God's help
has lately been brought to the Faith. You are therefore to follow
the way of life practised by our forefathers of the primitive
Church, among whom none said that anything which he
possessed was his own, but they had all things common. If there
are any clerics who have not received Sacred Orders and who
cannot accept a life of continence, let them marry and receive
their stipends outside the common fund; for it is written of the
fathers whom we have mentioned, that 'distribution was made
unto every man according as he had need'. So give consideration
to the provision of their stipends, and see that they observe the
Church's discipline and live orderly, attend to the singing of the
Psalter, and by God's help preserve themselves in thought,
word, and deed from everything unlawful. But to those who
live as a Community there should be no need for us to mention
allocating portions, exercising hospitality, and showing mercy.
Everything that can be spared is to be devoted to holy and
religious purposes, as the Lord and Master of all bids; *'Give alms
of such things as ye have; and behold, all things are clean unto you.'*

II. Augustine's second question: Since we hold the same
Faith, why do customs vary in different Churches? Why, for
instance, does the method of saying Mass differ in the holy
Roman Church and in the Churches of Gaul?

Pope Gregory's reply: My brother, you are familiar with the

usage of the Roman Church, in which you were brought up.
But if you have found customs, whether in the Church of Rome
or of Gaul or any other that may be more acceptable to God, I
wish you to make a careful selection of them, and teach the
Church of the English, which is still young in the Faith,
whatever you have been able to learn with profit from the
various Churches. For things should not be loved for the sake
of places, but places for the sake of good things. Therefore
select from each of the Churches whatever things are devout,
religious, and right; and when you have bound them, as it were,
into a sheaf,* let the minds of the English grow accustomed
to it.

III. Augustine's third question: What punishment should be
awarded to those who rob churches?

Pope Gregory's reply: The punishment must depend on the
circumstances of the offender. For some commit theft although
they have means of subsistence, and others out of poverty.
Some, therefore, should be punished by fines, others by beating;
some severely, and others more leniently. But when the punishment has to be severe, let it be administered in charity, not in
anger; for the purpose of such correction is to save the wicked
from hell-fire. We must maintain discipline among the faithful
as good fathers among their children, whom they beat for
wrongdoing, and yet choose for their heirs, while they preserve
their possessions for the benefit of those whom they appear to
treat harshly. So charity must always be our motive and indicate
the means of correction, so that we may do nothing unreason-
able. You may add that thieves are to restore whatever they
have taken from churches, but God forbid that the Church
should recover with interest any worldly goods she may lose,
or seek any gain from these empty things.*

IV. Augustine's fourth question: Is it permissible for two
brothers to marry two sisters, provided that there be no blood
ties between the families?

Pope Gregory's reply: This is quite permissible. There is
nothing in holy Scripture that seems to forbid it.

V. Augustine's fifth question: To what degree may the

faithful marry with their kindred? And is it lawful for a man to marry his step-mother or sister-in-law?

Pope Gregory's reply: an earthly law of the Roman state permits first-cousins to marry. But experience shows that such unions do not result in children, and sacred law forbids a man to *'uncover the nakedness of his kindred.'* Necessity therefore forbids a closer marriage than that between the third or fourth generation, while the second generation, as we have said, should wholly abstain from marriage. But to wed one's step-mother is a grave sin, for the Law says: *'Thou shalt not uncover the nakedness of thy father.'* Now the son cannot uncover the nakedness of his father; but since it says, *'They shall be one flesh'*, whosoever presumes to wed his step-mother, who was one flesh with his father, thereby commits this offence. It is also forbidden to marry a sister-in-law, since by a former union she had become one with his own brother: it was for denouncing this sin that John the Baptist was beheaded and met his holy martyrdom. For John was not ordered to deny Christ, but was in fact put to death as a confessor of Christ. For since our Lord Jesus Christ said: *'I am the Truth'*, John shed his blood for Christ in that he gave his life for the truth.

But since there are many among the English who, while they were still heathen, are said to have contracted these unlawful marriages, when they accept the Faith they are to be instructed that this is a grave offence and that they must abstain from it. Warn them of the terrible judgement of God lest for their bodily desires they incur the pains of eternal punishment. Nevertheless, they are not on that account to be deprived of the Communion of the Body and Blood of Christ, lest they appear to be punished for sins committed unknowingly before they received the purification of Baptism. For in these days the Church corrects some things strictly, and allows others out of leniency; others again she deliberately glosses over and tolerates and by so doing often succeeds in checking an evil of which she disapproves. But all who come to the Faith are to be warned against doing these things, and should any subsequently be guilty of them, they are to be forbidden to receive the Communion of the Body and Blood of our Lord. For while these offences may to some extent be condoned in those who acted in ignorance, they must be severely punished in those who presume to sin knowingly.

VI. Augustine's sixth question: If a long journey is involved, so that bishops cannot easily assemble, is it permissible for a bishop to be consecrated without other bishops being present?

Pope Gregory's reply: In the church of the English where as yet you are the only bishop, you cannot do otherwise than consecrate a bishop without other bishops being present. For when do bishops from Gaul pay a visit, so that they can be present as witnesses to the consecration? It is our wish, brother, that you should so establish bishops that they are not unnecessarily far apart: so that at a bishop's consecration other pastors, whose presence is certainly desirable, may be readily summoned. Therefore, when in God's good time bishops are appointed in various places at no great distance from one another, no consecration is to take place except in the presence of three or four bishops. For in spiritual matters we may often with advantage follow the customs of the world, so that we may arrange things carefully and wisely. When a wedding is celebrated, married folk are invited, so that those who have already travelled some way down the path of marriage may share the joy of the new couple. So, at this spiritual consecration, when a man is joined to God in the sacred ministry, why should not those be invited who will take pleasure in the elevation of the new bishop, or offer their prayers to God for his protection?

VII. Augustine's seventh question: What are to be our relations with the bishops of Gaul and Britain?

Pope Gregory's reply: We give you no authority over the bishops of Gaul, for since the time of my early predecessors the Bishop of Arles has received the *pallium*, and his authority is to be in no way impaired. If, therefore, you have occasion to cross over into the province of Gaul, you are to consult with the Bishop of Arles how to correct any faults among the bishops; and should he be remiss in administering discipline, inspire him with your own zeal. We have already written to him, requesting

him to offer you every assistance whenever you visit Gaul and
to ensure that his bishops observe no customs contrary to the
laws of God our Maker. Although we give you no authority
over the bishops of Gaul, you should nevertheless advise,
encourage and show them a good example. Recall the minds of
any wrong-doers to the pursuit of holiness, for it is written in
the Law: '*When thou comest into the standing corn of thy neighbour,
then thou mayest pluck the ears with thine hand; but thou shalt not
move a sickle into thy neighbour's standing corn.*' Similarly, you may
not use the sickle of authority in the field entrusted to another
man, but use your good influence to separate the Lord's wheat
from the chaff of their sins, and by your teaching and persuasion
assimilate them into the body of the Church. But no official
action is to be taken without the authority of the Bishop of
Arles, so that the long-established institutions of our fathers
may not fall into disuse. All the bishops of Britain, however,
we commit to your charge. Use your authority to instruct the
unlearned, to strengthen the weak, and correct the misguided.

VIII. Augustine's eighth question: May an expectant mother
be baptized? How soon after childbirth may she enter church?
And how soon after birth may a child be baptized if in danger
of death? How soon after child-birth may a husband have
relations with his wife? And may a woman properly enter
church at the time of menstruation? And may she receive
Communion at these times? And may a man enter church after
relations with his wife before he has washed? Or receive the
sacred mystery of Communion? These uncouth English people
require guidance on all these matters.

Pope Gregory's reply: I have no doubt, my brother, that
questions such as these have arisen, and I think I have already
answered you; but doubtless you desire my support for your
statements and rulings. Why should not an expectant mother be
baptized? – the fruitfulness of the flesh is no offence in the sight
of Almighty God. For when our first parents sinned in the
Garden, they justly forfeited God's gift of immortality. But
although God deprived man of immortality for his sin, he did
not destroy the human race on that account, but of his merciful

goodness left man his ability to continue the race. On what grounds, then, can Almighty God's free gift to man be excluded from the grace of Holy Baptism? For it would be foolish to suppose that his gift of grace is contrary to the sacred mystery by which all guilt is washed away.

As to the interval that must elapse after childbirth before a woman may enter church, you are familiar with the Old Testament rule: that is, for a male child thirty-three days and for a female, sixty-six. But this is to be understood as an allegory, for were a woman to enter church and return thanks in the very hour of her delivery, she would do nothing wrong. The fault lies in the bodily pleasure, not in the pain; the pleasure is in the bodily union, the pain is in the birth, so that Eve, the mother of us all, was told: '*In sorrow thou shalt bring forth children.*' If, then, we forbid a woman who is delivered of a child to enter church, we make this penalty into a sin. There is no obstacle to the Baptism either of a woman who has been delivered, or of a newborn babe, even if it is administered to her in the very hour of her delivery, or to the child at the hour of its birth, provided that there be danger of death. For as the grace of this sacred mystery is to be offered with great deliberation to the living and conscious, so is it to be administered without delay to the dying; for if we wait to offer them this mystery of redemption, it may be too late to find the one to be redeemed.

A man should not approach his wife until her child is weaned. But a bad custom has arisen in the behaviour of married people that women disdain to suckle their own children, and hand them over to other women to nurse. This custom seems to have arisen solely through incontinency; for when women are unwilling to be continent, they refuse to suckle their children. So those who observe this bad custom of giving their children to others to nurse must not approach their husbands until the time of their purification has elapsed. For even apart from childbirth, women are forbidden to do so during their monthly courses, and the Old Law prescribed death for any man who approached a woman during this time. But a woman should not be forbidden to enter church during these times; for the workings

of nature cannot be considered culpable, and it is not just that
she should be refused admittance, since her condition is beyond
her control. We know that the woman who suffered an issue of
blood, humbly approaching behind our Lord, touched the hem
of his robe and was at once healed of her sickness. If, therefore,
this woman was right to touch our Lord's robe, why may not
one who suffers nature's courses be permitted to enter the
church of God? And if it is objected that the woman in the
Gospels was compelled by disease while these latter are bound
by custom, then remember, my brother, that everything that
we suffer in this mortal body through the infirmity of its nature
is justly ordained by God since the Fall of man. For hunger,
thirst, heat, cold, and weariness originate in this infirmity of
our nature; and our search for food against hunger, drink against
thirst, coolness against heat, clothing against cold, and rest
against weariness is only our attempt to obtain some remedy in
our weakness. In this sense the menstrual flow in a woman is an
illness. So, if it was a laudable presumption in the woman who,
in her disease, touched our Lord's robe, why may not the same
concession be granted to all women who endure the weakness
of their nature?

A woman, therefore, should not be forbidden to receive the
mystery of Communion at these times. If any out of a deep
sense of reverence do not presume to do so, this is commendable; but if they do so, they do nothing blameworthy. Sincere
people often acknowledge their faults even when there is no
actual fault, because a blameless action may often spring from a
fault. For instance, eating when we are hungry is no fault, but
being hungry originates in Adam's sin; similarly, the monthly
courses of women are no fault, because nature causes them. But
the defilement of our nature is apparent even when we have no
deliberate intention to do evil, and this defilement springs from
sin; so may we recognize the judgement that our sin has brought
on us. And so may man, who sinned willingly, bear the
punishment of his sin unwillingly. Therefore, when women
after due consideration do not presume to approach the Sacrament of the Body and Blood of the Lord during their courses,

they are to be commended. But if they are moved by devout love of this holy mystery to receive it as pious custom suggests, they are not to be discouraged. For while the Old Testament makes outward observances important, the New Testament does not regard these things so highly as the inward disposition, which is the sole true criterion for allotting punishment. For instance, the Law forbids the eating of many things as unclean, but in the Gospel our Lord says: '*Not that which goeth into the mouth defileth a man; but that which cometh out of the mouth, this defileth a man.*' He also said: '*Out of the mouth proceed evil thoughts.*' Here Almighty God clearly shows us that evil actions spring from the root of evil thoughts. Similarly, Saint Paul says: '*Unto the pure all things are pure; but unto them that are defiled and unbelieving is nothing pure.*' And later, he indicates the cause of this corruption, adding: '*For even their mind and conscience is defiled.*' If, therefore, no food is unclean to one of a pure mind, how can a woman who endures the laws of nature with a pure mind be considered impure?

It is not fitting that a man who has approached his wife should enter church before he has washed, nor is he to enter at once, though washed. The ancient Law prescribed that a man in such cases should wash, and forbade him to enter a holy place before sunset. But this may be understood spiritually; for when a man's mind is attracted to those pleasures by lawless desire, he should not regard himself as fitted to join in Christian worship until these heated desires cool in the mind, and he has ceased to labour under wrongful passions. And although various nations have differing views on this matter and observe different customs, it was always the ancient Roman usage for such a man to seek purification and out of reverence to refrain awhile from entering a holy place. In making this observation, we do not condemn marriage itself, but since lawful intercourse must be accompanied by bodily desire, it is fitting to refrain from entering a holy place, since this desire itself is not blameless. For David, who said: '*Behold, I was shapen in iniquity, and in sin did my mother conceive me*', was not himself born of any illicit union, but in lawful wedlock. But knowing himself to have been conceived in iniquity, he grieved that he had been born in sin, like a tree bearing in its branches the sap of evil drawn up from its root. In saying this, he does not term the bodily union of married people iniquity, but the desire of such union. For there are many things that are lawful and legitimate, and yet in the doing of them we are to some extent contaminated. For example, we often correct faults under stress of anger and thereby disturb our peace of mind; and though we are right to do so, it is not good that we should lose our peace of mind in the process. He who said: '*Mine eye is troubled because of anger*'[1] had been roused by the crimes of evil men, and because only a quiet mind can rest in the light of contemplation, he regretted that his eye was troubled by anger, so that he was disquieted and prevented from contemplating heavenly things so long as he was distracted by indignation at the wicked doings of men. So while anger against evil is commendable, it is harmful to a man because in being disturbed by it he is conscious of some guilt. Lawful intercourse should be for the procreation of offspring, and not for mere pleasure; to obtain children, and not to satisfy lust. But if any man is not moved by a desire for pleasure, but only by a desire for children, he is to be left to his own judgement either as to entering church, or to receiving the Communion of the Body and Blood of our Lord; for we have no right to debar one who does not yield to the fires of temptation. But when lust takes the place of desire for children, the mere act of union becomes something that the pair have cause to regret; and although the holy teachings give them permission, yet this carries a warning with it. For when the Apostle Paul said: '*If they cannot contain, let them marry*', he at once added, '*I speak this by permission, and not of commandment.*' This concession makes it lawful, yet not good; so when he spoke of permission, he indicated that it was not blameless.

It should be carefully considered that, when God was about to speak to the people on Mount Sinai, he first ordered them to

---

[1] In the Authorized Version this passage (Psalm 6. 7) reads: 'Mine eye is consumed because of grief.'

abstain from women. And if such a degree of bodily purity was required in those who were to hear the word of God when he spoke to men through a subject creature, how much the more should women preserve themselves in purity of body when about to receive the Body of Almighty God himself, lest they be overwhelmed by the very greatness of this inestimable mystery? For this reason the priest instructed David that, if his men were clean in this respect, they might be given the shewbread, which would have been entirely forbidden had not David first certified that they had kept themselves from women. Similarly the man who has cleansed himself with water after intercourse with his wife is allowed to approach the mystery of Holy Communion, since he may enter church in accordance with this decision.

IX. Augustine's ninth question: May a man receive communion after a sexual illusion in a dream; or, if a priest, may he celebrate the holy mysteries?

Pope Gregory's reply: The Testament of the Old Law, as I have already mentioned, speaks of such a man as unclean and does not permit him to enter church until evening and after purification. But this is to be understood spiritually in another sense; for a man may be under a delusion and tempted to impurity in a dream, because, having yielded to temptation, he is defiled by real mental imaginings. Then he must cleanse himself with water, thus washing away his sinful thoughts with tears. And, unless the fire of temptation dies earlier, he should regard himself as unclean until evening. But we should carefully examine the origin of such illusions in the mind of a sleeper; for sometimes they arise from over-eating, sometimes from excess or lack of bodily vigour, and sometimes from impure thoughts. When such illusion occurs through excess or lack of bodily vigour, it need not be feared, because it is to be deplored rather as something the mind has unwittingly suffered than as something it has done. But when a greedy appetite runs riot and overloads the repositories of the bodily fluids, the mind is to blame, although not to the extent that a man must be forbidden to receive the holy mystery, or to say mass when a feast-day requires it, or when necessity demands that he administer the sacrament in the absence of another priest. But if there are others who can perform this ministry, then this illusion caused by greed need not debar a man from receiving the holy mystery unless the mind of the sleeper has been excited by impure thought; but I think that humility should move him to refrain from offering the holy mysteries under these circumstances. For there are some who are not mentally disturbed by impure thoughts, although subject to these illusions. In these things there is just one thing that shows that the mind is not innocent even in its own judgement: although it remembers nothing that occurs during sleep, yet it does remember its greedy appetites. But if the sleeper's illusion springs from indecent thoughts when awake, his guilt stands clear in his mind and he recognizes the source of his sin, because he has unconsciously experienced what has been in his conscious thoughts. But the question arises whether an evil thought merely suggests itself to a man, or whether he proceeds to take pleasure in it, or, worse still, to assent to it. For all sin is consummated in three ways, that is, by suggestion, pleasure, and consent. Suggestion comes through the devil, pleasure through the flesh, and consent through the will. The Serpent suggests the first sin, and Eve, as flesh, took physical pleasure in it, while Adam, as spirit, consented; and great discernment is needed if the mind, in judging itself, is to distinguish between suggestion and pleasure, and between pleasure and consent. For when the Evil Spirit suggests a sin, no sin is committed unless the flesh takes pleasure in it; but when the flesh begins to take pleasure, then sin is born; and if deliberate consent is given, sin is complete. The seed of sin, therefore, is in suggestion, its growth in pleasure, and its completion in consent. It often happens, however, that what the Evil Spirit sows in the mind and the flesh anticipates with pleasure, the soul rejects. And although the body cannot experience pleasure without the mind, yet the mind, in contending against the desires of the body, is to some extent unwillingly chained to them, having to oppose them for conscience sake, and strongly regretting its bondage to bodily desires. It was for

this reason that Paul, that great soldier in God's army, confessed
with sorrow: '*I see another law in my members warring against the
law of my mind, and bringing me into captivity to the law of sin,
which is in my members.*' Now if he was a captive, he fought but
little; yet he did fight. So he was both captive and also fighting
with the law of the mind, to which the law of the body is
opposed. And if he fought thus, he was no captive. So one may
say that a man is both captive and free; free through the law of
right which he loves, and captive through the law of bodily
pleasure, of which he is an unwilling victim.

CHAPTER 28: *Pope Gregory writes to the Bishop of Arles, asking
him to help Augustine in his work for God* [A.D. 601]

SUCH were the blessed Pope Gregory's replies to the questions of the most reverend Bishop Augustine. The Pope also
wrote a letter to the Bishop of Arles, which was delivered to
Vergilius, successor to Etherius. This ran as follows:

'To our most reverend and holy brother Vergilius, our
fellow-bishop: Gregory, servant of the servants of God.

'It is well established that brethren who visit us on their own
initiative should be warmly welcomed, since most visitors are
invited out of affection. Therefore, if Bishop Augustine, who is
brother to us both, happens to visit you, I beg you to receive
him with proper affection and kindness, so that he may be
encouraged by your goodwill and that others may learn how
brotherly love is to be cultivated. And since it often happens
that an independent observer sees what needs correction sooner
than the man on the spot, I ask that, should he bring to your
notice any wrong-doing among clergy or others, you make
careful enquiry into these matters with his help. In this way you
will show yourself strict and alert against all abuses that offend
God and incur His displeasure, so that the guilty may be
corrected, the innocent vindicated, and others mend their ways.
God keep you safe, most reverend brother.

'Dated the twenty-second day of June, in the nineteenth year of our most pious Lord and Emperor Maurice Tiberius Augustus, and the eighteenth year after his Consulship: the fourth indiction.

CHAPTER 29: *Gregory sends Augustine the* pallium, *a letter, and several clergy* [A.D. 601]

HEARING from Bishop Augustine that he had a rich harvest but few to help him gather it, Pope Gregory sent with his envoys several colleagues and clergy, of whom the principal and most outstanding were Mellitus, Justus, Paulinus, and Rufinianus. They brought with them everything necessary for the worship and service of the Church, including sacred vessels, altar coverings, church ornaments, vestments for priests and clergy, relics of the holy Apostles and martyrs, and many books.* Gregory also sent a letter to Augustine, telling him that he had dispatched the *pallium* to him, and giving him directions on the appointment of bishops in Britain. This letter runs as follows:

'To our most reverend and holy brother and fellow-bishop Augustine: Gregory, servant of the servants of God.

'While Almighty God alone can grant His servants the ineffable joys of the kingdom of heaven, it is proper that we should reward them with earthly honours, and encourage them by such recognition to devote themseves to their spiritual labours with redoubled zeal. And since the new Church of the English has now, through the goodness of God and your own efforts, been brought to the grace of God, we grant you the privilege of wearing the *pallium* in that Church whenever you perform the solemnities of the Mass. You are to consecrate twelve bishops in different places, who will be subject to your jurisdiction: the bishop of the city of London will thenceforward be consecrated by his own synod, and will receive the honour of the *pallium* from this apostolic See which, by divine decree, we at present occupy. We wish you also to send a bishop of your own choice to the city of York, and if that city with the adjoining territory accepts the word of God, this bishop is to consecrate twelve other bishops, and hold the dignity of Metropolitan. If we live to see this, we intend to grant him the *pallium* also, but he is to remain subject to your authority. After your death, however, he is to preside over the bishops whom he has consecrated and to be wholly independent of the Bishop of London. Thenceforward, seniority of consecration is to determine whether the Bishop of London or York takes precedence; but they are to consult one another and take united action in all matters concerning the Faith of Christ, and take and execute all decisions without mutual disharmony.

'You, my brother, are to exercise authority in the Name of our Lord and God Jesus Christ both over those bishops whom you shall consecrate, and any who shall be consecrated by the Bishop of York, and also over all the British bishops. Let Your Grace's words and example show them a pattern of right belief and holy life, so that they may execute their office in right belief and practice and, when God wills, attain the kingdom of heaven. God keep you safe, most reverend brother.

'Dated the twenty-second of June, in the nineteenth year of our most pious Lord and Emperor Maurice Tiberius Augustus, and the nineteenth after his Consulship: the fourth indiction.'

CHAPTER 30: *A copy of the letter sent by Pope Gregory to Abbot Mellitus on his departure for Britain* [A.D. 601]

WHEN these messengers had left, the holy father Gregory sent after them letters worthy of our notice, which show most clearly his unwearying interest in the salvation of our nation. The letter runs as follows:

'To our well loved son Abbot Mellitus: Gregory, servant of the servants of God.

'Since the departure of those of our fellowship who are bearing you company, we have been seriously anxious, because we have received no news of the success of your journey. Therefore, when by God's help you reach our most reverend

brother, Bishop Augustine, we wish you to inform him that we
have been giving careful thought to the affairs of the English,
and have come to the conclusion that the temples of the idols
among that people should on no account be destroyed. The
idols are to be destroyed, but the temples themselves are to be
aspersed with holy water, altars set up in them, and relics
deposited there.* For if these temples are well-built, they must
be purified from the worship of demons and dedicated to the
service of the true God. In this way, we hope that the people,
seeing that their temples are not destroyed, may abandon their
error and, flocking more readily to their accustomed resorts,
may come to know and adore the true God. And since they
have a custom of sacrificing many oxen to demons, let some
other solemnity be substituted in its place, such as a day of
Dedication or the Festivals of the holy martyrs whose relics are
enshrined there. On such occasions they might well construct
shelters of boughs for themselves around the churches that were
once temples, and celebrate the solemnity with devout feasting.
They are no longer to sacrifice beasts to the Devil, but they may
kill them for food to the praise of God, and give thanks to the
Giver of all gifts for the plenty they enjoy. If the people are
allowed some worldly pleasures in this way, they will more
readily come to desire the joys of the spirit. For it is certainly
impossible to eradicate all errors from obstinate minds at one
stroke, and whoever wishes to climb to a mountain top climbs
gradually step by step, and not in one leap. It was in this way
that the Lord revealed Himself to the Israelite people in Egypt,
permitting the sacrifices formerly offered to the Devil to be
offered thenceforward to Himself instead. So He bade them
sacrifice beasts to Him, so that, once they became enlightened,
they might abandon one element of sacrifice and retain another.
For, while they were to offer the same beasts as before, they
were to offer them to God instead of to idols, so that they
would no longer be offering the same sacrifices. Of your
kindness, you are to inform our brother Augustine of this
policy, so that he may consider how he may best implement it
on the spot. God keep you safe, my very dear son.

'Dated the seventeenth of June, in the nineteenth year of the reign of our most pious Lord and Emperor Maurice Tiberius Augustus, and the eighteenth after his Consulship: the fourth indiction.'

CHAPTER 31: *Pope Gregory writes to Augustine, warning him not to boast of his achievements* [A.D. 601]

A T the same time, hearing that Augustine had performed miracles, Pope Gregory sent him a letter in which he warned him not to fall into the peril of pride on this account. He wrote:

'My very dear brother, I hear that Almighty God has worked great wonders through you for the nation which He has chosen. Therefore let your feeling be one of fearful joy and joyful fear at God's heavenly gifts – joy that the souls of the English are being drawn through outward miracles to inward grace; fear lest the frail mind becomes proud because of these wonderful events. For when it receives public recognition, it is liable to fall through senseless conceit. We should remember how the disciples returned from their preaching full of joy, and said to their heavenly Master: '*Lord, even the devils are subject unto us, through thy name.*' But they received the prompt rejoinder: '*In this rejoice not. But rather rejoice because your names are written in heaven.*' For when the disciples rejoiced at these miracles, they were thinking of their transitory personal joy; but Christ recalled them from personal to universal, and from transitory to eternal joy, saying: '*In this rejoice, because your names are written in heaven.*' For God's chosen do not all work miracles, yet the names of all are written in heaven. For those who are disciples of the truth should rejoice only in that good thing which they share with all men, and which they shall enjoy for ever.

'Finally, dearest brother, in all the outward actions which by God's help you perform, always strictly examine your inner dispositions. Clearly understand your own character, and how much grace is in this nation for whose conversion God has given you the power to work miracles. And if you remember that you have ever offended our Creator by word or action, let the memory of your sin crush any temptation to pride that may arise in your heart. And bear in mind that whatever powers to perform miracles you have received or shall receive from God are entrusted to you solely for the salvation of your people.'

CHAPTER 32: *Pope Gregory sends letters and gifts to King Ethelbert* [A.D. 601]

POPE Gregory also sent a letter to King Ethelbert with many gifts of different kinds, wishing to bestow earthly honours on this king who by his exertions and zeal, and to his great joy, had been brought to knowledge of heavenly glory. A copy of this letter follows.

'To our excellent son, the most glorious King Ethelbert, King of the English: the Bishop Gregory.

'The reason why Almighty God raises good men to govern nations is that through them He may bestow the gifts of His mercy on all whom they rule. We know that this is so in the case of the English nation, over whom you reign so gloriously, so that by means of the good gifts that God grants to you He may bless your people as well. Therefore, my illustrious son, zealously foster the grace that God has given you, and press on with the task of extending the Christian Faith among the people committed to your charge. Make their conversion your first concern; suppress the worship of idols, and destroy their shrines; raise the moral standards of your subjects by your own innocence of life, encouraging, warning, persuading, correcting, and showing them an example by your good deeds. God will most surely grant you His rewards in heaven if you faithfully proclaim His Name and truth upon earth; and He whose honour you seek and uphold among your peoples will make your own name glorious to posterity.

'So it was that the devout Emperor Constantine in his day turned the Roman State from its ignorant worship of idols by his own submission to our mighty Lord and God Jesus Christ, and with his subjects accepted Him with all his heart. The result is that his glorious reputation has excelled that of all his predecessors, and he has outshone them in reputation as greatly as he surpassed them in good works. Now, therefore, let Your Majesty make all speed to bring to your subject princes and peoples the knowledge of the One God, Father, Son and Holy Spirit, so that your own merit and repute may excel that of all the former kings of your nation. And when you have thus cleansed your subjects from their sins, you will bear the load of your own sins with greater confidence before the judgement seat of God.

'Our most reverend brother Bishop Augustine has been trained under monastic Rule, has a complete knowledge of holy scripture, and, by the grace of God, is a man of holy life. Therefore I beg you to listen to his advice ungrudgingly, follow it exactly and store it carefully in your memory; for if you listen to him when he speaks in God's name, God himself will listen more readily to the prayers he utters on your behalf. But if you ignore his advice – which God forbid – and disregard him when he speaks for God, how should God pay attention when he speaks for you? Work sincerely and wholeheartedly with him in fervent faith, and support his efforts with all the strength God has given you, so that you may receive a place in the kingdom of Christ, whose Faith you profess and uphold in your own realm.

'We would also have Your Majesty know what we have learned from the words of Almighty God in holy Scripture, that the end of this present world is at hand and the everlasting kingdom of the Saints is approaching. When the end of the world is near, unprecedented things occur – portents in the sky, terrors from heaven, unseasonable tempests, wars, famines, pestilences, and widespread earthquakes. Not all these things will happen during our own lifetimes, but will all ensue in due course. Therefore, if any such things occur in your own country, do not be anxious, for these portents of the end are sent to warn us to consider the welfare of our souls and remember our last end, so that, when our Judge comes, He may find us prepared by good lives. I have mentioned these matters in this short letter, my illustrious son, in the hope that as the Christian Faith grows more strong in your kingdom, our correspondence with you may become more frequent. So my pleasure in addressing you will keep pace with the joy in my heart at the glad news of the complete conversion of your people.

'I have sent some small presents, which will not appear small to you, since you will receive them with the blessing of the blessed Apostle Peter. May Almighty God continue to perfect you in His grace, prolong your life for many years, and after this life receive you among the citizens of your heavenly home. May the grace of heaven preserve Your Majesty in safety.

'Dated the twenty-second day of June, in the nineteenth year of our most pious lord and Emperor Maurice Tiberius Augustus, and the eighteenth after his Consulship: the fourth indiction.'

CHAPTER 33: *Augustine repairs the Church of Our Saviour and builds a monastery of Saint Peter the Apostle. A note on Peter, its first Abbot* [A.D. 602]

HAVING been granted his episcopal see in the royal capital, as already recorded, Augustine proceeded with the king's help to repair a church which he was informed had been built long ago by Roman Christians. This he hallowed in the name of our Saviour, God, and Lord Jesus Christ,* and established there a dwelling for himself and his successors. He also built a monastery a short distance to the east of the city, where at his suggestion King Ethelbert erected from the foundations a church dedicated to the blessed Apostles Peter and Paul, enriching it with many gifts. It was here that the bodies of Augustine and all the Archbishops of Canterbury and of the Kings of Kent were to rest. This church was not consecrated by Augustine himself, however, but by Laurence his successor.

The first abbot of this monastery was the priest Peter, who was sent on a mission to Gaul and was drowned at sea in a bay called Amfleat,[1] where the local inhabitants buried him without

---

[1] Ambleteuse.

honour. But, as evidence of his holy life, Almighty God caused a heavenly light to appear over his grave every night, until the local people saw it and, realizing that a holy man lay buried there, made enquiries as to whose the body might be. Then they took up the body and interred it in a church in the city of Boulogne with the honours due to so great a man.

CHAPTER 34: *Ethelfrid, King of the Northumbrians, defeats the Irish and drives them out of England* [A.D. 603]

ABOUT this time, Ethelfrid, a very powerful and ambitious king, ruled the kingdom of the Northumbrians.* He ravaged the Britons more cruelly than all other English leaders, so that he might well be compared to Saul the King of Israel, except of course that he was ignorant of true religion. He overran a greater area than any other king or ealdorman, exterminating or enslaving the inhabitants, making their lands either tributary to the English or ready for English settlement. One might fairly apply to him the words of the patriarch Jacob's blessing of his son: '*Benjamin shall ravin as a wolf; in the morning he shall devour the prey, and at night he shall divide the spoil.*'

Alarmed at his advance, Aidan, king of those Irish who lived in Britain, came against him with a large and strong army, but was defeated and fled with very few, having lost almost his entire army at a famous place known as Degsastan, that is, Degsa's Stone. In this battle, Ethelfrid's brother Theodbald and all his following were killed. Ethelfrid won this fight in the year of our Lord 603, the eleventh of this reign, which lasted twenty-four years. It was also the first year of the reign of Phocas, who then occupied the throne of the Roman Empire. From that day until the present, no king of the Irish in Britain has dared to do battle with the English.

BOOK TWO

✤

CHAPTER I: *On the death of Pope Gregory*

ABOUT this time, in the year of our Lord 605, having ruled the apostolic Roman Church most illustriously for thirteen years, six months, and ten days, the blessed Pope Gregory died and was taken up to his eternal home in heaven. And it is fitting that he should receive fuller mention in this history, since it was through his zeal that our English nation was brought from the bondage of Satan to the Faith of Christ, and we may rightly term him our own apostle.* For during his pontificate, while he exercised supreme authority over all the churches of Christendom that had already long since been converted, he transformed our still idolatrous nation into a church of Christ. So, we may rightly describe him by the term apostle; for if he is not an apostle to others, yet doubtless he is to us, and we are *the seal of his apostleship in the Lord*.

Gregory was Roman-born, son of Gordian, and descended from ancestors not only noble but devout. Among them was Felix, once bishop of the same apostolic see, a man of high distinction in the Church of Christ, and Gregory maintained this family tradition by the nobility and devotion of his religious life. By God's grace, he turned his aptitude for worldly success wholly to the attainment of heavenly glory. For he suddenly retired from secular life and sought admission to a monastery. There he entered upon a life of such perfection in grace that in later years he used to recall with tears how his mind was set on high things, soaring above all that is transitory, and how he was able to devote himself entirely to thoughts of heaven. Remaining in the body, he could yet transcend its limitations in contemplation, and looked forward to death, which most men regard as a punishment, as the gateway to life and reward of his labours. He used to mention this, not in order to call attention to his increase in virtue, but lamenting rather the decrease in virtue that he believed himself to have suffered through his pastoral responsibilities. One day, in private conversation with his deacon Peter, Gregory described his former spiritual state, then sadly continued: 'My pastoral responsibilities now compel me to have dealings with worldly men, and after the unclouded beauty of my former peace, it seems that my mind is bespattered with the mire of daily affairs. For when it has squandered itself in attention to the worldly affairs of numberless people, even though it turns inward again to meditate on spiritual things, it does so with unmistakably lessened powers. So when I compare what I now endure with what I have lost, and when I weigh that loss, my burden seems greater than ever.'

Holy Gregory spoke in this way from deep humility. Yet we cannot but believe that he lost none of his monastic perfection through his pastoral cares, and indeed made greater spiritual progress by his labours for the conversion of souls than in his former peaceful life, especially since, even when he became Pope, he ordered his house as a monastery. When he was first summoned from his monastery, ordained to the ministry of the altar, and sent to Constantinople as representative of the apostolic see, he never abandoned his spiritual exercises even amid the concourse of an earthly palace. For some of his fellow-monks were so devoted to him that they accompanied him to the Imperial city, and he began to maintain a regular religious observance with them. In this way, as he records, their example proved an anchor-cable that held him fast to the peaceful shore of prayer while he was tossed on the restless waves of worldly affairs, and his studies in their company enabled him to refresh a mind distracted by earthly concerns. By their fellowship he was not only strengthened against the temptations of the world, but inspired to ever greater spiritual activity.

When these companions urged him to write a mystical commentary on the often obscure book of Job, he could not refuse a task imposed on him by brotherly affection, which would be of help to many people. So in a work of thirty-five sections he gave a marvellously clear exposition, showing first the literal meaning of the book, then how it refers to the sacraments of Christ and the Church, and in what sense it applies to each one of the faithful. He began this work when papal representative in the Imperial city, and completed it in Rome after he became Pope. During his stay in Constantinople he encountered a new heresy about our state at the resurrection and aided by the grace of Catholic truth crushed it in the very moment of birth. For Eutychius, bishop of that city, was proclaiming that our bodies will then be impalpable, of finer texture than wind and air: but when Gregory heard this, he proved both by the light of reason and by the example of our Lord's Resurrection that this opinion is utterly opposed to orthodox belief. For the Catholic belief is that the body, when transfigured in the glory of immortality, is indeed made finer by the operation of spiritual power, but remains palpable by reason of its nature. This is exemplified in our Lord's risen body, of which he said to the disciples: '*Handle Me, and see; for a spirit hath not flesh and bones as ye see Me have.*' In defence of the Faith, our venerable father Gregory contested this rising heresy so effectively that, with the help of the devout Emperor Tiberius Constantine, it was entirely suppressed, and no one has since been found to revive it.

Gregory also wrote a notable book, *The Pastoral Office*, in which he describes in clear terms the qualities essential in those who rule the Church, showing how they should live; with what discernment they should instruct their various pupils; and with what constant awareness they should daily call to mind their own frailty. He also compiled forty *Homilies* on the Gospel, which he divided into two volumes of equal size. He wrote four books of *Dialogue*, in which, at the request of his deacon Peter, he assembled the most splendid achievements of saints in Italy known or reported to him, to serve as patterns of holy life for posterity. So, whereas in his *Commentaries* he showed what virtues we should strive for, in describing the miracles of the saints he made clear the splendour of those virtues. In twenty-two homilies he also revealed the illumination latent in the early and latter parts of the prophet Ezekiel, which had hitherto remained very obscure. Further, he compiled a book of answers in reply to the questions of Saint Augustine, first bishop of the English nation, which I have already mentioned and quoted in full in this history. In conjunction with the bishops of Italy he also compiled the short *Synodical Book*, which deals with the administration of the Church. To these must be added his personal letters. The extent of his writings is all the more amazing when one considers that throughout his youth, to quote his own words, he was often in agony from gastric pain, perpetually worn out by internal exhaustion and frequently troubled by a slow but chronic fever. But in all these afflictions he reflected that holy scripture says: '*The Lord scourgeth every son whom he receiveth*', and the greater his worldly sufferings, the greater his assurance of eternal joy.

Much might be said of his imperishable genius, which was unimpaired even by the most severe physical afflictions; for while other popes devoted themselves to building churches and adorning them with gold and silver, Gregory's sole concern was to save souls. Whatever money he had he bestowed zealously to relieve the poor, in order that '*his righteousness might endure for ever, and his horn be exalted with honour*'. Like Job, he might justly claim, '*When the ear heard me, then it blessed me; and when the eye saw me, it gave witness to me, because I delivered the poor that cried, and the fatherless, and him that had none to help him. The blessing of him that was ready to perish came upon me, and I caused the widow's heart to sing for joy. I put on righteousness, and it clothed me; my judgement was as a robe and a diadem. I was eyes to the blind, and feet was I to the lame. I was a father to the poor; and the cause which I knew not I searched out. And I brake the jaws of the wicked, and plucked the spoil out of his teeth.*' And again, '*I have not withheld the poor from their desire, nor caused the eye of the widow to fail; nor have I eaten my morsel myself alone, and the fatherless hath not eaten thereof. For in my youth compassion grew up with me, and it came forth with me from my mother's womb.*

Among his deeds of kindness and justice, this also finds a place, that he saved our nation from the grasp of the ancient enemy by the preachers whom he sent us, and brought it into the abiding liberty of God. He was full of joy at its conversion and salvation, as he mentions with fitting commendation in his Commentary on Job: 'The tongue of Britain, which formerly knew only the utterance of barbarity, has some time since begun to cry the Hebrew *Alleluia* to the praise of God. The once restless sea now lies quiet beneath the feet of His saints, and its ungovernable rages, which no earthly princes could tame by the sword, are now quelled at the simple word of His priests in the fear of God. Heathen nations who never trembled before armed hosts now accept and obey the teachings of the humble. For now that the grace of the knowledge of God has enlightened them and His heavenly words are received and miracles too are published abroad, the fear of God restrains them from their former wickedness, and they desire with all their hearts to win the prize of eternal life.' In these words Gregory proclaims that the holy Augustine and his companions guided the English nation to knowledge of the truth not only by their preaching but also by the display of miracles.

Among many other matters, blessed Pope Gregory decreed that Mass should be said over the tombs of the holy Apostles Peter and Paul in their churches. He also introduced into the Canon of the Mass three petitions filled with the utmost perfection: *Order our days in Thy peace, preserve us from eternal damnation, and number us in the flock of Thine elect.*

Gregory ruled the Church during the reigns of the Emperors Maurice and Phocas, and in the second year of the latter's reign he passed from this life and entered the true life of heaven. His body was laid to rest on March the twelfth in the church of Saint Peter the Apostle before the sanctuary, whence he will one day rise in glory with other shepherds of Holy Church. On his tomb was inscribed this epitaph:

Receive, O earth, the body that you gave,
Till God's lifegiving power destroy the grave.
Over his heaven-bound soul death holds no sway
Who steps through death into a fairer day.
The life of this high Pontiff, here at rest,
With good deeds past all reckoning was blest.
He fed the hungry, and he clothed the chill,
And by his teaching shielded souls from ill.
Wisdom was in his words, and all he wrought
Was as a pattern, acting what he taught.
To Christ he led the Angles, by God's grace
Swelling Faith's armies with a new-won race.
O holy pastor, all your work and prayer
To God you offered with a shepherd's care.
Triumphant now you reap your just reward,
Raised to high place, the consul of the Lord.

I must here relate a story, handed down to us by the tradition of our forebears, which explains Gregory's deep desire for the salvation of our nation. We are told that one day some merchants who had recently arrived in Rome displayed their many wares in the market-place. Among the crowd who thronged to buy was Gregory, who saw among other merchandise some boys exposed for sale. These had fair complexions, fine-cut features, and beautiful hair. Looking at them with interest, he enquired from what country and what part of the world they came. 'They come from the island of Britain,' he was told, 'where all the people have this appearance.' He then asked whether the islanders were Christians, or whether they were still ignorant heathens. 'They are pagans,' he was informed. 'Alas!' said Gregory with a heartfelt sigh: 'how sad that such bright-faced folk are still in the grasp of the author of darkness, and that such graceful features conceal minds void of God's grace! What is the name of this race?' 'They are called Angles,' he was told. 'That is appropriate,' he said, 'for they have angelic faces, and it is right that they should become joint-heirs with the angels in heaven. And what is the name of the province from which they have been brought?' 'Deira,' was the answer,

'Good. They shall indeed be rescued *de ira* – from wrath – and called to the mercy of Christ. And what is the name of their king?' 'Aelle,' he was told. 'Then,' said Gregory, making play on the name, 'it is right that their land should echo the praise of God our Creator in the word *Alleluia*.'

Approaching the Pope of the apostolic Roman see – for he was not yet Pope himself – Gregory begged him to send preachers of the word to the English people in Britain to convert them to Christ, and declared his own eagerness to attempt the task should the Pope see fit to direct it. This permission was not forthcoming, for although the Pope himself was willing, the citizens of Rome would not allow Gregory to go so far away from the city. But directly Gregory succeeded to the Papacy himself, he put in hand this long cherished project. He sent other missionaries in his place; but it was his prayers and encouragement that made their mission fruitful. And I have thought it fitting to include this traditional story in the history of our Church.

CHAPTER 2: *Augustine urges the British bishops to cement Catholic unity, and performs a miracle in their presence. Retribution follows their refusal* [A.D. 603]

MEANWHILE, with the aid of King Ethelbert, Augustine summoned the bishops and teachers of the nearest British province* to a conference at a place still known to the English as Augustine's Oak, which lies on the border between the Hwiccas and the West Saxons. He began by urging them to establish brotherly relations with him in Catholic unity, and to join with him in God's work of preaching the Gospel to the heathen.

Now the Britons did not keep Easter at the correct time, but between the fourteenth and twentieth days of the moon – a calculation depending on a cycle of eighty-four years. Furthermore, certain other of their customs were at variance with the universal practice of the Church. But despite protracted discussions, neither the prayers nor the advice nor the censures of Augustine and his companions could obtain the compliance of the Britons, who stubbornly preferred their own customs to those in universal use among Christian Churches. Augustine then brought this lengthy and fruitless conference to a close, saying: 'Let us ask our Lord, *who makes men to be of one mind* in His Father's house, to grant us a sign from heaven and show us which tradition is to be followed, and by what roads we are to hasten our steps towards His kingdom. Bring in some sick person, and let the beliefs and practice of those who can heal him be accepted as pleasing to God and to be followed by all.' On the reluctant agreement of his opponents, a blind Englishman was led in and presented to the British priests, from whose ministry he obtained no healing or benefit. Then Augustine, as the occasion demanded, knelt in prayer to the Father of our Lord Jesus Christ, imploring that the man's lost sight be restored and prove the means of bringing the light of spiritual grace to the minds of countless believers. Immediately the blind man's sight was restored, and all acknowledged Augustine as the true herald of the light of Christ. The Britons declared that, while they had learnt that what Augustine taught was the true way of righteousness, they could not abandon their ancient customs without the consent and approval of their own people, and therefore asked that a second and fuller conference might be held.

This was arranged, and seven British bishops and many very learned men are said to have attended, who came mainly from their most famous monastery which the English call Bancornaburg,[1] then ruled by Abbot Dinoot. Those summoned to this council first visited a wise and prudent hermit, and enquired of him whether they should abandon their own traditions at Augustine's demand. He answered: 'If he is a man of God, follow him.' 'But how can we be sure of this?' they asked. 'Our Lord says, *Take My yoke upon you and learn of Me, for I am meek*

---

[1] Bangor-is-y-Coed, Clwyd.

and lowly in heart,' he replied. 'Therefore if Augustine is meek
and lowly in heart, it shows that he bears the yoke of Christ
himself, and offers it to you. But if he is haughty and unbend-
ing, then he is not of God, and we should not listen to him.'
Then they asked, 'But how can we know even this?' 'Arrange
that he and his followers arrive first at the place appointed for
the conference,' answered the hermit. 'If he rises courteously as
you approach, rest assured that he is the servant of Christ and
do as he asks. But if he ignores you and does not rise, then,
since you are in the majority, do not comply with his demands.'

The British bishops carried out his suggestion, and it happened that Augustine remained seated in his chair. Seeing this,
they became angry, accusing him of pride and taking pains to
contradict all that he said. Augustine then declared: 'There are
many points on which your customs conflict with ours, or
rather with those of the universal Church. Nevertheless, if you
will agree with me on three points, I am ready to countenance
all your other customs, although they are contrary to our own.
These points are: to keep Easter at the correct time;* to complete
the Sacrament of Baptism, by which we are reborn to God,
according to the rites of the holy, Roman, and apostolic Church;
and to join with us in preaching the word of God to the
English.' But the bishops refused these things, nor would they
recognize Augustine as their archbishop, saying among themselves that if he would not rise to greet them in the first instance,
he would have even less regard for them once they submitted to
his authority. Whereupon Augustine, that man of God, is said
to have answered with a threat that was also a prophecy: if they
refused to accept peace with fellow-Christians, they would be
forced to accept war at the hands of enemies; and if they refused
to preach to the English the way of life, they would eventually
suffer at their hands the penalty of death. And, by divine
judgement, all these things happened as Augustine foretold.

Some while after this, the powerful king Ethelfrid, whom I
have already mentioned, raised a great army at the City of
Legions – which the English call Legacestir[1], but which the

---

[1] Chester.

Britons more correctly named Carlegion – and made a great slaughter of the faithless Britons. Before battle was joined, he noticed that their priests were assembled apart in a safer place to pray for their soldiers, and he enquired who they were and what they had come there to do. Most of these priests came from the monastery of Bangor, where there are said to have been so many monks that although it was divided into seven sections, each under its own head, none of these sections contained less than three hundred monks, all of whom supported themselves by manual work. Most of these monks, who had kept a three-day fast, had gathered to pray at the battle, guarded by a certain Brocmail, who was there to protect them from the swords of the barbarians while they were intent on prayer. As soon as King Ethelfrid was informed of their purpose, he said: 'If they are crying to their God against us, they are fighting against us even if they do not bear arms.' He therefore directed his first attack against them, and then destroyed the rest of the accursed army, not without heavy loss to his own forces. It is said that of the monks who had come to pray about twelve hundred perished in this battle, and only fifty escaped by flight. Brocmail and his men took to their heels at the first assault, leaving those whom they should have protected unarmed and exposed to the sword-strokes of the enemy. Thus, long after his death, was fulfilled Bishop Augustine's prophecy that the faithless Britons, who had rejected the offer of eternal salvation, would incur the punishment of temporal destruction.

CHAPTER 3: *Augustine consecrates Mellitus and Justus as bishops: his own death* [A.D. 604]

IN the year of our Lord 604, Augustine, Archbishop of Britain, consecrated two bishops, Mellitus and Justus. Mellitus was appointed to preach in the province of the East Saxons, which is separated from Kent by the river Thames, and bounded on the east by the sea. Its capital is the city of London, which stands on the banks of the Thames, and is a trading centre for many nations who visit it by land and sea. At this time Sabert, Ethelbert's nephew through his sister Ricula, ruled the province under the suzerainty of Ethelbert, who, as already stated, governed all the English peoples as far north as the Humber. When this province too had received the faith through the preaching of Mellitus, King Ethelbert built a church dedicated to the holy Apostle Paul in the city of London, which he appointed as the episcopal see of Mellitus and his successors. Augustine also consecrated Justus as bishop of a Kentish city which the English call Hrofescaestir[1] after an early chieftain named Hrof. This lies nearly twenty-four miles west of Canterbury, and a church in honour of Saint Andrew the Apostle was built here by King Ethelbert, who made many gifts to the bishops of both these churches as well as to Canterbury; he later added lands and property for the maintenance of the bishop's household.

When our father Augustine, the beloved of God, died, his body was laid to rest just outside the church of the holy Apostles Peter and Paul, since the church was not yet completed or consecrated. But as soon as it was dedicated, his body was brought inside and buried in the north chapel with great honour. This is also the last resting-place of all succeeding archbishops except Theodore and Bertwald, whose bodies lie inside the church, no space remaining in the chapel. Almost in the centre of the church stands an altar dedicated in honour of blessed Pope Gregory, at which a priest of the place says solemn mass in their memory each Saturday. On the tomb of Augustine is inscribed this epitaph:

'Here rests the Lord Augustine, first Archbishop of Canterbury, who, having been sent here by blessed Gregory, Pontiff of the City of Rome, and supported by God with miracles, guided King Ethelbert and his people from the worship of idols to the Faith of Christ. He ended the days of his duty in peace, and died on the twenty-sixth day of May in the above King's reign.'*

---

[1] Rochester.

CHAPTER 4: *Laurence and his fellow-bishops urge the Irish to maintain the unity of the Church, particularly in the observance of Easter: Mellitus visits Rome* [A.D. 605–10]

AUGUSTINE was succeeded in the archbishopric by Laurence, whom he had consecrated during his own lifetime; for he feared that even a short interval without a pastor might cause a setback to the newly established Church. In so doing, he followed the precedent set by the Church's first Pastor, blessed Peter, Prince of the Apostles, who, having established the Church in Rome, is said to have consecrated Clement as his assistant and successor. On receiving the dignity of archbishop, Laurence gave constant encouragement and a holy example to his flock, working tirelessly to perfect the edifice of the Church whose foundations he had seen so nobly laid. Nor was his interest limited to the Church newly recruited from the English; for he sought also to extend his pastoral care to the original inhabitants of Britain, and to the Irish of Ireland adjacent to this island of Britain. For having learned that in their own country the life and practice of the Irish and of the Britons were in many respects unorthodox – particularly in the observance of Easter, which, as previously explained, they did not keep at the right time, but between the fourteenth and twentieth days of the moon – he wrote them a letter jointly with his fellow-bishops, urging them to join in maintaining the unity, peace, and Catholic customs of the Christian Church established throughout the world. This letter commences:

'To our dear brothers the lord bishops and abbots throughout Irish lands: from Laurence, Mellitus, and Justus, servants of the servants of God.

'When, in accordance with its custom, which holds good throughout the world, the apostolic see sent us to the western lands to preach the Gospel to the heathen peoples, we came to this island of Britain. Until we realized the true situation, we had a high regard for the devotion both of the Britons and of the Irish, believing that they followed the customs of the universal Church. On further acquaintance with the Britons, we imagined that the Irish must be better. We have now, however, learned through Bishop Dagan on his visit to this island, and through Abbot Columbanus in Gaul, that the Irish are no different from the Britons in their practices. For when Bishop Dagan visited us, he refused not only to eat with us but even to take his meal in the same house as ourselves.'

Laurence and his fellow-bishops also wrote a dignified letter to the British bishops, in which he tried to bring them into Catholic unity; but the present state of affairs shows how little he succeeded.

At this time Mellitus, Bishop of London, visited Rome to acquaint the Pope with the affairs of the Church of the English. This most reverend Pope had summoned a council of the bishops of Italy to draw up regulations for monastic life and discipline, and Mellitus sat with them at this council, which took place on the twenty-seventh of February 610 in the eighth year of the Emperor Phocas. The presence of Mellitus enabled him to subscribe to all the regular decisions of the council and confirm them with his authority, and to convey them to the Churches of the English for their acceptance and promulgation on his return to Britain. He also brought back letters from the Pope both to God's beloved Archbishop Laurence and all his clergy, and to King Ethelbert and his people. This Pope was Boniface [IV], third bishop of Rome after Gregory, who persuaded the Emperor Phocas to give the Christian Church the Roman temple anciently known as the *Pantheon*, as though it were emblematic of all the gods. After solemn purification, Boniface consecrated it as the Church of the Holy Mother of God and all Christian Martyrs; and once its company of devils had been cast out, it became a memorial to the company of Saints.

IN the year of our Lord 616 – the twenty-first year after Augustine and his companions were dispatched to preach to the English nation – King Ethelbert of the Kentish folk died after a glorious earthly reign of fifty-six years, and entered the eternal joys of the kingdom of heaven. He was the third English king to hold sway over all the provinces south of the river Humber, but he was the first to enter the kingdom of heaven. The first king to hold such overlordship was Aelle, King of the South Saxons; the second was Caelin, King of the West Saxons, known in the speech of his people as Ceaulin; the third, as I have mentioned, was Ethelbert, King of the Kentish folk; the fourth was Redwald, King of the East Angles, who in the lifetime of Ethelbert acted as the military leader of his own people. The fifth was Edwin, King of the Northumbrians, that is, the people living north of the Humber, who was a powerful king, and ruled all the peoples of Britain, both Angles and Britons, with the exception of the Kentish folk. He also brought under English rule the British Mevanian Isles,[1] which lie between Ireland and Britain. The sixth was Oswald, also King of the Northumbrians but a most Christian one, who maintained the same frontiers; the seventh was his brother Oswy, who for a while ruled the same territory, and to a large extent conquered and made tributary the Picts and Irish in the northern parts of Britain. But I shall speak of these kings later.*

King Ethelbert died on the twenty-fourth of February, twenty-one years after embracing the Faith, and was buried in Saint Martin's chapel in the Church of the blessed Apostles Peter and Paul, where Bertha his queen also rests. Among the many benefits that his wisdom conferred on the nation, he introduced with the consent of his counsellors a code of law inspired by the example of the Romans, which was written in

[1] Man and Anglesey.

English, and remains in force to this day. The first of his laws is designed to protect those whose persons and doctrines he had embraced, and prescribes what satisfaction must be made by any person who steals property from the Church, the bishop, or other clergy.

Ethelbert was son of Irminric, son of Octa, and after his grandfather Oeric, surnamed Oisc, the kings of the Kentish folk are commonly known as Oiscings. The father of Oeric was Hengist, who first came to Britain with his son Oeric at the invitation of Vortigern, as I have already related.

The death of Ethelbert and the accession of his son Eadbald proved to be a severe setback to the growth of the young Church; for not only did he refuse to accept the Faith of Christ, but he was also guilty of such fornication as the Apostle Paul mentions as being unheard of even among the heathen, in that he took his father's (second) wife as his own. His immorality was an incentive to those who, either out of fear or favour to the king his father, had submitted to the discipline of faith and chastity, to revert to their former uncleanness. However, this faithless king did not escape the scourge of God's punishment; for he was subject to frequent fits of insanity and possessed by an evil spirit.

The death of the Christian King Sabert of the East Saxons aggravated the upheaval; for, when he departed for the heavenly kingdom he left three sons, all pagans, to inherit his earthly kingdom. These were quick to profess idolatry, which they had pretended to abandon during the lifetime of their father, and encouraged their people to return to the old gods. It is told that when they saw Bishop Mellitus offering solemn Mass in church, they said with barbarous presumption: 'Why do you not offer us the white bread which you used to give to our father Saba (for so they used to call him), while you continue to give it to the people in church?' The Bishop answered, 'If you will be washed in the waters of salvation as your father was, you may share in the consecrated bread, as he did; but so long as you reject the water of life, you are quite unfit to receive the Bread of Life.' They retorted: 'We refuse to enter that font and see no need for it; but we want to be strengthened with this bread.' The Bishop then carefully and repeatedly explained that this was forbidden, and that no one was admitted to receive the most holy Communion without the most holy cleansing of Baptism. At last they grew very angry, and said: 'If you will not oblige us by granting such an easy request, you shall no longer remain in our kingdom.' And they drove him into exile, and ordered all his followers to leave their borders.

After his expulsion, Mellitus came to Kent to consult with his fellow-bishops Laurence and Justus on the best course of action; and they decided that it would be better for all of them to return to their own country and serve God in freedom, rather than to remain impotently among heathen who had rejected the Faith. Mellitus and Justus left first and settled in Gaul to await the outcome of events. But the kings who had driven out the herald of truth did not long remain unpunished for their worship of demons; for they and their army fell in battle against the West Saxons. Nevertheless, the fate of the instigators did not cause their people to abandon their evil practices, or to return to the simple faith and love to be found in Christ alone.

CHAPTER 6: *Laurence is reproved by Saint Peter, and converts King Eadbald to Christ. Mellitus and Justus are recalled* [A.D. 616]

ON the very night before Laurence too was to follow Mellitus and Justus from Britain, he ordered his bed to be placed in the Church of the blessed Apostles Peter and Paul, of which we have spoken several times. Here after long and fervent prayers for the sadly afflicted Church he lay down and fell asleep. At dead of night, blessed Peter, Prince of the Apostles, appeared to him, and set about him for a long time with a heavy scourge, demanding with apostolic sternness why he was abandoning the flock entrusted to his care, and to which of the shepherds he would commit Christ's sheep left among the wolves when he fled. 'Have you forgotten my example?' asked Peter. 'For the sake of the little ones whom Christ entrusted to me as proof of His love, I suffered chains, blows, imprisonment, and pain. Finally, I endured death, the death of crucifixion, at the hands of unbelievers and enemies of Christ, so that at last I might be crowned with Him.' Deeply moved by the words and scourging of blessed Peter, Christ's servant Laurence sought audience with the king early next morning, and removing his garment, showed him the marks of the lash. The king was astounded, and enquired who had dared to scourge so eminent a man; and when he learned that it was for his own salvation that the archbishop had suffered so severely at the hands of Christ's own Apostle, he was greatly alarmed. He renounced his idolatry, gave up his unlawful wife, accepted the Christian Faith, and was baptized, henceforward promoting the welfare of the Church with every means at his disposal.*

The king also sent to Gaul and recalled Mellitus and Justus, giving them free permission to return and set their churches in order: so, the year after they left, they returned. Justus came back to his own city of Rochester; but the people of London preferred their own idolatrous priests, and refused to accept Mellitus as bishop. And since the king's authority in the realm was not so effective as that of his father, he was powerless to restore the bishop to his see against the refusal and resistance of the pagans. After his conversion, however, he and his people were zealous to observe the teachings of our Lord, and in the monastery of the most blessed prince of the Apostles he built a church to the Holy Mother of God, which was consecrated by Archbishop Mellitus.

CHAPTER 7: *The prayers of Bishop Mellitus put out a fire in his city*
  [A.D. 619]

ON the second day of February in the same king's reign, the blessed Archbishop Laurence passed to the kingdom of heaven, and was buried in the monastery church of the holy Apostle Peter next to his predecessor. Mellitus, Bishop of London, became the third Archbishop of Canterbury in the succession of Augustine, while Justus, who was still living, ruled the Church of Rochester. While these bishops were guiding the Church of the English with great care and energy, they received letters of encouragement from Boniface, Bishop of the apostolic Roman see, who succeeded Deusdedit in the year of our Lord 619. And although Mellitus became crippled with the gout, his sound and ardent mind overcame his troublesome infirmity, ever reaching above earthly things to those that are heavenly in love and devotion. Noble by birth, he was even nobler in mind.

I record one among many instances of his virtue. One day the city of Canterbury was set on fire through carelessness, and the spreading flames threatened to destroy it. Water failed to extinguish the fire, and already a considerable area of the city was destroyed. As the raging flames were sweeping rapidly towards his residence, the bishop, trusting in the help of God where man's help had failed, ordered himself to be carried into the path of its leaping and darting advance. In the place where the flames were pressing most fiercely stood the Church of the Four Crowned Martyrs.* Hither the bishop was borne by his attendants, and here by his prayers this infirm man averted the danger which all the efforts of strong men had been powerless to check. For the southerly wind, which had been spreading the flames throughout the city, suddenly veered to the north, thus saving the places that lay in their path: then it dropped altogether, so that the fires burned out and died. Thus Mellitus, the man of God, afire with love for him, because it had been his practice by constant prayers and teaching to fend off storms of spiritual evil from himself and his people, was deservedly empowered to save them from material winds and flames.

Having ruled the Church five years, Mellitus likewise departed to the heavenly kingdom in the reign of King Eadbald, and was laid to rest with his predecessors in the same monastery church of the holy Apostle Peter on the twenty-fourth day of April, in the year of our Lord 624.

CHAPTER 8: *Pope Boniface [V] sends the pallium with a letter to Justus, Mellitus' successor* [A.D. 624]

JUSTUS, Bishop of Rochester, at once succeeded Mellitus as archbishop. He consecrated Romanus as Bishop of Rochester in his place, having received authority to consecrate bishops from Pope Boniface, successor to Pope Deusdedit. This letter of authority runs as follows:

'BONIFACE, to his well beloved brother Justus. The contents of your letter and the success granted to your work are double evidence of your devotion and diligence in spreading the Gospel of Christ. Almighty God has not been unmindful of the honour due to His Name, or of the reward due to your labours; for He has faithfully promised the preachers of the Gospel, "*Lo, I am with you always, even unto the end of the world.*" This promise He has of His mercy especially fulfilled in your own ministry, opening the hearts of the nations to receive the mystery of the Gospel through your preaching. For He has crowned the wonderful progress of your good work with His blessing, and has granted a plentiful increase to the faithful employment of the talents entrusted to you, which will set your seal on many generations to come. This is the just reward of the constancy with which you have held to your appointed mission, while with commendable patience you await the redemption of this nation, so that it may profit through the merits of those who work for its salvation; for our Lord Himself has said, "*He that endureth to the end shall be saved.*" By your patient hope and courageous endurance you have been saved, so that you may cleanse the hearts of the heathen from the ills implanted by nature and by superstition, and obtain mercy for them from their Saviour. We learn, furthermore, from the letters of our son King Ethelwald,[1] how your profound knowledge of God's holy word has guided him to a real conversion and acceptance of the true Faith. We firmly trust in God's patience and mercy, and are confident that your preaching and ministry will effect a

---

[1] i.e. Eadbald.

complete conversion of his own people and also of their neighbours. In this way, as the Scripture says, will you receive the reward of a task well done from the Lord and Giver of all good things, and the universal profession of the nations, after receiving the mysteries of the Christian Faith, will proclaim: *"Their sound is gone out through all the earth, and their words to the end of the world."*

'Moved by your devotion, my brother, we are sending you by the bearer of this letter the *pallium*, which we grant you the privilege of wearing only when you celebrate the Holy Mysteries. We also grant you authority, under the guiding mercy of our Lord, to consecrate bishops as occasion may require, in order that the Gospel of Christ may be diffused by the mouths of many preachers among all nations as yet unconverted. We are confident that you will maintain with whole-hearted sincerity this dignity granted you by the favour of the Apostolic See, bearing in mind all that is symbolized by this highest of honours which you have received to wear on your shoulders. And, as you implore God's mercy, endeavour so to live and labour that when you stand before the judgement seat of God, you may display this honour which we grant you not only unstained but enhanced by the witness of all the souls which you have won.

'God keep you in safety, my dearest brother.'

CHAPTER 9: *The reign of King Edwin: Paulinus comes to preach the Gospel to him, and first administers the Sacrament of Baptism to his daughter and others* [A.D. 625]

AT this time, the people of the Northumbrians, the English living north of the Humber, under Edwin their king received the Faith through the ministry of Paulinus, whom I have already mentioned. As a sign that he would come to the Faith and the heavenly kingdom, King Edwin received wide additions to his earthly realm, and brought under his sway all the territories inhabited either by English or by Britons, an achievement unmatched by any previous English king. He also brought the Isles of Anglesey and Man under English rule: of these, the southern island is the larger and more fertile, and by English reckoning, extends to nine hundred and sixty hides, while the other island extends to rather more than three hundred.*

The Northumbrian people's acceptance of the Faith of Christ came about through their king's alliance with the kings of Kent by his marriage to Ethelberga, known as Tata, a daughter of King Ethelbert. Edwin sent an embassy of nobles to her brother Eadbald, then king of the Kentish folk, to request her hand in marriage, but received the reply that it was not permissible for a Christian maiden to be given in marriage to a heathen husband, lest the Christian Faith and Sacraments be profaned by her association with a king who was wholly ignorant of the worship of the true God. When Edwin's messengers returned with this reply, he gave an assurance that he would place no obstacles in the way of the Christian Faith, and would afford complete freedom to Ethelberga and her attendants, both men and women, priests and servants, to live and worship in accordance with Christian belief and practice. He also professed himself willing to accept the religion of Christ if, on examination, his advisers decided that it appeared more holy and acceptable to God than their own.

On this understanding, the maiden was betrothed and sent to Edwin; and in accordance with the agreement Paulinus, a man beloved of God, was consecrated bishop, so that he could accompany the princess as her chaplain and by daily Mass and instruction preserve her and her companions from corruption by their association with the heathen.

Paulinus was consecrated bishop by Archbishop Justus on July 21st, 625, and came to Edwin with the princess as her spiritual counsellor in the marriage. But he was further determined to bring the nation to which he was sent to the knowledge of the Christian truth, and to fulfil the Apostle's saying, '*to espouse her to one husband, that he might present her as a chaste virgin to Christ*'. Therefore, directly he entered the province he began to toil unceasingly not only by God's help to maintain the faith of his companions unimpaired, but if possible to bring some of the heathen to grace and faith by his teaching. But although he laboured long, yet as the Apostle says, '*the god of this world blinded the minds of them which believed not, lest the light of the glorious Gospel of Christ should shine unto them*'.

During the following year, an assassin named Eumer was sent into the province by Cuichelm, King of the West Saxons, in order to rob Edwin both of his kingdom and his life. This man had a double-edged, poisoned dagger, to ensure that if the wound itself were not mortal, the poison would complete its work. On Easter Day Eumer arrived at the royal residence by the Derwent, and was admitted into the king's presence on the pretext of delivering a message from his master. And while he was artfully delivering his pretended message, he suddenly sprang up, and drawing the dagger from beneath his clothes, attacked the king. Swift to see the king's peril, Lilla, his thegn* and best friend, having no shield to protect the king, interposed his own body to receive the blow; but even so, it was delivered with such force that it wounded the king through the body of his warrior. The assassin was immediately attacked on all sides, but killed yet another of the king's men named Fordhere in the ensuing struggle.

On the same holy night of Easter Day, the queen was delivered of a daughter, to be named Eanfled; and as the king thanked his gods in the presence of Bishop Paulinus for the birth of his daughter, the bishop gave thanks to Christ, and told the king that it was Christ who had given the queen a safe and painless delivery in response to his prayers. The king was greatly pleased at his words, and promised that if God would grant him life and victory over the king his enemy who had sent the assassin, he would renounce his idols and serve Christ; and as a pledge that he would keep his word he gave his infant daughter to Paulinus to be consecrated to Christ. Accordingly, on the Feast of Pentecost this infant, together with twelve others of her household, was the first of the Northumbrians to receive Baptism.

When the king had recovered from the assassin's wound, he summoned his forces, marched against the West Saxons, and in the ensuing campaign either slew or forced to surrender all those who had plotted his murder. Returning home victorious, the king would not receive the Sacrament of Christian Baptism at once or without due consideration, although he had already abandoned idol-worship when he promised that he would serve Christ. But he wished first to receive a full course of instruction in the Faith from the venerable Paulinus, and to discuss his proper course with those of his counsellors on whose wisdom he placed most reliance. For the king was by nature a wise and prudent man, and often sat alone in silent converse with himself for long periods, turning over in his inmost heart what he should do and which religion he should follow.

CHAPTER 10: *Pope Boniface writes to the king, urging him to accept the Faith*

ABOUT this time, the king received a letter from Boniface, Bishop of the apostolic Roman see, urging him to accept the Faith. Here follows a copy of this letter, sent by the blessed and apostolic Pope Boniface of the Church and City of Rome to the illustrious Edwin, King of the English:

'To the illustrious Edwin, King of the English: Boniface, Bishop, servant of the servants of God.

'The words of man can never express the power of the supreme Divinity, abiding in His own greatness, invisible, inscrutable, eternal, such that no human intelligence can understand or define how great it is. Nevertheless, God's humanity having opened the doors of man's heart to admit Him, mercifully infuses into their minds by secret inspiration some knowledge of Himself. Accordingly, we have undertaken to extend our priestly responsibility to disclose to you the fullness of the Christian Faith, in order that we may impart to your sense also the Gospel of Christ, which our Saviour commanded to be preached to all nations, and may offer you the medicine of salvation.

'The clemency of the Divine Majesty, who by His Word alone created and established the heavens and the earth, the sea and all that in them is, has ordained the laws by which they subsist; and by the counsel of His co-eternal Word in the unity of the Holy Spirit He has formed man after His own image and likeness from the dust of the earth. He has further granted him a most excellent prerogative, placing him above all other creatures in order that he may inherit eternal life by obedience to His commandments. This God – Father, Son, and Holy Spirit – the undivided Trinity – is adored and worshipped by the human race from east to west, which confesses Him by the faith that brings salvation as Creator of all things and Maker of all men. To him are subject all imperial power and authority; for it is by him that kingship is conferred. Of His bountiful mercy and for the well-being of all his creatures, He has been pleased to warm with His Holy Spirit the frozen hearts of the most distant nations of the world in a most wonderful manner to knowledge of Himself.

'We presume that Your Majesty has heard in fuller detail, as from a neighbouring territory, how our Redeemer in His mercy has brought light to our excellent son Eadbald and the nations subject to him. We therefore trust that Heaven's mercy will grant this wonderful gift to you as it has to him, more especially as we understand that your gracious Queen and true partner is already endowed with the gift of eternal life through the regeneration of Holy Baptism. In this letter we affectionately urge Your Majesties to renounce idol-worship, reject the mummery of shrines and the deceitful flattery of omens, and believe in God the Father Almighty, and in His Son Jesus Christ, and in the Holy Spirit. This Faith will free you from Satan's bondage, and through the liberative power of the holy and undivided Trinity you will inherit eternal life.

'The profound guilt of those who perversely cling to pernicious superstition and idolatrous worship is clearly shown by the damnable example of those they adore. Of such the Psalmist says: "*All the gods of the nations are idols; but the Lord made the heavens.*" And again: "*Eyes have they, but they see not: they have ears, but they hear not: noses have they, but they smell not; they have hands, but they handle not; feet have they, but they walk not. They that make them are like unto them; so is everyone that trusteth in them.*" How can such objects have power to help you, when they are made for you from perishable materials by the labour of your own subjects and servants? Even their inanimate resemblance to living shapes is due solely to man's craftsmanship. Unless you move them they cannot move, but are like a stone fixed in its place: they are manufactured, but have no intelligence, being utterly insensible and having no power to hurt or help. We cannot understand how people can be so deluded as to worship as gods objects to which they themselves have given the likeness of a body.

'Accept therefore the sign of the Holy Cross, by which the entire human race has been redeemed, and exorcize from your heart the damnable crafts and devices of the Devil, who jealously opposes all the workings of God's goodness. Overthrow and destroy these artificial gods of your own making; and the very destruction of these things, which never drew the breath of life and could never receive understanding from their makers, will itself afford you clear evidence of the nothingness of these objects of your former worship. Consider, you yourselves, to whom God has given the breath of life, are nobler than these man-made things; for Almighty God has ordered your descent through countless generations from the first man that He created. Therefore accept the knowledge of your Creator, who breathed into your frame the breath of life, and who sent His only-begotten Son for your redemption, that He might deliver you from original sin and the evil power of the Devil, and grant you the prize of Heaven.

'Accept the message of the Christian teachers and the Gospel that they proclaim. Believe in God the Father Almighty, and in Jesus Christ His Son and in the Holy Spirit, the inseparable Trinity. Spurn the temptations of the Devil, and reject all the suggestions of our malicious and deceitful enemy. Thus, born again by water and the Holy Spirit, you will be empowered by God's generous aid to abide in the splendour of eternal glory with Him in whom you shall come to believe.

'We impart to you the blessing of your protector, blessed Peter, Prince of the Apostles. With it we send you a tunic with a golden ornament, and a cloak from Ancyra, asking Your Majesty to accept these gifts with the same goodwill as that with which we send them.'

CHAPTER 11: *The Pope writes to the Queen, urging her to exert her influence to obtain the king's salvation*

THE Pope also wrote to Queen Ethelberga as follows. A copy of the letter of the blessed and apostolic Boniface, Pope of the City of Rome, to Ethelberga, Queen of King Edwin:

'To his illustrious daughter, Queen Ethelberga, from Bishop Boniface, servant of the servants of God.

'In His great providence, our loving Redeemer has offered a saving remedy to the human race, which He has saved from the Devil's enslaving tyranny by the shedding of His own precious Blood. Christ has made His Name known to the nations in various ways, so that they may acknowledge their Creator by accepting the mysteries of the Christian Faith. God in His mercy has revealed this truth to Your Majesty's own mind in your own mystical cleansing and regeneration. We have been greatly encouraged by God's goodness in granting you, through your own profession of faith, an opportunity to kindle a spark of the true religion in your husband; for in this way He will more swiftly inspire not only the mind of your illustrious Consort to love of Him, but the minds of your subjects as well.

'We have been informed by those who came to report the laudable conversion of our glorious son King Eadbald that Your Majesty, who has also received the wonderful sacrament of the Christian Faith, shows a shining example of good works, pleasing to God. We also know that you carefully shun idol-worship and the allurements of temples and divinations; and that, having given your allegiance to Christ, you are unshakeably devoted to the love of our Redeemer and labour constantly to propagate the Christian Faith. Out of pastoral affection, we particularly enquired about your illustrious husband and learned that he still serves abominable idols and is slow to listen to the teaching of the preachers. It has caused us deep grief to hear that your partner remains a stranger to the knowledge of the most high and undivided Trinity. Our paternal responsibility moves us to urge Your Christian Majesty, imbued with the force of divine inspiration, not to avoid the duty imposed on us in season and out of season, in order that, with the assistance and strength of our Lord and Saviour Jesus Christ, the King also may be added to the Christian fold. Only in this way will you enjoy the full privileges of marriage in perfect union; for the Scripture says, "*The two shall become one flesh.*" But how can it be called a true union between you, so long as he remains alienated from the daylight of your Faith by the barrier of dark and lamentable error?

'Let it therefore be your constant prayer that God of His mercy will bless and enlighten the King, so that you, who are united in one flesh by the ties of bodily affection, may after this fleeting life remain united for ever in the bond of faith. My illustrious daughter, persevere in using every effort to soften his heart by teaching him the commandments of God. Help him to understand the excellence of the mystery that you have accepted by believing and the marvellous worth of the reward that you have been accounted worthy to receive in this new birth. Melt the coldness of his heart by teaching him about the Holy Spirit, so that the warmth of divine faith may set his mind on fire through your constant encouragement and remove the numbing and deadening errors of paganism. If you do this, the witness of the Holy Spirit will most certainly be fulfilled in you, that "*the unbelieving husband shall be saved through the believing wife.*" For this is why you have received our Lord's merciful goodness, in order that you may restore to your Redeemer with increase the fruits of faith and of the boundless blessings entrusted to you. We shall not cease from constant prayer that God will assist and guide you to accomplish this.

'Having mentioned this matter, as fatherly duty and affection demands, we beg you to inform us, as soon as a suitable messenger is available, what measure of success God's goodness grants you in the conversion of your husband and the people over whom you reign. Good news will greatly relieve your mind, which anxiously awaits the longed-for salvation of you and yours. And when we see the glory of the divine atonement spreading ever more widely among you, we shall give glad and heartfelt thanks to God, the Giver of all good things, and to blessed Peter, Prince of the Apostles.

'We impart to you the blessing of your protector, blessed Peter, Prince of the Apostles. With it we send you a silver mirror, together with a gold and ivory comb, asking Your Majesty to accept these gifts with the same goodwill as that with which we send them.'

CHAPTER 12: *King Edwin is moved to accept the Faith by a vision seen during his exile* [A.D. 625]

SUCH was the letter written by Pope Boniface on the salvation of King Edwin and his people. But the principal factor influencing the king to study and accept the truths of salvation was a heavenly vision which God in his mercy had once granted the king when he was an exile at the court of Redwald, King of the Angles. For although Paulinus found it difficult to bring the king's proud mind to accept the humility of the way of salvation or to acknowledge the mystery of the life-giving Cross, he nevertheless continued, by words of exhortation addressed to men and words of supplication addressed to the divine compassion, to strive for the conversion of the king and his nation. It seems most likely that Paulinus finally learnt in the spirit the nature of the vision previously vouchsafed to the king. Whereupon he lost no time in urging the king to

implement the promise that he had made at the time of the
vision, and which he had undertaken to fulfil should he be
delivered out of his troubles and ascend the throne of the
kingdom.

Now the vision was this. When his predecessor Ethelfrid was
persecuting him, Edwin wandered as an unknown fugitive for
many years through many lands and kingdoms, until at length
he came to Redwald and asked him for protection against the
plots of his powerful enemy. Redwald gave him a ready
welcome and promised to do everything he asked. But as soon
as Ethelfrid heard that he had arrived in that province and that
he and his companions were living at the king's court as his
friends, he sent messengers to offer Redwald a large sum of
money to murder him. Obtaining no satisfaction, he sent a
second and third time, offering even heavier bribes and threat-
ening war if his demand were refused. At length Redwald,
either intimidated by his threats or corrupted by his bribes,
agreed to his demand and promised either to kill Edwin or to
surrender him to Ethelfrid's envoys. This plot was discovered
by a loyal friend of Edwin, who went to his room early one
night when he was about to retire and, calling him out, warned
him of the king's wicked intentions, adding: 'If you are willing,
I will guide you at this very hour out of this province and take
you to some place where neither Redwald nor Ethelfrid can find
you.' Edwin replied: 'Thank you for your goodwill. But I
cannot act as you suggest. I cannot be the first to break the
agreement that I have made with so great a king, who has so far
done me no harm nor shown any hostility towards me. If I
must die, I would rather die by his hand than by a hand less
noble. For what refuge remains for me, who have already
wandered for so many years in every corner of Britain, trying
to escape the machinations of my enemies?' When his friend had
left, Edwin remained, sitting sadly alone outside the palace,
tossed upon conflicting tides of thought, and not knowing what
to do or where to turn.

He had remained for a long time in silent thought, tormented
by inward fires that brought no light, when suddenly, at dead

of night, he saw a man approaching whose face and appearance were strange to him and whose unexpected arrival caused him considerable alarm. But the stranger came up and greeted him, asking why he was sitting sadly on a stone, wakeful and alone at an hour when everyone else was at rest and asleep. Edwin asked what concern it might be of his whether he passed the night indoors or out of doors. In reply, the man said: 'Don't think that I am unaware why you are sad and sleepless and why you are keeping watch outside alone. I know very well who you are, what your troubles are, and what impending evils you dread. But tell me this: what reward will you give the man, whoever he may be, who can deliver you from your troubles and persuade Redwald not to harm you or betray you to death at the hands of your enemies?' Edwin answered that he would give any reward in his power in return for such an outstanding service. Then the other went on: 'And what if he also promised, and not in vain, that you should become king, crush your enemies, and enjoy greater power than any of your forbears, greater indeed than any king who has ever been among the English nation?' Heartened by these enquiries, Edwin readily promised that, in return for such blessings, he would give ample proofs of his gratitude. The stranger then asked a third question: 'If the man who can truthfully foretell such good fortune can also give you better and wiser guidance for your life and salvation than anything known to your parents and kinsfolk, will you promise to obey him and follow his salutary advice?' Edwin at once promised that he would faithfully follow the guidance of anyone who could save him out of so many troubles and raise him to a throne. On this assurance, the man who addressed him laid his right hand on Edwin's head, saying: 'When you receive this sign, remember this occasion and our conversation, and do not delay the fulfilment of your promise.' Hereupon, it is said, he vanished, and Edwin realized that it was not a man but a spirit who had appeared to him.

The young prince was still sitting there alone, greatly heartened by what he had heard, but puzzling over the identity and origin of the being who had talked with him, when his loyal

friend approached with a cheerful greeting, and said: 'Get up
and come inside. You can now cast aside your cares and sleep
without fear, for the king has had a change of heart. He now
intends you no harm, and means to keep the promise that he
made you. For when he privately told the queen of his intention
to deal with you as I warned, she dissuaded him, saying that it
was unworthy in a great king to sell his best friend in the hour
of need for gold, and worse still to sacrifice his royal honour,
the most valuable of all possessions, for love of money.' In
brief, the king did as she advised, and not only refused to
surrender the exiled prince to the envoys of his enemy but
assisted him to recover his kingdom. As soon as the envoys had
gone home, he raised a great army to make war on Ethelfrid
and allowing him no time to summon his full strength, encountered him with a great preponderance of force and killed him.
In this battle, which was fought in Mercian territory on the east
bank of the river Idle, Raegenhere, son of Redwald, also met
his death. So Edwin, as his vision had foretold, not only escaped
the plots of his enemy but succeeded to his throne at his death.

While King Edwin hesitated to accept the word of God at
Paulinus' preaching, he used to sit alone for hours, as I have
said, earnestly deliberating what he should do and what religion
he should follow. On one of these occasions, the man of God
came to him and, laying his right hand on his head, enquired
whether he remembered this sign. The king trembled and would
have fallen at his feet; but Paulinus raised him and said in a
friendly voice: 'God has helped you to escape from the hands of
the enemies whom you feared, and it is through His bounty
that you have received the kingdom that you desired. Remember the third promise that you made, and hesitate no longer.
Accept the Faith and keep the commands of Him who has
delivered you from all your earthly troubles and raised you to
the glory of an earthly kingdom. If you will henceforward obey
His will, which he reveals to you through me, he will save you
likewise from the everlasting doom of the wicked and give you
a place in His eternal kingdom in heaven.'

CHAPTER 13: *Edwin holds a council with his chief men about accepting the Faith of Christ. The high priest destroys his own altars* [A.D. 627]

WHEN he heard this, the king answered that it was his will as well as his duty to accept the Faith that Paulinus taught, but said that he must still discuss the matter with his principal advisers and friends,* so that, if they were in agreement with him, they might all be cleansed together in Christ the Fount of Life. Paulinus agreed, and the king kept his promise. He summoned a council of the wise men, and asked each in turn his opinion of this strange doctrine and this new way of worshipping the godhead that was being proclaimed to them.

Coifi, the chief Priest, replied without hesitation: 'Your Majesty, let us give careful consideration to this new teaching; for I frankly admit that, in my experience, the religion that we have hitherto professed seems valueless and powerless. None of your subjects has been more devoted to the service of our gods than myself; yet there are many to whom you show greater favour, who receive greater honours, and who are more successful in all their undertakings. Now, if the gods had any power, they would surely have favoured myself, who have been more zealous in their service. Therefore, if on examination you perceive that these new teachings are better and more effectual, let us not hesitate to accept them.'

Another of the king's chief men signified his agreement with this prudent argument, and went on to say: 'Your Majesty, when we compare the present life of man on earth with that time of which we have no knowledge, it seems to me like the swift flight of a single sparrow through the banqueting-hall where you are sitting at dinner on a winter's day with your thegns and counsellors. In the midst there is a comforting fire to warm the hall; outside, the storms of winter rain or snow are raging. This sparrow flies swiftly in through one door of the hall, and out through another. While he is inside, he is safe from the winter storms; but after a few moments of comfort, he vanishes from sight into the wintry world from which he came. Even so, man appears on earth for a little while; but of what went before this life or of what follows, we know nothing. Therefore, if this new teaching has brought any more certain knowledge, it seems only right that we should follow it.' The other elders and counsellors of the king, under God's guidance, gave similar advice.

Coifi then added that he wished to hear Paulinus' teaching about God in greater detail; and when, at the king's bidding, this had been given, he exclaimed: 'I have long realized that there is nothing in our way of worship; for the more diligently I thought after truth in our religion, the less I found. I now publicly confess that this teaching clearly reveals truths that will afford us the blessings of life, salvation, and eternal happiness. Therefore, Your Majesty, I submit that the temples and altars that we have dedicated to no advantage be immediately dese-crated and burned.' In short, the king granted blessed Paulinus full permission to preach, renounced idolatry, and professed his acceptance of the Faith of Christ. And when he asked the Chief Priest who should be the first to profane the altars and shrines of the idols, together with the enclosures that surrounded them, Coifi replied: 'I will do this myself; for now that the true God has granted me knowledge, who more suitably than I can set a public example and destroy the idols that I worshipped, in ignorance?' So he formally renounced his empty superstitions and asked the king to give him arms and a stallion – for hitherto it had not been lawful for the Chief Priest to carry arms or to ride anything but a mare – and, thus equipped, he set out to destroy the idols. Girded with a sword and with a spear in his hand, he mounted the king's stallion and rode up to the idols. When the crowd saw him, they thought he had gone mad; but without hesitation, as soon as he reached the shrine, he cast into it the spear he carried and thus profaned it. Then, full of joy at his knowledge of the worship of the true God, he told his companions to set fire to the shrine and its enclosures and destroy them. The site where these idols once stood is still shown, not far east of York, beyond the river Derwent, and is known today as Goodmanham. Here it was that the Chief Priest, inspired by the true God, desecrated and destroyed the altars that he had himself dedicated.

CHAPTER 14: *Edwin and his people accept the Faith, and are baptized by Paulinus* [A.D. 627]

So King Edwin, with all the nobility of his kingdom and a large number of humbler folk, accepted the Faith and were washed in the cleansing waters of Baptism in the eleventh year of his reign, which was the year of our Lord 627, and about one hundred and eighty years after the first arrival of the English in Britain. The king's baptism took place at York on Easter Day, the 12th of April, in the church of Saint Peter the Apostle, which the king had hastily built of timber* during the time of his instruction and preparation for baptism; and in this city he established the see of his teacher and bishop Paulinus. Soon after his baptism, at Paulinus' suggestion, he gave orders to build on the same site a larger and more noble basilica of stone, which was to enclose the little oratory he had built before. The foundations were laid, and the walls of a square church began to rise around this little oratory; but before they reached their appointed height, the cruel death of the king left the work to be completed by Oswald his successor. Thenceforward for six years, until the close of Edwin's reign, Paulinus preached the Word in that province with the king's full consent and approval, and as many as were predestined to eternal life believed and were baptized. Among these were Osfrid and Eadfrid, sons of King Edwin, who were both born to him in exile of Coenburg, daughter of Cearl, King of the Mercians.

At a later date, other children of his by Queen Ethelberga were also baptized: these included a son, Ethelhun; a daughter, Ethelthryd; and another son, Wuscfrea. The two former were snatched from life while still wearing their white baptismal robes, and were buried in the church at York. Yffi, son of Osfrid, was also baptized, and many others of noble and princely rank. Indeed, so great was the fervour of faith and desire for baptism among the Northumbrian people that Paulinus is said to have accompanied the king and queen to the royal residence at Ad-Gefrin[1] and remained there thirty-six days constantly occupied in instructing and baptizing. During this period, he did nothing from dawn to dusk but proclaim Christ's saving message to the people, who gathered from all the surrounding villages and countryside; and when he had instructed them, he washed them in the cleansing waters of Baptism in the nearby River Glen. This residence was abandoned by the later kings, who built another at a place called Maelmin.

These events took place in the province of Bernicia. In the province of Deira, where Paulinus often stayed with the king, he baptized in the River Swale, which flows near the village of Catterick; for during the infancy of the church in those parts it was not yet possible to build oratories or baptisteries. A basilica was built at the royal residence of Campodonum;[2] but this, together with all the buildings of the residence, was burned by the pagans who killed King Edwin, and later kings replaced this seat by another in the vicinity of Loidis.[3] The stone altar of this church survived the fire, and is preserved in the monastery that lies in Elmet Wood and is ruled by the most reverend priest and abbot Thrydwulf.

CHAPTER 15: *The Province of the East Angles accepts the Christian Faith* [A.D. 627]

So great was Edwin's zeal for the true Faith that he persuaded King Earpwald, son of Redwald, King of the East Angles, to abandon his superstitious idolatry and accept the Faith and Sacraments of Christ with his whole province. His father Redwald had in fact long before this received Christian Baptism

---

[1] Yeavering, in Glendale.
[2] Possibly Doncaster, or Slack near Huddersfield.   [3] Leeds.

in Kent, but to no good purpose; for on his return home his wife and certain perverse advisers persuaded him to apostatize from the true Faith. So his last state was worse than the first: for, like the ancient Samaritans, he tried to serve both Christ and the ancient gods, and he had in the same shrine an altar for the holy Sacrifice of Christ side by side with a small altar on which victims were offered to devils. Aldwulf, king of that province, who lived into our own times, testifies that this shrine was still standing in his day and that he had seen it when a boy. This King Redwald was a man of noble descent but ignoble in his actions: he was son of Tytila, and grandson of Wuffa, after whom all kings of the East Angles are called Wuffings.*

Not long after Earpwald's acceptance of Christianity, he was killed by a pagan named Ricbert, and for three years the province relapsed into heathendom, until Earpwald's brother Sigbert succeeded to the kingship. Sigbert was a devout Christian and a man of learning, who had been an exile in Gaul during his brother's lifetime, and was there converted to the Christian Faith, so that when he began his reign, he laboured to bring about the conversion of his whole realm. In this enterprise he was nobly assisted by Bishop Felix, who came to Archbishop Honorius from the Burgundian region, where he had been brought up and ordained, and, by his own desire, was sent by him to preach the word of life to this nation of the Angles. Nor did he fail in his purpose; for, like a good farmer, he reaped a rich harvest of believers. He delivered the entire province from its age-old wickedness and infelicity, brought it to the Christian Faith and works of righteousness and – in full accord with the significance of his own name – guided it towards eternal felicity. His episcopal see was established at Dunwich; and after ruling the province as its bishop for seventeen years, he ended his days there in peace.

PAULINUS also preached the word of God to the province of Lindsey, which lies immediately south of the Humber, and extends to the sea. His first convert was Blaecca, Reeve of the city of Lincoln, with all his family. In this city he also built a stone church of fine workmanship, which today, either through neglect or enemy damage, has lost its roof, although the walls are still standing. And each year miracles of healing occur in this place for the benefit of those who seek it in faith. When Justus had departed to Christ, it was in this church that Paulinus consecrated Honorius as bishop in his stead, as I will describe in due course.

The priest Deda, abbot of the monastery of Partney and a most reliable authority, when relating the story of the Faith in this province, told me that one of the oldest inhabitants had described to him how he and many others had been baptized by Paulinus in the presence of King Edwin, and how the ceremony took place at noon in the river Trent, close to the city which the English call Tiowulfingacaestir.* He used to paint a verbal portrait of Paulinus as a tall man having a slight stoop, with black hair, an ascetic face, a thin hooked nose, and a venerable and awe-inspiring presence. Paulinus was also assisted in his ministry by the deacon James, a man of great energy and repute in Christ's Church, who lived until our own day.

So peaceful was it in those parts of Britain under King Edwin's jurisdiction that the proverb still runs that a woman could carry her new-born babe across the island from sea to sea without any fear of harm. Such was the king's concern for the welfare of his people that in a number of places where he had noticed clear springs adjacent to the highway he ordered posts to be erected with brass bowls hanging from them, so that travellers could drink and refresh themselves. And so great was the people's affection for him, and so great the awe in which he was held, that no one wished or ventured to use these bowls for any other purpose. So royally was the king's dignity maintained throughout his realm that whether in battle or on a peaceful progress on horseback through city, town, and countryside in the company of his thegns, the royal standard was always borne before him. Even when he passed through the streets on foot, the standard known to the Romans as a *Tufa*,* and to the English as a *Tuf*, was carried in front of him.

CHAPTER 17: *Pope Honorius sends a letter of encouragement to King Edwin, and the* pallium *to Paulinus* [A.D. 634]

A T this time, Honorius had succeeded Boniface as Bishop of the apostolic see. Learning that the Northumbrian people and their king had been converted to the Faith and confession of Christ by the labours of Paulinus, he sent him the *pallium* and with it a letter of encouragement to King Edwin, urging him with fatherly affection to ensure that his people maintained and made progress in the true Faith that they had received. This letter ran as follows:

'To his most excellent son, the most illustrious Edwin, King of the English, from Bishop Honorius, servant of the servants of God, Greeting.

'Your sincere Christian character, afire with ardent faith in the worship of your Creator, has shone out far and wide. It has been spoken of throughout the world and has reaped a rich harvest for your labours. For you who are kings acknowledge your kingship when by your worship of God you express belief in your own king and creator according to the true teaching which you have received about Him and, so far as human nature allows, serve Him with a sincere and devout mind. And what more can we offer God than our perseverance in doing good, our worship and confession of Him as Creator of the human race, and the zealous fulfilment of our vows? Accordingly, most noble son, our paternal love rightly moves us to urge you to labour with vigilant mind and constant prayer to preserve yourself wholly in that state of grace to which God in His mercy has called you. He who in this world has deigned to deliver you from all error, and led you to the knowledge of His Name, will thus also prepare a place for you in our heavenly home. Make a regular study of the writings of your teacher and my master Gregory of apostolic memory, and constantly bear in mind the loving teaching which he so gladly gave for the benefit of your souls, so that his prayer may obtain an increase in your kingdom and people, and bring you blameless to Almighty God.

'We are glad to accede to your requests on behalf of your bishops without delay, and in so doing we pay tribute to the sincerity of your own faith, which has often been mostly high praised by the bearers of this letter. Accordingly, we have sent two *pallia*, one to each of the Metropolitans, Honorius and Paulinus, so that, whenever either of them shall be summoned from this world to his Maker, the survivor may have our authority to appoint another bishop in his place. We have been induced to grant this privilege not only out of regard for you, but also in the realization of the great and wide provinces that separate us, so that we may show our recognition of your devotion in all matters and accede to your pious wishes.

'May the grace of God preserve Your Majesty in safety.'

CHAPTER 18: *On succeeding Justus in the See of Canterbury* [A.D. 627–31], *Honorius receives the* pallium *and a letter from Pope Honorius* [A.D. 634]

MEANWHILE, Archbishop Justus was taken up into the heavenly kingdom on November the tenth, and Honorius was elected to the see in his place. He therefore came to Paulinus to be ordained and, meeting him at Lincoln, was there consecrated fourth successor to Augustine in the See of Canterbury. Pope Honorius sent him the *pallium* and a letter confirming the arrangement already made in his letter to King Edwin: namely, that on the death of either of the Archbishops of Canbterbury or York, the survivor was to have authority to appoint a successor in place of the deceased archbishop, which

privilege would obviate the necessity of a wearisome sea and
land journey to Rome on every occasion for consecration. I
have thought it proper to include the text of the letter in this
history.

'Honorius, to his well-beloved brother Honorius.

'Among the many good gifts which the mercy of our
Redeemer has deigned to grant His servants, His generous love
is never more evident than when He permits us to display our
mutual love in brotherly converse, as it were face to face. For
this blessing we constantly give thanks to His Divine Majesty
and earnestly pray that He will confirm your loving labours in
preaching the Gospel with constant and lasting results and that,
in following the rule of your master and patron the holy
Gregory, you may bear fruit, so that, through your ministry,
God will bless His Church with ever-increasing strength; that
the souls already won by you and your predecessors, beginning
with the Lord Gregory, may be established and grow ever
stronger in faith and good works, and in reverence and love for
God; and that in due time the promises of our Lord Jesus Christ
may be fulfilled in you, and His voice summon you to eternal
joy, saying: "*Come to Me, all ye that labour and are heavy-laden,
and I will give you rest.*" And again, "*Well done, thou good and
faithful servant; because thou hast been faithful over a few things, I
will make thee ruler over many things. Enter thou into the joy of thy
Lord.*" Our constant love urges us to offer you these preliminary
words of encouragement, dearest brothers, and we shall not fail
hereafter to grant any privileges that we think likely to benefit
your churches.

'In response to your request and that of our sons your kings,
we hereby, in the name of blessed Peter, Prince of the Apostles,
grant that whenever God's mercy shall summon either of you
to Himself, the survivor shall have authority to appoint a bishop
in his place. As proof of this authority we have sent to each of
your Lordships the *pallium* to wear at such a consecration, so
that by our permission and direction you may perform it in a
manner acceptable to God. The great expanses of land and sea
that separate us make it necessary for us to grant you this

authority, in order that troubles may not arise on every such occasion in your churches, but rather the devotion of the people committed to your charge may be further enlarged. God keep you in safety.

'Given the eleventh day of June, in the twenty-fourth year of the reign of our Lord Heraclius Augustus, and the twenty-third after his consulship: and in the twenty-third year of his son Constantine, and the third after his consulship; and in the third year of the most illustrious Caesar Heraclius, his son: the seventh indiction: the year of our Lord 634.'

CHAPTER 19: *Pope Honorius* [A.D. 634], *and later Pope John* [A.D. 640], *writes to the Irish about Easter and the Pelagian heresy*

POPE HONORIUS also wrote to the Irish, whom he learned to be in error about the observance of Easter, as I mentioned earlier. He earnestly warned them not to imagine that their little community, isolated at the uttermost ends of the earth, had a wisdom exceeding that of all churches ancient and modern throughout the world, and he urged them not to keep a different Easter, contrary to paschal calculations and the synodical decrees of all the bishops of the world.

Similarly John [IV], who succeeded Severinus, successor to Honorius, while still pontiff elect, sent them authoritative and learned letters to correct this error, showing clearly how Easter Day must be sought between the fifteenth and twenty-first days of the moon, as was agreed at the Council of Nicaea. In this letter he particularly warned them to beware of and suppress the heresy of Pelagius, which, he learned, was reviving among them. The letter begins as follows:

'To our well-beloved and holy Tomianus,* Columbanus. Cromanus, Dimnaus, and Baithanus, bishops: to Cromanus, Ernianus, Laistranus, Scellanus, and Segenus, priests: to Saranus and the other Irish teachers and abbots. Greetings from Hilarus, arch-priest and guardian (during its vacancy) of the holy Apostolic See: John, deacon and (Pope) elect in the Name of God:

John, first secretary and guardian of the holy Apostolic See: and John, servant of God, counsellor of the Apostolic See.

'Certain letters addressed to Pope Severinus, of blessed memory, remained unanswered at the time of his death. Therefore, lest any pressing matters should remain long unconsidered, we opened them and learned that certain persons in your province are attempting to revive a new heresy from an old one, contrary to the orthodox faith, and that in the dark cloud of their ignorance they refuse to observe our Easter on which Christ was sacrificed, arguing that it should be observed with the Hebrew Passover on the fourteenth day of the moon.'

From the beginning of this letter it is evident that this heresy had arisen in very recent times and that the error was restricted to a limited number of persons in the nation. Having therefore explained the proper calculation of Easter, they add this on Pelagianism:

'We learn also that the pernicious Pelagian heresy has once again revived among you, and we strongly urge you to expel the venom of this wicked superstition from your minds. You cannot be unaware that this detestable heresy has already been condemned; for not only has it been suppressed these two hundred years, but it is daily laid under the ban of our perpetual anathema. We therefore beg you not to rake up the ashes of controversies long since burned out. For who can do other than condemn the insolent and impious assertion that man can live without sin of his own free will and not of God's grace? In the first place, it is blasphemous folly to say that any man is sinless; for no one can be sinless save the one mediator between God and man, the Man Jesus Christ, who was conceived and born without sin. All other men are born in original sin and bear unmistakable evidence of Adam's fall, even when they are innocent of actual sin. For, as the prophet says, "*Behold, I was shapen in iniquity; and in sin did my mother conceive me.*"'

THE glorious reign of Edwin over England and Britons alike lasted seventeen years, during the last six of which, as I have said, he laboured for the kingdom of Christ. Then the British King Cadwalla★ rebelled against him, supported by Penda, a warrior of the Mercian royal house, who from then onwards ruled that nation with varying success for twenty-two years. In a fierce battle on the field called Haethfelth[1] on the twelfth of October 633, when he was 48 years old, Edwin was killed, and his entire army destroyed or scattered. In the same battle, Osfrid, a gallant young warrior, one of Edwin's sons, was killed before his father. Another son, Eadfrid, was compelled to submit to Penda, who subsequently in breach of a solemn promise put him to death during the reign of Oswald.

At this time a terrible slaughter took place among the Northumbrian church and nation, the more horrible because it was carried out by two commanders, one of whom was a pagan and the other a barbarian more savage than any pagan. For Penda and all his Mercians were idol-worshippers ignorant of the name of Christ; but Cadwalla, although he professed to call himself a Christian, was utterly barbarous in temperament and behaviour. He was set upon exterminating the entire English race in Britain, and spared neither women nor innocent children, putting them all to horrible deaths with ruthless savagery, and continuously ravaging their whole country. He had no respect for the newly established religion of Christ. Indeed even in our own days the Britons pay no respect to the faith and religion of the English and have no more dealings with them than with the heathen. The head of King Edwin was carried to York and subsequently placed in the church of the blessed Apostle Peter, which he had begun to build, but which his successor Oswald completed, as I have related above. It rested in the porch

[1] Hatfield, near Doncaster.

140

dedicated to the holy Pope Gregory, from whose disciples he
had received the Word of life.

As a result of this disaster, the affairs of the Northumbrians
were in such utter disorder that flight offered the sole hope of
safety. Paulinus took Queen Ethelberga, whom he had pre-
viously accompanied to the province, and returned by sea to
Kent, where he was most honourably received by Archbishop
Honorius and King Eadbald. On his journey he was escorted by
Bassus, a gallant warrior of King Edwin, and brought with him
Eanfled, Edwin's daughter, and Wuscfrea his son; also Yffi, son
of Osfrid his son, whom his mother, fearing Eadbald and
Oswald, later sent over to Gaul to be brought up by her friend,
King Dagobert. The two children, however, both died in
infancy and were buried in church with the honour due to royal
children and innocents in Christ. Paulinus also brought away
with him many precious things belonging to King Edwin,
among them a great cross of gold and a golden chalice hallowed
for the use of the altar. These are still preserved and can be seen
in the church at Canterbury.

At this time, the church of Rochester was in great need of a
pastor, since Romanus its bishop, who had been sent by
Archbishop Justus to Pope Honorius as his representative, had
been drowned at sea off Italy. Therefore, at the request of
Archbishop Honorius and King Eadbald, Paulinus assumed this
charge, which he held until he too departed to the kingdom of
heaven with the glorious fruit of his labours. When he died he
left in the church of Rochester the *pallium* that he had received
from the Roman Pontiff.

Paulinus left behind his deacon James to care for the church
of York. James was a holy churchman who remained a long
time in that church, teaching and baptizing, and snatching much
prey from the clutches of our old enemy the Devil. The village
close to Catterick, where he usually lived, bears his name to this
day. He had a wide knowledge of church music; and when
peace was at length restored to the province and the number of
believers increased, he began to teach many people to sing the

music of the Church after the Uses of Rome and Canterbury.
At last, old and *full of days* as the Scripture says, he went the
way of his fathers.

BOOK THREE

✤

CHAPTER 1: *King Edwin's immediate successors abandon their people's Faith and lose their kingdom: the most Christian King Oswald restores both* [A.D.633–4]

AFTER Edwin's death in battle, the kingdom of Deira, to which his family belonged and where he began his reign, devolved upon Osric, son of Edwin's uncle Elfric, who had been baptized into the Christian Faith by Paulinus. But the kingdom of Bernicia – for the kingdom of the Northumbrians had anciently been divided into these two provinces – fell to Eanfrid, son of Ethelfrid, who claimed descent from the royal family of that province.*

During the whole of Edwin's reign the sons of Ethelfrid his predecessor together with many young nobles lived in exile among the Irish or Picts and were there instructed in the teachings of the Irish Church and received the grace of Baptism. But on the death of their enemy Edwin, they received permission to return to their own land, and Eanfrid, as eldest son, inherited the crown of Bernicia. As soon as they had obtained control of their earthly kingdoms, however, both these kings apostatized from the faith of the kingdom of heaven which they had accepted, and reverted to the corruption and damnation of their former idolatry.

Not long afterwards they were justly punished by meeting their death at the hands of the godless Cadwalla, king of the Britons. First Osric next summer was rashly besieging him in a strong city when Cadwalla, making a sudden sally with his entire force, caught him off his guard and destroyed him with his whole army. After this, for a full year, Cadwalla ruled the Northumbrian provinces, not as a victorious king but as a savage tyrant, ravaging them with ghastly slaughter until at length he also destroyed Eanfrid, who had unwisely visited him to negotiate peace accompanied only by twelve picked soldiers. This year remains accursed and hateful to all good men, not only on account of the apostasy of the English kings, by which they divested themselves of the sacraments of the Faith, but also because of the savage tyranny of the British king. Hence all those calculating the reigns of kings have agreed to expunge the memory of these apostate kings and to assign this year to the reign of their successor King Oswald, a man beloved of God. This king, after the death of his brother Eanfrid, mustered an army small in numbers but strong in the faith of Christ; and despite Cadwalla's vast forces, which he boasted of as irresistible, the infamous British leader was killed at a place known by the English as Denisesburn, that is, the Brook of Denis.[1]

CHAPTER 2: *Before engaging the heathen in battle, King Oswald sets up a wooden cross: a young man is later healed by a portion of it, and innumerable other miracles take place* [A.D. 634]

WHEN King Oswald was about to give battle to the heathen, he set up the sign of the holy cross and, kneeling down, asked God that He would grant his heavenly aid to those who trusted in Him in their dire need. The place is pointed out to this day and held in great veneration. It is told that, when the cross had been hurriedly made and a hole dug to receive it, the devout king with ardent faith took the cross and placed it in position, holding it upright with his own hands until the soldiers had thrown in the earth and it stood firm. This done he summoned his army with a loud shout, crying, 'Let us all kneel together, and ask the true and living God Almighty of His mercy to protect us from the arrogant savagery of our enemies, since He knows that we fight in a just cause to save our nation.'

---

[1] New Rowley Water.

The whole army did as he ordered and, advancing against the enemy at the first light of dawn, won the victory that their faith deserved. At this spot where the king prayed, innumerable miracles of healing are known to have been performed, which serve as a reminder and a proof of the King's faith. Even to this day many folk take splinters of wood from this holy cross, which they put into water, and when any sick men or beasts drink of it or are sprinkled with it, they are at once restored to health.

This place is called in English *Hefenfelth*, meaning 'the heavenly field', which name, bestowed upon it long ago, was a sure omen of events to come, portending that there the heavenly sign would be set up, a heavenly victory won, and heavenly wonders shown. It lies on the northern side of the wall which the Romans built from sea to sea, as I have related, to protect Britain from the attacks of the barbarous peoples. The brothers of the church of Hexham, which lies not far away, have long been accustomed to make a yearly pilgrimage here on the eve of the anniversary of Oswald's death in order to keep vigil for the welfare of his soul, to recite the psalter, and to offer the Holy Sacrifice for him at dawn. By a further development of this good custom, the brothers have recently built a church on the spot, which has made it honoured and hallowed above all others. This is very fitting, for we know that there was no emblem of the Christian Faith, no church, and no altar in the whole of Bernicia until the new Christian leader Oswald, moved by his devotion to the Faith, set up this standard of the holy cross before giving battle to his relentless enemies.

It is not irrelevant to mention one of the many miracles that have taken place at this cross. A few years ago, one of the brothers of the church of Hexham named Bothelm, who is still living, was walking unwarily on the ice at night, when he suddenly fell and fractured an arm. He suffered such agonizing pain from it that he could not even raise his hand to his mouth. At length, hearing that another brother had decided to go up next day to the site of the cross, he begged him to bring back a piece of its revered wood, saying that by this means he trusted that God would grant him healing. The brother carried out his

145

request, and as he returned at night when the brothers were seated at their evening meal, he passed the sick man a bit of the old moss that grew on the surface of the cross. Being at table, the brother had nowhere to keep the proffered gift, so he thrust it next his breast, and when he retired, forgot to take it out. But, waking up in the middle of the night, he felt something cold at his side, and thrusting in his hand to feel what it was, found that his arm was whole and sound as if he had never suffered such great pain.

CHAPTER 3: *Oswald asks the Irish to send him a bishop: when Aidan arrives, he grants him the island of Lindisfarne as his episcopal see* [A.D. 635]

As soon as he became king, Oswald greatly wished that all the people whom he ruled should be imbued with the grace of the Christian Faith, of which he had received such signal proof in his victory over the heathen. So he sent to the Irish elders among whom he and his companions had received the sacrament of Baptism when in exile, asking them to send him a bishop by whose teaching and ministry the English people over whom he ruled might receive the blessings of the Christian Faith and the sacraments. His request was granted without delay, and they sent him Bishop Aidan, a man of outstanding gentleness, holiness, and moderation. He had *a zeal in God, but not according to knowledge,* in that he kept Easter in accordance with the customs of his own nation, which, as I have several times observed, was between the fourteenth and twentieth days of the moon. For the northern province of the Irish and all the Picts still observed these customs, believing that they were following the teachings of the holy and praiseworthy father Anatolius, although the true facts are evident to any scholar. But the Irish in the south of Ireland had already conformed to the injunctions of the Bishop of the apostolic see, and learnt to observe Easter at the canonical time.

On Aidan's arrival, the king appointed the island of Lindisfarne to be his see at his own request. As the tide ebbs and
flows, this place is surrounded by sea twice a day like an island,
and twice a day the sand dries and joins it to the mainland. The
king always listened humbly and readily to Aidan's advice and
diligently set himself to establish and extend the Church of
Christ throughout his kingdom. And while the bishop, who
was not fluent in the English language, preached the Gospel, it
was most delightful to see the king himself interpreting the
word of God to his ealdorman and thegns; for he himself had
obtained perfect command of the Irish tongue during his long
exile. Henceforward many Irishmen arrived day by day in
Britain and proclaimed the word of God with great devotion in
all the provinces under Oswald's rule, while those of them who
were in priest's orders ministered the grace of Baptism to those
who believed. Churches were built in several places, and the
people flocked gladly to hear the word of God, while the king
of his bounty gave lands and endowments to establish monasteries, and the English, both noble and simple, were instructed
by their Irish teachers to observe a monastic life.

For most of those who came to preach were monks, Aidan
himself being a monk sent from the island of Hii,[1] whose
monastery was for a long time the principal monastery of nearly
all the northern Irish and all the Picts and exercised a widespread
authority.* The island itself belongs to Britain, and is separated
from the mainland only by a narrow strait; but the Picts living
in that part of Britain gave it to the Irish monks long ago,
because they received the Faith of Christ through their
preaching.

[1] Iona.

IN the year of our Lord 565, when Justin the Younger succeeded Justinian and ruled as Emperor of Rome, a priest and abbot named Columba, distinguished by his monastic habit and life, came from Ireland to Britain to preach the word of God in the provinces of the northern Picts, which are separated from those of the southern Picts by a range of steep and desolate mountains.[1]

The southern Picts, who live on this side of the mountains, are said to have abandoned the errors of idolatry long before this date and accepted the true Faith through the preaching of Bishop Ninian,* a most reverend and holy man of British race, who had been regularly instructed in the mysteries of the Christian Faith in Rome. Ninian's own episcopal see, named after Saint Martin and famous for its stately church, is now held by the English, and it is here that his body and those of many saints lie at rest. The place belongs to the province of Bernicia and is commonly known as *Candida Casa*, the White House,[2] because he built the church of stone, which was unusual among the Britons.

Columba* arrived in Britain in the ninth year of the reign of the powerful Pictish king, Bride son of Meilochon; he converted that people to the Faith of Christ by his preaching and example, and received from them the island of Iona on which to found a monastery. Iona is a small island, with an area of about five hides according to English reckoning, and his successors hold it to this day. It was here that Columba died and was buried at the age of seventy-seven, some thirty-two years after he had come into Britain to preach. Before he came to Britain, he had founded a noble monastery in Ireland known in the Irish language as *Dearmach*, the Field of Oaks,[3] because of the oak forest in which it stands. From both of these monasteries Columba's disciples went out and founded many others in

---

[1] The Grampians.   [2] Whithorn.   [3] Durrow.

Britain and Ireland; but the monastery on the isle of Iona, where his body lies, remains the chief of them all.

Iona is always ruled by an abbot in priest's orders, to whose authority the whole province, including the bishops, is subject, contrary to the usual custom.* This practice was established by its first abbot Columba, who was not a bishop himself, but a priest and monk. His life and sayings are said to have been recorded in writing by his disciples. But whatever type of man he may have been, we know for certain that he left successors distinguished for their purity of life, their love of God, and their loyalty to the monastic rule. In observing the great Feast of Easter they followed doubtful rules; for being so isolated from the rest of the world, there was no one to acquaint them with the synodical decrees about the keeping of Easter. But they diligently followed whatever pure and devout customs they learned in the prophets, the Gospels, and the writings of the Apostles. They held to their own manner of keeping Easter for another 150 years, until the year of our Lord 715.

In that year the most reverend and holy father, Bishop Egbert, an Englishman, who had spent many years of exile in Ireland for love of Christ, and was most learned in the scriptures and renowned for lifelong holiness, came and corrected their error, and they changed to the right canonical customs for observing Easter. This error was that they kept Easter not, as some supposed, on the fourteenth day of the moon, as do the Jews, but on the Sunday of the wrong week. For as Christians they knew well that the Resurrection of our Lord took place on the first day after the Sabbath and should always be kept on that day. But being barbarous and simple, they had not learned when this first day after the Sabbath, which is now called the Lord's Day, should occur. Yet, since they did not fail in the fervent grace of charity, they were worthy to learn the full truth in this matter, in accordance with the Apostle's promise, when he said: '*And if in anything ye be otherwise minded, God shall reveal even this unto you.*' But I shall speak of this more fully in its proper place.

CHAPTER 5: *The Life of Bishop Aidan* [died A.D. 651]

I T was from this island and from this community of monks (while the abbot and priest Segenus was ruling there) that Aidan was sent, when he had been made bishop, to preach the Faith for Christ to a province of the English.* Among other evidences of holy life, he gave his clergy an inspiring example of self-discipline and continence, and the highest recommendation of his teaching to all was that he and his followers lived as they taught. He never sought or cared for any worldly possessions, and loved to give away to the poor who chanced to meet him whatever he received from kings or wealthy folk. Whether in town or country, he always travelled on foot unless compelled by necessity to ride; and whatever people he met on his walks, whether high or low, he stopped and spoke to them. If they were heathen, he urged them to be baptized; and if they were Christians, he strengthened their faith, and inspired them by word and deed to live a good life and to be generous to others.

His life is in marked contrast to the apathy of our own times, for all who walked with him, whether monks or lay-folk, were required to meditate, that is, either to read the scriptures or to learn the Psalms. This was their daily occupation wherever they went; and if, on rare occasions, he was invited to dine with the king, he went with one or two clerics, and when he had eaten sparingly, he left as soon as possible to read or pray with them. Many devout men and women of that day were inspired to follow his example, and adopted the practice of fasting until None on Wednesdays and Fridays throughout the year, except during the fifty days after Easter. If wealthy people did wrong, he never kept silent out of respect or fear, but corrected them outspokenly. Nor would he offer money to influential people, although he offered them food whenever he entertained them as host. But, if the wealthy ever gave him gifts of money, he either distributed it for the needs of the poor, as I have mentioned, or else used it to ransom any who had unjustly been sold as slaves. Many of those whom he had ransomed in this way later became his disciples; and when they had been instructed and trained, he ordained them to the priesthood.

It is said that when King Oswald originally asked the Irish to send a bishop to teach the Faith of Christ to himself and his people, they sent him another man of a more austere disposition. After some time, meeting with no success in his preaching to the English, who refused to listen to him, he returned home and reported to his superiors that he had been unable to achieve anything by teaching to the nation to whom they had sent him, because they were an ungovernable people of an obstinate and barbarous temperament. The Irish fathers therefore held a great conference to decide on the wisest course of action; for while they regretted that the preacher whom they had sent had not been acceptable to the English, they still wished to meet their desire for salvation. Then Aidan, who was present at the conference, said to the priest whose efforts had been unsuccessful: 'Brother, it seems to me that you were too severe on your ignorant hearers. You should have followed the practice of the Apostles, and begun by giving them the milk of simpler teaching, and gradually nourished them with the word of God until they were capable of greater perfection and able to follow the loftier precepts of Christ.' At this the faces and eyes of all who were at the conference were turned towards him; and they paid close attention to all he said, and realized that here was a fit person to be made bishop and sent to instruct the ignorant and unbelieving, since he was particularly endowed with the grace of discretion, the mother of virtues. They therefore consecrated him bishop, and sent him to preach. Time was to show that Aidan was remarkable not only for discretion, but for the other virtues as well.

CHAPTER 6: *The wonderful devotion and piety of King Oswald*

S UCH then was the bishop who brought knowledge of the
Faith to King Oswald and the English people under his rule.
Thus instructed, Oswald not only learned to hope for the
kingdom of heaven, which had been unknown to his ancestors,
but was also granted by Almighty God, Creator of heaven and
earth, an earthly kingdom greater than they enjoyed. For at
length he brought under his sceptre all the peoples and provinces
of Britain speaking the four languages, British, Pictish, Irish,
and English.

Although he reached such a height of power, Oswald was
always wonderfully humble, kindly, and generous to the poor
and strangers. The story is told how on the Feast of Easter one
year, Oswald sat down to dine with Bishop Aidan. A silver dish
of rich food was set before him, and they were on the point of
raising their hands to bless the food, when the servant who was
appointed to relieve the needs of the poor came in suddenly and
informed the king that a great crowd of needy folk were sitting
in the road outside begging alms of the king. Oswald at once
ordered his own food to be taken out to the poor, and the silver
dish to be broken up and distributed among them. The bishop,
who was sitting beside him, was deeply moved to see such
generosity, and taking hold of the king's right hand,
exclaimed, 'May this hand never wither with age.' Later events
proved that his prayer was heard; for when Oswald was killed
in battle, his hand and arm were severed from his body, and
they remain uncorrupted to this day. They are preserved as
venerated relics in a silver casket at the church of Saint Peter
in the royal city, which is called after a former queen named
Bebba.[1]

Through King Oswald's diplomacy the provinces of Deira
and Bernicia, formerly hostile to each other, were peacefully
united and became one people. Oswald was nephew to King

---

[1] Bebbanburh, now Bamburgh.

Edwin by his sister Acha; and it is fitting that so great a predecessor should have had so worthy a man of his own blood to maintain his religion and his throne.

CHAPTER 7: *The West Saxons accept the Faith through the teaching of Birinus and his successors Agilbert and Leutherius* [A.D. 635]

A T that time, during the reign of Cynigils, the West Saxons, anciently known as the Gewissae, accepted the Faith of Christ through the preaching of Bishop Birinus.* He had come to Britain at the direction of Pope Honorius [I], having promised in his presence that he would sow the seeds of our holy Faith in the most inland and remote regions of the English, where no other teacher had been before him. He was accordingly consecrated bishop by Asterius, Bishop of Genoa, at the Pope's command; but when he had reached Britain and entered the territory of the Gewissae, he found them completely heathen, and decided that it would be better to begin to preach the word of God among them rather than seek more distant converts. He therefore evangelized that province, and when he had instructed its king, he baptized him and his people. It happened at the time that the most holy and victorious Oswald was present, and greeted King Cynigils as he came from the font, and offered him an alliance most acceptable to God, taking him as his godson and giving his daughter as wife. The two kings gave Bishop Birinus the city of Dorcic[1] for his episcopal see, and there he built and dedicated several churches and brought many people to God by his holy labours. He also died and was buried there; and many years later, when Haeddi was bishop, his body was translated to Venta[2] and laid in the church of the blessed Apostles Peter and Paul.

On the death of Cynigils, his son Coenwalh succeeded to the throne, but refused to accept the faith and sacraments of the heavenly kingdom. Not long afterwards he lost his earthly

---

[1] Dorchester (Oxon.).   [2] Winchester.

kingdom also. For he put away his wife, who was sister of
Penda, King of the Mercians, and took another woman. This
led to war, and Coenwalh was driven out of his kingdom by
Penda and took refuge with Anna, King of the East Angles.
There he lived in exile for three years, during which he learned
the Christian Faith and received Baptism. For Anna his host
was a good man and blessed with good and holy children, as I
shall mention later.

When Coenwalh had been restored to his kingdom, there
arrived in the province a bishop from Gaul named Agilbert,*
who had been studying the scriptures in Ireland for many years.
This bishop came to the king and voluntarily undertook to
evangelize the country. Appreciating his learning and enthusiasm, the king asked him to accept an episcopal see and remain
in the province as his chief bishop. Agilbert acceded to the
king's request and presided as bishop for many years. Later,
however, the king, who understood only Saxon, grew tired of
the bishop's foreign speech, and invited to the province a bishop
of his own tongue called Wini, who had also been consecrated
in Gaul; and dividing his kingdom into two dioceses, he gave
Wini the city of Venta – known by the Saxons as Wintancaestir
– as his see. This action gravely offended Agilbert, as the king
had not consulted him in the matter, and he returned to Gaul,
where he became bishop of Paris and ended his days there at an
advanced age. Not many years after Agilbert's departure from
Britain, Wini was also driven from his bishopric by the king,
and took refuge with Wulfhere, King of the Mercians, to whom
he offered money for the bishopric of London, which he held
till his death. So for a considerable time the province of the
West Saxons remained without any bishop.

During this interval King Coenwalh often suffered great
damage to his kingdom from his enemies. Eventually he
remembered that he had formerly been driven from his throne
because of his infidelity and had been restored to it after his
acceptance of the Christian Faith, and realized that his kingdom
was now justly deprived of God's protection because it had no
bishop. He therefore sent his messengers to Agilbert in Gaul,

offering him satisfaction and requesting him to return to his bishopric. But Agilbert sent his regrets and said that it was impossible for him to return, since he was now responsible for his own bishopric and city of Paris. But, not wishing to reject such an urgent appeal for help, he sent in his place his nephew, the priest Leutherius,[1] to be consecrated as his bishop if the king were agreeable, recommending him as worthy of a bishopric. Both king and people welcomed Leutherius with honour, and asked Theodore, then Archbishop of Canterbury, to consecrate him their bishop. He was accordingly consecrated at Canterbury, and for many years wisely ruled the West Saxon see alone with the full support of the synod.

CHAPTER 8: *Earconbert, King of Kent, orders the destruction of idols. His daughter Earcongota and his kinswoman Ethelberga dedicate themselves to God as nuns* [A.D. 640]

IN the year of our Lord 640, King Eadbald of Kent departed this life, and his son Earconbert succeeded to the government of the realm, which he ruled most nobly for over twenty-four years and some months. He was the first of the English kings to give orders for the complete abandonment and destruction of idols throughout his realm, and for the observance of the Lenten fast, enforcing his decrees by suitable penalties for disobedience. His daughter Earcongota, who shared her father's zeal, was a nun of outstanding virtue, who served God in a convent in Frankish territory founded by the noble Abbess Fara at a place called Brie:* for as yet there were few monasteries built in English territory,* and many who wished to enter conventual life went from Britain to the Frankish realm or Gaul for the purpose. Girls of noble family were also sent there for their education, or to be betrothed to their heavenly Bridegroom, especially to the houses of Brie, Chelles, and Andelys; among such girls were Saethryd, step-daughter of King Anna of East

---

[1] A Latinized form of the name Hlothere.

Anglia, already mentioned, and Ethelberga his own daughter. Although foreigners, both were of such merit that they became abbesses of Brie. Sexburg, Anna's eldest daughter, and wife to King Earconbert of Kent, was the mother of Earcongota, who deserves especial mention.

To this day the people of the district tell stories of the wonderful deeds and miracles of the nun Earcongota; but I must restrict myself to a brief account of her passing to the heavenly kingdom. When she felt her call approaching, she set out to visit the cells of all the infirm handmaids of Christ, especially those who were of a great age or were most esteemed for their holiness of life, and humbly commending herself to their prayers, she revealed to them how she had received intimation of her coming death. She told how, in a vision, she had seen a company of men in white robes entering the monastery, and when she asked them what they were looking for and what they wanted, they replied: 'We have been sent to bring away with us the golden coin that was brought here from Kent.' And on the very night when, as dawn drew near, she left the darkness of this world and entered the light of heaven, many brethren of the monastery, who lived in separate buildings, said that they had clearly heard choirs of angels singing and a sound like that of a great throng entering the monastery. And when they came out to discover what it might be, they saw a great light coming down from heaven, which carried away the holy soul of Earcongota, freed from the bonds of the body, to the eternal joys of heaven. Other miracles are reported to have taken place in the monastery that night; but these I leave to her own people to recount, while I turn to other matters. The venerable body of this virgin and spouse of Christ was laid to rest in the church of the blessed Protomartyr Saint Stephen. Three days later it was decided to take up the stone slab covering the grave, and replace the body at a greater depth. While this was taking place, a perfume of such fragrance rose from below that it seemed to all the brethren and sisters standing round as though a store of balm had been unsealed.

Ethelberga, aunt of Earcongota, also preserved with strict self-discipline the glory of the perpetual virginity beloved by God, and the extent of her holiness became even more apparent after her death. For while she was abbess she began building within her monastery a church in honour of all the Apostles, in which she wished to be buried; but when the work was only half done, she was prevented by death from completing it and was buried within the church in a spot that she had chosen. After her death the brethren became wholly occupied in other matters, and the building of the church was discontinued for seven years. At the end of this period they decided to abandon an undertaking that had proved too great for their resources, and to remove the abbess' bones to another church that was already completed and consecrated. When they opened the tomb, they found the body untouched by decay as if it had been immune from the corruption of sinful desires. So having washed it, and clothed it in fresh garments, they removed it to the church of Saint Stephen the Martyr. Her feast-day is kept there with great splendour on the seventh of July.*

CHAPTER 9: *Miraculous cures take place at the site of Oswald's death. A traveller's horse is cured, and a paralytic girl healed.*

OSWALD, the most Christian king of the Northumbrians, reigned for nine years, if we include the fatal year made abhorrent by the callous impiety of the British king Cadwalla and the insane apostasy of the English kings (Osric and Eanfrid): for it has been generally agreed that the names of these apostates should be erased from the list of Christian kings and the year of their reign ignored. At the end of this period Oswald fell in a fierce battle fought at the place called in English Maserfelth[1] against the same heathen Mercians and their heathen king, who had also slain his predecessor Edwin. He died on the fifth of August 642, when he was thirty-eight years of age.

---

[1] Probably Oswestry (Shropshire).

Oswald's great devotion and faith in God was made evident
by the miracles that took place after his death. For at the place
where he was killed fighting for his country against the heathen,
sick men and beasts are healed to this day. Many people took
away the very dust from the place where his body fell, and put
it in water, from which sick folk who drank it received great
benefit. This practice became so popular that, as the earth was
gradually removed, a pit was left in which a man could stand.
But it is not to be wondered at that the sick received healing at
the place of his death; for during his lifetime he never failed to
provide for the sick and needy and to give them alms and aid.
Many miracles are reported as having occurred at this spot, or
by means of the earth taken from it; but I will content myself
with two, which I have heard from my elders.

Not long after Oswald's death, a man happened to be riding
near the place when his horse suddenly showed signs of distress.
It stopped and hung its head, foaming at the mouth, and as its
pains increased, it collapsed on the ground. The rider dismounted, removed the saddle, and waited to see whether the
beast was going to recover or to die. At length, having tossed
this way and that in great pain for a considerable time, it rolled
on to the spot where the great king had died. Immediately the
pain ceased, and the horse stopped its wild struggles; then,
having rolled on its other side, as tired beasts do, it got up fully
recovered and began to graze. The traveller, an observant man,
concluded that the place where his horse was cured must possess
especial sanctity, and when he had marked it, he mounted and
rode on to the inn where he intended to lodge. On his arrival he
found a girl, the niece of the landlord, who had long suffered
from paralysis; and when members of the household in his
presence were deploring the girl's disease, he began to tell them
about the place where his horse had been cured. So they put the
girl into a cart, took her to the place, and laid her down. Once
there she fell asleep for a short while; and, on awakening, she
found herself restored to health. She asked for water and washed
her face; then she tidied her hair, adjusted her linen headgear,

and returned home on foot in perfect health with those who had
brought her.

CHAPTER 10: *How the earth from this place has power over fire*

ABOUT this time another man, a Briton by race, is said to
have been crossing the ground where this battle had been
fought, and noticing that one spot was more green and beautiful
than the rest of the field, he came to the wise conclusion that
there could be no other explanation for this exceptional greenness but that some person of greater sanctity than anyone else in
the army had been slain there. So he took away some of the
earth wrapped up in a linen cloth, thinking that, as the event
proved, it might have power to heal the sick. Proceeding on his
journey, he arrived that night at a village and entered a house
where some neighbours were having a feast. He was welcomed
by the owners of the house, and when he had hung the cloth
containing the earth on a beam of the wall, he sat down to share
their meal. They had sat eating and drinking for a long while
around a blazing fire in the centre of the room, when sparks
flew up into the roof of the house, which was made of wattles
thatched with hay, and quickly burst into flame. When the
fuddled revellers realized this, they rushed out of the burning
house in terror, powerless to extinguish the blaze. The house
burned down, and only the beam from which the earth hung
remained whole and untouched by the flames. When they saw
this miracle, they were all astonished, and after making careful
enquiry, they found that the man had taken the earth from the
place where Oswald's blood had been shed. These marvels were
reported far and wide, and many folk began to visit the place
each day and obtained healing for themselves and their families.

CHAPTER 11: *A heavenly light appears all night over Oswald's tomb, and folk are healed from demonic possession*

IT would not be right to omit mention of the favours and miracles that were shown when Oswald's bones were discovered and translated into the church where they are now enshrined. This took place through the devout interest of Queen Osthryd of the Mercians, daughter of his brother Oswy who succeeded him on the throne, as I shall mention in due course.

In the province of Lindsey there is a noble monastery called Beardaneu,[1] which was greatly loved, favoured, and enriched by the queen and her husband Ethelred. She wished that the honoured bones of her uncle should be reinterred there. But when the waggon carrying the bones arrived towards evening at the abbey, the monks were reluctant to admit it; for although they acknowledged Oswald's holiness, they were influenced by old prejudices against him even after his death, because he originally came from a different province and had ruled them as an alien king. So it came about that the king's bones remained outside the gates all night, with only a large awning spread over the waggon in which they lay. But a sign from heaven showed them that the bones should be welcomed with respect by all the faithful: for throughout the night a pillar of light shone skywards from the waggon, and was seen by nearly all the inhabitants of the province of Lindsey. Early next morning, therefore, the monks who had previously refused to admit it, began to pray earnestly that the holy relics so dear to God should find a resting-place in their midst. Accordingly the bones were washed and laid in a casket made for the purpose, which was placed in the church with fitting honour. And to furnish a lasting memorial of the royal saint, they hung the king's banner of purple and gold over his tomb. The water in which the bones had been washed was poured away in a corner of the cemetery, and from that time on the very earth that had received this

---

[1] Bardney Abbey, Lincs.

venerated water had the saving power to expel devils from the bodies of those who were possessed.

Some while later, when Queen Osthryd was staying in the monastery, the venerable Ethelhild, abbess of a neighbouring house, visited her to pay her respects. This lady, who is still living, is sister of Bishop Ethelwin of Lindsey and of Abbot Aldwin of Partney, which lies not far away. While she was talking with the queen, the conversation turned to Oswald, and the abbess told her how she had herself seen the light reaching heavenwards from Oswald's relics on that night. And the queen informed her how the dust from the pavement, on which the water that had washed the bones had been spilt, had already healed many sick people. The abbess then asked that she might be given some of this healing dust; and when it had been given her, she tied it up in a cloth, and put it into a little casket which she took away with her. Some while later, a guest visited her abbey who was often horribly tormented by an evil spirit during the night hours. This man was hospitably welcomed, and had retired to bed after supper, when he was suddenly possessed by the devil and began to cry out, grind his teeth, foam at the mouth, and toss his limbs in wild contortions. No one could hold or bind him, so a servant ran and knocked at the abbess' door to inform her. She opened the monastery gate herself and went out with one of the nuns to the men's quarters, where she called one of the priests to accompany her to the sufferer. On their arrival, they found a crowd already present, none of whom had been able to control the man's wild convulsions. The priest therefore employed exorcism and did all he could to allay the sufferer's frenzy; but all his efforts were useless. When there seemed no hope left of easing his frenzy, the abbess suddenly remembered this dust, and told a maidservant to go at once and fetch the casket containing it. As soon as she returned from her errand and entered the porch of the house where the possessed man lay writhing, he immediately became silent, laying down his head as though to sleep, and relaxing his whole body. 'All in rapt silence stood, with gaze intent,'* watching anxiously to see the outcome of this affair. After some while, the man who had been so tormented sat up with a deep sigh, saying: 'I am now restored to health and in my right mind.' They eagerly asked him what had happened, and he replied: 'As soon as the maid carrying the casket approached the porch of the house, all the evil spirits who were tormenting me went away and left me and were nowhere to be seen.' Then the abbess gave him a portion of the dust, and after the priest had offered prayers, the man spent a quiet night and was never again troubled by the old enemy.

CHAPTER 12: *A little boy is cured of ague at Saint Oswald's tomb*

SOME while after this, there was a little boy in the monastery who had been seriously troubled by ague. One day he was anxiously awaiting the hour of an attack, when one of the brothers came in to him and said: 'My boy, shall I tell you how you may be cured of this complaint? Get up, and go to Oswald's tomb in the church. Remain there quietly and mind you don't stir from it until the time that your fever is due to leave you. Then I will come and fetch you.' The boy did as the brother advised, and while he sat by the saint's tomb the fever dared not touch him: furthermore, it was so completely scared that it never recurred, either on the second or the third day, or ever after. A brother of that monastery who told me this story added that the boy who had been so miraculously cured was by then a young man and still living in the monastery. But it need cause no surprise that the prayers of this king, who now reigns with God, should be acceptable to him, since when he was a king on earth he always used to work and pray fervently for the eternal kingdom.

It is said that Oswald often remained in prayer from the early hour of Lauds until dawn, and that through his practice of constant prayer and thanksgiving to God he always sat with his hands palm upwards on his knees. It is also said, and has become proverbial, that his life even closed in prayer; for when he saw the enemy forces surrounding him and knew that his end was near, he prayed for the souls of his soldiers. 'God have mercy on their souls, said Oswald as he fell' is now a proverb. As I have already mentioned, his bones were taken up and buried in the Abbey of Bardney; but the king who slew him ordered that his head and hands with the forearms be hacked off and fixed on stakes. The following year, Oswald's successor Oswy came to the place with his army and removed them, placing the head in the church at Lindisfarne, and the hands and arms in his own royal city of Bamburgh.

CHAPTER 13: *A man in Ireland is recalled from death's door by means of Oswald's relics*

THE fame of this illustrious hero was not confined to Britain, for the rays of his beneficent light shone far overseas, and reached Germany and Ireland. The most reverend Bishop Acca★ tells how, on a journey to Rome, Bishop Wilfrid and he stayed a while with the most holy Willibrord, then Archbishop of the Frisians, and how he heard him speak of the miracles that had been done by the relics of the venerated king in his own province. Willibrord also told them that when he was still a priest in Ireland, and living the life of a pilgrim out of love for his heavenly home, stories of the king's holiness were already current far and wide. I include in this history one of the stories that he told.

'At the time of the great plague that swept Britain and Ireland,' he said, 'one of its many victims was a scholar of Irish race, who was well read in literature but utterly uninterested and careless in the matter of his eternal salvation. When he realized that his death was near, he began to fear that as soon as he died his sins would drag him down to hell. As I was in the neighbourhood, he sent for me and said with tears in his voice, sighing and trembling: "You can see how this disease has tightened its hold and brought me to the point of death. I have no doubt that after the death of my body I shall immediately be condemned to the eternal death of the soul and endure all the torments of hell; for although I have made a great study of the scriptures, I have for a long time devoted myself to evil-doing rather than to keeping God's Commandments. But, if God's mercy allows me to survive, I solemnly resolve to amend my evil ways and will completely reform my character and way of life in submission to the will of God. I am fully aware that I do not deserve any prolongation of my life, nor can I expect it, unless it pleases God to pardon a wretched sinner through the intercession of those who have served Him faithfully. I have heard the well-known story of your most saintly King Oswald, whose wonderful faith and virtue have become renowned even after his death by the working of miracles. I therefore beg you, if you possess any of his relics, to bring them to me, and perhaps God will have pity on me for his sake." I told him: "I have a portion of the stake to which the king's head was fixed by the heathen after his death, and if you will make a sincere act of faith, God of His mercy and through the merits of this great saint may grant you a long term of earthly life and render you fitted to enter into life eternal." The man then assured me that he had complete faith in this. Then I blessed some water, and put in it a chip of this oak, and gave it to the sick man to drink. He quickly began to feel better, and having recovered from his illness, he lived many years after. He gave his heart and life entirely to God, and wherever he went he proclaimed the mercy of our kind Creator and the glory of His faithful servant Oswald.'*

CHAPTER 14: *On the death of Paulinus, Ithamar succeeds to his Bishopric of Rochester. An account of the wonderful humility of King Oswin, who was treacherously murdered by Oswy* [A.D. 642–651]

WHEN Oswald departed to the kingdom of heaven, his brother Oswy, a young man of about thirty, succeeded to his earthly throne and ruled for twenty-eight troubled years. He was attacked both by the pagan Mercians, who had already killed his brother, and also by his own son Alchfrid and his nephew Ethelwald, son of his brother and predecessor. In the year of our Lord 644, the second year of Oswy's reign, the most reverend father Paulinus, formerly Bishop of York and subsequently Bishop of Rochester, died on the tenth of October, after an episcopate lasting nineteen years, two months, and twenty-one days. He was buried in the sacristy of the church of the blessed Apostle Andrew, which had been founded and built in Rochester by King Ethelbert. In his place Archbishop Honorius consecrated Ithamar, a man of Kent, but as worthy and learned as his predecessors.

During the first part of his reign, Oswy shared the royal dignity with Oswin, who came of Edwin's royal line and was son of the above-mentioned Osric. This prince, who was a man of great holiness and piety, ruled the province of Deira most prosperously for seven years and was deeply loved by all. But even with him Oswy, who ruled the province of Bernicia, that is, the northern part of the Transhumbrian people, could not live peaceably; and when their differences grew more acute, he most treacherously murdered him. For, when the kings had raised armies against each other, Oswin realized that his opponent's forces were far stronger than his own, and decided not to risk an engagement but to await a more favourable opportunity. So he disbanded the army that he had raised at Wilfaresdun, that is, Wilfar's Hill, ten miles north-west of the village of Cataract,[1] and sent all his men to their homes. He himself, accompanied by a single trusted soldier named Tondhere, went back and lay concealed in the house of the nobleman Hunwald, whom he regarded as his greatest friend. Alas, it was far otherwise: for Hunwald betrayed Oswin and his man to Oswy, who amid universal disgust ordered his commander Ethelwin to put them both to death. This crime took place on the twentieth of August at In-Getlingum[2] in the ninth year of his reign, and here at a later date, in atonement for this crime, a

---

[1] Catterick.   [2] Gilling, Yorks.

monastery was built in which prayers were to be offered to God daily for the souls of the two kings, both slayer and slain alike.

King Oswin was a man of handsome appearance and lofty stature, pleasant in speech and courteous in manner. He was generous to high and low alike, and soon won the affection of everyone by his regal qualities of mind and body, so that nobles came from almost every province to enter his service. But among his other especial endowments of virtue and moderation the greatest was what one may describe as the singular blessing of humility, of which a single instance will be sufficient.

He had given Bishop Aidan a very fine horse, in order that he could ride whenever he had to cross a river or undertake any difficult or urgent journey, although the bishop ordinarily travelled on foot. Not long afterwards, when a poor man met the bishop and asked for alms, the bishop immediately dismounted and ordered the horse with all its royal trappings to be given to the beggar; for he was most compassionate, a protector of the poor and a father to the wretched. When this action came to the king's ears, he asked the bishop as they were going in to dine: 'My lord bishop, why did you give away the royal horse which was necessary for your own use? Have we not many less valuable horses or other belongings which would have been good enough for beggars, without giving away a horse that I had specially selected for your personal use?' The bishop at once answered, 'What are you saying, Your Majesty? Is this child of a mare more valuable to you than this child of God?' At this they went in to dinner, and the bishop sat down in his place; but the king, who had come in from hunting, stood warming himself by the fire with his attendants. As he stood by the fire, the king turned over in his mind what the bishop had said; then suddenly unbuckling his sword and handing it to a servant, he impulsively knelt at the bishop's feet and begged his forgiveness, saying: 'I will not refer to this matter again, nor will I enquire how much of our bounty you give away to God's children.' The bishop was deeply moved, and immediately stood up and raised him to his feet, assuring him of his high regard and begging him to sit down to his food without regrets. At the bishop's urgent request, the king sat down and began to be merry; but Aidan on the contrary grew so sad that he began to shed tears. His chaplain asked him in his own language, which the king and his servants did not understand, why he wept. Aidan replied: 'I know that the king will not live very long; for I have never before seen a humble king. I feel that he will soon be taken from us, because this nation is not worthy of such a king.' Not very long afterwards, as I have related, the bishop's foreboding was borne out by the king's death. And Bishop Aidan himself was taken from this world only eleven days after his beloved king, and received the eternal reward of his labours from our Lord on the thirty-first of August 651.

CHAPTER 15: *Bishop Aidan foretells a coming storm, and gives seafarers holy oil to calm the waves* [*c.* A.D. 651]

ALMIGHTY God made known the greatness of Aidan's merits by the evidence of miracles, of which it must suffice to mention three in his memory. A priest named Utta, a truthful and serious man, who on that account was generally respected by all, even by worldly princes, was sent to Kent to bring back Eanfled as wife for King Oswy: she was the daughter of King Edwin and had been taken to Kent when her father was killed. Intending to make the outward journey by land and to return with the princess by sea, he went to Bishop Aidan and asked him to pray for him and his companions as they set out on their long journey. When Aidan had blessed them and commended them to God, he gave them some holy oil, saying: 'When you set sail, you will encounter a storm and contrary winds. Remember then to pour the oil that I am giving you on the sea, and the wind will immediately drop, giving you a pleasant, calm voyage and a safe return home.' Everything happened as the bishop foretold. In a rising gale, the sailors dropped anchor, hoping to ride out the storm. This proved impossible; for the roaring seas broke into the ship from every side, and it began to fill. Everyone felt that his last hour had come, when at last the priest remembered the bishop's words. He took out the flask of oil, and poured some of it over the sea, which immediately ceased its raging as Aidan had foretold. So it came about that the man of God through the spirit of prophecy both foretold the storm and, although absent, calmed its fury. The story of this miracle is no groundless fable; for it was related to me by Cynimund, a most faithful priest of our own church [Jarrow], who had it from the mouth of the priest Utta, on and through whom the miracle was performed.

CHAPTER 16: *Aidan's prayers save the royal city when fired by the enemy*

ANOTHER notable miracle of the same father Aidan is told by those in a position to know the facts. While he was bishop, Penda and his enemy army of Mercians spread ruin far and wide throughout the lands of the Northumbrians and reached the very gates of the royal city, which takes its name from Bebba, a former queen. Unable to enter it either by force or after a siege. Penda attempted to set fire to it. Pulling down all the neighbouring villages, he carried to Bamburgh a vast quantity of beams, rafters, wattled walls, and thatched roofs, piling it high around the city wall on the landward side. Directly the wind became favourable, he set fire to this mass, intending to destroy the city. Now, while all this was happening, the most reverend Bishop Aidan was living on Farne Island, which lies nearly two miles from the city, and which was his retreat when he wished to pray alone and undisturbed: indeed, his lonely hermitage can be seen there to this day. When the saint saw the column of smoke and flame wafted by the winds above the city walls, he is said to have raised his eyes and hands to heaven, saying with tears: 'Lord, see what evil Penda does!' No sooner had he spoken than the wind shifted away from the city, and drove back the flames on to those who had kindled them, so injuring some and unnerving all that they abandoned their assault on a city so clearly under God's protection.*

CHAPTER 17: *The wooden buttress of the church against which Aidan leaned as he died is untouched when the rest of the church is burned down. His spiritual life* [A.D. 651]

DEATH came to Aidan when he had completed sixteen years of his episcopate, while he was staying at a royal residence near the town we have described. Having a church and lodging there, Aidan often used to go and stay at the place, travelling about the surrounding countryside to preach. This was his practice at all the king's country-seats, for he had no personal possessions except his church and a few fields around it. When he fell ill, a tent was erected for him on the west side of the church, so that the tent was actually attached to the church wall. And so it happened that, as he drew his last breath, he was leaning against a post that buttressed the wall on the outside. He passed away on the last day of August, in the seventeenth year of his episcopate, and his body was soon taken across to Lindisfarne Island and buried in the monks' cemetery. When a larger church, dedicated to the most blessed prince of the Apostles, was built there some while later, his bones were transferred to it and buried at the right side of the altar in accordance with the honours due to so great a prelate.

Finan, who had also come from the Irish island and monastery of Iona, succeeded him as bishop and held the office for a considerable time. Some years later, Penda, King of the Mercians, came into these parts with an invading army and destroyed everything that he found with fire and sword; and he burned down the village and the church where Aidan had died. But, in a wonderful manner, the beam against which he was leaning at his death was the only object untouched by the flames which devoured everything around it. This miracle was noticed and a church was soon rebuilt on the same site, with the beam supporting the structure from the outside as before. Sometime later in another fire, caused this time by carelessness, the village and church were again destroyed; but even on this occasion the beam remained undamaged. For, although in a most extraordinary way the flames licked through the very holes of the pins that secured it to the building, they were not permitted to destroy the beam. When the church was rebuilt for the third time, the beam was not employed as an outside support again, but was set up inside the church as a memorial of this miracle, so that those who entered might kneel there and ask God's mercy. Since that day many are known to have obtained the grace of healing at this spot, and many have cut chips of wood from the beam and put them in water, by which means many have been cured of their diseases.

I have dealt at length with the character and life of Aidan, although one cannot commend or approve his inadequate knowledge of the proper observance of Easter; indeed, as I have made clear in my book on the seasons, I strongly disapprove of these practices. None the less, as a truthful historian, I have given an accurate account of his life, commending all that was excellent and preserving his memory for the benefit of my readers. He cultivated peace and love, purity and humility; he was above anger and greed, and despised pride and conceit; he set himself to keep as well as to teach the laws of God, and was diligent in study and prayer. He used his priestly authority to check the proud and powerful; he tenderly comforted the sick; he relieved and protected the poor. To sum up in brief what I have learned from those who knew him, he took pains never to neglect anything that he had learned from the writings of the evangelists, apostles and prophets, and he set himself to carry them out with all his powers.

I greatly admire and love all these things about Aidan, because I have no doubt that they are pleasing to God; but I cannot approve or commend his failure to observe Easter at the proper time, whether he did it through ignorance of the canonical times or in deference to the customs of his own nation. But this in him I do approve, that in keeping his Easter he believed, worshipped, and taught exactly what we do, namely the redemption of the human race through the Passion, Resurrection, and Ascension into heaven of the Man Jesus Christ, the Mediator between God and man. He always kept Easter, not as some mistakenly suppose, on the fourteenth moon whatever the day was, as the Jews do, but on the Lord's Day falling between the fourteenth and twentieth days of the moon. He did so because he held that the Resurrection of our Lord took place on the day following the Sabbath and because, like the rest of Holy Church, he rightly expected our own resurrection to take place on the same day after the Sabbath, which we now call the Lord's Day.

CHAPTER 18: *The life and death of the devout King Sigbert* [*c.* A.D. 635]

ABOUT this time, after the death of Earpwald, successor to Redwald, the kingdom of the East Angles was ruled by his brother Sigbert, a good and religious man who had been baptized long previously in Gaul while he had been living in exile to escape the hostility of Redwald. When he returned home and became king, he wished to copy what he had seen well contrived in Gaul, and was quick to found a school for the education of boys in the study of letters. In this project he was assisted by Bishop Felix, who had come to him from Kent and provided him with teachers and masters according to the practice of Canterbury.

King Sigbert became so ardent in his love for the kingdom of heaven that he abandoned the affairs of his earthly kingdom, and entrusted them to his kinsman Egric, who had already governed part of the kingdom.* He then entered a monastery that he had founded and, after receiving the tonsure, devoted his energies to winning an everlasting kingdom. A considerable while later, the Mercians led by King Penda attacked the East Angles who, finding themselves less experienced in warfare than their enemies, asked Sigbert to go into battle with them and foster the morale of the fighting men. When he refused, they dragged him out of the monastery regardless of his protests, and took him into battle with them in the hope that their men would be less likely to panic or think of flight if they were under the eye of one who had once been a gallant and distinguished commander. But, mindful of his monastic vows, Sigbert, surrounded by a well-armed host, refused to carry anything more than a stick, and when the heathen charged, both he and King Egric were killed and the army scattered.

These kings were succeeded by Anna son of Eni, an excellent man of royal stock, and father of a distinguished family, of whom I shall give an account in due course. Anna also was later killed by the same pagan king of the Mercians who had slain his predecessors.

CHAPTER 19: *Fursey establishes a monastery among the East Angles: the incorruption of his body after death attests to his visions and holiness* [A.D. 633]

DURING Sigbert's reign there came from Ireland a holy man named Fursey, renowned for his words and doings and outstanding in virtue. His purpose was to spend his life as a pilgrim for love of our Lord, and to go wherever he found an opening. On his arrival in the province of the East Angles, he was honourably received by the king and preached the Gospel as he always did. Inspired by the example of his goodness and the effectiveness of his teaching, many unbelievers were converted to Christ, and many who already believed were drawn to greater love and faith in him.

Once when he was ill, God granted Fursey to enjoy a vision, in which he was directed to continue his diligent preaching of the word and to maintain his accustomed vigils and prayers with indefatigable zeal; for although death is certain, its coming is unpredictable, as our Lord says: '*Watch therefore, for ye know neither the day nor the hour.*' Stimulated by this vision, Fursey set himself with all speed to build a monastery on a site given him by King Sigbert, and to establish a regular observance in it. This monastery was pleasantly situated in some woods close to the sea, within the area of a fortification that the English call Cnobheresburg, meaning Cnobhere's Town. Subsequently,

Anna, king of the province, and his nobles endowed the house with finer buildings and gifts.*

Fursey was of noble Irish blood and even more noble in mind than in birth; for from his boyhood he had not only read sacred books and observed monastic discipline but, as is fitting in saints, had also diligently practised all that he learned.

In course of time he had built himself a monastery in which he might devote himself more freely to sacred studies. There, as the book on his life informs us, he fell ill and entered a trance; and quitting his body from sunset to cockcrow, was privileged to see the choirs of angels, and to hear the songs of the blessed. He used to say that, among other things, he clearly heard them sing: '*The saints shall go from strength to strength*', and '*The God of gods shall be seen in Sion*'. Then he returned to bodily consciousness; but three days later he was again withdrawn from it, and saw not only the greater joys of the blessed, but the amazing struggles of evil spirits, who fought to prevent his approach to heaven by constant wicked accusations: nevertheless, under the protection of the angels, he reached his goal. And if any one wishes to learn about these experiences in greater detail, let him read the above-mentioned little book on his life, and I think that he will reap great benefit from it. It describes the deceitful cunning with which the devils threw back at him his actions, his idle words, and even his thoughts, as though they were recorded in a book; and it tells of the joyful and sorrowful things that he learned both from the angels and from the saints who appeared among the angels.

I have, however, thought it proper to record in this history one happening which may be helpful to many. When Fursey had been carried up to a great height, he was told by his angel guides to look back at the world. As he looked down, he saw what appeared to be a gloomy valley beneath him, and four fires in the air, not far from one another. Asking what these were, the angels told him that they were the fires which were to burn and consume the world. 'One of them is Falsehood, when we do not renounce Satan and all his works as we promised at our Baptism. The next is Covetousness, when we put the love

173

of worldly wealth before the love of God. The third is Discord,
when we needlessly offend our neighbours, even in small
matters. The fourth is Cruelty, when we think it no crime to
rob and defraud the weak.' These fires gradually grew together
and merged into one vast conflagration, so that Fursey in alarm
cried to the angel: 'Master, the fire is coming near me!' To
which the angel replied: 'It will not burn you, because you did
not kindle it; for although it appears as a great and terrible fire,
it tests everyone according to his deserts, and will burn away
his sinful desires. For as every man's body is set on fire by
unlawful desire, so when death frees him from the body, he
must make due atonement for his sins by fire.' Then he saw one
of the three angels who had been his guides in both his visions
go forward and divide the flames, while the other two flew on
each side of him to protect him from harm. He also saw devils,
who flew through the flames stirring up the fires of war against
the just. These evil spirits made accusations against him, while
the good spirits spoke in his defence. Fursey also saw a greater
vision of the heavenly hosts of the saints of his own nation who
had once worthily adorned the dignity of priesthood, and from
them he learned many things of spiritual benefit both to himself
and to those who were ready to listen. And when they had
ended speaking and returned to heaven with the other angelic
spirits, there remained with Fursey the three angels who were
to restore him to his body. As they approached the great fire,
the angel divided the flames as before for him to pass. But when
the man of God came to the passage opened among the flames,
wicked spirits seized one of those whom they had been tormenting in the fire, and thrust him against Fursey, so that he
was burned on his shoulder and jaw. He recognized this man,
and remembered that he had received some of his clothing when
he died. And when the holy angel quickly took the man and
cast him back into the flames, the malicious devil said: 'Don't
reject one of your own friends; for since you accepted the
property of this sinner, you must share his punishment.' But
the angel defended Fursey, saying: 'He did not accept them out
of greed, but in order to save the man's soul.' The fire then died

down, and the angel turned to Fursey, saying: 'You lit this fire, so you were burned: had you not accepted property from one who died in his sins, you would not have shared his punishment.' And he went on to instruct Fursey in salutary words what should be done for the salvation of those who repented on their death-bed. And when Fursey had been restored to his body, he found that the burn that he had received in his soul had left a permanent and visible scar on his shoulder and jaw; and in this strange way his body afforded visible evidence of the inward sufferings of his soul. He continued to set an example of virtue to others in his life and teaching as before, but he would relate his visions only to those who were moved by penitence to ask him. An old brother of our monastery, who is still living, testifies that he once knew a truthful and devout man who had met Fursey in the province of the East Angles, and heard of these visions from his own mouth. He added that it was a frosty and bitter winter's day when Fursey told his story; and yet, though he wore only a thin garment, he was sweating profusely as though it had been summer, either because of the consolation or the terror of his recollections.

To return to my original narrative, when Fursey had preached the word of God among the Irish for many years, he could no longer endure the crowds that thronged him. So he abandoned everything he seemed to possess and, leaving his native island with a few companions, crossed into Britain to the province of the Angles, where he preached the word of God and built the above-mentioned noble monastery. Having done this with success, he began to long to be rid of all worldly business, even to the affairs of the monastery; and having entrusted the care of souls to his brother Foillan and the priests Gobban and Dicul, he freed himself of all worldly responsibilities and resolved to end his life as a hermit. Now Fursey had another brother named Ultan, who after many years in a monastery had adopted the life of a hermit. So Fursey sought him out alone and for a year shared his life of prayer and austerity, supporting himself by daily manual labour.

At this period, the province was again distressed by the

attacks of the heathen, and Fursey, foreseeing that even monasteries would be endangered, set his affairs in order and sailed over to Gaul, where he was honourably received by King Clovis [II] and his chamberlain Earconwald, and built a monastery at Latiniacum.* Not long afterwards, when he fell sick and died, the noble Earconwald took his body and placed it in the porch of a church he was building in his estate called Péronne, until the church itself should be consecrated. This took place twenty-seven days later, and when the body was taken from the porch to be buried near the altar, it was found to be as free from decay as on the day of his death. Four years later a more suitable chapel was built for his resting-place to the east of the altar, and his still uncorrupt body was transferred to it with great honour. In this chapel God has granted many miracles as evidence of the saint's merits. I have briefly recorded these events and the incorruption of his body, so that the reader may understand more clearly how great a man Fursey was. But he will find a fuller account of Fursey and his companions in the book on his life which I have mentioned.

CHAPTER 20: *On the death of Honorius* [A.D. 653], *Deusdedit succeeds him as Archbishop of Canterbury. The succession of the bishops of the East Angles and of Rochester*

MEANWHILE Felix, Bishop of the East Angles, died after an episcopate of seventeen years, and Archbishop Honorius consecrated Thomas his deacon from the province of the Gyrwas* to succeed him. He died after five years in the bishopric, and was followed by Bertgils, a man of Kent known as Boniface. Archbishop Honorius himself, having run his course, died on the thirtieth of September 653, and after a vacancy of eighteen months Deusdedit, a West Saxon, was elected to the archiepiscopal see and so became the sixth Archbishop. He was consecrated by Ithamar, Bishop of Rochester, on the twenty-sixth of March (655), and ruled the see until his death nine years, four months, and two days later. And on the death of Ithamar, Deusdedit himself consecrated Damian, a South Saxon, in his place.

CHAPTER 21: *The Province of the Middle Angles, under its king Peada, becomes christian* [A.D. 653]

ABOUT this time the Middle Angles, ruled by their king Peada, son of Penda, accepted the true Faith and its sacraments. Peada, who was a noble young man, well deserving the title and dignity of a king, whom his father had appointed to the kingship of this people, went to Oswy King of the Northumbrians and requested the hand of his daughter Alchfled in marriage. Oswy, however, would not agree to this unless the king and his people accepted the Christian Faith and were baptized. So when Peada had received instruction in the true Faith, and had learned of the promises of the kingdom of heaven and of man's hope of resurrection and eternal life to come, he said that he would gladly become a Christian, even if he were refused the princess. He was chiefly influenced to accept the Faith by King Oswy's son Alchfrid, who was his kinsman and friend, and had married his sister Cyniburg, daughter of King Penda.*

Accordingly, Peada was baptized by Bishop Finan, together with his companions and thegns and all their servants, at a well-known village belonging to the king known as At-Wall. Then, taking with him four priests, chosen for their learning and holy life, to instruct and baptize his people, he returned home full of joy. These priests were Cedd, Adda, Betti, and Diuma, all of whom were English except Diuma, who was Irish. As I have said, Adda was brother of Utta, a well-known priest and Abbot of Gateshead. On their arrival in the province with the king, these priests preached the word of God and found a ready hearing, both noble and common folk alike coming in great numbers daily to renounce their idols and receive Baptism.

King Penda himself did not forbid the preaching of the Faith to any even of his own Mercians who wished to listen; but he hated and despised any whom he knew to be insincere in their practice of Christianity once they had accepted it, and said that any who despised the commandments of the God in whom they professed to believe were themselves despicable wretches. This Christian mission was begun two years before Penda's death. And when Penda was killed, and was succeeded by the Christian King Oswy, as I shall tell later, Diuma, one of these four priests, was consecrated Bishop of the Middle Angles and Mercians by Bishop Finan, since a shortage of priests made it necessary for one bishop to preside over two peoples. During his short episcopate, Diuma converted many to the Faith, and died among the Middle Angles in the district known as In-Feppingum. He was succeeded by Ceollach, an Irishman who relinquished the see after a short time and returned to the Isle of Iona, the chief and mother-house of many Irish monasteries. His successor was Bishop Trumhere, a devout man trained as a monk, English by race but consecrated bishop by the Irish. This took place during the reign of King Wulfhere, of whom I shall speak later.

CHAPTER 22: *The East Saxons, who had apostatized from the Faith under King Sigbert, are re-converted by the preaching of Cedd* [A.D. 653]

ABOUT this time also, the East Saxons, who had once rejected the Faith and driven out Bishop Mellitus, again accepted it under the influence of King Oswy. For Sigbert their king, successor to Sigbert the Small, was a friend of Oswy and often used to visit him in the province of the Northumbrians. Oswy used to reason with him how gods made by man's handiwork could not be gods, and how a god could not be made from a log or block of stone, the rest of which might be burned or made into articles of everyday use or possibly thrown away as rubbish to be trampled underfoot and reduced to dust. He showed him how God is rather to be understood as a being of boundless majesty, invisible to human eyes, almighty, ever-lasting, creator of heaven and earth and of the human race. He told him that he rules and will judge the world in justice, abiding in eternity, not in base and perishable metal; and that it should be rightly understood that all who know and do the will of their Creator will receive an eternal reward from him. King Oswy advanced these and other arguments during friendly and brotherly talks with Sigbert, who, encouraged by the agreement of his friends, was at length convinced. So he talked it over with his advisers, and with one accord they accepted the Faith and were baptized with him by Bishop Finan in the king's village at At-Wall, so named because it stands close to the wall which the Romans once built to protect Britain, about twelve miles from the eastern coast.

Having now become a citizen of the kingdom of heaven, Sigbert returned to the capital of his earthly kingdom after asking Oswy to send him teachers to convert his people to the Faith of Christ and baptize them. Accordingly Oswy sent to the province of the Middle Angles and summoned the man of God, Cedd, whom he dispatched with another priest as companion to evangelize the East Saxons. When these priests had visited the entire province and established a strong Christian community, Cedd returned home to Lindisfarne for consultations with Bishop Finan. When the latter learned the great success of his preaching, he invited two other bishops to assist him, and consecrated Cedd Bishop of the East Saxons. And when Cedd had been raised to the dignity of bishop, he returned to his province and used his increased authority to promote the work already begun. He built churches in several places and ordained priests and deacons to assist in teaching the Faith and baptizing the people, especially in the city which the Saxons call Ythan-caestir* and that called Tilaburg.[1] The former place stands on the bank of the River Pant, the latter on the River Thames. Here Cedd established communities of the servants of Christ

---

[1] Tilbury.

and taught them to maintain the discipline of the regular life so far as these untutored folk were then capable of doing.

To the great joy of the king and all his people, the Gospel of eternal life made daily headway throughout the province for a considerable time until, at the instigation of the Enemy of all good men, the king was murdered by his own kinsmen. This horrid crime was committed by two brothers who, on being asked their motive, had no answer to make except that they hated the king because he was too lenient towards his enemies and too readily forgave injuries when offenders asked pardon. This then was the fault for which the king was killed, that he sincerely observed the teachings of the Gospel. Yet in this undeserved fate he was overtaken by punishment for his real fault, as the man of God had once foretold. For one of the nobles who murdered him had contracted an illicit marriage, and the bishop, being unable to prevent or correct this, had therefore excommunicated him, forbidding anyone to enter his house or eat at his table. But the king had disregarded this ban and had accepted the noble's invitation to a feast. As he was leaving the house, the bishop met him, and the king immediately dismounted from his horse and fell trembling at his feet, begging pardon for his fault. The bishop, for he too had been on horseback, also dismounted in great anger and, touching the prostrate king with the staff in his hand, exercised his pontifical authority and said: 'I tell you that, since you have refused to avoid the house of a man who is lost and damned, this very house will be the place of your death.' However, since the death of this religious king was due to his loyal obedience to Christ's commandments, we may believe that it atoned for his earlier offence and increased his merits.

Sigbert was succeeded as king by Swidhelm, son of Sexbald, who had been baptized by Cedd in the province of the East Angles at the king's country-seat of Rendlesham, that is, Rendil's House: his godfather was Ethelwald, King of the East Angles, brother of King Anna.

DURING his episcopate among the East Saxons, God's servant Cedd often visited his own province, that is the province of the Northumbrians, to preach. Ethelwald, son of King Oswald, who ruled in the region of Deira, knowing Cedd to be a wise, holy, and virtuous man, asked him to accept a grant of land to found a monastery, to which he himself might often come to pray and hear the word of God and where he might be buried: for he firmly believed that the daily prayers of those who would serve God there would be of great help to him. The king's chaplain had been Cedd's brother, a priest named Caelin, a man equally devoted to God, who had ministered the Word and Sacraments to himself and his family, and it was mainly through him that the king came to know and love the bishop. In accordance with the king's wishes, Cedd chose a site for the monastery among some high and remote hills, which seemed more suitable for the dens of robbers and haunts of wild beasts than for human habitation. His purpose in this was to fulfil the prophecy of Isaiah: '*In the habitation of dragons, where each lay, shall be grass, with reeds and rushes*', so that the fruits of good works might spring up where formerly lived only wild beasts, or men who lived like wild beasts.

The man of God wished first of all to purify the site of the monastery from the taint of earlier crimes by prayer and fasting and make it acceptable to God before laying the foundations. He therefore asked the king's permission to remain there throughout the approaching season of Lent, and during this time he fasted until evening every day except Sunday according to custom. Even then, he took no food but a morsel of bread, a hen's egg and a little watered milk. He explained that it was the custom of those who had trained him in the rule of regular discipline to dedicate the site of any monastery or church to God with prayer and fasting. But ten days before the end of Lent a messenger arrived to summon him to the king. So in order that the king's business should not interrupt the work of dedication, Cedd asked his brother the priest Cynibil to complete this holy task. The latter readily consented, and when the period of prayer, and fasting came to an end, he built the monastery now called Laestingaeu,[1] and established there the observance of the usages of Lindisfarne where he had been trained.

When Cedd had been bishop of the province for many years and ruled the monastery through the priors he had chosen, he happened to visit the monastery during a time of plague, and there fell sick and died. He was first buried in the open, but in the course of time a stone church was built, dedicated to the blessed Mother of God, and in it his body was reinterred on the right side of the altar.

The bishop bequeathed the abbacy of the monastery to his brother Chad, who subsequently became a bishop as I shall record later.* The four brothers I have mentioned – Cedd, Cynibil, Caelin, and Chad – all became famous priests of our Lord, and two became bishops, which is a rare occurrence in one family. When the brethren of Cedd's monastery in the province of the East Saxons heard that their founder had died and been buried in the province of the Northumbrians, about thirty of them came there visiting wishing either, God willing, to live near the body of their Father, or else to die and be laid to rest at his side. They were kindly welcomed by their brothers and fellow-soldiers of Christ, and all of them died there of the plague with the exception of one little boy who must surely have been preserved from death by the prayers of his Father Chad. For many years afterwards, when this boy was still alive and applying himself to the study of the Scriptures, he suddenly learned that he had never been baptized; so he at once sought salvation in the waters of the font, and was subsequently admitted to the priesthood and proved himself a support to many in the Church. So I have no doubt that, when the boy visited the tomb of his beloved Father, he was saved from

---

[1] Lastingham, near Whitby.

imminent death by his prayers, in order that he might escape
eternal death and by his witness exercise a ministry of life and
salvation to the other brethren.

CHAPTER 24: *On the death of Penda, the Province of the Mercians*
accepts the Faith of Christ: in gratitude for his victory, Oswy gives
endowments and lands to God for the building of monasteries
[A.D. 655]

A T this period King Oswy was subjected to savage and
intolerable attacks by Penda, the above-mentioned King of
the Mercians who had slain his brother. At length dire need
compelled him to offer Penda an incalculable quantity of regalia
and presents as the price of peace, on condition that he returned
home and ceased his ruinous devastation of the provinces of his
kingdom. But the treacherous king refused to consider his offer,
and declared his intention of wiping out the entire nation from
the highest to the humblest in the land. Accordingly Oswy
turned for help to the mercy of God, who alone could save the
land from its barbarous and godless enemy; and he bound
himself with an oath, saying: 'If the heathen refuses to accept
our gifts, let us offer them to the Lord our God.' So he vowed
that, if he were victorious, he would offer his daughter to God
as a consecrated virgin and give twelve estates to build monasteries. This done, he gave battle with an insignificant force to
the pagan armies, which are said to have been thirty times
greater than his own and comprised thirty battle-hardened
legions under famous commanders. Oswy and his son Alchfrid,
trusting in Christ as their leader, met them, as I have said, with
very small forces. His other son Egfrid was at the time held
hostage at the court of Queen Cynwise in the province of the
Mercians. But Oswald's son Ethelwald, who should have
helped them, had gone over to the enemy and had acted as
guide to Penda's army against his own kin and country,
although during the actual battle he withdrew and awaited the
outcome in a place of safety. When battle had been joined, the

pagans suffered defeat. Almost all the thirty commanders who had come to Penda's aid were killed. Among them Ethelhere, brother and successor of King Anna of the East Angles, who had been responsible for the war, fell with all his men. This battle was fought close by the River Winwaed, which at the time was swollen by heavy rains and had flooded the surrounding country: as a result, many more were drowned while attempting to escape than perished by the sword.*

In fulfilment of his vow to the Lord, King Oswy gave thanks to God for his victory and dedicated his daughter Aelffled, who was scarcely a year old, to his service in perpetual virginity. He also gave twelve small grants of land, where heavenly warfare was to take the place of earthly, and to provide for the needs of monks to make constant intercession for the perpetual peace of his nation. Six of these lay in the province of Deira, and six in Bernicia, each of ten hides in extent, making one hundred and twenty in all. The daughter whom King Oswy had in this way dedicated to God entered the monastery of Heruteu[1] or Hart's Island, at that time ruled by Abbess Hilda. Two years later, the Abbess acquired a property of ten hides at a place called Streanaeshalch,[2]* where she founded a monastery. In this the king's daughter became first a novice and later a mistress of the monastic life, until at fifty-nine years of age this holy virgin departed to the wedding-feast and embrace of her heavenly Bridegroom. In the church of this monastery, dedicated to the holy Apostle Peter, she herself, her father Oswy, her mother Eanfled, her mother's father Edwin, and many other noble folk are buried. This battle was won by King Oswy in the region of Loidis[3] on the fifteenth of November in the thirteenth year of his reign, to the great benefit of both nations. For not only did he deliver his own people from the hostile attacks of the heathen, but after cutting off their infidel head he converted the Mercians and their neighbours to the Christian Faith.

The first Bishop in the province of the Mercians, together with the people of Lindsey and the Middle Angles, was the

---

[1] Hartlepool.   [2] Whitby.   [3] Leeds.

above-mentioned Diuma, who died and was buried among the Middle Angles. The second was Ceollach, who resigned the bishopric and returned to the land of the Irish; for both he and Diuma were of Irish race. The third was Trumhere, an English-man trained and ordained by the Irish, who was abbot of the monastery of In-Getlingum.[1] As I have said, this was the place where King Oswin had been killed and where his kinswoman Queen Eanfled, in expiation for his unjust death, petitioned King Oswy to grant God's servant Trumhere, who was also a near relative of the king, land on which to build a monastery; in this way, prayer could be offered for the eternal salvation of both kings, slayer and slain alike. For three years after the death of Penda, King Oswy ruled both the Mercians and the other peoples of the southern provinces; he also subjected most of the Picts to English rule.

At this time he granted Peada, son of Penda, because he was his kinsman, the Kingdom of the South Mercians, which consists of five thousand hides of land and is divided by the River Trent from the land of the North Mercians, which consists of seven thousand hides. In the following spring, however, during the Festival of Easter, Peada was foully assas-sinated through the treachery, it is said, of his own wife. And three years after Penda's death the Mercian leaders Immin, Eafa, and Eadbert rebelled against Oswy and proclaimed as king Wulfhere, son of Penda, a youth whom they had kept hidden; and having driven out the representatives of a king whom they refused to acknowledge, they boldly recovered their liberty and lands. Free under their own king, they gave willing allegiance to Christ their true King, so that they might win his eternal kingdom in heaven. King Wulfhere ruled the Mercians for seventeen years and, as I have said, had Trumhere as his first bishop. The second bishop was Jaruman; the third, Chad; the fourth, Wynfrid. All these in turn held the bishopric of the Mercians under King Wulfhere.

[1] Gilling, near Richmond.

WHEN Bishop Aidan departed this life, he was succeeded in the Bishopric by Finan, who had been consecrated and sent by the Irish. He built a church in the Isle of Lindisfarne suitable for an episcopal see, constructing it, however, not of stone, but of hewn oak, thatched with reeds after the Irish manner. It was later dedicated by the most reverend Archbishop Theodore in honour of the blessed Apostle Peter. But Eadbert, a later Bishop of Lindisfarne, removed the thatch, and covered both roof and walls with sheets of lead.*

About this time there arose a great and recurrent controversy on the observance of Easter, those trained in Kent and Gaul maintaining that the Irish observance was contrary to that of the universal Church. The most zealous champion of the true Easter was an Irishman named Ronan, who had been instructed in Gaul and Italy in the authentic practice of the Church. He disputed against Finan and convinced many, or at least persuaded them to make more careful enquiry into the truth. But he entirely failed to move Finan, a hot-tempered man whom reproof made more obstinate and openly hostile to the truth. James, formerly the deacon of the venerable Archbishop Paulinus, of whom I have spoken, kept the true and Catholic Easter with all whom he could persuade to adopt the right observance. Also Queen Eanfled and her court, having a Kentish priest named Romanus who followed the Catholic practice, observed the customs she had seen in Kent. It is said that the confusion in those days was such that Easter was sometimes kept twice in one year, so that when the King had ended Lent and was keeping Easter, the Queen and her attendants were still fasting and keeping Palm Sunday. During Aidan's lifetime these differences of Easter observance were patiently tolerated by everyone; for it was realized that, although he was in loyalty bound to retain the customs of those who sent him, he nevertheless laboured diligently to cultivate the faith, piety, and love that marks out God's saints. He was therefore rightly loved by all, even by those who differed from his opinion on Easter, and was held in high respect not only by ordinary folk, but by Honorius of Canterbury and Felix of the East Angles.

When Finan, who followed Aidan as bishop, died, he was succeeded by another Irishman, Colman, under whom an even more serious controversy arose about Easter and also about other rules of Church discipline. This dispute rightly began to trouble the minds and consciences of many people, who feared that they might have received the name of Christians in vain. Eventually the matter came to the notice of King Oswy and his son Alchfrid. Oswy thought nothing could be better than the Irish teaching, having been instructed and baptized by the Irish and having a complete grasp of their language. But Alchfrid, who had been instructed in the Faith by Wilfrid – a very learned man who had gone to Rome to study the doctrine of the Church, and spent a long time at Lyons under Dalfin,* Archbishop of Gaul, from whom he had received the tonsure – knew that Wilfrid's doctrine was in fact preferable to all the traditions of the Irish. He had therefore given him a monastery with forty hides of land at In-Hrypum.[1] Actually, he had given this not long previously to the adherents of the Irish customs; but since, when offered the alternative, these preferred to give up the place rather than alter their customs, he then offered it to Wilfrid, whose life and teaching made him a worthy recipient. About this time, Agilbert, Bishop of the West Saxons, whom I have mentioned, had come to visit the province of the Northumbrians. He was a friend both of King Alchfrid and of Abbot Wilfrid and stayed with them for some time, and at the king's request he made Wilfrid a priest in his monastery. He also had with him a priest named Agatho. So when discussion arose there on the questions of Easter, the tonsure, and various other church matters, it was decided to hold a synod to put an end to this dispute at the monastery of Streanaeshalch,* which means The Bay of the Beacon, then ruled by the Abbess Hilda, a woman devoted to God. Both kings, father and son, came to this synod,

---

[1] Ripon.

and so did Bishop Colman with his Irish clergy, and Bishop
Agilbert with the priests Agatho and Wilfrid. James and
Romanus supported the latter, while Abbess Hilda and her
community, together with the venerable bishop Cedd, supported the Irish. Cedd, who as already mentioned had long ago
been ordained by the Irish, acted as a most careful interpreter
for both parties at the council.

King Oswy opened by observing that all who served the One
God should observe one rule of life, and since they all hoped for
one kingdom in heaven, they should not differ in celebrating
the sacraments of heaven. The synod now had the task of
determining which was the truer tradition, and this should be
loyally accepted by all. He then directed his own bishop Colman
to speak first, and to explain his own rite and its origin. Then
Colman said: 'The Easter customs which I observe were taught
me by my superiors, who sent me here as a bishop; and all our
forefathers, men beloved of God, are known to have observed
these customs. And lest anyone condemn or reject them as
wrong, it is recorded that they owe their origin to the blessed
evangelist Saint John, the disciple especially loved by our Lord,
and all the churches over which he presided.' When he had
concluded these and similar arguments, the king directed Agilbert to explain the origin and authority of his own customs.
Agilbert replied: 'May I request that my disciple the priest
Wilfrid be allowed to speak in my place? For we are both in full
agreement with all those here present who support the traditions
of our Church, and he can explain our view in the English
language more competently and clearly than I can do through
an interpreter.' When Wilfrid had received the king's command
to speak, he said: 'Our Easter customs are those that we have
seen universally observed in Rome, where the blessed Apostles
Peter and Paul lived, taught, suffered, and are buried. We have
also seen the same customs generally observed throughout Italy
and Gaul when we travelled through these countries for study
and prayer. Furthermore, we have learnt that Easter is observed
by men of different nations and languages at one and the same
time, in Africa, Asia, Egypt, Greece, and throughout the world

wherever the Church of Christ has spread. The only people who stupidly contend against the whole world are those Irishmen and their partners in obstinacy the Picts and Britons, who inhabit only a portion of these the two uttermost islands of the ocean.'* In reply to this statement, Colman answered: 'It is strange that you call us stupid when we uphold customs that rest on the authority of so great an Apostle, who was considered worthy to lean on our Lord's breast, and whose great wisdom is acknowledged throughout the world.' Wilfrid replied: 'Far be it from us to charge John with stupidity, because he literally observed the Law of Moses at a time when the Church followed many Jewish practices, and the Apostles were not able immediately to abrogate the observances of the Law once given by God, lest they gave offence to believers who were Jews (whereas idols, on the other hand, being inventions of the devil, must be renounced by all converts). For this reason Paul circumcised Timothy, offered sacrifice in the Temple, and shaved his head at Corinth with Aquila and Priscilla, for no other reason than that of avoiding offence to the Jews. For James said to Paul: "*Thou seest, brother, how many thousands of Jews there are which believe; and they are all zealous of the law.*" But today, as the Gospel spreads throughout the world, it is unnecessary and indeed unlawful for the faithful to be circumcised or to offer animals to God in sacrifice. John, following the custom of the law, used to begin the Feast of Easter on the evening of the fourteenth day of the first month, not caring whether it fell on the Sabbath or on any other day. But Peter, when he preached in Rome, remembering that it was on the day after the Sabbath that our Lord rose from the dead and gave the world the hope of resurrection, realized that Easter should be kept as follows: like John, in accordance with the Law, he waited for moonrise on the evening of the fourteenth day of the first month. And if the Lord's Day, then called the morrow of the Sabbath, fell on the following day, he began to observe Easter the same evening, as we all do today. But, if the Lord's Day did not fall on the day following the fourteenth day of the moon, but on the sixteenth, seventeenth, or any other day up to the twenty-first, he waited until that day, and on the Sabbath evening preceding it he began the observance of the Easter Festival. This evangelical and apostolical tradition does not abrogate but fulfil the Law, which ordained that the Passover be kept between the eve of the fourteenth and twenty-first days of the moon of that month. And this is the custom of all the successors of blessed John in Asia since his death, and is also that of the world-wide Church. This is the true and only Easter to be observed by the faithful. It was not newly decreed by the Council of Nicaea, but reaffirmed by it, as Church history records. It is quite apparent, Colman, that you follow neither the example of John, as you imagine, nor that of Peter, whose tradition you deliberately contradict. Your keeping of Easter agrees neither with the Law nor with the Gospel. For John, who kept Easter in accordance with the decrees of Moses, did not keep to the first day after the Sabbath; but this is not your practice, for you keep Easter only on the first day after the Sabbath. Peter kept Easter between the fifteenth and twenty-first days of the moon; you do not, for you keep it between the fourteenth and twentieth days of the moon. As a result, you often begin Easter on the evening of the thirteenth day, which is not mentioned in the Law. Nor did our Lord, the Author and giver of the Gospel, eat the old Passover or institute the Sacrament of the New Testament to be celebrated by the Church in memory of His Passion on that day, but on the fourteenth. Furthermore, when you keep Easter, you totally exclude the twenty-first day, which the Law of Moses particularly ordered to be observed. Therefore, I repeat, you follow neither John nor Peter, the Law nor the Gospel, in your keeping of our greatest Festival.'

Colman in reply said: 'Do you maintain that Anatolius, a holy man highly spoken of in Church history, taught contrary to the Law and the Gospel, when he wrote that Easter should be kept between the fourteenth and twentieth days of the moon? Are we to believe that our most revered Father Columba and his successors, men so dear to God, thought or acted contrary to Holy Scripture when they followed this custom? The holiness of many of them is confirmed by heavenly signs, and their virtues by miracles; and having no doubt that they are Saints, I shall never cease to emulate their lives, customs, and discipline.'

'It is well established that Anatolius was a most holy, learned, and praiseworthy man,' answered Wilfrid; 'but how can you claim his authority when you do not follow his directions? For he followed the correct rule about Easter, and observed a cycle of nineteen years; but either you do not know of this general custom of the Christian Church, or else you ignore it. He calculated the fourteenth day of the moon at Easter according to the Egyptian method, counting it on the evening as the fifteenth day; similarly, he assigned the twentieth to Easter Sunday, regarding it after sunset as the twenty-first day. But it appears that you do not realize this distinction, since you sometimes keep Easter before full moon, that is, on the thirteenth day. And with regard to your Father Columba and his followers, whose holiness you claim to imitate and whose rules and customs you claim to have been supported by heavenly signs, I can only say that when many shall say to our Lord at the day of Judgement: *"Have we not prophesied in thy name, and cast out devils, and done many wonderful works?"* the Lord will reply, *"I never knew you."* Far be it from me to apply these words to your fathers; for it is more just to believe good rather than evil of those whom one does not know. So I do not deny that they are true servants of God and dear to Him, and that they loved Him in primitive simplicity but in devout sincerity. Nor do I think that their ways of keeping Easter were seriously harmful, so long as no one came to show them a more perfect way to follow. Indeed, I feel certain that, if any Catholic reckoner had come to them, they would readily have accepted his guidance, as we know that they readily observed such of God's ordinances as they already knew. But you and your colleagues are most certainly guilty of sin if you reject the decrees of the Apostolic See, indeed of the universal Church, which are confirmed by Holy Writ. For, although your Fathers were holy men, do you imagine that they, a few men in a corner of a remote island, are to be preferred before the universal Church of Christ throughout the world? And even if your Columba – or, may I say, ours also if he was the servant of Christ – was a Saint potent in miracles, can he take precedence before the most blessed Prince of the Apostles, to whom our Lord said: "*Thou art Peter, and upon this rock I will build my Church, and the gates of hell shall not prevail against it, and I will give unto thee the keys of the kingdom of heaven*"?'

When Wilfrid had ended, the king asked: 'Is it true, Colman, that these words were spoken to that Peter by our Lord?' He answered: 'It is true, Your Majesty.' Then the king said: 'Can you show that a similar authority was given to your Columba?' 'No,' replied Colman. 'Do you both agree', the king continued, 'that these words were indisputably addressed to Peter in the first place, and that our Lord gave him the keys of the kingdom of heaven?' Both answered: 'We do.' At this, the king concluded: 'Then, I tell you, Peter is guardian of the gates of heaven, and I shall not contradict him. I shall obey his commands in everything to the best of my knowledge and ability; otherwise, when I come to the gates of heaven, there may be no one to open them, because he who holds the keys has turned away.'*

When the king said this, all present, both high and low, signified their agreement and, abandoning their imperfect customs, hastened to adopt those which they had learned to be better.

CHAPTER 26: *After his defeat Colman returns home and Tuda succeeds to his bishopric* [A.D. 664]: *the condition of the Church under these teachers*

IN this way the controversy was terminated, the company dispersed, and Agilbert returned home. Colman, seeing his teachings rejected and his following discounted, took away with him all who wished to follow him, that is, all who still dissented from the Catholic Easter and tonsure* – for there was no small argument about this as well – and returned to the land of the Irish[1] in order to consult his compatriots on their future course

[1] Iona.

of action. Cedd, on the other hand, having abandoned the Irish customs and accepted the Catholic, returned to his own bishopric. This Synod took place in the year of our Lord 664, which was the twenty-second year of King Oswy's reign, and the thirtieth anniversary of the coming of the Irish bishops to England, Aidan having held his bishopric for seventeen years, Finan for ten, and Colman for three.

On Colman's return to his own land, the servant of God, Tuda, became bishop of the Northumbrians in his place. He had been trained and consecrated bishop by the southern Irish, and had worn the ecclesiastical tonsure according to the customs of the province, and observed the Catholic Easter customs. He was a good devout man, but ruled the diocese only for a short time. He had arrived from the land of the Irish during Colman's episcopate, and taught the truths of the Faith diligently in word and deed. Then Eata, abbot of the monastery of Mailros,[1] a gentle man and greatly revered, was appointed Abbot of Lindisfarne to rule the brethren who elected to remain there when the Irish withdrew. It is said that before Colman left, he asked and obtained this favour from King Oswy, because Eata had been one of the twelve English boys whom Aidan received to be taught the Christian Faith when he first became bishop; for the king greatly loved Bishop Colman for his innate discernment. This is the same Eata who not long afterwards was raised to the bishopric of the church of Lindisfarne. On his return home, Colman took with him a portion of the bones of the most reverend Father Aidan; but he left some of them in the church over which he had ruled, directing that they be enshrined in the sanctuary.

So frugal and austere were Colman and his predecessors that when they left the seat of their authority there were very few buildings except the church; indeed, no more than met the bare requirements of a seemly way of life. They had no property except cattle, and whenever they received any money from rich folk, they immediately gave it to the poor; for they had no need to amass money or provide lodging for important people, since

---

[1] Melrose.

such visited the church only in order to pray or hear the word
of God. Whenever opportunity offered, the king himself used
to come with only five or six attendants; and when he had
completed his prayer in the church, he used to leave. But if they
happened to remain for a meal, they were content with the plain
daily food of the brothers and asked nothing more. For in those
days the sole concern of these teachers was to serve God, not
the world; to satisfy the soul, not the belly. Accordingly the
religious habit at that time was held in high esteem. Wherever
any priest or monk paid a visit, he was joyfully welcomed by
all as the servant of God. And if people met him on the road,
they ran to him and bowed, eager to be signed by his hand or
receive a blessing from his lips. Whenever he spoke a word of
encouragement, he was given an attentive hearing. On Sundays
the people flocked to the churches and monasteries, not to
obtain food, but to hear the word of God. When a priest visited
a village, the people were quick to gather together to receive the
word of life; for priests and clerics always came to a village
solely to preach, baptize, visit the sick, and, in short, to care for
the souls of its people. They were so free from the sin of avarice
that none of them would accept lands or gifts for the building
of monasteries unless expressly directed to do so by the secular
authorities. This continued to be the general practice for some
years among the churches of the Northumbrians. But enough
has been said on such matters.*

CHAPTER 27: *Egbert, an Englishman of holy life, becomes a monk
in Ireland*

IN the same year of our Lord 664 an eclipse of the sun occurred
about ten o'clock in the morning on the third of May; and a
sudden plague, which first decimated the southern parts of
Britain and later spread into the province of the Northumbrians,
raged for a long time and brought widespread death to many
people. Bishop Tuda fell a victim to this plague, and was buried
with honour in the monastery of Paegnalaech. The plague was

equally destructive in Ireland. At this period there were many English nobles and lesser folk in Ireland who had left their own land during the episcopates of Bishops Finan and Colman, either to pursue religious studies or to lead a life of stricter discipline. Some of these soon devoted themselves to the monastic life, while others preferred to travel, studying under various teachers in turn. The Irish welcomed them all kindly, and without asking for payment, provided them with daily food, books, and instruction.

Among these English nobles were Ethelhun and Egbert, two young men of outstanding ability. The former was brother of Ethelwin, a man no less dear to God, who at a later date also travelled to study in Ireland and, after a full course of instruction, returned home and was made Bishop of Lindsey, where he enjoyed a long and illustrious episcopate. These two young men, who were studying in the monastery which the Irish call Rathmelsigi, having lost all their companions either through the plague or through their dispersal to other places, were themselves stricken by the same disease and fell dangerously ill. And I am told by a most dependable priest of venerable age, who says that he learnt the story at first hand, that Egbert,* believing himself about to die, went out one morning from the room where the sick were lying and, sitting down in a place by himself, began seriously to examine his past life. Tears fell from his eyes as he sorrowfully recalled his sins, and he begged God from the bottom of his heart not to let him die until he could atone for the offences of his boyhood and youth, and exert himself to better purpose in good deeds. He also made a vow that he would remain an exile and never return to his native island of Britain; and that, unless prevented by sickness, in addition to the canonical hours of prayer, he would recite the entire Psalter daily to the praise of God and would fast once a week for a day and a night. When he had ended his tears, vows and prayers, he returned to the house where he found his companion asleep; and lying down on his pallet, he composed himself to rest. When he had lain there a short while, his companion awoke, and looking at him, said: 'O brother Egbert,

what have you done? I was hoping that we should enter eternal
life together; but now you may be sure that what you have
prayed for will be granted.' For he had learned in a vision what
his friend had prayed for, and that his prayer was heard. The
rest is soon told. Ethelhun died the following night; but Egbert
threw off the disease, recovered, and lived for many years. He
became a worthy ornament of the priestly order, and, as he had
prayed, lived a life of great merit, entering the kingdom of
heaven at the age of ninety in the year of our Lord 729. Egbert
led a life of great humility, gentleness, purity, simplicity, and
uprightness. He brought great blessings both to his own nation,
and to the Picts and Irish among whom he exiled himself,
setting them an example of holy life. He was indefatigable in
teaching, firm in administering reproof, and generous in distrib-
uting whatever he received from the rich. In addition to his
earlier vows, he ate only one meal a day during Lent, allowing
himself a scanty ration of bread and skim milk; for he used to
keep the previous day's fresh milk in a flask, and having
skimmed off the cream next day, he drank what was left with a
little bread. He practised a similar abstinence for forty days
before Christmas, and as many after the Feast of Pentecost.

CHAPTER 28: *On Tuda's death, Wilfrid is consecrated bishop in
Gaul and Chad among the West Saxons, to be bishops in the
Province of the Northumbrians* [A.D. 665]

MEANWHILE King Alchfrid sent Wilfrid, then a priest, to
the King of the Gauls* to be consecrated bishop for
himself and his people. He sent him for consecration to Agilbert,
who, as I have said, had been made Bishop of Paris after his
return from Britain. Summoning several other bishops to the
royal country-seat at Compiègne, he consecrated Wilfrid with
great splendour. But since Wilfrid remained overseas for a
considerable time on account of his consecration, King Oswy
meanwhile, following his son's example, sent to Canterbury to
be consecrated Bishop of York, a holy man, modest in his ways,

learned in the Scriptures, and careful to practise all that he found in them. This was a priest named Chad, a brother of the above-mentioned most reverend Bishop Cedd, and at that time Abbot of Lastingham. With Chad the king sent a priest named Ead-haed, who later, during the reign of Egfrid, became Bishop of Ripon. On arriving in Kent, they found that Archbishop Deusdedit had died and that no successor had yet been appointed. They therefore went on to bishop Wini in the province of the West Saxons, consecrated Chad as bishop with the assist-ance of two bishops of the British, who, as I have often observed, keep Easter contrary to canonical practice between the fourteenth and twentieth days of the moon. For at that time Wini was the only bishop in all Britain who had been canonically consecrated.

When he became bishop, Chad immediately devoted himself to maintaining the truth and purity of the Church, and set himself to practise humility and continence and to study. After the example of the Apostles, he travelled on foot and not on horseback when he went to preach the Gospel, whether in towns or country, in cottages, villages, or strongholds; for he was one of Aidan's disciples and always sought to instruct his people by the same methods as Aidan and his own brother Cedd. And Wilfrid too, when he returned to Britain as a bishop, introduced into the English churches many Catholic customs, with the result that the Catholic Rite daily gained support and all the Irish then living among the English either conformed to it or returned to their own land.

CHAPTER 29: *The priest Wighard is sent from Britain to Rome to be made archbishop: letters from the apostolic Pope tell of his death there* [A.D. 655]

A T this time, the most noble English kings Oswy of the Northumbrians and Egbert of the Kentish folk conferred together on the state of the Church of the English; for Oswy, although educated by the Irish, was fully aware that the Roman Church was the Catholic and Apostolic Church.* With the

choice and approval of the holy Church of the English, the two
kings accepted the priest Wighard, one of Archbishop Deusdedit's clergy, a good man well fitted to be a bishop, and sent him
to Rome to be consecrated bishop, so that, when he had received
the rank of Archbishop, he could consecrate Catholic bishops
for the churches of the English throughout Britain. Wighard
arrived in Rome, but died before he could be consecrated; and
the following letter was sent to Oswy in Britain:

'To our son, the most excellent Lord Oswy, King of the
Saxons, from Bishop Vitalian, servant of the servants of God.

'We have read Your Excellency's welcome letter, in which
we recognize your very sincere devotion and fervent desire for
eternal life. And we know how you have been converted to the
true and apostolic Faith by the guiding hand of God, and trust
that, as you now reign over your own nation, so you will one
day reign with Christ. Your nation is fortunate to have a king
so wise and devoted to the worship of God, who not only
adores God himself, but labours day and night to lead all his
people to the Catholic Apostolic faith, and to save his own soul.
Who can help being glad to hear such encouraging news? And
who will not be delighted at such works of devotion? For your
nation has come to believe in Christ our mighty God in
fulfilment of the words of God's prophets, as Isaiah says: "*In
that day there shall be a root of Jesse, which shall stand as an ensign of
the people; to it shall the Gentiles seek.*" And again: "*Listen, O isles,
unto Me; and hearken, ye people from far.*" And a little later he
says: "*It is a light thing that thou shouldest be My servant, to raise up
the tribes of Jacob, and to restore the preserved of Israel. I will also
give thee for a light to the Gentiles, that thou mayest be My salvation
unto the end of the earth.*" And again: "*Kings shall see, princes also
shall arise and worship.*" And later: "*I have given thee for a covenant
of the people, to establish the earth and possess the desolate heritages;
that thou mayest say to the prisoners, Go forth; to them that are in
darkness, Show yourselves.*" And again: "*I, the Lord, have called
thee in righteousness, and will hold thine hand, and will keep thee, and
give thee for a covenant of the people, for a light of the Gentiles; to*

*open the blind eyes, to bring out the prisoners from prison, and them
that sit in darkness out of the prison-house.*"

'Here you may see, most excellent son, how clearly it is
prophesied, not only of you but of all nations, that they shall
believe in Christ the Maker of all things. It must therefore be
the task of Your Majesty, as a living member of Christ, always
to observe the holy precepts of the Prince of the Apostles, both
in keeping Easter, and in everything transmitted to us by the
holy Apostles Peter and Paul, who, as the two heavenly bodies
light the world, give daily light to their teaching to the hearts of
all believers.'

And after some observations on the keeping of one true Easter
throughout the world, the Pope continues:

'In view of the lengthy journey involved, we have not yet
been able to discover a man wholly suitable to be your bishop,
as you request in your letters. But as soon as such a man can be
found, we will give him instructions and send him to your
country, so that under God's guidance, through his own witness
and the teachings of God, he may uproot the tares sown by the
Enemy throughout your island. We gratefully acknowledge the
gifts sent by Your Highness to the blessed Prince of the Apostles
in tribute to his immortal memory, and pray for your safety
together with the Christian clergy. But the bearer of your gifts
has departed this life, and is buried in the Church of the
Apostles. We are deeply distressed that he should have died
here. We have directed, however, that blessings of the Saints –
that is, relics of the blessed Apostles Peter and Paul, and of the
holy martyrs Laurence, John, and Paul, Gregory and Pancras –
be given to the bearers of this letter for delivery to Your
Excellency. By the same bearers we send to our spiritual
daughter, your queen, a cross made from the fetters of the
blessed Apostles Peter and Paul with a golden key. Learning of
her pious zeal, the entire apostolic see rejoices with us as greatly
as her holy deeds shine and blossom in the sight of God. We
trust that Your Highness will soon fulfil our hope, and dedicate
your whole island to Christ our God. For assuredly you have as
your protector the Redeemer of the human race, our Lord Jesus

Christ, who will support all your efforts to draw together a new people in Christ, and establish there the Catholic and Apostolic Faith. For Scripture says: "*Seek first the kingdom of God and His righteousness, and all these things shall be added unto you*"; and you assuredly seek, and will obtain what we too desire, that is, the conversion of all your islands. We greet Your Excellency with fatherly affection, constantly praying that God of His mercy will assist you and yours in all good works, so that you may reign with Christ in the world to come. May Heaven's grace preserve your Excellency in health.'

The next book will provide a more suitable place to tell who was actually discovered and consecrated in place of Wighard.

CHAPTER 30: *During a plague the East Saxons lapse into idolatry, but are quickly recalled from their errors by Bishop Jaruman* [A.D. 665]

AT the same time, the kings Sighere and Sebbi succeeded Swidhelm, of whom I have spoken, as rulers of the East Saxons under Wulfhere, King of the Mercians.* While the plague was causing a heavy death-roll in the province, Sighere and his people abandoned the mysteries of the Christian Faith and relapsed into paganism. For the king himself, together with many of the nobles and common folk, loved this life and sought no other, or even disbelieved in its existence. Hoping for protection against the plague by this means, they therefore began to rebuild the ruined temples and restore the worship of idols. But Sebbi his fellow-king and colleague held with all his people loyally to the Faith they had accepted, and, as will appear later, remained faithful and ended his days happily.

As soon as King Wulfhere learned that part of the province had apostatized from the Faith, he sent Bishop Jaruman, Trumhere's successor, to correct their error and recall the province to the true Faith. I am told by a priest who accompanied him on his journey and shared his preaching that Jaruman proceeded with great energy, for he was a good devout man, who travelled far and wide and succeeded in bringing back both king and people to the path of righteousness. As a result, they abandoned or destroyed the temples and altars they had erected, and opened the churches, glad to confess the name of Christ whom they had denied, and more ready to die with him believing in the Resurrection than to continue living among their idols in the degradation of apostasy. Their task accomplished, these priests and teacher then returned home full of joy.

BOOK FOUR

✤

CHAPTER I: *On the death of Archbishop Deusdedit, Wighard is sent to Rome to be consecrated in his stead: on the latter's death there, Theodore is consecrated Archbishop and sent to Britain with Abbot Hadrian* [A.D. 664]

ON the fourteenth of July in the above-mentioned year, when an eclipse was quickly followed by plague, and during which Bishop Colman was refuted by the unanimous decisions of the Catholics and returned to his own country, Deusdedit the sixth Archbishop of Canterbury died. Earconbert, King of the Kentish folk, died on the same day, and was succeeded by his son Egbert, who reigned for nine years. The See of Canterbury was then vacant for a considerable time, until Wighard, an English priest with great experience in church administration, was sent to Rome by the common consent of Egbert and King Oswy of the Northumbrians, with the request that he be consecrated Archbishop of the Church of the English. This I have already briefly noted in the preceding book. At the same time the two kings sent presents to the apostolic Pope, including many gold and silver vessels. On his arrival in Rome, where Vitalian was ruling the apostolic see, Wighard explained to the Pope the reason for his journey; but shortly afterwards he and nearly all his companions fell victim to a plague that broke out at the time.

The apostolic Pope therefore took advice on the situation, and made careful enquiry as to whom he could send as Archbishop of the churches of the English. Not far from Naples in Campania is the monastery of Niridano, whose Abbot Hadrian, a native of Africa, was very learned in the Scriptures, experienced in ecclesiastical and monastic administration, and a great scholar in Greek and Latin. So the Pope summoned Hadrian, and directed him to accept the bishopric and go to Britain. Hadrian excused himself on the grounds that he was not fitted for such high dignity, but said that he could recommend another, whose learning and age were more suited to the office of bishop. He proposed to the Pope a monk named Andrew, who was chaplain to a neighbouring convent of women, and was considered as worthy of a bishopric by all who knew him; but Andrew excused himself on the grounds of ill health. Then Hadrian was again pressed to accept the bishopric; but he asked for a delay in order to make a fresh attempt to find a more suitable man.

At this time there was in Rome a monk named Theodore, a native of Tarsus in Cilicia, who was well known to Hadrian. He was learned both in sacred and in secular literature, in Greek and in Latin, of proved integrity, and of the venerable age of sixty-six. Hadrian, therefore, suggested the name of Theodore to the Pope, who agreed to consecrate him, but made it a condition that Hadrian himself should accompany him to Britain, since he had already travelled through Gaul twice on various missions and had both a better knowledge of the road and sufficient men of his own available. The Pope also ordered Hadrian to give full support to Theodore in his teaching, and to ensure that he did not introduce into the Church which he was to rule any Greek customs which conflicted with 'the teachings of the true Faith. On receiving the subdiaconate, Theodore waited four months for his hair to grow so that he could receive the circular tonsure; for hitherto he had worn the tonsure of the holy Apostolic Paul in conformity to Eastern custom. He was then consecrated bishop by Pope Vitalian on Sunday the 26th of March 668, and on the 27th of May he set out for Britain, accompanied by Hadrian.

The travellers crossed by sea to Massilia,[1] and thence overland

---

[1] Marseilles.

to Arles, where they delivered Pope Vitalian's letters of commendation to John, Archbishop of that city, who gave them hospitality until Ebroin, Mayor of the king's palace, gave them a permit to travel wherever they wished. Armed with this Theodore then went on to Agilbert, Bishop of Paris, of whom I have already spoken, who welcomed him kindly and entertained him for a considerable time. Hadrian meanwhile went first to Emme, Bishop of Sens, and then to Faro, Bishop of Meaux, and made lengthy stays with them, since the approach of winter obliged travellers to remain quietly wherever they could. When messengers informed King Egbert that the bishop whom they had requested from the Pope was now in the kingdom of the Franks, he at once sent his High Reeve Raedfrid to escort him; and when the Reeve arrived, he obtained Ebroin's permission to escort Theodore to the port of Quentavic.[1] Here exhaustion compelled Theodore to rest for a while; but as soon as he began to recover, he took ship for Britain. But Hadrian was detained by Ebroin, who suspected that he bore some message from the Emperor to the kings of Britain, which might be to the disadvantage of the kingdom for whose interests he was largely responsible. But when he ascertained that Hadrian had in fact no such mission, he released him and allowed him to follow Theodore. And as soon as Hadrian arrived, Theodore appointed him abbot of the monastery of blessed Peter the Apostle, where, as I have said, the Archbishops of Canterbury are buried. For when he left Rome the apostolic Pope had instructed Theodore to provide for him in his diocese, and give him a suitable place to live with his followers.

[1] Étaples.

CHAPTER 2: *Theodore makes a general visitation: the English churches begin to receive instruction in Catholic truth, and sacred study is fostered. Putta succeeds Damian as Bishop of Rochester* [A.D. 669]

THEODORE arrived in his see on Sunday May 27th in the second year after his consecration, and held it for twenty-one years, three months, and twenty-six days. Soon after his arrival, he visited every part of the island occupied by the English peoples, and received a ready welcome and hearing everywhere. He was accompanied and assisted throughout his journey by Hadrian, and he taught the Christian way of life and the canonical method of keeping Easter. Theodore was the first archbishop whom the entire Church of the English obeyed, and since, as I have observed, both he and Hadrian were men of learning both in sacred and in secular literature, they attracted a large number of students, into whose minds they poured the waters of wholesome knowledge day by day. In addition to instructing them in the holy Scriptures, they also taught their pupils poetry, astronomy, and the calculation of the church calendar. In proof of this, some of their students still alive today are as proficient in Latin and Greek as in their native tongue. Never had there been such happy times as these since the English settled in Britain; for the Christian kings were so strong that they daunted all the barbarous tribes. The people eagerly sought the new-found joys of the kingdom of heaven, and all who wished for instruction in the reading of the Scriptures found teachers ready at hand.*

The knowledge of sacred music, hitherto limited to Kent, now began to spread to all the churches of the English. With the exception of the deacon James, already mentioned, the first singing-master in the Northumbrian churches was Eddi, known as Stephen, who was invited from Kent by the most reverend Wilfrid, the first bishop of English blood to teach the churches of the English the Catholic way of life.

During his visitation, Theodore consecrated bishops in suitable places, and with their assistance he corrected abuses wherever he found them. When he informed Bishop Chad that his

consecration was irregular, the latter replied with the greatest
humility: 'If you know that my consecration as bishop was
irregular, I willingly resign the office, for I have never thought
myself worthy of it. Although unworthy, I accepted it solely
under obedience.' At this humble reply, Theodore assured him
that there was no need for him to give up his office, and himself
completed his consecration according to Catholic rites. About
the time that Deusdedit died and a successor for the See of
Canterbury was sought for, consecrated, and sent, Wilfrid also
was sent from Britain to Gaul for consecration. Returning
before Theodore, he ordained certain priests and deacons in
Kent, pending the archbishop's arrival in his own see. Shortly
afterwards Theodore himself came to Rochester, where the see
had been vacant ever since the death of Damian, and there
consecrated Putta as its bishop. He was a man of simple life,
who was well acquainted with church affairs, but had little
experience in worldly matters. He was a most skilled exponent
of the Roman chant, which he had learnt from pupils of blessed
Pope Gregory.

CHAPTER 3: *Chad is appointed Bishop of the Mercians* [c.
A.D. 667]: *his life, death* [A.D. 672], *and burial*

THE Mercians at this time were ruled by King Wulfhere,
who on the death of Jaruman asked Theodore to provide
him and his people with a bishop. Theodore, however, did not
wish to consecrate a new bishop for them, but asked King
Oswy to give them Chad as their bishop. Chad was then living
quietly in his monastery at Lastingham, while Wilfrid ruled the
Bishopric of York, and indeed of all the lands of the Northumbrians and Picts to the borders of Oswy's realms. The most
reverend Bishop Chad always preferred to undertake his preaching missions on foot rather than on horseback; but Theodore
ordered him to ride whenever he undertook a long journey. He
was most reluctant to forgo this pious exercise which he loved,
but the archbishop, who recognized his outstanding holiness

and considered it more proper for him to ride, himself insisted on helping him to mount his horse. So Chad received the Bishopric of the Mercians and the people of Lindsey, and administered the diocese in great holiness of life after the example of the early Fathers. King Wulfhere gave him fifty hides of land to build a monastery at a place called At-Barwe – that is, At the Wood – in the province of Lindsey, and evidences of the regular observance that he established remain to this day.

Chad established his episcopal seat in the town of Lyccid-felth,[1] where he also died and was buried, and where the succeeding bishops of the province have their see to this day. There he built himself a house near the church, where he used to retire privately with seven or eight brethren in order to pray or study whenever his work and preaching permitted. When he had ruled the church of the province with great success for two and a half years, divine providence ordained a time such as is spoken of in Ecclesiastes: '*There is a time to cast away stones, and a time to gather stones together.*' For heaven sent a plague which, bringing bodily death, bore away the living stones of the Church from their earthly stations to the temple in heaven. And when death had freed many members of the reverend bishop's church from the burden of the flesh, the hour drew near when Chad himself was to pass out of this world to our Lord. One day he was alone in his house with a brother whose name was Owini, his other companions having had occasion to return to the church. This Owini was a monk of great merit, who had renounced the world with the pure intention of winning a heavenly reward, so that he was altogether a fit person to receive a revelation of God's secrets, and one whose word everyone could trust. He had accompanied Queen Etheldreda from the province of the East Angles, and had been her chief thegn and steward of her household. Growing in devotion to the Faith, he decided to renounce the world, which he did in no half-hearted fashion; for he rid himself so completely of worldly ties that he abandoned all his possessions, put on a simple garment, and

---

[1] Lichfield.

carrying in his hand an axe and an adze, set off for the reverend father Chad's monastery at Lastingham. This he did to show that he was entering the monastery not for the sake of an idle life, as some do, but in order to work, and he demonstrated this in practice; for since he found himself less able to meditate on the Scriptures with profit, he undertook a larger amount of manual labour. In short, recognizing his reverence and devotion, the bishop admitted him to his house among the brethren; and whenever they were engaged in study, he used to busy himself in essential tasks out of doors. One day, while Owini was working outside and the other brethren had departed to the church, the bishop was reading and praying alone in his oratory. Suddenly, as he used afterwards to relate, he heard the sound of sweet and joyful singing coming down from heaven to earth. The sound seemed at first to emanate from the south-east, gradually coming closer to him until it centred over the roof of the oratory where the bishop was at prayer. It then entered the oratory, and seemed to fill both it and the surrounding air. He listened with rapt attention to what he heard, and after about half an hour he heard the song of joy rise from the roof of the oratory, and return to heaven as it had come with inexpressible sweetness. Owini stood astonished for a while, turning over in his mind what this might portend, when the bishop threw open the oratory window and, clapping his hands, as he often used to do if someone was outside, summoned him indoors. When he hurried in, the bishop said: 'Go at once to the church, and fetch these seven brethren here, and come back with them yourself.' On their arrival, he first urged them to live in love and peace with each other and with all the faithful, and to be constant and tireless in keeping the rules of monastic discipline that he had taught them and they knew him to observe, and those that they had learned from the lives and teachings of former abbots. He then announced that his own death was drawing near, saying: 'The welcome guest who has visited many of our brethren has come to me today, and has deigned to summon me out of this world. Therefore return to the church, and ask the brethren to commend my passing to our

Lord in their prayers. And let each prepare for his own passing by vigils, prayers, and good deeds; for no man knows the hour of his death.' Having said this and much besides, he gave them his blessing, and they left him sadly; but the brother who had heard the heavenly music came back alone and flung himself to the ground, saying: 'Father, I beg you to let me ask you a question.' 'Ask what you wish,' Chad replied. 'Tell me, I pray,' he asked, 'what was the glad song that I heard of singers coming down from heaven upon this oratory and later returning to heaven?' 'Since you heard the singing and were aware of the coming of the heavenly company,' Chad answered, 'I command you in the name of our Lord not to tell anyone of this before my death. The truth is that they were angelic spirits, who came to summon me to the heavenly reward that I have always hoped and longed for, and they promised to return in seven days and take me with them.' All took place as he had been told: for Chad was quickly attacked by a disease which steadily grew worse until the seventh day. Then he prepared for death by receiving the Body and Blood of our Lord, his holy soul was released from the prison-house of the body and, one may rightly believe, was taken by the angels to the joys of heaven. Nor is it strange that he regarded death with joy as the Day of the Lord; for he had always been careful to prepare for his coming.

In addition to Chad's many virtues of continence, humility, right preaching, prayer, voluntary poverty, and many others, he was so filled with the fear of God and so mindful of his last end in all that he did, that I was told by one of his monks named Trumbert – who was one of my tutors in the Scriptures and had been trained in the monastery under Chad's direction – that, if a gale arose while he was reading or doing anything else, he would at once call upon God for mercy and pray him to show mercy on mankind. And if the wind increased in violence, he would close his book and prostrate himself on the ground, praying even more earnestly. But if there was a violent storm of wind and rain, or thunder and lightning startled earth and air, he would go to the church and devote all his thoughts to prayers and psalms continuously until the tempest had passed.

When his monks asked him why he did this, Chad replied:
'Have you not read, "*The Lord thundered in the heavens, and the
Highest gave His voice. He sent out His arrows and scattered them;
He shot out lightnings and discomfited them*"? For God stirs the air
and raises the winds; He makes the lightning flash and thunders
out of heaven, to move the inhabitants of the earth to fear Him,
and to remind them of judgement to come. He shatters their
conceit and subdues their presumption by recalling to their
minds that awful Day when heaven and earth will flame as He
comes in the clouds with great power and majesty to judge the
living and the dead. Therefore we should respond to His
heavenly warnings with the fear and love we owe Him,' said
Chad. 'And whenever He raises His hands in the trembling air
as if to strike, yet spares us still, we should hasten to implore
His mercy, examining our inmost hearts and purging the
vileness of our sins, watchful over our lives lest we incur His
just displeasure.'

This brother's account of the bishop's death is supported by
the evidence of the above-mentioned most reverend Father
Egbert, who lived the monastic life in Ireland with Chad when
they were both youths, constantly occupied in prayer, fasting,
and meditation on the sacred scriptures. But when Chad
returned to his own country, Egbert remained an exile for God's
sake until the end of his life. A long time afterwards, Hygbald,
a very holy and austere man who was an abbot in the province
of Lindsey, came from Britain to visit him. And while they
were discussing the lives of the early Fathers and delighting to
imitate them as was fitting in holy men, the name of the most
holy Bishop Chad was mentioned. Whereupon Egbert said: 'I
know a man still living in this island who, when the bishop
died, saw the soul of his brother Cedd descend from heaven
accompanied by angels, and carry away his soul to the heavenly
kingdom.' Whether he was speaking of himself or another is
uncertain; but the truth of a statement by so great a man cannot
be doubted.

Chad died on the second of March [672], and was first buried
close by Saint Mary's church; but when a church of the most

blessed Peter, Prince of the Apostles, was built there later, his body was transferred to it. In both of these places, frequent miracles of healing attested to his virtues. More recently, a madman wandering at large arrived there one evening, and passed the night in church unnoticed and unheeded by the watchmen. And in the morning, to the amazement and delight of all, he left the place in his right mind, showing clearly what healing he had been granted there by the goodness of God. Chad's burial place is covered by a wooden tomb made in the form of a little house with an aperture in the wall through which those who visit it out of devotion may insert their hand and take out some of the dust. They mix this in water and give it to sick men or beasts to drink, by which means their ailment is quickly relieved and they are restored to the longed for joys of health.

In Chad's place Theodore consecrated Wynfrid, a good and modest man, who like his predecessors, presided over the provinces of the Mercians, Middle Angles, and Lindsey folk, all of which were subject to King Wulfhere, who was still living. Wynfrid was one of his predecessor's clergy, and had been his deacon for a considerable time.

CHAPTER 4: *Bishop Colman leaves Britain, and founds two monasteries in the land of the Irish, one for the Irish, and another for the English whom he had taken with him* [A.D. 667]

MEANWHILE the Irish bishop Colman left Britain, taking with him all the Irish he had collected at Lindisfarne, together with about thirty English whom he had likewise trained in the monastic life. Leaving some brethren in his own church, he first visited the isle of Hii,[1] from which he had originally been sent to preach the word to the English. He subsequently retired to a small island at some distance from the west coast of Ireland, known in the Irish tongue as Inisboufinde,[2] meaning the Isle of the White Heifer. On his arrival, he

[1] Iona.   [2] Inishboffin.

founded a monastery, and established there the monks of both races whom he had gathered. But a dispute arose among them because in summer the Irish went off to wander on their own around places they knew instead of assisting at harvest, and then, as winter approached, came back and wanted to share whatever the English monks had gathered. Colman sought a remedy for this dispute, and after searching near and far, discovered a site suitable for a monastery on the Irish mainland, a place which the Irish call Mageo.* Here he bought a small tract of land from the nobleman who owned the land, who made it a condition of sale that the monks who settled there should pray for him. So a monastery was promptly built with the help of the nobleman and all the neighbours, and Colman established the English monks thre, leaving the Irish on the original island. This monastery is still occupied by English monks. For this is the place, grown large from small beginnings, that is now usually known as Muigeo and, under an improved constitution houses a distinguished community of monks drawn from the English provinces. After the example of the venerable Fathers, they live devoutly and austerely by the labour of their own hands and observe a Rule under a canonically elected abbot.

CHAPTER 5: *The death of King Oswy and King Egbert. Archbishop Theodore presides over a Synod held at Hertford* [A.D. 673]

IN the year of our Lord 670, the second year after Archbishop Theodore's arrival in Britain, King Oswy of the Northumbrians was stricken with an illness, of which he died at the age of fifty-eight. At this time the King held the apostolic Roman see in such high esteem that, had he recovered from his illness, it was his intention to travel to Rome and end his life among its holy places, and he had persuaded Bishop Wilfrid to conduct him on the journey with the promise of a considerable gift. He died on February 15th, leaving his son Egfrid to succeed him as king. In the third year of the latter's reign, Theodore summoned a council of bishops and the many other teachers of the Church who both understood and loved the canonical statutes of the Fathers. As befitted his authority as archbishop, when they were assembled, he began by charging them to observe whatsoever things were conducive to the peace and unity of the Church. The decisions of the Council are in the following form:*

'In the name of the Lord God and our Saviour Jesus Christ, and under the everlasting governance and guidance of His Church by the same Lord Jesus Christ, it was thought right that we should assemble in accordance with the custom of venerable canons to deliberate concerning the necessary affairs of the Church. We therefore assembled on the 24th day of September, the first indiction, at the place called Hertford; that is, myself, Theodore, though unworthy, Bishop of the See of Canterbury by the authority of the apostolic see; our fellow-bishop and brother the most reverend Bisi, Bishop of the East Angles; also our brother the Bishop Wilfrid, Bishop of the Northumbrian people, who is represented by his own proxies. Also present were our brothers and fellow-bishops Putta, Bishop of the Kentish fortress of Rochester; Leutherius, Bishop of the West Saxons, and Wynfrid, Bishop of the province of the Mercians. When all the above had assembled and taken their places in due order, I said: "My dearest brothers, for the love and reverence you bear our Redeemer, I beg that we may all deliberate in harmony for our Faith, preserving inviolate the decrees and definitions of our holy and respected Fathers." I dealt with these and many other matters relating to charity and the preservation of the Church's unity. And having concluded this introductory address, I asked each in turn whether they agreed to observe all the canonical decrees of the ancient Fathers. To which all our fellow-priests replied: "We are all resolved that we will cheerfully and willingly obey whatever is laid down in the canons of the holy Fathers." I then produced the said book of canons, and publicly showed them ten chapters which I had marked in certain places, because I knew them to be of the greatest importance to us, and I asked that all should devote special attention to them.

'*Chapter* 1. "That we all unite in observing the holy day of Easter on the Sunday after the fourteenth day of the moon of the first month."

Chapter 2. "That no bishop intrude into the diocese of another, but confine himself to the guidance of the people committed to his charge."

'*Chapter* 3. "That no bishop shall interfere in any way with monasteries dedicated to God, nor take anything from them forcibly."

'*Chapter* 4. "That monks shall not wander from place to place, that is, from monastery to monastery, except with letters dimissory from their own abbot; and that they keep the promise of obedience which they made at the time of their profession."

'*Chapter* 5. "That no clergy shall leave their own bishop and wander about at will, nor be received anywhere without letters of commendation from their own bishop. And should such a person, once received, refuse to return when so directed, both receiver and received shall incur excommunication."

'*Chapter* 6. "That bishops and clergy when travelling shall be content with whatever hospitality is offered them; and that it shall be unlawful for any of them to exercise any priestly function without permission from the bishop in whose diocese they are known to be."

'*Chapter* 7. "That a synod be held twice a year." In view of various obstacles, however, it was unanimously agreed that we should meet once a year on the first of August at the place called Clofeshoch.[1]

'*Chapter* 8. "That no bishop claim precedence over another out of ambition: seniority of consecration shall alone determine precedence."

'*Chapter* 9. It was generally discussed, "That more bishops shall be consecrated as the number of the faithful increases." But we have announced no decision in the matter for the present.

'*Chapter* 10. On marriages: "That lawful wedlock alone is permissible; incest is forbidden; and no man may leave his

---

[1] Clovesho (probably near London).

lawful wife except, as the gospel provides, for fornication. And if a man puts away his own wife who is joined to him in lawful marriage, he may not take another if he wishes to be a good Christian. He must either remain as he is, or else be reconciled to his wife."

'After discussing these chapters and reaching decisions by our common consent, in order that no occasion for unedifying controversy or differences between ourselves may arise, it has been thought right that each of us should ratify our decisions by his own signature. I have dictated this expression of our decisions to Titillus our secretary to be written down, and this has been done in the month and indiction mentioned above. Therefore, if anyone shall presume in any way to contravene or disobey these decisions confirmed by our agreement and ratified by our signatures, according to canonical decrees, let him take notice that he incurs suspension from every priestly function and exclusion from our fellowship.

'May divine grace preserve us all in safety, who live in the unity of His Holy Church.'

This synod took place in the year of our Lord 673, in July of which year King Egbert died and was succeeded by his brother Hlothere, who reigned eleven years and seven months. Bisi, bishop of the East Angles, who is said to have attended this synod, was successor to Boniface, of whom I have spoken, and was a man of great holiness and devotion; for when Boniface died in the eighteenth year of his episcopate, Theodore consecrated Bisi in his place. And when severe illness prevented him from administering his diocese, two bishops, Aecci and Badwin, were chosen and consecrated to carry out his duties, and from then until the present day this province has had two bishops.

CHAPTER 6: *Wynfrid is deposed, and Sexwulf appointed to his see: Earconwald is made Bishop of the East Saxons* [A.D. 675]

Not long afterwards Archbishop Theodore, displeased at some disobedience on the part of Bishop Wynfrid of the Mercians, deposed him from the bishopric which he had held only a few years, and appointed in his place Sexwulf, founder and abbot of the monastery of Medeshamstedi[1] in the Gyrwas' country. On his deposition, Wynfrid retired to his own monastery of At-Barwe, and lived a most holy life there until his death.

Theodore also made Earconwald Bishop of the East Saxons, whose kings were the above-mentioned Sebbi and Sighere, with the city of London as his see. Both before and after his consecration as bishop, Earconwald is said to have lived so holy a life that heaven still affords proofs of his virtues. To this day, the horse-litter in which he travelled when ill is preserved by his disciples, and continues to cure many folk troubled by fever and other complaints. Sick people are cured when placed under or against the litter, and even chips cut from it bring speedy recovery when taken to the sick.

Before he became bishop, Earconwald had built two well-known monasteries, one for himself and the other for his sister Ethelburga, and had established an excellent regular discipline in both houses. His own monastery stood by the river Thames at Cerotaesei[2] – meaning Cerot's island – in the district of Surrey. The convent where his sister was to rule as mother and instructress of women devoted to God was at a place called In-Berecingum[3] in the province of the East Saxons. Entrusted with the affairs of this convent, she always bore herself in a manner worthy of her brother the bishop, upright of life and constantly planning for the needs of her community, as heavenly miracles attest.

[1] Now Peterborough.   [2] Chertsey.   [3] Barking.

IN this convent many proofs of holiness were effected, which many people have recorded from the testimony of eyewitnesses in order that the memory of them might edify future generations; I have therefore been careful to include some of this history of the Church. When the plague that I have often mentioned was at its height, it attacked the men's part of the monastery, and daily carried off some to meet their God. The watchful Mother of the Community therefore began to ask the sisters of the convent where they wished their bodies to be buried, and where the cemetery should be made when the plague should enter the enclosure where these handmaids of God lived separately from the men, and snatch them out of this world by the same deadly stroke. But when her frequent enquiries of the sisters had elicited no definite reply, both she and the whole Community received a very clear indication of the wishes of heaven. For one night when they had finished singing the morning psalms of praise to God, these servants of Christ left the oratory to visit the graves of the brothers who had departed this life before them. And as they were singing their customary praises to our Lord, a light from heaven like a great sheet suddenly appeared and shone over them all, so alarming them that they even broke off their singing in consternation. After a short while, this brilliant light, compared to which the noonday sun would appear dark, rose and travelled to the south side of the convent westward of the oratory and, having remained over that area for a time, withdrew heavenwards in the sight of them all. This occurrence left no doubt in their minds that the light, which was to guide or receive the souls of Christ's servants into heaven, had also indicated the spot where their bodies were to rest and await the day of resurrection. So brilliant was this light that one of the older brothers, who was in the oratory at the time with another younger brother, reported next morning that the rays of light penetrating the chinks of doors and windows seemed brighter than the brightest daylight.

CHAPTER 8: *A little boy, dying in the convent, announces the approaching death of one of the sisters. A nun, about to depart this life, sees a glimpse of future glory*

I N this convent lived a little boy named Aesica, not more than three years old, who, being so young, was being brought up and taught his lessons in the cell of these virgins vowed to God. Attacked by the plague and about to die, he three times called the name of one of Christ's virgins as though she were present, saying: 'Edith! Edith! Edith!' Then he left this present world, and passed to eternal life. The nun whose name he had called with his dying breath was at once stricken where she was by the same disease, and departed this life, following the child who had called her to the kingdom of heaven.

Again, one of the handmaids of God was brought to her last hour by this disease, and in the middle of the night she began to call to those who attended her to put out the lamp that burned by her bed. But in spite of her repeated requests, none of them paid any attention. At length she said: 'I know that you think that my mind is wandering, but I assure you that it is not so. I tell you truthfully that I see the house filled with such brilliant light that your lamp appears to me only as darkness.' And when they still disregarded her request and made no reply, she said again: 'Let the lamp burn as long as you wish; but I assure you that it gives me no light. My light will come to me when dawn draws near.' She then told them how a man of God, who had died the same year, had appeared to her and informed her that at daybreak she would depart to eternal light. The reality of this vision was quickly confirmed; for the nun died at dawn.

W HEN Ethelburga, the devout Mother of this God-fearing Community, was herself about to be taken out of this world, one of the sisters whose name was Tortgyth saw a wonderful vision. This nun had lived for many years in the convent, humbly and sincerely striving to serve God, and had helped the Mother to maintain the regular observances by instructing and correcting the younger sisters. In order that her strength might be '*made perfect in weakness*' as the Apostle says, she was suddenly attacked by a serious disease. Under the good providence of our Redeemer, this caused her great distress for nine years, in order that any traces of sin that remained among her virtues through ignorance or neglect might be burned away in the fires of prolonged suffering. Leaving her cell one night at first light of dawn, the sister saw distinctly what appeared to be a human body wrapped in a shroud and shining more brightly than the sun. This was raised up and carried out of the house where the sisters used to sleep. She observed closely to see how this appearance of a shining body was being raised, and saw what appeared to be cords brighter than gold which drew it upwards until it entered the open heavens and she could see it no longer. When she thought about this vision, there remained no doubt in her mind that some member of the Community was shortly to die, and that her soul would be drawn up to heaven by her good deeds as though by golden cords. And so it proved not many days later, when God's beloved Ethelburga, the Mother of the Community, was set free from her bodily prison. And none who knew her holy life can doubt that when she departed this life the gates of our heavenly home opened at her coming.

In the same convent there was also a nun of noble family in the world, who was yet more noble in her love for the world to come. For many years she had been so crippled that she could not move a single limb; and hearing that the venerable abbess' body had been carried into the church until its burial, she asked to be carried there, and to be bowed towards it in an attitude of prayer. Then she spoke to Ethelburga as though she were still alive, and begged her to pray to God on her behalf, and ask him of his mercy to release her from her continual pain. Her request received a swift reply; for twelve days later she was set free from the body, and exchanged her earthly troubles for a heavenly reward.

Three years after the death of the abbess, Christ's servant Tortgyth was so wasted away by the disease that I mentioned earlier that her bones scarcely held together, until finally, as death drew near, she lost the use of her limbs and even of her tongue. After three days and nights in this condition, she was suddenly refreshed by a vision from heaven, opened her eyes, and spoke. Looking up to heaven, she began to address the vision that she saw: 'I am so glad that you have come; you are most welcome.' She then remained silent for awhile, as if awaiting an answer from the person whom she saw and spoke to; then, seeming a little displeased, she said: 'This is not happy news.' After another interval of silence, she spoke a third time: 'If it cannot be today, I beg that it may not be long delayed.' Then she kept silent a little while as before, and ended: 'If it cannot be today, I beg that it may not be long delayed.' Then she kept silent a little while as before, and ended: 'If this decision is final and unalterable, I implore that it may not be delayed beyond the coming night.' When she had finished, those around her asked her to whom she had spoken. 'To my dearest Mother Ethelburga', she replied; and from this they understood that she had come to announce that the hour of her passing was near. So after a day and a night her prayers were answered, and she was delivered from the burden of the body and entered the joys of eternal salvation.

ETHELBURGA was succeeded in the office of abbess by a devout servant of God named Hildilid, who ruled the convent with great energy until extreme old age, promoting observance of the regular discipline and making provisions for the needs of the Community. Owing to the restricted space on which the convent was built, she decided that the bones of Christ's servants buried there, both men and women, should be exhumed and transferred to a single tomb within the church of the blessed Mother of God. And whoever wishes to read about the wonderful things that happened there will find in the book which is the source of my information how a bright, heavenly light was often seen there, and how a wonderfully fragrant scent was often evident.

It would not be right to omit mention of a miraculous cure which this same book records as having taken place in the cemetery of this God-serving Community. In the neighbourhood there lived a nobleman whose wife was afflicted by a gradual loss of sight, which daily grew worse until she could no longer see the faintest glimmer of light. When she had been totally blind for some while, it suddenly occurred to her that if she were taken to the convent of these holy nuns and prayed before the relics of the saint, she might recover her lost sight. She lost no time in putting this inspiration into effect. Professing a firm belief that she would be healed, she was taken by her maids to the near-by convent and guided to the burial ground, where she remained a long while on her knees in prayer. Her petition was quickly granted; for as she rose from prayer and before she left the place, her sight was restored. And whereas she had been led there by the hands of her maids, she walked home unaided and full of delight. It might almost seem that she had lost her bodily sight solely in order that its restoration might show how great a light is enjoyed by the saints in heaven, and how great a power their virtues possess.

THE same little book informs us that Sebbi, a man who dearly loved God and of whom I have already spoken, ruled the kingdom of the East Saxons at this time. He devoted himself to religious exercises, frequent prayer, and acts of mercy, and he preferred a retired, monastic life to all the riches and honours of a kingdom. In fact, had not his wife absolutely refused to be separated from him, he would long before have abdicated and entered a monastery. For this reason many people thought and often said that a man of such disposition should have been a bishop rather than a king. When this soldier of the heavenly kingdom had ruled his earthly kingdom for thirty years, he was attacked by the serious disease that was to cause his death. He therefore urged his wife that, since they could no longer enjoy or serve the world, they should both devote themselves to the service of God. Having obtained her reluctant consent, the king went to Waldhere, bishop of London, successor to Earconwald, and with his blessing received the monastic habit that he had so long desired. He brought the bishop a considerable sum of money to be distributed among the poor, and kept nothing at all for himself, wishing to be *poor in spirit* for the sake of the kingdom of heaven.

As his malady gained ground and he felt the day of his death approaching, Sebbi, who was a man of kingly spirit, became apprehensive that the sufferings of a painful death might wring from him some word or gesture unbecoming to his dignity. He therefore summoned the bishop of London, in which city he was living, and asked that none but the bishop himself and two attendants might be present at his death. The bishop readily promised this, and not long afterwards this godly man saw in his sleep a comforting vision, which removed his anxiety on this score, and also revealed to him on what day he was to depart this life. As he subsequently related, he saw three men in bright robes come to him, one of whom sat down in front of his pallet while his companions remained standing and enquired about the condition of the sick man they had come to visit. The first man replied that his soul would leave his body without pain in a splendour of light, and that he would die in three days' time. Both of these things happened as he had learned in the vision; for on the third day, at the hour of None, he seemed suddenly to fall into a light sleep and breathed out his spirit without any feeling of pain.

A stone sarcophagus had been made ready for the burial; but when they came to lay his body in it, they found it a hand's breadth too long for the sarcophagus. So they chiselled out sufficient stone to add a further two fingers in length to it; but it still proved too short to receive the body. In this quandary, they wondered whether to look for another coffin, or whether, if possible, to shorten the body by bending the knees until it fitted the sarcophagus. But an amazing thing happened, undoubtedly caused by providence, that rendered both these alternatives unnecessary; for in the presence of the bishop and of Sighard, son of the monk-king – who succeeded him as king jointly with his brother Swefred – and a considerable number of men, the sarcophagus was suddenly found to be the correct length for the body, so much so that a pillow could be placed at the head, while the feet rested four fingers short of the end of the sarcophagus. Sebbi was buried in the church of the blessed Apostle of the Gentiles,[1] through whose teachings he had learned to aspire to heavenly things.

CHAPTER 12: *Haeddi succeeds Leutherius as Bishop of the West Saxons: Cuichelm succeeds Putta in the See of Rochester, and is himself succeeded by Gebmund. The succession of the Northumbrian bishops*

LEUTHERIUS was the fourth Bishop of the West Saxons, Birinus being the first, Agilbert the second, and Wini the third. On the death of Coenwalh, during whose reign Leutherius was made bishop, under-kings took over the government of

---

[1] St Paul's, London.

the realm, which they divided amongst them and ruled for
about ten years. During this period Leutherius died and was
succeeded in the bishopric by Haeddi, who had been consecrated
by Theodore in the city of London. During Haeddi's episcopate,
Cadwalla defeated and deposed these under-kings and assumed
control himself; but after a reign of two years, while the same
bishop remained in authority, desire for the kingdom of heaven
moved the king to resign his powers, and, as I shall record more
fully later, he went away to end his days in Rome.

In the year of our Lord's incarnation 676, Ethelred, King of
the Mercians, ravaged Kent with his wicked soldiery, profaning
churches and monasteries without fear of God or respect to
religion, and among the rest he destroyed the city of Rochester,
Putta's see, the bishop being absent at the time. When he learned
that his church was looted and destroyed, Putta went to
Sexwulf, Bishop of the Mercians, who granted him a church
and a small plot of land, where he ended his days quietly,
making no attempt to re-establish his see. As I have said, he was
more at home in religious than in worldly matters, and therefore
served God only in his own church, travelling about wherever
invited to teach church music. In his place Theodore consecrated
Cuichelm as Bishop of Rochester, but after a short time he
resigned this see because of its poverty and withdrew elsewhere;
Theodore appointed Gebmund in his place.

In the month of August 678, in the eighth year of Egfrid's
reign, there appeared a star known as a comet, which remained
visible for three months, rising in the morning and emitting
what seemed to be a tall column of bright flame. In the same
year a dispute arose between King Egfrid and the most reverend
Bishop Wilfrid, who was driven from his diocese, and two
bishops were appointed to preside over the Northumbrian
people in his place. These were Bosa, Bishop of Deira, and
Eata, Bishop of Bernicia; the former had the city of York as his
see, and the latter had Hexham or Lindisfarne. Both of them
were monks before their elevation to the episcopate. At the
same time Eadhaed was made bishop of the province of Lindsey,
which King Egfrid had recently annexed after defeating and

driving out Wulfhere. So for the first time this province had its own bishop; the second was Ethelwin, the third, Edgar, and the fourth, Cynibert, the present bishop. Before Eadhaed, Sexwulf had been bishop not only of Lindsey, but also of the Mercians and Middle Angles; when he was expelled from Lindsey, he continued to preside over the other two provinces. Eadhaed, Bosa, and Eata were consecrated at York by Archbishop Theodore, who, three years after Wilfrid's departure, consecrated two others, Tunbert to the see of Hexham – Eata remaining at Lindisfarne – and Trumwine to be bishop of those Picts who were then subject to English rule. When Ethelred recovered the province of Lindsey, Eadhaed returned and was appointed by Theodore as Bishop of Ripon.*

CHAPTER 13: *Wilfrid converts the Province of the South Saxons to Christ* [see also v. 19]

D RIVEN out of his see, Wilfrid spent a considerable time travelling in various parts and also went to Rome. When he returned to Britain, the hostility of King Egfrid made it impossible for him to return to his own province or diocese, but nothing could deter him from preaching the Gospel. He therefore made his way to the province of the South Saxons, which stretches west and south from Kent as far as the land of the West Saxons, and covers an area of seven thousand hides. As the province was still pagan, Wilfrid preached the Christian Faith there, and administered the baptism of salvation. Ethelwalh its king had been baptized in the province of the Mercians not long previously under the influence of King Wulfhere, who was present at his baptism and became his godfather at the font. In token of their relationship, Wulfhere gave him two provinces, the Isle of Wight and the province of the Meanwaras[1] in the territory of the West Saxons. With the king's approval and greatly to his satisfaction, the bishop batpized the leading thegns

---

[1] Eastern Hampshire (Meonstoke).

and soldiers of the province. The remainder of the people were baptized either then or subsequently by the priests Eappa, Padda, Burghelm, and Oiddi. Queen Eabae, who had already received baptism in her own province of the Hwiccas, was the daughter of Eanfrid, brother of Aenheri, both of whom were Christians, as were their people. Otherwise the whole South Saxon province was ignorant of the Name and Faith of Christ. There was, however, an Irish monk named Dicul, who had a very small monastery at a place called Bosanham,[1] surrounded by woods and the sea, where five or six brothers served the Lord in a life of humility and poverty: but none of the natives was willing to follow their way of life or listen to their preaching.

By preaching to these folk, Bishop Wilfrid not only delivered them from the penalty of eternal damnation, but also saved them from a cruel and horrible extinction in his life. For no rain had fallen in the province for three years prior to his arrival, and a terrible famine had ensued, which reduced many to an awful death. It is said that frequently forty or fifty emaciated and starving people would go to a precipice, or to the edge of the sea, where they would join hands and leap over, to die by the fall or by drowning. But on the very day that the nation received the baptism of faith a soft but ample rainfall refreshed the earth, restoring greenness to the cornfields and giving a happy and fruitful season. Having once abandoned their earlier superstition and rejected idolatry, '*the heart and flesh of all cried out for the living God*', and they came to understand how He who is true God, had of his divine mercy granted them both spiritual and material blessings. For when Wilfrid had first arrived in the province and found so much misery from famine, he taught the people to obtain food by fishing; for although fish were plentiful in the sea and rivers, the people had no knowledge of fishing and caught only eels. So the bishop's men collected eel-nets from all sides and cast them into the sea, where, by the aid of

---

[1] Bosham, near Chichester.

God's grace, they quickly caught three hundred fishes of various kinds. These they divided into three portions, giving a hundred to the poor, a hundred to those who had lent their nets, and retaining a hundred for their own needs. By this good turn the bishop won the hearts of all, and the people began to listen more readily to his teaching, hoping to obtain heavenly blessings through the ministry of one to whom they already owed these material benefits.

At this time, King Ethelwalh granted the most reverend Bishop Wilfrid eighty-seven hides of land so that he could maintain his exiled companions. This land lay at Selsey, which means the seal's island, a place surrounded by the sea on all sides except to the west, where there is an approach about a sling's cast in width. A place of this description is known as a *peninsula* by the Latins, and as a *chersonese* by the Greeks. Bishop Wilfrid accepted this land, and having built a monastery there, established the regular life, most of the monks being his own companions: his successors are known to occupy the place to this day. Until the death of King Egfrid five years later, Wilfrid performed the duties of a bishop in word and deed in these parts, and was held in high esteem by all. And since the king had given him not only the land but all the property and inhabitants on it, Wilfrid instructed and baptized them all in the Faith of Christ. Among them were two hundred and fifty male and female slaves, all of whom he released from the slavery of Satan by baptism and by granting them their freedom released them from the yoke of human slavery as well.

CHAPTER 14: *A fatal epidemic is halted by the intercession of King Oswald*

CERTAIN proofs of heaven's especial favour are said to have been shown to this monastery; for once the tyranny of the Devil had been overthrown, the rule of Christ began. I have thought it fitting to preserve the memory of one of these stories, often told me by the very reverend Bishop Acca, who said that it was vouched for by some very reliable brethren of the monastery.

About the time that this province accepted the Faith of Christ, a dangerous epidemic struck many provinces of Britain. When, by God's dispensation, it reached the monastery, ruled at the time by the most religious priest of Christ, Eappa, it swept from this life many of the brethren, some of whom had come with the bishop, while others were South Saxons recently converted by the Faith. The brethren therefore decided to observe a three-day fast and implore God in his mercy to show pity on them, that he would preserve those who were in danger of death by disease, and deliver the souls of those already departed this life from eternal damnation.

In the monastery at this time lived a little Saxon boy, who had recently been converted to the Faith; this child had caught the disease, and for a long time had been confined to bed. About the second hour on the second day of prayer and fasting, he was alone in the place where he lay sick, when, under divine providence, the most blessed Princes of the Apostles deigned to appear to him; for he was a boy of innocent and gentle disposition, who sincerely believed the truths of the Faith that had been accepted. The Apostles greeted him very lovingly, and said: 'Son, put aside the fear of death that is troubling you; for today we are going to take you with us to the kingdom of heaven. But first of all you must wait until the Masses are said, and you have received the Viaticum of the Body and Blood of our Lord. Then you shall be set free from sickness and death, and carried up to the endless joys of heaven. So call the priest Eappa, and tell him that our Lord has heard the prayers of the brethren and regarded their fasting and devotion with favour. No one else in this monastery and its possessions is to die of this disease, and all who are now suffering from it will recover and be restored to their former health. You alone are to be set free by death today, and shall be taken to heaven to see the Lord Christ whom you have served so faithfully. God in his mercy has granted you this favour at the intercession of the devout

King Oswald, so beloved by God, who once ruled the people of the Northumbrians with outstanding devotion as their early king and whose Christian piety has won him an everlasting kingdom. For today is the anniversary of the king's death in battle at the hands of the heathen, when he was taken up to the joys of the souls in heaven and enrolled among the company of the Saints. If the brethren will consult the annals that record the burials of the dead, they will find that this is the day on which he departed this life, as we have said. So let them say Masses in all the oratories of the monastery, either in thanksgiving for God's answer to their prayers, or in commemoration of King Oswald the former ruler of their nation, who has prayed for them as newcomers of his nation. Let all the brethren assemble in church, and join in offering the heavenly Sacrifice; and let them end their fast and take food to restore their strength.'

When the boy had called Eappa and told him all that the Apostles had said, the priest particularly asked him to describe the clothes and appearance of these men who had appeared to him. 'They wore wonderful robes,' the boy replied, 'and their faces were very kindly and handsome, such as I have never seen before. I did not believe that there could be men so distinguished and wonderful. One of them was tonsured like a priest and the other had a long beard; and they said that one of them was Peter and the other Paul, and that they were servants of our Lord and Saviour Jesus Christ, sent by Him to protect our monastery.' The priest then believed the boy's statement, and went off at once to consult his annals, where he found that King Oswald had indeed been killed on that very day. So he summoned the brethren, ordered a meal to be prepared, Masses to be said, and all the brethren to communicate as usual. He also directed that a particle of the Lord's Offering should be taken to the sick boy at the time of the holy Sacrifice.

A little while later the same day the boy died, and his death proved the truth of what Christ's Apostles had told him. In further confirmation of his statement, no one except himself died in the monastery at that time. Many who heard about the vision were wonderfully inspired to implore God's mercy in every trouble, and to adopt the wholesome remedy of fasting. And from that time the heavenly birthday of Christ's warrior King Oswald was commemorated each year by the offering of Masses, not only in this monastery but in many other places as well.

CHAPTER 15: *King Cadwalla of the Gewissae kills King Ethelwalh and devastates his province with plundering and slaughter*

MEANWHILE Cadwalla, a daring young man of the royal house of the Gewissae, exiled from his own country, came with an army and killed King Ethelwalh, wasting the province with slaughtering and plunder. But the last king's ealdormen Berthun and Andhun soon drove him out, and administered the country from then on. The former was subsequently killed by Cadwalla when he had become king of the Gewissae, and the province was reduced to a worse state of subjection. Similarly Ini, who succeeded Cadwalla, held the province in subjection for several years. For this reason, it had no bishop of its own during all this period; for when Wilfrid its first bishop had been recalled home, it became dependent on the Bishop of the Gewissae, that is, the West Saxons, whose see was at Winchester.

CHAPTER 16: *The Isle of Wight receives Christian settlers. Two young princes of the island are killed immediately after Baptism* [A.D. 686]

AFTER Cadwalla became king of the Gewissae, he captured the Isle of Wight, which was entirely devoted to idolatry and strove to exterminate all the natives and replace them by settlers from his own province. Although not yet baptized, he is said to have bound himself by an oath to dedicate a quarter of the land and spoils to the Lord if he conquered the island; and he fulfilled this oath by offering it for God's use to Bishop

Wilfrid, who chanced at this time to have left his own people in order to visit the island. By English reckoning, the island has an area of twelve hundred hides, so that the bishop was given three hundred hides of land. This share he entrusted to Bernwini, one of his clerks who was his own sister's son, and he appointed a priest named Hiddila to preach and administer Baptism to all who sought salvation.

It would not be right to omit mention of two young princes, brothers of Arwald, king of the island, who were especially favoured by God's grace, and became the first natives of the island to believe and be saved. On the approach of the invaders, these princes had escaped from the island and crossed to the adjoining province of the Jutes. Here they were guided to a place called At-the-Stone,[1] where they hoped to remain hidden from the victorious king; and they were betrayed and ordered to be put to death. This was reported to the priest Cynibert, Abbot of a not far distant monastery at a place called Hreutford, that is, the Ford of Reeds;[2] so he sought out the king, who was living in seclusion in the district while he recovered from wounds received while fighting in the Isle of Wight, and begged him that, if it was necessary for these lads to die, he might first be allowed to instruct them in the mysteries of the Christian Faith. The king consented to this, and when Cynibert had taught them the word of truth, he baptized them in the fount of salvation, and assured their entry into the kingdom of heaven. So when the executioner arrived, they met bodily death gladly, in the firm faith that through it their souls would pass to eternal life. So last of all the provinces of Britain, the Isle of Wight accepted the Faith of Christ; but owing to its subjection to an alien rule, it had no bishop or see of its own until the time of Daniel, who is now Bishop of the West Saxons.

The Isle of Wight lies opposite the boundary between the South Saxons and the Gewissae, and is separated from it by three miles of sea, known as the Solent. In this strait, two ocean tides that flow round Britain from the boundless northern seas

---

[1] Stoneham, Hants.   [2] Redbridge.

meet in daily opposition off the mouth of the River Homelea.[1]
This enters the sea after flowing through the lands of the Jutes
who lived in the Gewissae country; and when the turbulence
ceases, they flow back into the ocean whence they spring.

CHAPTER 17: *Theodore presides over a Synod held in the Plain of*
Haethfeld (Hatfield) [A.D. 680]

ABOUT this time, Theodore learned that the faith of the
Church at Constantinople was greatly disturbed by the
heresy of Eutyches. Wishing to preserve the churches of the
English that he ruled untainted by this error, he summoned a
large number of venerable bishops and teachers to a conference;
and when he had carefully ascertained their individual beliefs,
he found them all united in support of the Catholic Faith. He
therefore took pains to record this fact in a synodical letter, to
serve as a reminder and guide to future generations. This letter
opens as follows:

'In the Name of our Lord and Saviour Jesus Christ. On the
seventeenth of September in the eighth indiction; in the tenth
year of the reign of our most devout lord Egfrid, King of the
Northumbrians; in the sixth year of King Ethelfrid of the
Mercians; in the seventeenth year of King Aldwulf of the East
Angles; and in the seventh year of King Hlothere of the Kentish
people. Under the presidency of Theodore, by the grace of God
Archbishop of the island of Britain and the City of Canterbury,
we the venerable bishops of the island of Britain assembled in
conclave at the place which is called in the Saxon language
Haethfeld, having the most holy Gospels before us, hereby unite
to proclaim the true and orthodox faith. This same faith our
Lord Jesus Christ delivered in the flesh to His disciples, who
saw Him in person and heard His teaching. This is now set
forth in the Creed of the holy fathers, and by all the sacred
General Councils, and by the united voice of the accredited

[1] The Hamble.

doctors of the Catholic Church. We follow them in devotion and right faith, professing our belief in their divinely inspired teachings; and we unite with the holy fathers in acknowledging the Father, the Son, and the Holy Spirit, the Trinity consubstantial in Unity, and Unity in Trinity, that is, One God subsisting in three consubstantial Persons of equal glory and honour.'

And after a great deal more to this effect, in which they affirm their confession of the true Faith, the letter of this holy synod continues: 'We accept the decisions of the five holy General Councils of the blessed fathers who were acceptable to God; that is, the Council of three hundred and eighteen bishops assembled at Nicaea, which condemned the impious Arius and his teachings; the Council of one hundred and fifty bishops at Constantinople, which condemned the madness of Macedonius and Eudoxius and their teachings; the first Council of two hundred bishops at Ephesus, which condemned the wicked Nestorius and his teachings; the Council of six hundred and thirty bishops at Chalcedon, which condemned Eutyches and Nestorius and their teachings; and the fifth Council at Constantinople in the reign of Justinian the younger, which condemned Theodorus, Theodoret, the epistles of Ibas, and their teachings against Cyril.'

Shortly after this, the letter continues: 'We also accept the decisions of the Council held in Rome under the blessed Pope Martin in the eighth indiction and ninth year of the reign of the most pious Emperor Constantine [IV]. We glorify our Lord Jesus Christ as they glorified Him, neither adding nor withdrawing anything; we anathematize with heart and voice those whom they anathematized, and accept those whom they accepted. And we glorify God the Father, who is without beginning, and His only-begotten Son, begotten of the Father before all worlds, and the Holy Spirit ineffably proceeding from the Father and the Son, as proclaimed by all the holy Apostles, prophets, and teachers whom we have already mentioned. And we who have all joined with Archbishop Theodore in proclaiming the Catholic Faith affix our signatures hereto.'

AMONG those who signed the affirmation of the Catholic Faith at this Synod was the venerable John, Arch-cantor of the church of the holy Apostle Peter and Abbot of the monastery of Saint Martin, who had recently come from Rome under instructions from Pope Agatho with the most reverend Abbot Benedict, of whom I have spoken. For when Benedict had built a monastery in Britain near the mouth of the River Wear[1] in honour of the blessed Prince of the Apostles, he travelled to Rome with his colleague and partner in the work, Ceolfrid, who later succeeded him as abbot of the monastery. As he had made several earlier visits to Rome, he was received with honour by Pope Agatho of blessed memory. From him he asked and obtained a letter of privilege, granted with his apostolic authority, which confirmed the independence of the monastery that he had founded; for he knew this to accord with the wishes of King Egfrid, with whose approval and grant he had built the monastery.

Benedict received Abbot John and conducted him to Britain, where he was to teach his monks the chant for the liturgical year as it was sung at Saint Peter's, Rome. In accordance with the Pope's instructions, Abbot John taught the cantors of the monastery the theory and practice of singing and reading aloud, and he put into writing all that was necessary for the proper observance of festivals throughout the year. This document is still preserved in this monastery, and many copies have been made for other places. John's instruction was not limited to the brethren of this monastery alone; for men who were proficient singers came from nearly all the monasteries of the province to hear him, and he received many invitations to teach elsewhere.

In addition to his task of teaching the arts of singing and reading, John had also been directed by the apostolic Pope to make careful enquiries about the faith of the Church of the

---

[1] Monkwearmouth.

English, and report on it when he returned to Rome. He had brought with him the decisions of the Council recently held in Rome by blessed Pope Martin and one hundred and five bishops, which particularly condemned those who taught that only one will operated in Christ, and he handed this over for a transcript to be made in the monastery of the most religious Abbot Benedict. Those who supported such views had caused great confusion in the Church of Constantinople at the time, but by God's help they were exposed and refuted. For this reason, Pope Agatho wished to be informed on the state of the Church in Britain as well as in other provinces, and whether it was free from contamination by heretics; so he entrusted this mission to the most reverend Abbot John, who had already been ordered to visit Britain. After the above-mentioned Synod had been summoned for the purpose in Britain, the Catholic Faith was shown to be held untainted by all, and a copy of its decisions was given to John to take back to Rome.

Not long after crossing the sea, on his return journey to his own country, John fell sick and died; and out of devotion to Saint Martin, of whose monastery he was abbot, his friends carried his body to Tours, where he was buried with great honour. For on his journey to Britain he had been courteously welcomed there by the brethren, who begged him to travel by the same route on his return to Rome and pay another visit to their house. They also provided him with assistants to accompany him on his journey and help him in his appointed task. And although he died on his journey, John's testimony to the Catholic Faith of the English was taken on to Rome, where it was received with great satisfaction by the apostolic Pope and by all who heard or read it.

KING Egfrid married Etheldreda,* a daughter of Anna, King of the East Angles, of whom I have often spoken; he was a very devout man, noble in mind and deed. Before her marriage to Egfrid, Etheldreda had been married to Tondbert, a prince of the South Gyrwas; but he died shortly after the wedding, and she was given to King Egfrid. Although she lived with him for twelve years, she preserved the glory of perpetual virginity. This fact is absolutely vouched for by Bishop Wilfrid of blessed memory, of whom I made enquiry when some people doubted it. He said that Egfrid promised to give estates and much wealth to him if he could persuade the queen to consummate the marriage, knowing that there was no man for whom she had a higher regard. And there is no reason to doubt that such a thing could happen in our own day, since reliable histories record it as having happened on several occasions in the past through the grace of the same Lord who has promised to remain with us until the end of the world. For the miraculous preservation of her body from corruption in the tomb is evidence that she had remained untainted by bodily intercourse.

For a long time Etheldreda begged the king to allow her to retire from worldly affairs and serve Christ the only true King in a convent. And having at length obtained his reluctant consent, she entered the convent of the Abbess Ebba, King Egfrid's aunt, at Coludesbyrig,[1] where she received the veil and clothing of a nun from the hands of Bishop Wilfrid. A year later she was herself made Abbess in the district called Ely, where she built a convent and became the virgin mother of many virgins vowed to God and displayed the pattern of a heavenly life in word and deed. It is said that from the time of her entry into the convent she never wore linen but only woollen garments, and that she would seldom wash in hot water except on the eve of the greater festivals such as Easter, Pentecost, and the

---

[1] Coldingham: see also iv, 25.

Epiphany, and then only after she and her assistants had helped
the other handmaids of Christ to wash. She seldom had more
than one meal a day except at the greater festivals or under
urgent necessity, and she always remained at prayer in the
church from the hour of Matins until dawn unless prevented by
serious illness. Some say that she possessed the spirit of prophecy, and that in the presence of all the community, she not only
foretold the plague that was to cause her death, but also the
number who would die of it in the convent. She was taken to
Christ in the presence of her nuns seven years after her appointment as abbess, and in accordance with her instructions she was
buried among them in the wooden coffin in which she died.

Etheldreda was succeeded in the office of abbess by her sister
Sexburg,* who had been wife of King Earconbert of Kent.
Sixteen years after Etheldreda's burial, this abbess decided to
have her bones exhumed, placed in a new coffin, and transferred
into the church. She therefore directed some of the brethren to
search for stone to make this coffin. And since the district of
Ely was surrounded on all sides by sea and fens and had no large
stones, they took a boat and came to a small ruined city not far
distant which the English call Grantchester. After a short while
they discovered near the city walls a white marble sarcophagus
of very beautiful workmanship with a close-fitting lid of similar
stone; and realizing that God had prospered their journey, they
returned thanks to him and brought it back to the convent.

When the tomb of the holy and virginal spouse of Christ was
opened and her body brought to light, it was found as free from
decay as if she had died and been buried that very day; this is
vouched for by Bishop Wilfrid and many others of their own
knowledge. But even fuller proof is given by the physician
Cynifrid, who was present at both her death and her exhuma-
tion. Cynifrid used to relate that during her last illness she had a
large tumour under the jaw. 'I was asked,' he said, 'to open the
tumour and drain away the poisonous matter in it. I did this,
and for two days she seemed somewhat easier, so that many
thought that she would recover from her illness. But on the
third day her earlier pain returned, and she was taken from this

world, and exchanged all pain and death for everlasting life and health. When her bones were to be taken up out of the grave so many years later, a pavilion was raised over it, and the whole community stood around it chanting, the brothers on one side, and the sisters on the other. The abbess herself, with a few others, went in to take up and wash the bones, when we suddenly heard her cry out in a loud voice, "Glory to the Name of the Lord!" Shortly afterwards they opened the door of the pavilion and called me in. There I saw the body of the holy virgin taken from its grave and laid on a bed as though asleep; and when they had uncovered her face, they showed me that the incision which I had made had healed. This astounded me; for in place of the open gaping wound with which she was buried, there remained only the faint mark of a scar. All the linen clothes in which the body had been enfolded appeared so fresh and new that they looked as if they had been wrapped that very day around her pure body.'

It is said that when she was affected by this tumour and pain in her jaw and neck, she welcomed pain of this kind, and used to say: 'I realize very well that I deserve this wearisome disease in my neck, on which, as I well remember, when I was a girl, I used to wear the needless burden of jewellery. And I believe that God in His goodness wishes me to endure this pain in my neck so that I may be absolved from the guilt of my needless vanity. So now I wear a burning red tumour on my neck instead of gold and pearls.' At the touch of these robes devils were expelled from the bodies of those whom they possessed, and other complaints were sometimes cured. And the coffin in which she was first buried is said to have cured diseases of the eye, relieving pain and failing sight in those who placed their heads on the coffin as they prayed. When the sisters had washed the virgin's body and clothed it in new robes, they carried it into the church and laid it in the sarcophagus which had been brought, where it is held in great veneration to this day. This same sarcophagus was found to fit the virgin's body in a marvellous way, as though it had been especially made for her, and the special place cut out for the head exactly fitted the measurements of her own.

Ely lies in the province of the East Angles, an area of about six hundred hides. As I have said, it resembles an island surrounded by water and marshes, and it derives its name from the vast quantity of eels that are caught in the marshes. And the servant of Christ wished to have her monastery in this place because, as already mentioned, her forbears came from the province of the East Angles.

CHAPTER 20: *A hymn in honour of Etheldreda*

IT seems appropriate to insert in this History an elegiac hymn in praise of virginity which I composed many years ago in honour of this same queen and bride of Christ – all the more a queen because a bride of Christ. In this I am following the example of Holy Scripture, in which the narrative is frequently interspersed with songs which are known to have been composed in verse.*

> All-guiding Trinity, guide my design.
> Battles were Virgil's theme; let peace be mine,
> Chanting in lieu of Helen's wantonness
> Divine compassion, to redeem and bless,
> Entering a virgin's womb, God's gate to earth.
> Fair maid, who gav'st the whole world's Parent birth,
> God gave thee grace. And by that grace empowered
> How many virgin blossoms since have flowered!
> In fiery torment stood chaste Agatha
> Joyful to death; so stood Eulalia.
> Kindled with love, Thecla with virgin breast
> Laughed at wild beasts; so was Euphemia blest.
> More strong than steel, Agnes disdained its thrust;
> Nor did Cecilia's strength betray her trust.
> Our age at length in triumphs such as these
> Partakes through ETHELDREDA's victories.
> Queenly by birth, an earthly crown she wore
> Right nobly; but a heavenly pleased her more.
> Scorning the marriage bed, a virgin wife
> Twelve years she reigned, then sought a cloistered life.

> Unspotted to her heavenly spouse she came,
> Virgin in soul, her virgin robe and frame,
> Whom sixteen winters they had lain entombed,
> Xrist willing it, still fresh and unconsumed.
> Yea, from their touch Eve's Tempter flees dismayed,
> Zealous for evil, vanquished by a maid.
>
> Ah bride of Christ, bright fame on earth is thine.
> More bright in Heaven thy bridal torches shine.
> Exultant hymns proclaim in glad accord:
> No power henceforth may part thee from thy Lord.

CHAPTER 21: *Archbishop Theodore makes peace between King Egfrid and King Ethelred* [A.D. 679]

IN the ninth year of his reign, King Egfrid fought a great battle near the river Trent against King Ethelred of the Mercians, in which Egfrid's brother Elfwin was killed. The latter was a young man of about eighteen, who was much loved in both provinces since Ethelred had married his sister Osthryd. This gave every indication of causing fiercer strife and more lasting hatred between the two warlike kings and peoples, until Archbishop Theodore, the beloved of God, enlisting God's help, smothered the flames of this awful peril by his wholesome advice. As a result, peace was restored between the kings and peoples, and in lieu of further bloodshed the customary compensation* was paid to King Egfrid for his brother's death. The peace thus made was maintained between these kings and their peoples for many years.

IN the above battle in which King Elfwin was killed, a remarkable thing occurred, which I should not fail to mention, since it will further the salvation of many. During the battle, a young thegn named Imma belonging to Elfwin's forces was struck down, and lay apparently dead all that day and the following night among the bodies of the slain. At length he recovered consciousness, sat up, and bandaged his wounds as well as he could; then when he had rested awhile, he got up and tried to find some friends to help him. While so engaged he was found and captured by men of the enemy forces, and taken before their leader, who was a nobleman of King Ethelred. When asked his identity, he was afraid to reveal that he was a soldier, and answered that he was a poor married peasant who had come with others of his kind to bring provisions to the army. The nobleman ordered him to be given shelter and treatment for his wounds; and when he began to recover, he ordered him to be chained at night to prevent his escape. But this proved impossible, for no sooner had those who chained him left than the fetters fell off.

Now this young man had a brother named Tunna, who was a priest and abbot of a monastery that is still called Tunnacaestir after him. And when he heard that his brother had been killed in battle, he went to see whether he could find his body. Finding another very similar to him, he concluded that it was his; so he took the body back to his monastery, gave it honourable burial, and offered many Masses for the repose of his brother's soul. And it was on account of these Masses that, as I have said, when anyone tried to chain him, he was immediately set free. The nobleman, whose prisoner he was, was astonished, and asked why he could not be bound, and whether he possessed any written charms to protect him from binding like those mentioned in fables. He replied: 'I know nothing about such things. But I have a brother who is a priest in my own province, and I am sure that, thinking me killed, he is saying many Masses for me; and were I now in another life, my soul would be freed from its pains by his prayers.' After he had been held some time in the nobleman's custody, those who observed the young man closely realized from his appearance, clothing, and speech that he was no common peasant as he said, but of noble birth. The nobleman then sent for him privately, and pressed him to disclose his identity, promising that he would do him no harm if he told him the truth about who he was. On this assurance, the young man revealed that he was a king's thegn. At this the nobleman said: 'I realized by all your answers that you were no peasant. You deserve to die, because all my brothers and kinsmen were killed in that battle: but I will not put you to death, because I have given you my promise.'

As soon as Imma recovered, the nobleman sold him to a Frisian in London, who took him away, but found that he was unable to fetter him. When one kind of fetter after another had been put on him and none could hold him, his buyer gave him permission to ransom himself if he could. It was at the hour of Terce, the customary time of saying Mass, that his chains were most frequently loosed. Promising either to return or to send his ransom money, Imma went to King Hlothere of Kent, who was nephew to the above Queen Etheldreda, because he had once been one of the queen's thegns. From him he obained the money for his ransom, and sent it to his master as he had promised.

When Imma returned to his own country, he visited his brother and gave him a full account of all his troubles and how he had been helped in them; and from him he learned that his chains had been loosed at the times when Mass was being said on his behalf. He also realized how he had received comfort and strength from heaven in many other dangers through the prayers of his brother and his offering of Christ's saving Sacrifice. He related his experiences to many people, who were thereby inspired to greater faith and devotion and gave them-selves to prayer, almsgiving, and offering the Holy Sacrifice to God for the deliverance of their friends who had departed this life; for they understood how this saving Sacrifice availed for the eternal redemption of soul and body.

Among those who told me this story were some who had actually heard it from the mouth of the man to whom these things had happened, so that I have no hesitation about including it in this history of the Church as it was related.*

CHAPTER 23: *The life and death of Abbess Hilda* [A.D. 680]

IN the following year, that is the year of our Lord 680, Hilda, abbess of the monastery of Streanaeshalch, of which I have already spoken, a most religious servant of Christ, after an earthly life devoted to the work of heaven passed away to receive the reward of a heavenly life on the seventeenth of November at the age of sixty-six. Her life on earth fell into two equal parts: for she spent thirty-three years most nobly in secular occupations, and dedicated the ensuing thirty-three even more nobly to our Lord in the monastic life. She was nobly born, the daughter of Hereric, nephew to King Edwin. With Edwin she received the Faith and sacraments of Christ through the preaching of Paulinus of blessed memory, first bishop of the Northumbrians, and she preserved this Faith inviolate until she was found worthy to see her Master in heaven.*

When she decided to abandon the secular life and serve God alone, she went to the province of the East Angles, whose king was her kinsman; for having renounced her home and all that she possessed, she wished if possible to travel on from there into Gaul, and to live an exile for our Lord's sake in the monastery of Cale,[1] so that she might the more easily attain her eternal heavenly home. For her sister Hereswith, mother of Aldwulf, King of the East Angles, was already living there as a professed nun and awaiting her eternal crown. Inspired by her example, Hilda remained in the province a full year, intending to join her overseas; but she was recalled home by Bishop Aidan

---

[1] Chelles, near Paris.

and was granted one hide of land on the north bank of the River Wear, where she observed the monastic rule with a handful of companions for another year.

After this, Hilda was made abbess of the monastery of Heruteu,[1] founded not long previously by Heiu, a devout servant of Christ, said to have been the first woman in the province of the Northumbrians to take vows and be clothed as a nun, which she did with the blessing of Bishop Aidan. But soon after establishing the monastery she left for the town of Calcaria, which the English call Kaelcacaestir,[2] and settled there. Then Christ's servant Hilda was appointed to rule this monastery, and quickly set herself to establish a regular observance, following the instructions of learned men; for Bishop Aidan and other devout men, who knew her and admired her innate wisdom and love of God's service, often used to visit her, to express their affection and offer thoughtful guidance.

When she had ruled this monastery for some years, constantly occupied in establishing the regular life, she further undertook to found or organize a monastery at a place known as Streanaeshalch, and carried out this appointed task with great energy. She established the same regular life as in her former monastery, and taught the observance of righteousness, mercy, purity, and other virtues, but especially of peace and charity. After the example of the primitive Church, no one there was rich, no one was needy, for everything was held in common, and nothing was considered to be anyone's personal property. So great was her prudence that not only ordinary folk, but kings and princes used to come and ask her advice in their difficulties and take it. Those under her direction were required to make a thorough study of the Scriptures and occupy themselves in good works, to such good effect that many were found fitted for Holy Orders and the service of God's altar.

Five men from this monastery later became bishops – Bosa, Aetla, Oftfor, John, and Wilfrid – all of them men of outstanding merit and holiness. As already mentioned, Bosa was consecrated Bishop of York; of Aetla let it suffice to note that he

---

[1] Hartlepool.   [2] Possibly Tadcaster.

became Bishop of Dorchester; and I shall tell in due course how John became Bishop of Hexham, and Wilfrid Bishop of York. Meanwhile I wish to speak of Oftfor, who having devoted himself to reading and applying the Scriptures in both Hilda's monasteries, wished to win greater perfection, and travelled to Kent in order to visit Archbishop Theodore, of blessed memory. When he had continued his studies under him for some while, he decided to visit Rome, which in those days was considered an act of great merit. On his return to Britain he visited the province of the Hwiccas, then ruled by King Osric, where he remained a long time, preaching the word of faith and setting an example of holy life to all who met and heard him. At this time Bosel, bishop of the province, was in such ill health that he was unable to carry out his duties in person, and Oftfor was therefore unanimously elected bishop in his place. At the request of King Ethelred, he was consecrated by Bishop Wilfrid of blessed memory, who was acting as Bishop of the Middle Angles, since Theodore had died and as yet no bishop had been appointed to succeed him. A little earlier, before the man of God Bosel, an energetic and very learned man of great ability named Tatfrid had been elected bishop while a monk in Hilda's monastery, but met an untimely death before he could be consecrated.

Christ's servant Abbess Hilda, whom all her acquaintances called Mother because of her wonderful devotion and grace, was not only an example of holy life to members of her own community; for she also brought about the amendment and salvation of many living at a distance, who heard the inspiring story of her industry and goodness. Her life was the fulfilment of a dream which her mother Breguswith had when Hilda was an infant, during the time that her husband Hereric was living in banishment under the protection of the British king Cerdic, where he died of poison. In this dream she fancied that he was suddenly taken away, and although she searched everywhere, she could find no trace of him. When all her efforts had failed, she discovered a most valuable jewel under her garments; and as she looked closely, it emitted such a brilliant light that all

Britain was lit by its splendour. This dream was fulfilled in her daughter, whose life afforded a shining example not only to herself but to all who wished to live a good life.

When Hilda had ruled this monastery for many years, it pleased the Author of our salvation to try her holy soul by a long sickness, in order that, as with the Apostle, her strength might be *made perfect in weakness*. She was attacked by a burning fever that racked her continually for six years; but during all this time she never ceased to give thanks to her Maker or to instruct the flock committed to her, both privately and publicly. For her own example taught them all to serve God obediently when in health, and to render thanks to him faithfully when in trouble or bodily weakness. In the seventh year of her illness the pain passed into her innermost parts, and her last day came. About cockcrow she received the Viaticum of the holy Communion, and when she had summoned all the handmaids of Christ in the monastery, she urged them to maintain the gospel peace among themselves and with others. And while she was still speaking, she joyfully welcomed death, or rather, in the words of our Lord, passed from death to life.

That same night it pleased Almighty God to make her death known by means of a vision in a monastery some considerable distance away, which she had founded that same year at Hackness. In this place there was a devout nun named Begu, who had vowed herself to God in virginity in the monastic life over thirty years previously. As she was resting in the sisters' dormitory, she suddenly heard in the air the well-known note of the bell that used to wake and call them to prayer when any of the sisters had died. Opening her eyes, as she thought, she saw the roof open, and a great light pour in from above and flood the room. While she gazed into this light, she saw the soul of God's servant Hilda borne up to heaven in the midst of the light accompanied and guided by angels. Then she awoke, and seeing the other sisters lying around her, realized that what she had seen was either a dream or a vision. Rising at once in alarm, she ran to Frigyth, who was Prioress at the time, and with many sighs and tears told her that their Mother the Abbess

Hilda had departed this life, and that she had seen her surrounded by angels in a great light, and ascending to the abode of eternal light to join the company of the saints in heaven. When she had heard the nun's story Frigyth roused all the sisters, and when she had gathered them into the church, she enjoined them to pray and recite the psalter for the soul of their Mother. They did this for the remainder of the night, and at daybreak some brothers arrived from the monastery where she had died with news of her passing. The sisters replied that they already knew, and when they explained how and when they had heard it, it was evident that her death had been revealed to them by means of a vision at the very hour that the brothers said she had died. Thus with fitting harmony the mercy of heaven ordained that while some of her Community attended her death-bed, the others were made aware of her soul's entry into eternal life, although these monasteries are about thirteen miles apart.

It is said that Hilda's death was revealed also on the same night in a vision to one of the sisters in the actual monastery where the servant of God passed away. This sister, who loved her dearly, saw her soul ascend to heaven in the company of angels, and immediately awoke the servants of Christ with her and told them to pray for her soul. This was at the very hour of her death, even before the rest of the Community knew of it; for it was only made known to them early in the morning. At this time the nun was with certain other handmaids of Christ in a remote part of the monastery, where novices were admitted to test their vocation until they were fully instructed and admitted to membership of the Community.

CHAPTER 24: *A brother of the monastery is found to possess God's gift of poetry* [A.D. 680]

IN this monastery of Streanaeshalch lived a brother singularly gifted by God's grace. So skilful was he in composing religious and devotional songs that, when any passage of Scripture was explained to him by interpreters, he could quickly turn it into delightful and moving poetry in his own English tongue. These verses of his have stirred the hearts of many folk to despise the world and aspire to heavenly things. Others after him tried to compose religious poems in English, but none could compare with him; for he did not acquire the art of poetry from men or through any human teacher but received it as a free gift from God. For this reason he could never compose any frivolous or profane verses; but only such as had a religious theme fell fittingly from his devout lips. He had followed a secular occupation until well advanced in years without ever learning anything about poetry. Indeed it sometimes happened at a feast that all the guests in turn would be invited to sing and entertain the company; then, when he saw the harp coming his way, he would get up from table and go home.

On one such occasion he had left the house in which the entertainment was being held and went out to the stable where it was his duty that night to look after the beasts. There when the time came he settled down to sleep. Suddenly in a dream he saw a man standing beside him who called him by name. 'Caedmon,' he said, 'sing me a song.' 'I don't know how to sing,' he replied. 'It is because I cannot sing that I left the feast and came here.' The man who addressed him then said: 'But you shall sing to me.' 'What should I sing about?' he replied. 'Sing about the Creation of all things,' the other answered. And Caedmon immediately began to sing verses in praise of God the Creator that he had never heard before, and their theme ran thus:

> Praise we the Fashioner now of Heaven's fabric,
> The majesty of his might and his mind's wisdom,

Work of the world-warden, worker of all wonders,
How he the Lord of Glory everlasting,
Wrought first for the race of men Heaven as a rooftree,
Then made he Middle Earth to be their mansion.

This is the general sense, but not the actual words that Caedmon sang in his dream; for verses, however masterly, cannot be translated literally from one language into another without losing much of their beauty and dignity. When Caedmon awoke, he remembered everything that he had sung in his dream, and soon added more verses in the same style to a song truly worthy of God.

Early in the morning he went to his superior the reeve, and told him about this gift that he had received. The reeve took him before the abbess, who ordered him to give an account of his dream and repeat the verses in the presence of many learned men, so that a decision might be reached by common consent as to their quality and origin. All of them agreed that Caedmon's gift had been given him by our Lord. And they explained to him a passage of scriptural history or doctrine and asked him to render it into verse if he could. He promised to do this, and returned next morning with excellent verses as they had ordered him. The abbess was delighted that God had given such grace to the man, and advised him to abandon secular life and adopt the monastic state. And when she had admitted him into the Community as a brother, she ordered him to be instructed in the events of sacred history. So Caedmon stored up in his memory all that he learned, and like one of the clean animals chewing the cud, turned it into such melodious verse that his delightful renderings turned his instructors into auditors. He sang of the creation of the world, the origin of the human race, and the whole story of Genesis. He sang of Israel's exodus from Egypt, the entry into the Promised Land, and many other events of scriptural history. He sang of the Lord's Incarnation, Passion, Resurrection, and Ascension into heaven, the coming of the Holy Spirit, and the teaching of the Apostles. He also made poems on the terrors of the Last Judgement, the horrible pains of Hell, and the joys of the Kingdom of Heaven. In addition to these, he composed several others on the blessings and judgements of God, by which he sought to turn his hearers from delight in wickedness and to inspire them to love and do good. For Caedmon was a deeply religious man, who humbly submitted to regular discipline and hotly rebuked all who tried to follow another course. And so he crowned his life with a happy end.*

For, when the time of his death drew near, he felt the onset of physical weakness for fourteen days, but not seriously enough to prevent his walking or talking the whole time. Close by there was a house to which all who were sick or likely to die were taken. Towards nightfall on the day when he was to depart this life, Caedmon asked his attendant to prepare a resting-place for him in this house. The attendant was surprised at this request from a man who did not appear likely to die yet; nevertheless, he did as he was asked. So Caedmon went to the house, and conversed and jested cheerfully with those who were already there; and when it was past midnight, he asked: 'Is the Eucharist in the house?' 'Why do you want the Eucharist?' they enquired; 'you are not likely to die yet, when you are talking so cheerfully to us and seem to be in perfect health.' 'Nevertheless,' he said, 'bring me the Eucharist.' And taking It in his hands, Caedmon asked whether they were all charitably disposed towards him, and whether they had any complaint or ill-feeling against him. They replied that they were all most kindly disposed towards him, and free from all bitterness. Then in turn they asked him to clear his heart of bitterness towards them. At once he answered: 'Dear sons, my heart is at peace with all the servants of God.' Then, when he had fortified himself with the heavenly Viaticum, he prepared to enter the other life, and asked how long it would be before the brothers were roused to sing God's praises in the Night Office. 'Not long,' they replied. 'Good, then let us wait until then,' he answered; and signing himself with the holy Cross, he laid his head on the pillow and passed away quietly in his sleep. So, having served God with a simple and pure mind, and with tranquil devotion, he left the world and departed to his presence by a tranquil death. His tongue, which had sung so many inspiring verses in praise of his Maker, uttered its last words in his praise as he signed himself with the Cross and commended his soul into his hands. For, as I have already said, Caedmon seems to have had a premonition of his death.

CHAPTER 25: *A man of God sees a vision portending the destruction of Coldingham monastery by fire*

A T this time, the monastery of nuns called Coludesbyrig, which I have already mentioned, was burned down through carelessness. However, all who knew the facts could readily perceive that it happened because of the wickedness of its members, and in particular of those who were supposed to be in authority. But God's mercy gave them a warning of punishment, and if they had followed the example of the Ninevites in fasting, prayers, and tears, they could have averted the anger of the just Judge.

In this monastery lived an Irishman named Adamnan, who led a life so devoted to God in prayer and austerity that he took no food or drink except on Sundays and Thursdays, and often spent the entire night in vigil and prayer. He had originally adopted this severe life from necessity, to overcome his evil inclinations; but as time went on, this necessity became his custom. During his youth he had committed some crime for which, when he came to his senses, he was thoroughly ashamed, and dreaded punishment by the strict Judge. So he visited a priest from whom he hoped to learn a way of salvation, confessed his sins to him, and asked for advice how he might escape the wrath to come. When he had heard his confession, the priest said: 'A severe wound calls for an ever more severe remedy. Therefore spend your time as far as possible in fasting, reciting the psalter, and prayer, so that you may avert God's anger in confession, and deserve to find His mercy.' Already deeply smitten in conscience and longing for speedy release

from the inward fetters of the sin that burdened him, he replied:
'I am still young and strong in body, and I will readily undergo
whatever penance you impose on me, if only I may be saved at
Judgement Day. Even if you order me to remain standing in
prayer all night, or to remain the whole week fasting, I will do
it.' But the priest answered: 'To remain the whole week without
food is too severe a penance: it will be sufficient if you fast for
two or three days. Do this until I return shortly, when I will
explain more fully what you should do, and how long you
should continue this penance.' So, having prescribed the extent
of his penance, the priest went away; but he was suddenly called
by an urgent need to Ireland, which was his native land, and
never returned to him as he had arranged. But Adamnan bore
in mind his directions and his own promise, and earnestly
applied himself to penitent tears, holy vigils, and fasting. He
took food only on Sundays and Thursdays, as I have said, and
ate nothing on the other days of the week. And when he heard
that his priest had left for Ireland and died there, he continued
to observe the austerity that he had imposed; what he had
undertaken through fear of God in remorse for his sin he
continued without flagging through love of God in enjoyment
of his reward.

When he had followed this way of life for a considerable time,
it happened one day that he had travelled some distance from
the monastery accompanied by one of the brothers. On the
return journey, as they were approaching the monastery and
saw its buildings towering up, the man of God burst into tears,
and his face betrayed the sorrow of his heart. Seeing this, his
companion enquired the reason, and he replied: 'The time is
near when all the public and private buildings that you see in
front of you will be burned to ashes.' When his companion
heard this, he went and informed Ebba, the Mother of the
Community, as soon as he reached the monastery. She was
naturally alarmed, and summoning Adamnan, pressed him to
tell her how he knew such a thing. He answered: 'One night
recently I was occupied in keeping vigil and reciting the psalter,
when a stranger suddenly appeared beside me, and I was greatly

startled. He told me not to be afraid, and spoke kindly to me, saying, "You do well to employ these night hours of rest in vigil and prayer instead of indulging in sleep." I answered, "I am aware that I have great need of wholesome vigils and earnest prayer to God to pardon my sins." He said, "You are right; and many besides yourself need to atone for their sins by good works, and employ the time of their release from worldly occupations in seeking their eternal welfare. But there are very few who do this. For I have visited every room and every bed of this monastery, and entered every building and dormitory. Nowhere have I found anyone except yourself concerned with the health of his own soul. All of them, men and women alike, are either sunk in unprofitable sleep, or else awake only to sin. Even the cells, which were built for prayer and study, are now converted into places for eating, drinking, gossip, or other amusements. When they have leisure, even the nuns vowed to God abandon the propriety of their calling and spend their time weaving fine clothes, which they employ to the peril of their calling, either to adorn themselves like brides or to attract attention from strange men. For this reason a heavy and well-deserved punishment is about to fall on this place and its people in the form of a terrible fire."' The abbess asked: 'Why did you not reveal this to me earlier?' Adamnan replied: 'I hesitated to do so out of regard for you, lest it should cause you grave distress: but let it be some comfort to you that this calamity will not happen in your own time.' Once the vision became known, the Community was somewhat alarmed for a few days, and began to refrain from wrong-doing and undergo penance. But after the death of the abbess they relapsed into their earlier sins and became even more wicked. And when they said 'Peace and safety', then sudden destruction came upon them.

My informant in all these events was my fellow-priest, Edgils, who was living in the monastery at the time. And when the majority of the inhabitants had left the ruined building, he lived a long while in our own monastery, and died there. I have thought it desirable to include this in my history to warn the reader of the workings of God, and how terrible he is in his doings towards the children of men.★ Let us beware lest at some time we should indulge in the pleasures of the flesh, and pay such scant heed to the judgements of God that we incur his sudden anger. For we shall either be justly and severely punished by losses in this world, or else be even more strictly judged and carried away to eternal perdition.

CHAPTER 26: *On the death of King Egfrid and King Hlothere* [A.D. 685]

I N the year of our Lord 684, King Egfrid of the Northumbri-ans sent an army into Ireland under the command of Bert, which brutally harassed an inoffensive people who had always been friendly to the English, sparing neither churches nor monasteries from the ravages of war. The islanders resisted force by force as well as they could, and implored the merciful aid of God, praying Heaven long and earnestly to avenge them. And although those who curse may not inherit the kingdom of God, one may well believe that those who were justly cursed for their wickedness quickly suffered the penalty of their guilt at the hands of God their Judge. For in the following year King Egfrid, ignoring the advice of his friends and in particular of Cuthbert, of blessed memory, who had recently been made bishop, rashly led an army to ravage the province of the Picts. The enemy pretended to retreat, and lured the king into narrow mountain passes, where he was killed with the greater part of his forces on the twentieth of May in his fortieth year and the fifteenth of his reign.★ As I have said, his friends had warned him against this campaign; but in the previous year he had refused to listen to the reverend Father Egbert, who begged him not to attack the Irish who had done him no harm; and this was his punishment, that he now refused to listen to those who tried to save him from destruction.

Henceforward the hopes and strength of the English realm began

'to waver and slip backward ever lower.'★

The Picts recovered their own lands that had been occupied by the English, while the Irish living in Britain and a proportion of the Britons themselves regained their freedom, which they have now preserved for about forty-six years. Many of the English at this time were killed, enslaved, or forced to flee from Pictish territory. Among them, the most reverend man of God Trumwine, who had been appointed their bishop, withdrew with his people from the monastery of Abercurnig, which was situated in English territory but stood close to the firth that divides the lands of the English from those of the Picts. Wherever he could, he recommended his own people to friends in various monasteries. He himself chose to live in the often-mentioned monastery of Streanaeshalch. There, for several years, he lived an austere life with a few of his own folk, to the benefit of many besides himself. On his death, he was buried in the church of blessed Peter the Apostle with the honours due to his life and dignity. The royal nun Aelffled, with her mother Eanfled whom I mentioned earlier, ruled the monastery at this period: and when Bishop Trumwine came, she found him a great help in the administration of the monastery and a great comfort in her own life. Egfrid's successor on the throne was Aldfrid, a man well-read in the Scriptures, who was said to be brother of Egfrid and son of King Oswy. He ably restored the shattered fortunes of the kingdom, though within smaller boundaries.

On the sixth of February in the same year of our Lord 685, King Hlothere of Kent died after a reign of twelve years, his brother Egbert having reigned nine years. He was wounded in battle against the South Saxons, whom Edric, son of Egbert, had raised against him, and he died as his wound was being dressed. This Edric succeeded him and reigned a year and a half; on his death, various alien kings and usurpers plundered the kingdom for a while, until Wictred, son of Egbert, its rightful king, established himself on the throne, and freed the nation from foreign invasion by his devotion and diligence.

IN the year of his death, King Egfrid appointed as Bishop of Lindisfarne the holy and venerable Cuthbert, who for many years had lived a solitary life in great self-mastery of mind and body on a tiny island known as Farne, which lies in the ocean about nine miles from the church. From his earliest boyhood he had always longed to enter the religious life, and as soon as he became a youth was clothed and professed as a monk. He first entered the monastery of Melrose on the banks of the River Tweed, then ruled by Abbot Eata, the gentlest and simplest of men, who later became Bishop of the church of Hexham or Lindisfarne, as already noted. The prior of Melrose was Boisil, a priest of great virtues and prophetic spirit. Cuthbert humbly submitted himself to the direction of Boisil, who gave him instruction in the Scriptures and showed him an example of holy life.

When Boisil departed to our Lord, Cuthbert was made prior in his place and trained many men in the monastic life with masterly authority and by his personal example. He did not restrict his teaching and influence to the monastery, but worked to rouse the ordinary folk far and near to exchange their foolish customs for a love of heavenly joys. For many profaned the Faith that they professed by a wicked life, and at a time of plague some had even abandoned the Christian sacraments and had recourse to the delusive remedies of idolatry, as though they could expect to halt a plague ordained of God by spells, amulets, and other devilish secret arts. Following Boisil's example, in order to correct such errors he often used to leave the monastery, sometimes on horseback but more frequently on foot, and visit the neighbouring towns, where he preached the way of truth to those who had gone astray. In those days, whenever a clerk or priest visited a town, English folk always used to gather at his call to hear the Word, eager to hear his message and even more eager to carry out whatever they had heard and understood. But Cuthbert was so skilful a speaker,

and had such a light in his angelic face, and such a love for
proclaiming his message, that none presumed to hide his inmost
secrets, but all openly confessed their wrong-doing; for they felt
it impossible to conceal their guilt from him, and at his direction
they blotted out by works of penance the sins that they had
confessed. He used mainly to visit and preach in the villages
that lay far distant among high and inaccessible mountains,
which others feared to visit and whose barbarity and squalor
daunted other teachers. Cuthbert, however, gladly undertook
this pious task, and taught with such patience and skill that
when he left the monastery it would sometimes be a week,
sometimes two or three, and occasionally an entire month,
before he returned home, after staying in the mountains to
guide the peasants heavenward by his teachings and virtuous
example.

When this venerable servant of our Lord had spent many
years in the monastery of Melrose and become renowned for
his wonderful acts of virtue, the most reverend Abbot Eata
transferred him to Lindisfarne to instruct the brethren there in
the observance of regular discipline, both in his official capacity
as prior and by his personal example. For the most reverend
Father Eata was then Abbot of Lindisfarne as well. And in
ancient times, the bishop used to reside at Lindisfarne with his
clergy and the abbot with his monks, the latter being regarded
as part of the bishop's household. For Aidan, first Bishop of
Lindisfarne, himself a monk, brought monks with him and
established the regular life there. The blessed Father Augustine
is known to have done the same earlier in Kent, which is shown
in the letter addressed to him by the most reverend Pope
Gregory, which I included earlier: 'In your case, my brother,
having been trained under monastic rule, you should not live
apart from your clergy in the Church of the English, which by
God's help has lately been brought to the Faith. You are to
follow the way of life practised by our forefathers of the
primitive Church, among whom none said that anything which
he possessed was his own, but they had all things common.'

CHAPTER 28: *Cuthbert becomes a hermit: his prayers obtain a spring from dry ground, and a crop from seed sown out of season*

THEN Cuthbert with a growing sense of his religious vocation entered, as I have said, upon a life of solitary contemplation and silence. But, as I wrote a full account of his life and virtues both in heroic verse and prose a few years ago, it may suffice to record here a single incident. When he was about to leave for the island, he assured the brethren: 'If God's grace will enable me to live in this place by the labour of my own hands, I shall gladly remain there; but if it proves otherwise, then, God willing, I will soon return to you.' Now the island had no water, corn, or trees, and being the haunt of evil spirits was very ill-suited to human habitation. But when the man of God came, he ordered the evil spirits to withdraw, and the island became quite habitable. And when he had expelled these hostile forces, the brethren helped him to build a tiny dwelling surrounded with a ditch, and such essential buildings as an oratory and a communal shelter. He then directed the brethren to dig a well in the floor of the shelter, although the ground was hard and stony and there seemed no hope whatever of finding a spring. But they did so, and through the faith and prayers of God's servant it was found full of water next day; and this spring still provides an ample supply of its heaven-sent bounty for those who come here. Cuthbert also asked for farming implements and wheat to be brought him; but although he prepared the ground and sowed at the right season, when summer came, not a single ear of corn had come up, not even so much as a blade. So when the brethren paid their accustomed visit, he asked them to bring some barley, in case the nature of the soil and the laws of the divine Giver required that a crop of this grain rather than wheat should be sown. This he planted in the same soil as soon as it was brought, but after the proper season, when there was no hope of its maturing; nevertheless, a rich crop quickly sprang up, and gave the man of God the much desired opportunity to support himself by his own labour.

Thus Cuthbert served God in solitude for many years in a hut surrounded by an embankment so high that he could see nothing but the heavens for which he longed so ardently. Then it came about that a great Synod was held under the presidency of Archbishop Theodore of blessed memory, and in the presence of King Egfrid. This assembled near the river Alne at a place called Twyford, or the Two Fords; and the whole company unanimously elected Cuthbert as bishop of the church of Lindisfarne. But although many messengers and letters were sent to him, nothing would induce him to abandon his hermitage. At length the king in person, accompanied by the most holy Bishop Trumwine and other devout and distinguished men, took boat to the island. There they were joined by many of the Lindisfarne brethren, and the whole company knelt before him and adjured him in God's name and begged him with tears to consent, until eventually they drew him, also in tears, from his dearly loved retreat, and brought him to the Synod. Still profoundly reluctant, he at length bowed to the unanimous decision of the whole assembly, and was persuaded to assume the burden of episcopal dignity. He was chiefly influenced to do so by the prophetic words of God's servant Boisil, who had foretold all that was to happen to him, and how he would become a bishop. His consecration did not take place at once; but after the winter, which was then approaching, it was performed at York on Easter Day in the presence of King Egfrid by the Primate Theodore of blessed memory, assisted by six other bishops. In the first instance, Cuthbert was appointed to the Bishopric of Hexham in place of Tunbert, who had been deposed: but since he much preferred to rule the church of Lindisfarne, where he had been trained, it was arranged that Eata should return to the See of Hexham, to which he had originally been appointed, and that Cuthbert should assume the direction of the church of Lindisfarne.

As bishop he followed the example of the blessed Apostles and enhanced his dignity by his holy actions, protecting the people entrusted to him by his constant prayer and inspiring them to heavenly things by his salutary teachings. Like a good teacher, he taught others to do only what he first practised himself. Above all else, he was afire with heavenly love, unassumingly patient, devoted to unceasing prayer, and kindly to all who came to him for comfort. He regarded as equivalent to prayer the labour of helping the weaker brethren with advice, remembering that he who said, '*Thou shalt love the Lord thy God*', also said, '*Love thy neighbour*'. His self-discipline and fasting were exceptional, and through the grace of contrition he was always intent on the things of heaven. Lastly, whenever he offered the sacrifice of the Saving Victim of God, he offered his prayers to God not in a loud voice but with tears welling up from the depths of his heart.

CHAPTER 29: *Cuthbert foretells his own death to the hermit Herebert*
[A.D. 687]

WHEN he had spent two years in his bishopric, Cuthbert returned to his island hermitage, God having made known to him that the day of his death was drawing near, or rather, the day of his entry into that life which alone may be called life. In his usual simple way, he mentioned this fact to some people at the time in somewhat veiled terms, though such that they could be clearly understood later; but to others he spoke openly.

There was a priest of praiseworthy life named Herebert, who had for a long time been linked in a spiritual friendship with the man of God. He lived the life of a hermit on an island in the great lake which is the source of the river Derwent, and used to visit Cuthbert each year to seek his advice on matters of eternal salvation. Hearing that Cuthbert had come to the city of Lugubalia,[1] he went to visit him as usual, wishing to be ever more fervently inspired to heavenly desires by his salutary guidance. As each in turn regaled the other with exhilarating draughts of heavenly life, Cuthbert said among other things: 'Brother Herebert, remember that, whatever you wish to ask or

[1] Carlisle.

tell me, you must do before we part, because we shall not see one another again in this world. For I know that the day of my death is approaching, and I shall soon put off this earthly tabernacle.' At these words, the other fell at his feet with sighs and tears, saying: 'In the Name of our Lord, I beg you not to leave me! Remember that I am your most devoted friend, and ask God of His mercy to grant that, as we have served Him together on earth, we may pass away together to the vision of heavenly grace. You know how I have always tried to live as you directed; and whenever I have sinned out of ignorance or frailty, I have at once tried to make amends in any way you enjoined.' So the bishop prostrated himself in prayer, and soon received inward intimation that God had granted his request. 'Rise, my brother, and do not weep. Be glad. For God in His mercy has heard our prayer.'

Subsequent events proved the truths of this prophecy; for when they parted, they never saw one another again in this life and on the twentieth of March, their souls left their bodies on the same day and were together borne by angels to see the beatific vision in the kingdom of heaven. But Herebert was first tried by a long illness. And one may believe that God's mercy decreed this in order that, if his merits were inferior to those of blessed Cuthbert, the chastening of a long illness might supply whatever was lacking: in this way, he would be made equal in grace with his intercessor and in departing this life at the same time would merit to enter into the same state of eternal blessedness.

The most reverend Father Cuthbert died on Farne Island, earnestly requesting the brethren to bury him in this place where he had served God so long. But at length he yielded to their entreaties and consented that his body should be taken back to Lindisfarne and buried within the church. This was accordingly done; and the venerable Bishop Wilfrid held the see for a year until a successor could be appointed. Subsequently Eadbert was consecrated, a man who was well known for his knowledge of the Scriptures, his obedience to God's commandments, and especially for his generosity in almsgiving. For each year, in

accordance with the Law, he used to give a tenth not only of all
his beasts but also of all his grain, fruit and clothing to the poor.

CHAPTER 30: *After eleven years in the grave, Cuthbert's body is
found incorrupt. His successor departs this life soon afterwards*
[A.D. 698]

IN order to make more widely known the height of glory
attained after death by God's servant Cuthbert, whose illustrious life on earth had been marked by so many miracles even
before his death, Divine Providence guided the brethren to
exhume his bones. After eleven years, they expected to find his
flesh reduced to dust and the remains withered, as is usual in
dead bodies; and they proposed to place them in a new coffin
on the same site but above ground level, so that he might
receive the honours due to him. When they informed Bishop
Eadbert of their wish, he gave approval and directed that it
should be carried out on the anniversary of his burial. This was
done; and when they opened the grave, they found the body
whole and incorrupt as though still living and the limbs flexible,
so that he looked as if he were asleep rather than dead.
Furthermore, all the vestments in which he was clothed
appeared not only spotless but wonderfully fresh and fair. At
this sight the brothers were awestruck, and hastened to inform
the bishop of their discovery. At that time he was living alone
at some distance from the church in a place surrounded by the
sea, where he always used to spend Lent and the forty days
before the Nativity of our Lord in fasting, prayer, and penitence.
It was here that his venerable predecessor Cuthbert had served
God in solitude for a period before he went to Farne Island.

The brothers brought with them some of the garments in
which the holy body had been clothed. The bishop received
these gifts with gratitude, and as he listened with joy to their
account of the miracle, he lovingly kissed the garments as
though they were still on the father's body. 'Clothe the body in
new garments,' he said, 'in place of those that you have

removed, and place it in the coffin you have prepared. I have certain knowledge that the grave hallowed by so great and heavenly a miracle will not remain empty for long. And blessed is the man to whom our Lord, the Author and Giver of all bliss, shall grant the privilege of resting in it.' When the bishop had said this and more to the same effect in a trembling voice with tears and deep feeling, the brethren carried out his instructions: having clothed the body in fresh garments, they laid it in a new coffin, which they placed on the pavement of the sanctuary.

Not long afterwards, God's beloved Bishop Eadbert was attacked by an illness that rapidly grew more serious, and in a short time he departed to our Lord on the sixth of May. Whereupon the brethren laid his body in the tomb of the blessed Father Cuthbert, and above it they placed the coffin containing the uncorrupt body of the Father. The miracles of healing that take place from time to time at the tomb bear witness to the holiness of them both. I have recorded some instances in my book on his life. And in this present history I have included further examples that have recently come to my knowledge.

CHAPTER 31: *A brother is cured of paralysis at Cuthbert's tomb*

IN the monastery was a brother named Baduthegn, who served for a considerable time in the guest-house and is still alive. All the brethren and visitors testify that he was a very devout and religious man, who did his appointed task solely for the sake of a heavenly reward. One day he had washed the cloaks used in the guest-house in the sea. As he was returning homewards, he had a sudden seizure and fell to the ground, where he lay prostrate for some time before he could rise. When at last he got up, he found that one side of his body was paralysed from head to foot, and made his way home with the greatest difficulty leaning on a stick. The disease gradually increased and at nightfall became even more serious, so that next day he could hardly rise or walk without help. Crippled as he was, he conceived the excellent plan of making his way to

the church as best he could to visit the tomb of the most
reverend Father Cuthbert. There on bended knee he would
implore God's mercy either to heal his disease, if this were to
his good, or else to give him grace to bear his affliction calmly
and with patience should Divine Providence decree that he be
afflicted with it longer. Acting on this resolve and supporting
his feeble limbs with a staff, he entered the church and prostrated
himself before the body of the man of God, earnestly praying
that at Cuthbert's intercession our Lord would show mercy. As
he prayed, he fell into a deep sleep and, as he used afterwards to
relate, seemed to feel a great, broad hand rest on the seat of the
pain in his head. At this touch, the entire area of his body
affected by the disease was gradually eased of its pain, and health
was restored right down to his feet. He soon awoke and rose
completely cured and after giving thanks to God for his recovery, told the brethren what had happened to him. And to the
joy of all he returned to the duties that he had always carried
out so faithfully, as though chastened by the scourge of
suffering.

The garments that had clothed Cuthbert's hallowed body
both before and after his death continued to possess healing
virtues, as anyone may read in the book of his life and miracles.

CHAPTER 32: *The relics of Saint Cuthbert heal another brother's
diseased eye*

I CANNOT omit mention of a cure that took place through his
relics three years ago and was told me by the very brother to
whom it happened. It occurred in a monastery which was in
course of construction near the river Dacore,[1] from which it
took its name, and whose head was the devout Abbot Swidbert.
In this house lived a young man who developed a tumour on
his eyelid, which daily increased in size and threatened to
destroy the eye. Although the physicians applied poultices to

[1] Dacre, near Penrith.

reduce it, they had no success: some advised cutting it out, while others opposed this, fearing graver complications. So the brother suffered great pain for a long time, and it seemed that no human skill could prevent the loss of his eye, whose condition was deteriorating daily, till he was suddenly cured by the goodness of God and by means of the relics of the most holy father Cuthbert. This came about because, when the brethren found his body uncorrupt after many years in the grave, they had taken some of his hair to provide relics for their friends and to show as evidence of this miracle.

At that time a small portion of these relics was in the possession of Thruidred, then one of the priests of the monastery and now its abbot. And one day, when he went into the church and opened the casket of relics in order to give a portion to a friend who had requested it, the young man with the diseased eye happened to be present. Having given the required portion to his friend, Thruidred handed the remainder to the young man to replace in their casket. Moved by a beneficent impulse, the youth took the hairs of holy Cuthbert's head in his hand and applied them to his eyelid, and tried by holding them there for a while to soften and reduce the swelling. He then replaced the relics in their casket as he had been directed, confident that, now that his eye had been touched by the hair of the man of God, it would soon be cured. Nor was his faith in vain. For, as he tells, it was then about Terce, and thenceforward he was busy about the day's duties until nearly Sext, when he suddenly felt his eye and found both it and the lid sound, as though there had never been any deformity or swelling on it.

BOOK FIVE

✤

CHAPTER I: *The hermit Ethelwald, Cuthbert's successor, calms a storm by his prayer when some brethren are in danger at sea*

CUTHBERT, the man of God, had a successor in the solitary life that he had lived on Farne Island before he became a bishop. This was a venerable man named Ethelwald who had received the priesthood many years previously in the monastery of Ripon and adorned the office by conduct worthy of it. To illustrate more clearly his virtue and the kind of life that he led, I will relate a miracle of his that was told me by one of the brethren among whom and for whose benefit it was performed; this was the venerable priest and servant of Christ Guthfrid, who afterwards presided as abbot over the brethren of the church of Lindisfarne where he had been brought up.

'I came with two other brothers to Farne Island,' he said, 'wishing to speak with the most reverend Father Ethelwald. We were greatly inspired by his discourse and, having asked his blessing, were returning homewards. Then, while we were in the middle of the sea, the calm weather that was favouring our crossing suddenly changed. There followed a storm of such ferocity and violence that sail and oars were useless and we expected nothing but death. Having struggled unavailingly against the wind and waves for a long time, we looked back to see whether it were practicable to fight our way back to the island we had left, but found the storm equally violent on all sides, so that in ourselves there was no hope for us of escape. But, as we looked into the distance, we saw that Father Ethelwald, the beloved of God, had come out of his cell on

Farne and was watching our progress; for he had heard the roar of the gale and raging of the sea and had come out to discover how we were faring. When he saw us in distress and despair, he fell on his knees to the Father of our Lord Jesus Christ and prayed for our safety. Directly his prayer was ended, the raging sea grew calm, the severity of the storm lessened on all sides, and a following wind bore us over calm water towards the land. As soon as we had reached the shore and were lifting our little boat out of the surf, the wind that had dropped awhile for our sakes at once began to blow again and continued strongly all that day. So we realized that the short interval of calm had been granted by the mercy of heaven at the prayer of the man of God so that we might escape.'

The man of God remained on Farne Island for twelve years and died there; but he was buried on the island of Lindisfarne in the church of the blessed Apostle Peter next to the bodies of the above-mentioned bishops. These events took place in the time of King Aldfrid, who succeeded his brother Egfrid as King of the Northumbrians and reigned for nineteen years.

CHAPTER 2: *The blessing of Bishop John cures a dumb man*

A T the beginning of King Aldfrid's reign Bishop Eata died, and was succeeded as Bishop of Hexham by a holy man named John.* Many miracles are told of him by those who knew him well, and in particular by Berthun, a most reverend and truthful man, formerly John's deacon and now abbot of the monastery known as In-Derawuda, which means 'In the wood of the Deiri'.[1] I have thought it fitting to preserve the memory of some of these miracles for posterity.

Whenever opportunity offered and especially during Lent, this man of God used to retire with a few companions to read and pray quietly in an isolated house surrounded by open woodland and a dyke. It stood about a mile and a half from the

---

[1] Now Beverley.

church at Hexham across the river Tyne, and had a burial-
ground dedicated to Saint Michael the Archangel. John once
came to stay here at the beginning of Lent and, as was his
invariable custom, told his companions to find some poor
person who was either seriously infirm or in dire want, so that
he might live with them during their stay and benefit from their
alms.

In a village not far distant lived a dumb youth known to the
bishop; for he had often visited him to receive alms and had
never been able to utter a single word. In addition, he had so
many scabs and scales on his head that no hair ever grew on the
crown, but only a few wisps stood up in a ragged circle round
it. So the bishop ordered this youth to be fetched, and a little
hut to be made for him in the enclosure round the house where
he could live and receive his daily allowance. When one week
of Lent was past, on the following Sunday John told the poor
lad to come to him, and when he had entered he ordered him to
put out his tongue and show it to him; then he took him by the
chin, and making the sign of the holy cross on his tongue, told
him to retract it and speak. 'Pronounce some word,' he said:
'say *yea*,' which is the English word of agreement and assent,
i.e. 'Yes'. The lad's tongue was loosed, and at once he did what
he was told. The bishop then proceeded to the names of letters:
'Say A.' And he said 'A'. 'Now say B,' he said, which the youth
did. And when he had repeated the names of each of the letters
after the bishop, the latter added syllables and words for him to
repeat after him. When he had uttered every word accordingly,
the bishop set him to repeat longer sentences, and he did so. All
those who were present say that all that day and the next night,
as long as he could keep awake, the youth never stopped saying
something and expressing his own inner thoughts and wishes to
others, which he had never been able to do previously. He was
like the cripple healed by the Apostles Peter and John, who
stood up, leaped, and walked, entering the temple with them,
walking, and leaping, and praising God, rejoicing in the use of his
feet, of which he had been so long deprived. The bishop was

delighted at his cure, and directed the physician to undertake the cure of the youth's scabby head.

The physician did as he was asked, and with the assistance of the bishop's blessing and prayers his skin healed, and a vigorous growth of hair appeared. So the youth obtained a clear complexion, readiness of speech, and a beautiful head of hair, whereas he had formerly been deformed, destitute, and dumb. In his joy at this recovery, he declined an offer from the bishop of a permanent place in his household, preferring to return to his own home.

CHAPTER 3: *Bishop John heals a sick girl by his prayers*

BERTHUN described another miracle done by the bishop. When the most reverend Wilfrid became Bishop of Hexham after his long exile, and John became Bishop of York on the death of the holy and humble Bosa, he came one day to a convent of nuns at a place called Wetadun,[1] ruled at the time by the Abbess Heriburg. 'When we had arrived and been welcomed with general rejoicing, the abbess informed us that one of the nuns, her own daughter, was very seriously ill. She told us that the nun had recently been bled in the arm and that, while she was being treated, she was suddenly seized by a violent pain which rapidly increased, so that the wounded arm grew worse and became so swollen that it could hardly be encircled with two hands. In consequence, the nun was lying in bed in terrible pain and seemed likely to die. The abbess therefore begged the bishop to visit her and give her his blessing, being sure that she would improve if the bishop blessed or touched her. He enquired when the girl had been bled, and when he learned that it had been on the fourth day of the moon, he said: "You have acted most foolishly and unwisely to carry out blood-letting on the fourth day of the moon. I remember that Archbishop Theodore, of blessed memory, said that it was

---

[1] Watton, near Beverley.

very dangerous to bleed at a time when the light of the moon and the pull of the tide is increasing. And what can I do for the girl if she is going to die?" But the abbess pressed him most earnestly on behalf of her daughter, who was very dear to her, and whom she intended to appoint abbess in her own place, and at length she prevailed on him to visit the sick girl. So he went in, taking me with him to see the girl who, as I have said, lay helpless and in great pain, with her arm swollen to such a size that she could not bend her elbow. The bishop stood and said a prayer over her, and having given her his blessing, went out. Some while later, as we were sitting at table, someone came in and asked me to come outside, saying: "Coenburg" – for that was the girl's name – "wishes you to come back to her room at once." I did so, and when I entered, I found her looking cheerful and apparently in sound health. And when I sat down by her, she said: "Would you like me to ask for a drink?" "Certainly," I replied, "I shall be delighted if you will." When a cup had been brought and we had both drunk, she began to tell me what had happened. "As soon as the bishop had blessed me and gone away, I began to feel better; and although I have not yet recovered my full strength, the pain has entirely left my arm where it was most intense, and all my body. It was as though the bishop took it away with him entirely when he left, although the swelling on my arm seems to remain." As we were leaving the convent, the disappearance of the pain in her limbs was promptly followed by a subsidence of the swelling, and the girl, saved from pain and death, gave thanks to our Lord and Saviour with all the other servants of God in the place.'

CHAPTER 4: *The Bishop cures a thegn's wife with holy water*

ABBOT BERTHUN also told the story of another miracle not unlike the previous one performed by the bishop. He said: 'Not far from our monastery, about two miles distant, stood the country house of a thegn named Puch, whose wife had been suffering from an acute complaint for forty days, and for three

weeks it had been impossible to move her from the room where
she lay. It had happened at the time that the man of God had
been invited there by the thegn to dedicate a church; and when
he had done this, the thegn asked him to dine in his house. The
bishop declined, saying that he must return to the monastery,
which was close by. But the thegn pressed him even more
earnestly, promising to give alms to the poor if only the bishop
would consent to come into his house to break his fast. I
supported the thegn's request and also promised to give alms to
the poor if he would go in to have a meal in the thegn's house
and give his blessing. After much difficulty, we persuaded him,
and went in for some food. Meanwhile, at the hands of one of
the brethren who had come with us, the bishop had sent the
sick woman some of the holy water that he had blessed for the
dedication of the church, telling him to give her some of it to
drink and to apply some as a lotion to the place where the worst
pain lay. When this had been done, the woman immediately got
up cured. Then finding herself not only relieved of her long
illness but restored to her former strength, she brought a cup to
the bishop and us and, having performed this duty, continued
to serve us with drink until the close of the meal. In this she
followed the example of Saint Peter's wife's mother, who after
being troubled by a burning fever was restored to health and
activity at the touch of the Lord's hand and immediately arose
and ministered to them.'

CHAPTER 5: *The Bishop's prayers recall the servant of a thegn from
death's door*

O N another occasion, the bishop was invited to consecrate
the church of a thegn named Addi. When he had completed the ceremony, the thegn requested him to visit one of his
serving-lads who was so seriously ill that he had completely lost
the use of all his limbs and now seemed about to die: indeed, a
coffin had already been prepared to receive his corpse. The
thegn pressed him with tears, earnestly begging him to go in

and pray for the boy, saying that his life was of great concern to him. He was sure that, if only the bishop were willing to lay his hands on him and bless him, he would recover immediately. So the bishop went in and found the boy at death's door, with the coffin in which he was to be buried lying beside him. All present were in tears. After saying a prayer and giving the boy his blessing, the bishop went out with the stock formula of encouragement: 'Hurry up and get well.' Later, while the company were sitting at table, the boy sent to his master saying he was thirsty and asking if he might have a cup of wine. Delighted that he could drink, the thegn sent him a cup of wine blessed by the bishop, and as soon as he had drunk it he got up, threw off his disease, and put on his clothes. Then he left his room and came in to greet the bishop, saying that he would be glad to join them in eating and drinking. They were delighted at his recovery, and told him to sit down to dine with them; so he sat down and made merry as one of the company. He lived for many years afterwards, and retained the good health that had been restored to him. Abbot Berthun says that he was not present when this miracle took place, but that he had an account of it from those who were.

CHAPTER 6: *By his prayers and blessing, Bishop John saves from death one of his clergy who had been bruised in a fall*

I CANNOT leave unmentioned a miracle that God's servant Heribald relates as having been performed for his benefit by Bishop John. At the time he was one of the bishop's clergy, but is now abbot of a monastery near the mouth of the river Tyne. 'Living with him, and knowing his way of life very intimately,' he says, 'I knew it to be wholly worthy of a bishop, so far as it is permissible for a man to judge. But I also proved by the experience of many others, and more especially by my own, how great his merit was in the eyes of Him who sees the heart; for by his prayer and blessing, as I shall tell, he brought me back from death's door and restored me to life. In my early youth I lived among his clergy, occupied in learning to read and sing; but my heart had not yet entirely abandoned youthful follies. As we were travelling with him one day, we happened to come to a level open road, well suited for galloping our horses. The young men with him, mainly layfolk, began to ask the bishop's permission to gallop and try out their horses against each other. At first he refused their request, saying that it was an unprofitable occupation; but at length he gave in to their unanimous wish, saying: "Do so if you wish; but Heribald is not to take part in the race." I begged him persistently to let me race with the rest, for I had confidence in an excellent horse he had given me; but I could not obtain his consent.

'When they had galloped to and fro several times, and came back spurring their horses in a race while the bishop and I watched, my hot-headed wilfulness got the better of me, and I could not restrain myself. Despite his prohibition, I joined in the sport and began to race with the others at full speed. As I did so, I heard the bishop behind me say in a sorrowful voice: "Oh, how you grieve me by riding like that!" But, although I heard him, I went on against his orders. Shortly afterwards, as my spirited horse took off in a powerful jump across a hollow in the path, I fell, and at once lost all feeling and power of movement as though I were dying; for at the spot lay a stone, level with the ground, lightly covered by turf, the only stone to be found in the whole of that level plain. And it happened by chance, or rather by the disposition of divine providence as a punishment for my disobedience, that I struck my head, and the hand which I had put under my head as I fell, on this stone. As a consequence, my thumb was broken and my skull cracked, and, as I said, I lay as though dead. As I was unable to move, they stretched an awning over me for protection; and from an hour after midday until evening I lay motionless as a corpse. Then I revived slightly, and my companions carried me home, where I lay speechless all night, vomiting blood as a result of some internal injury. The bishop was greatly distressed about my accident and possible death, because he was especially fond of me; and he did not remain with his clergy that night as was his usual custom, but spent all night in vigil and prayer, as I understand, asking God of His mercy to restore me to health. Early next morning he came and said a prayer over me, calling me by name, and waking me out of what seemed to be a heavy sleep. "Do you know who it is speaking to you?" he asked. Opening my eyes, I replied: "I do. You are my beloved bishop." "Can you live?" he asked. "I can do so with the help of your prayers, God willing," I replied.

'Having laid his hand on my head and blessed me, he went back to his prayers. On his return after a short while, he found me sitting up and well enough to talk. Then, inspired by God – as was soon evident – he asked me if I knew for certain whether I had been baptized. I answered that I was sure beyond a doubt that I had been washed in the waters of salvation for the forgiveness of sins; and I told him the name of the priest who had baptized me. But he said: "If you were baptized by that priest, you were not validly baptized. For I know him. When he was ordained priest, he was so slow-witted that he could not learn how to catechize and baptize. For this reason, I ordered him to cease presuming to exercise this ministry, because he was too ignorant to carry it out properly." He then proceeded to catechize me on the spot; and when he happened to breathe on my face, I immediately began to feel better. He called the surgeon, and told him to close and bandage up the crack in my skull. After receiving his blessing, I was so much better next day that I mounted my horse and journeyed on with him to another town. I was soon completely recovered, and was then cleansed in the lifegiving waters of Baptism.'

John remained in his bishopric for thirty-three years, and then entered the kingdom of heaven. He was buried in Saint Peter's porch in his own monastery of In-Derawuda in the year of our Lord 721. When his advanced years prevented him from administering his bishopric, he consecrated his priest Wilfrid to the See of York, and retired to his monastery to end his days in a manner pleasing to God.

CHAPTER 7: *Cadwalla, King of the West Saxons, goes to Rome for Baptism: his successor Ini also makes a pilgrimage of devotion to the shrine of the Apostles* [A.D. 688]

IN the third year of King Aldfrid's reign, Cadwalla, King of the West Saxons, who had governed his people most ably for two years, abdicated from his throne for the sake of our Lord and his eternal kingdom and travelled to Rome. For, having learned that the road to heaven lies open to mankind only through baptism, he wished to obtain the particular privilege of receiving the cleansing of baptism at the shrine of the blessed Apostles. At the same time, he hoped to die shortly after his baptism, and pass from this world to everlasting happiness. By God's grace, both of these hopes were realized. Arriving in Rome during the pontificate of Sergius, he was baptized on Holy Saturday before Easter in the year of our Lord 689, and he fell ill and while still wearing his white robes departed this life on the twentieth of April and joined the company of the blessed in heaven. At the time of his baptism, the aforesaid Pope had given him the name of Peter, in order that he might be linked by name to the most blessed Prince of the Apostles, to whose most sacred body the king's devotion had brought him from the ends of the earth. He was buried in the Apostle's church, and the Pope directed that an epitaph be inscribed on his tomb to preserve the memory of his devotion for ever and inspire all who read or heard of it to religious fervour. This inscription was as follows:

> High rank and wealth, offspring, and mighty realms,
> Triumphs and spoils, great nobles, cities, halls,
> Won by his forbears' prowess and his own –
> All these great Cadwal left for love of God.
> This royal pilgrim then sought Peter's Chair
> To slake his thirst at Peter's vital spring,
> And in his splendid, glowing light to bathe
> From whom life-giving radiance ever streams.
> Eager to win the prize of life renewed,
> Converted, he converts his barbarous ways

And then his name itself to Peter's own
At father Sergius' word, that at the font
Christ's grace may wash him from all taint of sin
And bring him clothed in white to heaven's gate.
Great was his faith; Christ's mercy greater still
Whose secret purpose mortals may not know.
Safely he came from Britain's utmost shores
Through many peoples, over land and sea,
Bearing his mystic gifts, to visit Rome
And in the shrine of Peter lay them down.
Now, robed in white, he moves among Christ's sheep:
His body lies entombed, his soul on high.
Wise king, his earthly sceptre to resign,
And win from Christ in heaven His promised crown.

Cadwalla, also known as Peter, King of the Saxons, was buried here on the twelfth day before the Kalends of May, the second indiction. He lived about thirty years, during the reign of the most pious Emperor Justinian Augustus, in the fourth year of his Consulship, and in the seond year of the pontificate of our apostolic lord Pope Sergius.

On Cadwalla's departure for Rome, he was succeeded as king by Ine, who was of the blood royal. Having ruled the nation for thirty-seven years, Ine also abdicated and handed over the government to younger men.* He then set out to visit the shrines of the blessed Apostles during the pontificate of Gregory [II], wishing to spend some of the time of his earthly pilgrimage in the vicinity of the holy places, hoping thereby to merit a warmer welcome from the saints in heaven. At this period, many English people vied with one another in following this custom, both noble and simple, layfolk and clergy, men and women alike.

CHAPTER 8: *On the death of Theodore, Bertwald becomes archbishop* [A.D. 690]: *among bishops consecrated by him is Tobias, Bishop of Rochester, a man of great learning*

I N the year after Cadwalla's death in Rome, that is, the year of our Lord 690, Archbishop Theodore, of blessed memory, died old and full of years at the age of eighty-eight. He had long previously told his friends that he would die at this age, which had been foretold to him in a dream. He had held the archbishopric for twenty-two years, and was buried in the church of Saint Peter, where all the bodies of the Archbishops of Canterbury are buried. It may be said of him, as of all his colleagues in the same dignity, that *'their bodies are buried in peace, but their name liveth for evermore.'* To summarize briefly, the churches of the English made greater progress during his pontificate than they had ever done before. His epitaph publicly and clearly describes his character, life, age, and death to all who visit his tomb. This consists of thirty-four heroic verses, the first of which run:

> Here rests the holy Primate in his tomb –
> Great Theodore, a Greek by race and name.
> A prince of pontiffs, and a blest high priest
> Who taught to all his flock the light of truth.

And the last verses are:

> The nineteenth of September was the day
> That saw his spirit burst its earthly bonds
> Rising in rapture to a newer life
> In sweet communion with the saints on high.

Theodore's successor in the archbishopric was Bertwald, Abbot of the monastery of Reculver, which stands on the north bank at the mouth of the river Genlade. Although he can hardly be compared with his predecessor, he was learned in the Scriptures and well versed in ecclesiastical and monastic affairs. He was elected bishop on the first of July in the year of our Lord 692, when Wictred and Swaebhard were kings of Kent: but he

was consecrated the following year on Sunday June the twenty-
ninth by Godwin, Metropolitan of Gaul, and occupied his see
on Sunday the thirty-first of August. Berttwald consecrated
many bishops, including Tobias, a man of wide learning and a
scholar of Latin, Greek, and Saxon, who became Bishop of
Rochester on the death of Gebmund.

CHAPTER 9: *Egbert, a holy man, plans to travel to Germany and
preach, but is prevented. Subsequently Wictbert goes, but meeting
with no success, returns to his native Ireland*

A T this time, the venerable servant of Christ, Bishop Egbert,
a man whose name deserves high honour, was living a life
of exile in Ireland, as I have already mentioned, in order to
attain his heavenly home. He planned to bring blessings to more
people by undertaking the apostolic work of preaching the word
of God to some of the nations who had not heard it. He had
learned that there were many such nations in Germany, of
whose stock came the Angles or Saxons now settled in Britain,
who are for this reason still miscalled 'Garmans' by their
neighbours the Britons. These nations include the Frisians,
Rugians, Danes, Huns, Old Saxons, and Boructuars besides
many other races in that region who still observe pagan rites.
So this warrior of Christ planned to sail around Britain and
attempt to snatch some of them from Satan and bring them to
Christ. If this proved impossible, he proposed to travel to
Rome, to visit and venerate the shrines of the blessed Apostles
and martyrs of Christ.*

From the execution of either of these projects, however, he
was stayed by heavenly portents and manifestations. He had
already chosen the boldest of his companions, whose distinguished lives and learning rendered them well fitted to preach
the Gospel, and all preparations for the voyage were complete.
Then early one morning he received a visit from one of the
brethren, who had formerly been a disciple and assistant in
Britain to God's beloved priest Boisil, when, as already related,

he was Prior of the monastery of Melrose under Abbot Eata. This brother told him of a vision which he had seen that night: 'After the morning hymns,' he said, 'I had lain down on my pallet and fallen into a light sleep, when my old master and most loving teacher Boisil appeared to me, and asked whether I recognized him. "Of course I do," I said: "you are Boisil." He then said: "I have come to bring a message from our Lord and Saviour to Egbert, which you must deliver to him. Tell him that he is not to go on the journey that he has in mind; for it is God's will that he should go and instruct the monks of Columba."' Now Columba was the first teacher of the Christian Faith to the Picts living north of the mountains, and founder of the monastery on the Isle of Iona, which long remained venerated by the people of the Picts and Irish. For this reason, Columba is now known by some people as Columbkill, a name compounded from 'Columba' and 'cell'. When Egbert had heard about this vision, he ordered the brother who had related it not to tell anyone else, in case the vision were a delusion; but silently turning it over in his own mind, Egbert feared that it was true. But he did not abandon his preparations for his voyage to evangelize the heathen.

After a few days, this brother came to him once more, saying that Boisil had again appeared to him in a vision after Matins, saying: 'Why did you convey the message that I gave you for Egbert in such a careless and offhand fashion? Now go and tell him that, whether he wishes it or not, he is to visit the monks of Columba, because their ploughs do not run stráight and it is his duty to recall them to the right way.' Hearing this, Egbert again enjoined the brother not to disclose the vision to anyone. But although he was now convinced of the vision's reality, he none the less attempted to carry out his projected voyage with the brethren. Then, when they had stored the ship with everything necessary for the voyage and had waited some days for a favourable wind, a storm of such violence arose one night that the ship was left lying on her beam ends among the breakers, and part of her stores was lost. However, everything that belonged to Egbert and his companions was salvaged. Then, like the prophet Jonah, Egbert said: '*For my sake this great tempest is upon you.*' So he abandoned his plan, and resigned himself to staying at home.

But among Egbert's companions was one called Wictbert, well known for his contempt for worldly things and for his knowledge of doctrine, who had lived the life of a hermit in great perfection for many years as an exile in Ireland. Wictbert took ship and arrived in Frisia, where he preached the word of life constantly for two years to the people and their king Radbod; but his great efforts produced no results among his barbaric hearers. He then returned to his beloved land of exile and began to give himself to our Lord in his accustomed silence. And since he had been unable to help foreigners towards the Faith, he sought to be of more help to his own people by setting them a holy example.

CHAPTER 10: *Willibrord preaches in Frisia and converts many to Christ: his companions the Hewalds suffer martyrdom* [A.D. 692]

So the man of God, Egbert, realized that he was not permitted to go and preach to the heathen, and that he was retained to be of some other service to the Holy Church, as he had been forewarned by the vision. But, although he knew that Wictbert had enjoyed no success when he visited those parts, he still attempted to send other holy and zealous men for the work of preaching, among whom the outstanding figure by his priestly rank and his merit was one named Willibrord.* When he and his twelve companions arrived, they made a detour to visit Pippin, Duke of the Franks, by whom they were graciously received. Since Pippin had recently conquered western Frisia and driven out King Radbod, he dispatched them to preach there, supporting them with his imperial authority so that no one should interfere with their preaching, and granting many favours to those who wished to embrace the Faith. Consequently, aided by God's grace, they converted many folk in a short while from idolatry to belief in Christ.

Two other priests of English race, who had long lived as exiles in Ireland for the sake of the eternal kingdom, followed their lead and went to the province of the Old Saxons in order to try and win them for Christ by their teaching. They shared the same name and the same zeal, but with the distinction that, since their hair was of different colour, one was known as Hewald the Black, and the other as Hewald the White. Both men were devout and religious, but Hewald the Black was more learned in the holy scriptures. On entering the province, they were given hospitality by a certain reeve, whom they asked to conduct them to his lord, as they had a message to his advantage which they were bound to communicate to him. For these Old Saxons have no king, but several lords who are set over the nation. Whenever war is imminent, these cast lots impartially, and the one on whom the lot falls is followed and obeyed by all for the duration of the war; but as soon as the war ends, the lords revert to equality of status. So the reeve received and kept them with him for some days, promising to send them as they had asked to the lord to whom he was subject.

Now the Hewalds devoted themselves to psalms and prayers, and daily offered the sacrifice of the saving Victim to God, having with them sacred vessels and a consecrated table for use as an altar. And when the barbarous people realized that they belonged to a different religion, they began to distrust them, fearing that if they went to their lord and spoke to him, they might turn him from his gods and convert him to the new practice of the Christian Faith, so that the whole province would gradually be compelled to change its old religion for new. So they suddenly seized them and put them to death: Hewald the White was killed outright with a sword, and Hewald the Black was put to lingering torture and torn agonizingly limb from limb. Then they flung the murdered men into the Rhine. When the lord whom they had wished to see heard of this, he was extremely angry that strangers desiring to see him had not been allowed to do so; and he sent and slew all the villagers and burned down their village. These priests and servants of Christ suffered on the third of October.*

Their martyrdom was not unmarked by heavenly signs; for when their bodies were thrown into the Rhine by the heathen, as I have described, they were carried upstream against the current for nearly forty miles to the place where their companions were. And a great ray of light reaching high into the sky shone all night above the spot where the bodies had arrived, and was also seen by the heathen who had murdered them. Moreover one of the two appeared by night in a vision to one of their companions, a distinguished man of noble family named Tilmon, a soldier turned monk, and told him that their bodies would be found at the spot where he saw the light shining from heaven to earth. This happened as he said: their bodies were found and buried with the honour due to martyrs, and the day of their death, or of the finding of their bodies, is observed in those parts with fitting respect. When Pippin, the most illustrious Duke of the Franks, later heard of these events, he directed that the bodies be brought to him, and buried them with great splendour in the church of the city of Cologne on the Rhine. It is said that a spring bubbled up at the scene of the martyrdom, which affords a plentiful supply of water to this day.

CHAPTER 11: *The venerable Swidbert in Britain, and Willibrord in Rome, are consecrated bishops for Frisia* [A.D 692]

ON their first arrival in Frisia, as soon as Willibrord learned that the prince had granted him permission to preach, he hurried to Rome, where Pope Sergius then ruled the apostolic see, in order to obtain his approval and blessing on the evangelistic work he wished to undertake. He also hoped to obtain from him relics of the blessed Apostles and martyrs of Christ, so that when he had destroyed the idols and built churches among the people to whom he preached, he might have the relics of the saints ready to put in them. And when he had deposited them, he intended to dedicate these places fittingly in honour of each of the saints whose relics they were. He also wished to learn and obtain many other things required for carrying out so formidable a task. And having obtained all that he wanted, he returned to preach.

At this time the brethren who were engaged in the ministry of the word in Frisia elected one of their number named Swidbert, who was modest in his ways and humble-hearted, to be consecrated their bishop. And they sent him to Britain, where, at their request, he was consecrated by the most reverend Bishop Wilfrid, who happened to be driven out of his own country at the time and was living in exile among the Mercians. For there was no bishop in Kent at this juncture, Theodore having died and Bertwald his successor, who had crossed the sea to be consecrated, having not yet returned to his episcopal see.

When he had been made bishop, Swidbert returned from Britain and shortly afterwards went to the Boructuars, many of whom he guided into the way of truth by his teaching. But after a short while, the Boructuars were defeated by the Old Saxons, and those who had accepted the word of God were scattered. The bishop himself went with certain others to Pippin, who at the request of his wife Plectrude, gave them a place of residence on an island in the Rhine, which in their language is called 'On the shore'.[1] Here he established a monastery, which is still occupied by his successors, and after leading a most austere life for some while, he ended his days there.

When those who had come over had taught in Frisia for a number of years, Pippin with their unanimous consent dispatched the venerable Willibrord to Rome, where Sergius was still Pope, with the request that he might be consecrated Archbishop of the Frisian nation. His request was carried out in the year of our Lord 696, and Willibrord was consecrated in the church of the holy martyr Cecilia on her feast day, when the Pope gave him the name of Clement. He was sent back to his bishopric without delay, fourteen days after his arrival in the city.

[1] Now Kaiserswerth.

Pippin assigned him a place for his see in his own famous castle, which is known in the ancient language of that people as Wiltaburg, that is, the Town of the Wilts; but it is known in the Gallic tongue as Utrecht. Having built a church here, the most reverend prelate preached the word of God far and wide, recalling many from their errors and establishing several churches and a number of monasteries in those parts. And now long afterwards he appointed a number of bishops, choosing them from among the brethren who had come with him or after him to preach. Some of these have now fallen asleep in the Lord, but Willibrord himself, surnamed Clement, is still living, and is much revered for his great age. He has been thirty-six years a bishop, and after the countless spiritual battles he has fought, longs with all his heart for the prize of a heavenly reward.

CHAPTER 12: *A man in the Province of the Northumbrians returns from the dead, and tells of the many dreadful and many desirable things that he saw*

ABOUT this time, a noteworthy miracle, like those of olden days, occurred in Britain.* For, in order to arouse the living from spiritual death, a man already dead returned to bodily life and related many notable things that he had seen, some of which I have thought it valuable to mention here in brief. There was a head of a family living in a place in the country of the Northumbrians known as Cunningham, who led a devout life with all his household. He fell ill and grew steadily worse until the crisis came, and in the early hours of one night he died. But at daybreak he returned to life and suddenly sat up to the great consternation of those weeping around the body, who ran away; only his wife, who loved him more dearly, remained with him, though trembling and fearful. The man reassured her and said: 'Do not be frightened; for I have truly risen from the grasp of death, and I am allowed to live among men again. But henceforward I must not live as I used to, and

. must adopt a very different way of life.' Then he rose and went
off to the village church, where he continued in prayer until
daybreak. He then divided all his property into three parts, one of
which he allotted to his wife, another to his sons, and the third he
retained and distributed at once to the poor. Not long afterwards,
he abandoned all worldly responsibilities and entered the monastery of Melrose, which is almost completely surrounded by a
bend in the river Tweed. There he was given the tonsure and
entered a separate part of the house allotted him by the abbot,
where he entered upon a life of such physical and spiritual
penance to the day of his death that, even if he had kept silence,
his life would have witnessed that he had seen many dreadful
and many desirable things that remained hidden from others.

This was the account he used to give of his experience: 'A
handsome man in a shining robe was my guide, and we walked
in silence in what appeared to be a north-easterly direction. As
we travelled onwards, we came to a very broad and deep valley
of infinite length. The side to our left was dreadful with burning
flames, while the opposite side was equally horrible with raging
hail and bitter snow blowing and driving in all directions. Both
sides were filled with men's souls, which seemed to be hurled
from one side to the other by the fury of the tempest. For when
the wretches could no longer endure the blast of the terrible
heat, they leaped into the heart of the terrible cold; and finding
no refuge there, they leaped back again to be burned in the
middle of the unquenchable flames. A countless host of
deformed spirits were tormented far and wide in this wretched
condition without any interval of respite as far as the eye could
see, and I began to think that perhaps this was Hell, of whose
intolerable torments I had often heard tell. But, as if in response
to my thoughts, the guide who preceded me said: "Do not think
this; for this is not Hell as you imagine."

'When he had led me gradually to the further end, much
alarmed by the terrible scene, I saw the place suddenly begin to
grow dim, and darkness concealed everything. As we entered
it, this darkness gradually grew so dense that I could see nothing
except it and the outline and robes of my guide. And as we

went on "through the nocturnal, solitary gloom",★ frequent
masses of dusky flame suddenly appeared before us, rising as
though from a great pit and falling back into it again. When my
guide had brought me to this place, he suddenly disappeared
and left me alone in the midst of the darkness before this
horrible scene. Meanwhile these masses of flame continued
ceaselessly leaping up and falling back again into the depths of
the chasm, and I saw that, as the tongues of flame rose, they
were filled with the souls of men which, like sparks flying up
with the smoke, were sometimes flung high in the air, and at
others dropped back into the depths as the vapours of the fire
died down. Furthermore, an indescribable stench welled up
with these vapours, and filled the whole of this gloomy place.

'When I had stood there a long time terrified, not knowing
what to do, where to turn, or what would happen to me, I
suddenly heard behind me the sound of a most hideous and
desperate lamentation, accompanied by harsh laughter, as
though a rough mob were mocking captured enemies. As the
noise increased and drew nearer, I saw a throng of wicked spirits
dragging with them five human souls howling and lamenting
into the depths of the darkness while the devils laughed and
exulted. I saw among them one man tonsured like a clerk, a
layman, and a woman. The wicked spirits dragged them down
into the centre of the burning chasm, and as they descended
deeper, I could no longer distinguish the weeping of the men
from the laughter of the devils, but heard only a confused noise
in my ears. Meanwhile, some of the dark spirits emerged from
the fiery depths and rushed to surround me, harassing me with
their glowing eyes and foul flames issuing from their mouths
and nostrils. They threatened to seize me with the glowing
tongs that they brandished in their hands, but although they
frightened me, they did not dare to touch me. While I was thus
beset about by enemies and black darkness and looked everywhere for some means of help to save me, there appeared behind
me on the road by which I had come what seemed to be a bright
star shining in the gloom, which grew in size and came swiftly

towards me. As it approached, all the evil spirits who had tried
to drag me away with their tongs, scattered and took to flight.

'The newcomer whose approach put them to flight was my
former guide, who took a road to the right and began to lead
me towards the south-east. He soon brought me out of darkness
into an atmosphere of clear light, and as he led me forwards in
bright light, I saw before us a tremendous wall which seemed
to be of infinite length and height in all directions. As I could
see no gate, window, or entrance in it, I began to wonder why
we went up to the wall. But when we reached it, all at once – I
know not by what means – we were on top of it. Within lay a
very broad and pleasant meadow, so filled with the scent of
flowers that its wonderful fragrance quickly dispelled all the
stench of the gloomy furnace that had overcome me. Such was
the light flooding all this place that it seemed greater than the
brightness of daylight or of the sun's rays at noon. In this
meadow were innumerable companies of men in white robes,
and many parties of happy people were sitting together. And as
my guide led me through these crowds of happy citizens, I
began to wonder whether this was the Kingdom of Heaven, of
which I had heard so often. But in response to my thought he
said: "No, this is not the Kingdom of Heaven as you imagine."

'When we had passed through these abodes of blessed spirits
and progressed further, I saw ahead of us a much more lovely
light than before, and heard in it a sweet sound of people
singing, while a scent of such surpassing fragrance emanated
from the place that the earlier scent that I had thought so
wonderful now seemed quite trifling. And even the wonderful
light that had flooded the flowery meadow seemed thin and dim
when compared with that now visible. As I was hoping that we
should enter this delightful place, my guide suddenly halted
and, without stopping, retraced his steps and led me back along
the road by which we had come.

'When we returned to the happy dwellings of the souls robed
in white, he asked me: "Do you know what all these things are
that you have seen?" "No," I replied. Then he said: "The valley
that you saw, with its horrible burning flames and icy cold, is

the place where souls are tried and punished who have delayed
to confess and amend their wicked ways, and who at last had
recourse to penitence at the hour of death, and so depart this
life. Because they confessed and were penitent, although only at
death, they will all be admitted into the Kingdom of Heaven on
the Day of Judgement. But many are helped by the prayers,
alms, and fasting of the living, and especially by the offering of
Masses, and are therefore set free before the Day of Judgement.
The fiery, noisome pit that you saw is the mouth of Hell, and
whosoever falls into it will never be delivered throughout
eternity. This flowery place, where you see these fair young
people so happy and resplendent, is where souls are received
who die having done good, but are not so perfect as to merit
immediate entry into the Kingdom of Heaven. But at the Day
of Judgement they shall all see Christ and enter upon the joys of
His heavenly Kingdom. And whoever are perfect in word,
deed, and thought, enter the Kingdom of Heaven as soon as
they leave the body. The Kingdom is situated near the place
where you heard the sound of sweet singing, with the sweet
fragrance and glorious light. You must now return to your
body and live among men once more; but, if you will weigh
your actions with greater care and study to keep your words
and ways virtuous and simple, then when you die you too will
win a home among these happy spirits that you see. For, when
I left you for a while, I did so in order to discover what your
future would be." When he told me this, I was most reluctant
to return to my body; for I was entranced by the pleasantness
and beauty of the place I could see and the company that I saw
there. But I did not dare to question my guide, and meanwhile,
I know not how, I suddenly found myself alive among men
once more.'

This man of God would not discuss these and other things
that he had seen with any apathetic or careless-living people,
but only with those who were haunted by fear of punishment
or gladdened by the hope of eternal joys, and were willing to
take his words to heart and grow in holiness. But in the vicinity
of his cell lived a monk named Haemgils, an eminent priest who

adorned his office with good deeds: he is still living, and leads the life of a hermit in Ireland, supporting his latter years on a diet of bread and cold water. He often used to visit this man, and by repeated questioning learned from him what sort of things he had seen when freed from the body; and it is from this account that I have come to know these details that I have briefly described. He also related his vision to King Aldfrid, a man of wide learning, who listened so readily and attentively to him that, at his request, he was admitted to the above monastery and received the monastic tonsure. And whenever the king visited those parts, he frequently went to listen to him. At the time of these events, the ruler of the monastery was the religious and humble abbot and priest Ethelwald, who at present most worthily occupies the episcopal see of the church of Lindisfarne.

This man was given a more secluded dwelling in the monastery, so that he could devote himself more freely to the service of his Maker in unbroken prayer. And since this place stands on the bank of a river, he often used to enter it for severe bodily penance, and plunge repeatedly beneath the water while he recited psalms and prayers for as long as he could endure it, standing motionless with the water up to his loins and sometimes to his neck. When he returned to shore, he never removed his dripping, chilly garments, but let them warm and dry on his body. And in winter, when the half-broken cakes of ice were swirling around him which he had broken to make a place to stand and dip himself in the water, those who saw him used to say: 'Brother Drythelm (for that was his name), it is wonderful how you can manage to bear such bitter cold.' To which he, being a man of simple disposition and self-restraint, would reply simply: 'I have known it colder.' And when they said: 'It is extraordinary that you are willing to practise such severe discipline', he used to answer: 'I have seen greater suffering.' So until the day of his summons from this life he tamed his aged body by daily fasting, inspired by an insatiable longing for the blessings of heaven, and by his words and life he helped many people to salvation.

CHAPTER 13: *Devils show another man a record of his sins before his death*

QUITE the reverse happened in the case of a man living in the province of the Mercians, whose visions and words – although not his way of life – benefited many others, but not himself. For in the reign of Coenred, Ethelred's successor, there was a layman who held a military command, and pleased the king as greatly by his public diligence as he displeased him by the carelessness of his private life. The king repeatedly warned him to confess and amend, and to abandon his wicked ways before a sudden death deprived him of any time for repentance and amendment. But, although frequently warned, he rejected his salutary advice, and promised that he would do penance at some future date. Meanwhile he fell ill and, taking to his bed, began to suffer severe pains. The king, who was fond of him, visited him and urged him even then to repent of his sins before he died. But he answered that he did not wish to confess his sins at this time, but would do so when he recovered from his illness; for he did not wish his friends to accuse him of doing in fear of death what he had refused to do when he was well. He thought that he had spoken bravely, but it soon became clear that he had been deceived by the Devil's tricks.

As his illness grew more serious, the king again came to visit and reason with him; but the man at once cried out in a miserable voice: 'What do you want now? Why have you come here? There is nothing that you can do to help or save me now.' The king answered: 'Do not talk like that. Stop acting like a madman.' 'I am not mad,' he replied, 'but I have the knowledge of my wickedness set clearly before my eyes.' 'What do you mean by that?' the king asked. 'A short time ago,' the man said, 'two very handsome youths entered this house and sat down beside me, one at my head and the other at my feet. One of them produced a tiny but very beautiful book and gave it to me to read. When I looked at it, I found all the good deeds that I had ever done recorded; but they were few and trifling. Then they took back the book, but said nothing to me. Suddenly there arrived a horde of wicked spirits with horrible faces, who surrounded the house and occupied the greater part of it. Then one, who from the blackness of his dusky face and his exalted position seemed to be their chief, produced a horrible-looking book of enormous size and almost unbearable weight, which he ordered one of his satellites to bring me to read. When I read it, I found all my crimes clearly recorded there in black letters, not only sins of act and word, but even of the least thought. And he said to the glorious white-robed men who were sitting beside me: "Why are you sitting here? You know very well that this man belongs to us." They replied: "You are right. Take him, and enrol him in your company of the damned." With these words, they immediately vanished, and two wicked spirits rose and struck me with the tridents in their hands, one on the head and the other on the foot. These blows are now penetrating the inmost parts of my body with awful agony, and when they meet, I shall die. The devils will be waiting to snatch me away, and I shall be dragged down through the gates of Hell.'

So spoke the wretched man in his despair, and died shortly afterwards. So he is now vainly undergoing everlasting torments because he refused to undergo penance for a short while to win the grace of pardon. In his case it is clear – as Pope Gregory writes of certain people – that he did not see these things for his own benefit, since they did not help him, but for the benefit of others. For, when people learned of his death, they would fear to delay their penance while they still had time, lest the intervention of sudden death might cause them to perish unrepentant. When this man saw good and evil spirits offering him different records, this was done by divine providence in order that we should remember that our actions and thoughts are not scattered by the wind, but are all preserved to be examined by the Supreme Judge, and will be shown to us at the last either by our friends the angels or by our enemies. And whereas the white-robed angels first produced a white record, and the devils a black, the former tiny and the latter enormous, let it be noted that in his early years he did some good deeds which he completely obscured by his evil-doing as a grown man. In contrast, if in his manhood he had taken care to correct the errors of his childhood and cancel them in God's eyes by well-doing, he might have been assigned to the company of those mentioned in the psalm: '*Blessed are they whose transgression is forgiven, and whose sin is covered.*' I have thought that this story should be told in a straightforward way, as I have heard it from the venerable Bishop Pecthelm, to further the salvation of those who may read or hear it.

CHAPTER 14: *Another man about to die sees the place of punishment reserved for him in Hell*

I MYSELF know a brother – Ah, how I wish I had never known him! – whose name I could mention were it desirable, who lived in a noble monastery but lived an ignoble life. He was often taken to task by the brethren and authorities of the house and warned to adopt a more disciplined life; and although he refused to listen to them, they bore with him patiently because they had need of his manual labour; for he was a skilled worker in metal. But he was much addicted to drunkenness and the other pleasures of a loose life, and used to remain in his workshop day and night rather than enter the church to sing and pray and to listen to the word of life with the brethren. So it happened to him according to the proverb that 'he that will not go through the church door in contrition willingly must needs be thrust through Hell', door in damnation unwillingly'. Falling ill, he summoned the brethren to his death-bed and, groaning like one already damned, began to describe to them how he saw Hell open, and Satan in the depths of the abyss, with Caiaphas and others who had slain our Lord condemned like him to the avenging flames. 'Close to them, alas,' he cried, 'I see a place of eternal doom prepared for my wretched self!' As the brethren listened, they began earnestly to urge him to repent while he remained in the body, but he answered in despair: 'There is no time left for me to amend my ways. I have already seen my judgement pronounced.'

With these words, he died without receiving the saving Viaticum, and his body was buried in the remote part of the monastery, nor did anyone dare to say masses or sing psalms for him, or even to pray for him. Oh, by how vast a distance has God divided the light from the darkness! When the blessed Proto-martyr Stephen was about to die for the truth, he *saw the heavens opened, the glory of God revealed, and Jesus standing on the right hand of God.* And in order that he might die the happier, he fixed his mental gaze before death on the place where he hoped to be after death. In contrast the metal worker, a man of dark thoughts and deeds, saw Hell open as death drew near, and saw the damnation of the Devil and his followers. The unhappy man even saw his own place of punishment among them, so that he might despair of salvation and die in greater misery, but also that through his own perdition he might bequeath a means of salvation to the living who learned of his fate. This happened recently in the Province of the Bernicians, and was talked of far and wide, rousing many people to do penance for their sins without delay. And may the reading of this account have the same effect.

CHAPTER 15: *Under Adamnan's influence, many churches of the Irish adopt the Catholic Easter. He writes a book on the Holy Places* [*c.* A.D. 703]

AT this period, by the grace of God, the majority of the Irish in Ireland, together with some of the Britons in Britain, conformed to the logical and canonical time of keeping Easter. Adamnan,★ priest and abbot of the monks who lived on the Isle of Iona, was sent by his nation on a mission to Aldfrid, King of the English, and remained in his province for some while, where he observed the rites of the Church canonically performed. He was earnestly advised by many who were more learned than himself not to presume to act contrary to the universal customs of the Church, whether in the keeping of Easter or in any other observances, seeing that his following was very small and situated in a remote corner of the world. As a result he changed his opinions, and readily adopted what he saw and heard in the churches of the English in place of the customs of his own people. For he was a wise and worthy man, excellently grounded in knowledge of the Scriptures.

On his return home, he tried to lead his own people in Iona and those who were under the jurisdiction of that monastery into the correct ways that he had himself learned and whole-heartedly accepted; but in this he failed. Then he sailed over to preach in Ireland, and by his simple teaching showed its people the proper time of Easter. He corrected their ancient error and restored nearly all who were not under the jurisdiction of Iona to Catholic unity, teaching them to observe Easter at the proper time. Having observed the canonical Easter in Ireland, he returned to his own island, where he vigorously pressed his own monastery to conform to the Catholic observance of Easter, but had no success in his attempts. Before the close of the next year he departed this life. For God in his goodness decreed that so great a champion of peace and unity should be received into everlasting life before the time of Easter returned once more, and before he should be obliged to enter upon more serious controversy with those who refused to follow him in the truth.

Adamnan also wrote a book about the Holy Places, which is most valuable to many readers. The man who dictated the information to him was Arculf, a bishop from Gaul who had visited Jerusalem to see the Holy Places. Having toured all the Promised Land, Arculf had travelled to Damascus, Constantinople, Alexandria, and many islands; but as he was returning home, his ship was driven by a violent storm on the western coast of Britain. After many adventures, he visited Christ's servant Adamnan, who, finding him learned in the Scriptures and well acquainted with the Holy Places, was glad to welcome him and even more glad to listen to him. As a result, he rapidly committed to writing everything of interest that Arculf said that he had seen at the Holy Places. And by this means, as I have said, he compiled a work of great value to many people,

especially those who live at a great distance from the places
where the patriarchs and Apostles lived, and whose only source
of information about them lies in books. Adamnan presented
this book to King Aldfrid, and through his generosity it was
circulated for lesser folk to read. The writer himself was sent
back to his own land richer by many gifts. And I think it will
be valuable to readers of this history if I make some extracts
from this book, and include them in this history.

CHAPTER 16: *Descriptions from this book of the sites of our Lord's
Birth, Passion, and Resurrection*

A DAMNAN wrote about our Lord's birthplace as follows:
'Bethlehem, the city of David, is situated on a narrow ridge
almost entirely enclosed by valleys. It is a thousand paces in
length from east to west, and has a low wall without towers
built around the circumference of the plateau. At the eastern
corner is a kind of natural grotto, the outer part of which is said
to have been the place of our Lord's birth while the inner part is
known as our Lord's manger. The interior of this grotto is
entirely faced with precious marble over the exact spot where
our Lord is said to have been born, and above it stands the lofty
church of Saint Mary.'

On the site of Christ's Passion and Resurrection, he writes as
follows:

'For those entering the city of Jerusalem from the northern
side, the lay-out of the streets makes the Church of Constantine,
known as the Martyrdom, the first of the Holy Places to be
visited. This was erected by the Emperor Constantine in a
magnificent regal style, for this is the place where his mother
Helena discovered the Cross of our Lord. To the west, the
Church of Golgotha comes into view, where can be seen the
rock on which once stood the Cross, with the Body of our Lord
nailed to it: it now supports an enormous silver cross, over
which hangs a great bronze wheel bearing lamps. Beneath the
site of our Lord's Cross a crypt has been hewn out of the rock,

and the Holy Sacrifice is offered for the honoured dead on an altar here, while their bodies are left for the time outside in the street. To the west of this stands the Church of the Anastasis, which is the church of our Lord's Resurrection, circular in shape, surrounded by three walls, and supported on twelve columns. Between the walls are two broad passages, where three altars stand at three places against the central wall, to the north, south, and west. There are eight doors or entrances through the three walls, four facing east and four facing west. In the centre is the circular Tomb of our Lord, cut out of the rock, and a man standing inside it can touch the roof with his hand. The entrance faces eastward, and against it stands the great stone, which still bears the marks of iron tools. The exterior is completely covered with marble to the top of the roof, which is adorned with gold and bears a great golden cross. The Sepulchre of our Lord is cut out of the north side of the Tomb; it is seven feet in length, and raised three palms' breadth above the pavement. The entrance is on the south side, where twelve lamps burn day and night, four inside the sepulchre itself, and eight above it on the right-hand side. The stone that once formed the door of the Tomb has now been broken, but the smaller portion stands as a small square altar in front of the Tomb, while the larger portion forms another altar at the eastern end of the same Church, and is draped with linen cloths. The colour of the Tomb and Sepulchre is a mingled white and red.'

CHAPTER 17: *The site of our Lord's Ascension, and the tombs of the patriarchs*

ON the site of our Lord's Ascension, Adamnan writes: 'The Mount of Olives is the same height as Mount Sion but is broader and longer. It is sparsely wooded, except for olives and vines, but grows wheat and barley for the soil is thin and suitable only for grass and flowers. On the very top of the hill, where our Lord ascended into heaven, stands a lofty circular church, with three roofed-in porches on the outside. The interior of the building could not be roofed and vaulted because of the upward flight of our Lord's body; but it has an altar on the east side, protected by a narrow canopy. In the centre of the Church, where our Lord ascended, can be seen His last footprints, exposed to the sky above. And although the earth is daily removed by the faithful, it remains undiminished, and still retains these marks resembling footprints. Round these lies a bronze wheel, as high as a man's neck, with great lamps hanging above it on a pulley and burning day and night. On the west side of the Church are eight windows and as many lamps hanging opposite them on cords. These cast their rays through the glass as far as Jerusalem, and their light is said to evoke a feeling of ardour and penitence in the hearts of all who see it. Each year on the day of our Lord's Ascension, at the end of Mass, a powerful rush of wind descends from above and throws to the ground all who are in the Church.'

On the situation of Hebron, and the tombs of the patriarchs, Adamnan writes:

'Hebron, once a city and the capital of David's kingdom, now only shows what it was by its ruins. In a valley one furlong to the east of it is a double cave, where the tombs of the patriarchs are enclosed in a square wall with their heads to the north. Each tomb is covered by a single stone slab, cut like those in a church: those of the three patriarchs are white, while that of Adam is of humbler and inferior workmanship, and lies not far from the others at the northern extremity of the wall. There are also three smaller and plainer monuments to three women. The hill of Mamre rises a thousand paces away from these monuments to the north, and is covered with grass and flowers. There is a level plateau at the summit, to the north of which stands Abraham's Oak – a trunk twice the height of a man, enclosed in a church.'

I have thought it useful to include these extracts from the works of the above author for the benefit of those who read this history, and have retained the sense of his words but summarized them in a shorter form. Should anyone wish to know more about this book, they may either study it in the original form or read the abridgement containing short extracts which I have recently compiled.

CHAPTER 18: *The South Saxons receive as their bishops Eadbert and Ealla, and the West Saxons Daniel and Aldhelm. The writings of Aldhelm* [c. A.D. 705]

IN the year of our Lord 705, Aldfrid, King of the Northumbrians, died after a reign of nearly twenty years, and was succeeded on the throne by his son Osred, a boy of about eight years of age, who reigned eleven years. At the commencement of his reign, Bishop Haeddi of the West Saxons departed to the life of heaven. He was a good, just man, who carried out his duties as bishop guided by an inborn love of goodness rather than by anything learned from books. The most reverend Bishop Pecthelm – of whom more will be said in due course – who was a fellow-monk or deacon for a long time with Haeddi's successor Aldhelm, relates how many miracles of healing occurred through Haeddi's holiness at the place where he died. He says that the people of that province used to carry away earth from it to mix in water for the sick, and that many sick men and beasts who drank or were sprinkled with it were restored to health. In consequence, there was a considerable pit created there by the continual removal of the hallowed soil.

At his death, the bishopric of the province was divided into two dioceses, one of which was assigned to Daniel,★ who rules it to this day, and the other to Aldhelm,★ who administered it with great energy for four years. Both bishops were well acquainted with church matters and learned in the study of the Scriptures. While Aldhelm was still a priest, and abbot of the monastery known as Maelduib's Town,[1] he was directed by a synod of his own people to write a notable treatise against the errors of the Britons in observing Easter at the wrong time and doing other things contrary to the orthodoxy and unity of the

---

[1] Malmesbury, Wiltshire.

Church. By means of this book he persuaded many of those Britons who were subject to the West Saxons to conform to the Catholic observance of our Lord's Resurrection. He also wrote an excellent book *On Virginity*, which he composed in a double form in hexameter verse and prose on the model of Sedulius. He also wrote other books; for he was a man of wide learning, with a polished style and, as I have said, extremely well-read both in biblical and general literature. At his death, Forthere, who is also a man of great learning in the scriptures, was appointed to the bishopric in his place and is still living today.

During their episcopates, it was decided by synodical decree that the province of the South Saxons, which had hitherto belonged to the diocese of Winchester under Bishop Daniel, should have an episcopal see and bishop of its own. Eadbert, who was Abbot of Selsey, a monastery founded by Bishop Wilfrid of blessed memory, was consecrated its first bishop, and at his death Eolla succeeded him in the office. After some years he also departed this life, and the bishopric has fallen into abeyance to this day.

CHAPTER 19: *Coenred, King of the Mercians, and Offa, King of the East Saxons, end their days in Rome as monks. The life and death of Bishop Wilfrid* [A.D. 709]

IN the fourth year of Osred's reign, Coenred, who had ruled the kingdom of Mercia with great renown for some while, resigned his kingly sceptre for a yet more noble kingdom. During the pontificate of Constantine, he went to Rome, received the tonsure, and became a monk at the shrine of the Apostles, passing the remainder of his days in prayer, fasting, and acts of mercy. He was succeeded on the throne by Ceolred, son of Ethelred who had ruled the kingdom before Coenred. With Coenred went Offa, son of Sighere the above-mentioned king of the East Saxons, a very handsome and lovable young man who the entire nation greatly hoped would inherit and uphold the sceptre of the kingdom. But, fired by an equal ardour, he left his wife, lands, family, and country for the sake of Christ and his Gospel, hoping *to receive an hundred-fold in this life, and in the world to come life everlasting.* So, when they had arrived at the holy places in Rome, he received the tonsure, entered upon the monastic life, and at last attained the long-desired vision of the blessed Apostles in heaven.

During the same year in which these two left Britain, the renowned Bishop Wilfrid ended his days in the region of Oundle, after forty-five years as a bishop. The coffin containing his body was carried to his own monastery at Ripon and buried in the church of the blessed Apostle Peter with the honours due to so eminent a prelate. I will now turn back and recall briefly some of the events of his life.* As a boy, he was of a good disposition and behaviour for his age, always bearing himself modestly and thoughtfully, so that he was deservedly loved, admired, and welcomed by his elders as one of themselves. When he reached the age of fourteen, he chose monastic life rather than secular, and when he informed his father – for his mother was dead – he readily agreed to his heavenly desires and aspirations, and encouraged him to persevere in this laudable decision. He therefore went to the Isle of Lindisfarne and offered himself for the service of the monks, diligently setting himself to learn and practise all that conduces to monastic purity and devotion. Having a quick mind, he very soon learned the psalms and certain other books, before he received the tonsure, but not before he had become remarkable for monastic attributes more important than the tonsure, for humility and obedience, which naturally endeared him to the older monks as well as to his contemporaries. When he had served God in that monastery for some years, being a thoughtful youth, he gradually came to realize that the way of life taught by the Irish was far from perfect; so he decided to visit Rome and see what ecclesiastical and monastic customs were in use at the apostolic see. When he acquainted the brethren with his wish, they commended his proposal and encouraged him to carry out whatever he had in mind. Without further delay, he went to Queen Eanfled, who knew him and at whose request he had been accepted into the monastery, and told her of his desire to visit the shrines of the blessed Apostles. The youth's plan pleased the queen, who sent him to King Earconbert of Kent, her uncle's son, with the request that he would send him honourably to Rome. At this time Honorius, one of the disciples of blessed Pope Gregory and a man of great experience in church matters, was occupying the archbishopric with great distinction. And while he was waiting there, Wilfrid, being an active-minded young man, diligently set himself to study everything that he saw. Another young man then arrived named Biscop, known as Benedict, whom I have already mentioned: he came of noble English family, and also wished to travel to Rome. So the king gave Wilfrid to Benedict as his companion, with instructions to accompany him to Rome. On their arrival at Lugdunum,[1] Wilfrid was detained there by Dalfin,★ bishop of the city; but Benedict continued on his journey to Rome without staying. For the bishop took great pleasure in the young man's wise conversation, graceful appearance, and enthusiasm for action, as well as in his balanced and mature opinions. He therefore made ample provision for all the needs of Wilfrid and his companions for as long as they stayed with him, and offered to entrust to him, if he were willing, the administration of a considerable area of Gaul, to give him his young niece as wife, and make him his own adopted son. Wilfrid thanked him for the kindness that he had been pleased to show a stranger, but told him that he had set his heart on a different way of life, which was the reason why he had left his own country and set out on the journey to Rome.

Hearing this, the bishop sent him on to Rome, providing him with a guide and generously supplying everything that the needs of the journey demanded. And he earnestly pressed him to remember to come that way on his return journey to his own country. When Wilfrid arrived in Rome, he devoted himself daily to constant prayer and study of church matters, as he had intended, and won the friendship of the most holy and learned

[1] Lyons.

archdeacon Boniface, who was also a papal counsellor. Under
his guidance he mastered each of the Gospels in turn and the
correct method of calculating Easter, while through this tutor
he came to understand many other things relating to church
order which he had no means of learning in his own country;
and having spent some months engrossed in profitable study,
he returned to Dalfin in Gaul. He remained with him three
years, received the tonsure at his hands, and so won his affection
that the bishop considered making him his heir. But the bishop's
cruel death intervened to prevent this, and Wilfrid was destined
rather to become a bishop of his own people the English. For
Queen Baldhild sent soldiers with orders to kill the bishop, and
Wilfrid as his clerk accompanied him to the place of execution,
wishing to die with him, although the bishop strongly opposed
this. But when the executioners learned that he was a foreigner
and an Englishman, they spared him and refused to put him to
death with his bishop.

On his return to Britain, Wilfrid was admitted to the friendship of King Alchfrid, who had learned to love and follow the
Catholic laws of the Church. When he found Wilfrid was also a
Catholic, the king gave him ten hides of land at a place called
Stanford, and not long afterwards, a monastery with thirty
hides at Ripon. This place had been formerly granted to monks
who followed the Irish custom in order to build a monastery
there. But since, when offered the alternative, they had preferred
to abandon the place rather than adopt the Catholic Easter and
other canonical rites in accordance with the usage of the Roman
and apostolic Church, the king gave it to one whom he knew
to be trained in better doctrines and customs.

At this time, under instructions from the king, Wilfrid was
ordained priest at this monastery by the above-mentioned
Agilbert, Bishop of the Gewissae, because the king wished to
retain a man of such great learning and devotion as a priest and
counsellor for his own special companionship. Shortly after the
exposure and removal of the Irish sect that I mentioned, and
with the approval and advice of his father Oswy, the king sent
Wilfrid to Gaul, asking that he be consecrated as his bishop,

Wilfrid being at the time about thirty years of age. And when Agilbert, then Bishop of Paris, and eleven other bishops had gathered to make him a bishop, they carried out the rite of his consecration with great splendour. But since Wilfrid remained overseas for some while, a holy man named Chad was consecrated Bishop of York at the orders of King Oswy, as I have already described. Chad, having ruled the church very ably for three years, resigned the see and retired to his monastery of Lastingham, and Wilfrid then became bishop of the whole province of the Northumbrians.

Subsequently, as I have already told, Wilfrid was expelled from his bishopric during the reign of Egfrid, and other bishops were consecrated in his place. Intending to travel to Rome and plead his case before the apostolic Pope, he therefore took ship, but a strong westerly wind drove him to Frisia, where he was honourably received by the barbarous people and their king Aldgils. He preached Christ among them, teaching the word of truth to many thousands, and cleansing them from the guilt of their sins in the font of our Saviour. He was the first to attempt the work of their evangelization, which was later completed so zealously by the most reverend Christian Bishop Willibrord. Having spent the winter happily there with God's new people, Wilfrid set out once more for Rome. There his case was heard before Pope Agatho and several bishops, who were unanimous in acquitting him of the charges laid against him and declared him worthy of his bishopric.

At this time Pope Agatho summoned a hundred and twenty-five bishops to a Synod in Rome in order to combat those who were teaching that there was only one will and action in our Lord and Saviour. He ordered Wilfrid to be summoned to take his place among the bishops, and to state his own belief and that of the province or island whence he had come. And when both he and his nation were shown to be Catholic in their belief, it was thought fitting to include this among the other findings of the synod in the following form: 'Wilfrid, beloved of God, Bishop of the city of York, having brought his case before the apostolic see, has been acquitted by its authority from all charges

against him, both definite and indefinite. Appointed to take his
seat in consultation with one hundred and twenty-five bishops
in synod, he affirmed the true and Catholic Faith on behalf of
all the northern part of Britain, Ireland, and the islands inhabited
by the English, Britons, Irish, and Picts, ratifying this by his
own signature.'

After this, Wilfrid returned to Britain and converted the
province of the South Saxons from their idolatrous rites to the
Faith of Christ. He also sent preachers to the Isle of Wight, and
during the second year of King Aldfrid, Egfrid's successor, he
was restored to his own see and bishopric at the king's invitation. But five years later he was again accused and expelled from
his diocese by the king and several bishops. He travelled to
Rome, and was given opportunity to defend himself in the
presence of his accusers before the apostolic Pope John [VI] and
several bishops. It was unanimously decided that his accusers
had brought partially false charges against him; and the Pope
wrote to the English kings Ethelred and Aldfrid that he had
been unjustly condemned and that they should restore him to
his bishopric.

His acquittal was greatly forwarded by the reading of the
transactions of the synod held by Pope Agatho of blessed
memory during Wilfrid's former visit to the city, when he had
sat at the council with the other bishops, as I have already
described. For when as need required and at the direction of the
apostolic Pope, the transactions of this Synod were read for
some days in the presence of the nobility and many of the
people, they came to the passage where it is written: 'Wilfrid,
beloved of God and Bishop of the city of York, having brought
his case before the apostolic see, has by its authority been
acquitted from all charges etc.,' as already recorded. When this
was read, those who listened were surprised; and when the
reader finished, they began to ask one another, 'Who was this
Bishop Wilfrid?' Then Boniface, counsellor to the apostolic
Pope, and many others who had met him there in Pope Agatho's
time, explained that he was the same bishop who had been
accused by his own people and had recently come to Rome to

be tried by the apostolic see. 'He came here long ago under a similar accusation,' they said, 'and the dispute between the two parties was quickly heard and decided. Pope Agatho of blessed memory showed that he had been unjustly expelled from his bishopric, and had so high a regard for Wilfrid that he ordered him to sit in the council of bishops which he had summoned, as a man of blameless faith and honest mind.' Hearing this, the Pope and all the assembly declared that a man of such authority, who had been a bishop for nearly forty years, should certainly not be condemned, but should be cleared of all charges laid against him and returned home with honour.

As Wilfrid was crossing Gaul on his return to Britain, he was suddenly overtaken by an illness, which grew so serious that he was unable to ride and had to be carried by his attendants in a litter. He was brought to Maeldum,[1] a city of Gaul, where he lay four days and nights as though dead, and only his faint breathing showed that he was still alive. He remained like this for four days without food or drink, speech or hearing, but at daybreak on the fifth day he sat up as though waking from a deep sleep. When he opened his eyes and saw around him a crowd of brethren singing psalms and weeping, he sighed and asked for the priest Acca, who came in at once when summoned and, seeing Wilfrid better and able to speak, fell on his knees and thanked God with all the brethren present. And when they had sat down, and began with some hesitation to talk of the judgements of heaven, the bishop told the others to leave them for an hour, and said to the priest Acca:

'I have seen a momentous vision, which I want you to keep secret until I know God's will for me. There stood beside me a noble being in white robes, who told me that he was Michael the Archangel. "I am come to recall you from death," he said, "for our Lord has granted you life at the prayers of your brethren and the intercession of His blessed Mother the ever-virgin Mary. So I now pronounce that you shall be healed of this sickness: but be prepared, for I shall return to visit you after

[1] Meaux.

four years. When you return to your own country, you shall recover the greater portion of the possessions that were taken from you and end your life in perfect peace."' And to the delight of all, who gave thanks to God, the bishop recovered, resumed his journey, and arrived in Britain.

When they had studied the letters that Wilfrid had brought from the apostolic Pope, Archbishop Bertwald and Ethelred very readily supported him. The latter, formerly king but now an abbot, sent for Coenred, whom he had appointed king in his own place, and asked him to be a friend to Wilfrid, to which he agreed. Aldfrid, King of the Northumbrians, still refused to receive him; but he died shortly afterwards, and was succeeded by his son Osred. A synod was soon held near the river Nidd, and after some argument between the parties, it was generally agreed that Wilfrid should be restored to the bishopric of his own church. And so for four years, until the day of his death, he lived his life in peace. He died in his monastery in the region of Oundle during the rule of Abbot Cuthbald and was carried by the brethren to his first monastery at Ripon, where he was buried in the church of the blessed Apostle Peter close to the altar on the south side, as already recorded, and the following epitaph was inscribed above him:

> Here Wilfrid, mighty prelate, lies at peace
> Who, spurred by love of God, this temple raised,
> And hallowed it in Peter's noble name,
> To whom our Master Christ bequeathed the keys.
> Fair gold and purple vestments he bestowed,
> A noble cross of richly shining ore
> He placed aloft as sign of victory won.
> The Gospels four in golden letters writ
> At his command and in due order bound
> Were fitly cased in covers of red gold.
> Easter's mistimed observance he set right
> In due conformity with canon law
> Fixed by the Fathers, and to all his folk
> Banishing doubt, made manifest the truth.
> Here he established many flocks of monks

And as a watchful shpeherd bade them keep
The rule established by the saints of old.
In his long life he weathered many storms,
Discords at home and perils overseas.
He ruled as bishop five and forty years,
And passed rejoicing to God's heavenly realm.
Grant us, O Jesus, his true flock to be,
And tread with him the road that leads to Thee.

CHAPTER 20: *Albinus succeeds the devout Abbot Hadrian, and Acca succeeds to Wilfrid's bishopric* [A.D. 709]

IN the year following the death of the above Father Wilfrid, that is, the fifth year of King Osred, the most reverend father, Abbot Hadrian, fellow-worker in the word of God with Archbishop Theodore of blessed memory, died and was buried in the church of the blessed Mother of God in his own monastery. This was the forty-first year after his dispatch by Pope Vitalian with Theodore, and the thirty-ninth after his arrival in Britain. Among other testimonies to his learning and that of Archbishop Theodore is the fact that his disciple Albinus, who succeeded him as abbot of his monastery, was so well grounded in the study of the Scriptures that he had no small grasp of Greek, while he understood Latin as thoroughly as his native English tongue.*

Wilfrid's successor as Bishop of the church of Hexham was his priest Acca, a man of great energy and noble in the sight of God and man. He greatly beautified and enlarged the structure of his church, which was dedicated in honour of blessed Andrew the Apostle. He devoted much care, as he still does, to obtaining relics of the blessed Apostles and martyrs of Christ from various places, and builds altars for their veneration, placed for this purpose in recesses within the walls of his church. He has also collected accounts of their sufferings and other books on religious subjects, to form a very complete and excellent library. And he has been diligent in providing sacred vessels, lights, and

similar articles necessary for the furnishing of God's house. He
also invited a famous singer named Maban, who had been
trained in vocal music by the successors of blessed Pope
Gregory's disciples in Kent, to come and instruct him and his
clergy. He retained his services for twelve years, to teach them
whatever church music they did not know, and also to restore
to their original form any familiar chants that had become
imperfect through lapse of time or neglect; for the bishop
himself was a singer of great experience. He was also most
learned in the holy Scriptures, orthodox in his profession to the
Catholic Faith, and well acquainted with the rules of church
administration. And in all these activities he remains unflagging
until the time comes for him to receive the reward of his piety
and devotion. For he was reared and trained from boyhood
among the clergy of the most holy Bosa, God's beloved Bishop
of York; he later came to Bishop Wilfrid in the hope of
improving himself, and remained under him continuously until
the latter's death, travelling to Rome with him, and there
learning many valuable things about the organization of Holy
Church which he had no means of learning in his own country.

CHAPTER 21: *Abbot Ceolfrid sends church architects to the King of*
the Picts, and with them a letter about the Catholic Easter and
tonsure [*c.* A.D. 710]

A T this time, Nechtan, King of the Picts, living in the
northern parts of Britain, convinced after assiduous study
of Church writings, renounced the error hitherto maintained by
his nation about the observance of Easter and adopted the
Catholic time of keeping our Lord's Resurrection with all his
people. In order to do this more smoothly and with greater
authority, the king asked help from the English people, whom
he knew to have based their practice long previously on the
pattern of the holy Roman apostolic Church. So he sent
messengers to the venerable Ceolfrid, Abbot of the monastery
of the blessed Apostles Peter and Paul, which he ruled most

illustriously as successor of the above-mentioned Benedict. This monastery stands at the mouth of the river Wear, and also close to the river Tyne at a place called In-Gyrwum.[1] The king requested Ceolfrid to write him a letter of guidance that would help him to refute those who presume to keep Easter at the wrong time; and although he was relatively well informed on these matters himself, he also required information about the form and reason for the tonsure that clergy should wear. In addition, he asked that architects be sent him in order to build a stone church for his people in the Roman style, promising that he would dedicate it in honour of the blessed Prince of the Apostles and that he and his people would follow the customs of the holy apostolic Roman Church, as far as they could learn them in view of their remoteness from the Roman people and from Roman speech. The most reverend Abbot Ceolfrid complied with his devout wishes and requests, sending him the architects he asked for, together with the following letter.*

'To the most excellent and illustrious lord, King Nechtan, from Abbot Ceolfrid – Greetings in our Lord.

'In response to your devout enquiries as a God-fearing king, I am most willing and ready to attempt to explain the Catholic observance of Easter in accordance with the rulings of the apostolic see; for we know that whenever Holy Church sets itself to learn, teach, or maintain the truth concerning our Lord, this truth is revealed to it from heaven. As a secular writer very truly said, the world would be in the happiest possible state if kings were philosophers or philosophers were kings.* And if a man of the world could make a true estimate of this world's philosophy and judge rightly about the state of this world, how much more is it to be desired and sincerely prayed for by the citizens of our heavenly home, who are pilgrims in this world, that the greater any man's position in this world, the more he should exert himself to obey the commands of the Supreme Judge, and by his example and authority induce those committed to his charge to follow him in observing them!

---

[1] Wearmouth and Jarrow are here treated as constituting a single monastery.

'There are three rules in holy scripture that determine the
time of keeping Easter, and which no human authority may
change. Two of these are decreed by God in the Law of Moses,
and the third is added in the Gospel as a consequence of the
Passion and Resurrection of our Lord. For the Law directed that
the Passover should be kept in the first month of the year, and
in the third week of that month, that is, between the fifteenth
and twenty-first days of the month. To this, the apostolic
ordinance in the Gospels adds that we are to wait for the Lord's
Day in this third week and begin to observe Eastertide on that
day. Whoever keeps this three-fold rule correctly will never
make a mistake in fixing the Feast of Easter. But if you wish to
hear more clear and detailed information about this, it is written
in Exodus, where the people of Israel, before their deliverance
from Egypt, are directed to keep the first Passover, that "*The
Lord said to Moses and Aaron: This month shall be unto you the
beginning of months; it shall be the first month of the year to you.
Speak ye unto all the congregation of Israel, saying, In the tenth day
of this month they shall take to them every man a lamb, according to
the house of their father.*" And a little later, "*And ye shall keep it up
until the fourteenth day of the same month: and the whole assembly of
the congregation of Israel shall kill it in the evening.*" These words
make it very clear that, in the paschal observance, the fourteenth
day is mentioned not because it was the day on which the
Passover is commanded to be kept, but because the lamb is
commanded to be killed on the evening of the fourteenth day,
that is, at the fifteenth rising of the moon (which marks the
beginning of the third week): and because it was on the night of
the fifteenth moon that the Egyptians were smitten, and Israel
redeemed out of its long slavery. "*Seven days shall ye eat
unleavened bread,*" it is said. In these words, all the third week of
the first month is directed to be solemnly observed. But lest we
should think that those seven days were to be reckoned from
the fourteenth to the twentieth day, it is added: "*On the first day
ye shall put away leaven out of your house; for whosoever eateth
leavened bread from the first day until the seventh day, that soul shall*

be cut off from Israel" and so on, until he says: "*For in this selfsame day I will bring your army out of the land of Egypt.*"

'So the day on which God was to bring out their army from Egypt is called the first day of unleavened bread. It is clear, however, that they were not brought up out of Egypt on the fourteenth day, on the evening of which the lamb was killed and which is properly known as the *Pascha* or *Phase*, that is, the Passover, but on the fifteenth day, as is quite plainly recorded in the Book of Numbers; "*So they departed from Rameses in the first month, on the fifteenth day of the month; on the morrow after the Passover the children of Israel went out with an high hand.*" So the seven days of unleavened bread, on the first of which the Lord's people were led up out of Egypt, are to be reckoned from the beginning of the third week, as I have said: that is, from the fifteenth day of the month to the twenty-first day of the same month inclusive. But the fourteenth day is noted down separately from this number under the title of the Passover, as is clearly defined in the ensuing passage of *Exodus*, where it is said: "*For in this selfsame day I will bring your army out of the land of Egypt,*" and immediately adds: "*Therefore shall ye observe this day in your generations by an ordinance for ever. In the first month, on the fourteenth day of the month at even, ye shall eat unleavened bread, until the one and twentieth day of the month at even. Seven days there shall be no leaven found in your houses.*" Who can fail to see that, if the fourteenth day is included, there are not seven but eight days from the fourteenth to the twenty-first days? But if, as careful study of the scriptures reveals the truth, we reckon from the evening of the fourteenth day to the evening of the twenty-first, we shall at once see that this fourteenth day gives its evening to the beginning of the Paschal feast, so that the entire sacred solemnity comprises no more than seven days and nights. Accordingly our definition is shown to be correct, in which we stated that the Paschal period should be celebrated during the first month of the year and in its third week. For it is in fact the third week, because it begins on the evening of the fourteenth day, and closes on the evening of the twenty-first.

'After the sacrifice of Christ our Passover, the Lord's Day

(which the ancients called the first day after the Sabbath) was
made holy for us by the joy of his resurrection: and the tradition
of the Apostles established this day for the Easter feast, in such
a way that the lawful Paschal period should be neither forestalled
nor cut short. Rather it is laid down that, according to the Law,
the first month of the year and its fourteenth day and the
evening of that day should be awaited. And if by chance this
day fell on the Sabbath, *They shall take to them every man a lamb
according to the house of their fathers* and sacrifice it in the evening
– that is to say, all churches throughout the world, who
constitute the one Catholic church, should prepare bread and
wine as a sacrament of the Body and Blood of the spotless Lamb
who *taketh away the sins of the world*. And after suitable prayers,
in the solemn celebration of Easter, they should offer these to
the Lord in the hope of their future redemption. For that is the
very night on which the people of Israel were snatched out of
Egypt by the blood of the Lamb, and the very night on which
all God's people was freed from eternal death by Christ's
resurrection. And when the Lord's Day dawns on the morrow,
they should celebrate the first day of the Easter feast. For that is
the very day on which the glory of the Lord's resurrection was
joyfully revealed to his disciples, and is also the first day of
unleavened bread, of which it is clearly written in Leviticus: "*In
the fourteenth day of the first month at even is the Passover; and on the
fifteenth day is the feast of unleavened bread unto the Lord; seven days
ye must eat unleavened bread. The first day shall be the most renowned
and holy.*"

'Therefore if it could be brought about that a Sunday should
always fall on the fifteenth day of the first month, that is, on the
fifteenth appearance of the moon, we should be able always to
celebrate our Easter at the very same time as the ancient people
of God, as we do by the very same faith, although by a different
kind of sacrament. But because the days of the week do not
keep pace with the phases of the moon, the apostolic tradition
(preached by the blessed Peter at Rome and confirmed by the
evangelist Mark, his interpreter, at Alexandria) decreed that,
when the first month came round and the evening of its

fourteenth day, they should wait further for a Sunday, from the fifteenth to the twenty-first day of that month. And on whatever of those days Sunday should occur, Easter should be celebrated on that day, because this falls within the seven days of unleavened bread. So it comes about that our Easter never diverges in either direction from the third week of the first month, but either occupies the whole of it, that is, all the Law's seven days of unleavened bread, or at any rate occupies some of these days. For even if only one of them is included, that is, the seventh day (which scripture commends so highly, saying "*the seventh day shall be more renowned and holy; ye shall do no servile work therein*"), no one can accuse us of not keeping correctly the Easter Day, which we have received from the Gospel, in the third week of the first month as the Law decrees.

'The reasons for the Catholic practice are therefore evident: equally evident is the irrational error of those who presume without real necessity to anticipate or to overrun the periods prescribed in the Law. Those who consider that the day of our Lord's Resurrection should be kept between the fourteenth day of the month and the twentieth day of the moon anticipate without any reasonable necessity the time prescribed in the Law; for when they begin to keep the vigil of the holy night from the evening of the thirteenth day, it is evident that they regard that day as the beginning of their Easter, and they cannot show any authority for this in the decrees of the Law. And when they refuse to keep the Lord's Easter on the twenty-first day of the month, they clearly exclude from their observance a day which the Law often recommends as suitable for greater festivity than the other days. Consequently, they disarrange the proper order, sometimes even placing Easter entirely in the second week and never keeping it on the seventh day of the third week.

Those who consider that Easter should be celebrated between the sixteenth day of the said month and the twenty-second, no less incorrectly, deviate from the correct course on the other side and, as though avoiding shipwreck on Scylla, are sucked down and drowned in the whirlpool of Charybdis. For when they teach that Easter is to begin at moonrise on the sixteenth

day of the first month, that is, from the evening of the fifteenth
day, it follows that they entirely exclude from their solemnity
the fourteenth day of the month, which the Law particularly
recommends. Consequently, they barely include the evening of
the fifteenth day – the day on which God's people were
redeemed from slavery in Egypt, on which our Lord redeemed
the world from the darkness of sin by His own Blood, and on
which He was buried, bestowing on us the hope of blessedness
and peace after death. When they place the Lord's day of Easter
on the twenty-second day of the month, these people *receive in
themselves the recompense of their error* and openly violate the
legitimate limits of Easter, beginning it on the evening of the
day on which the Law had directed that it should be finished
and completed. They also appoint as the first day of Easter a
day of which no mention is made in the Law, that is, the first
day of the fourth week.

'Both these factions are sometimes mistaken not only in
defining and calculating the age of the moon, but even in
discovering the first month. However, this controversy is too
lengthy to be dealt with fully in this letter. I will say only that
the first and last months of the lunar year can always be
accurately determined by reference to the vernal equinox.
According to the views of all the eastern nations, and in
particular of the Egyptians, who are especially skilled in such
calculation, the vernal equinox occurs on the twenty-first of
March, as we can prove by horological observation. Therefore,
whatever moon is at the full (that is, in its fourteenth or fifteenth
day) before the equinox, this rightly belongs to the last month
of the preceding year and consequently is not suitable for
keeping Easter. But the full moon falling either on or after the
equinox itself certainly belongs to the first month; on it the
ancients used to keep the Passover, and on it, when the Lord's
day comes, we should keep Easter. There is a very convincing
reason why this should be so, because it is written in *Genesis*:
"*God made two lights, the greater light to rule the day, and the lesser
light to rule the night;*" or, as it appears in another version: "*the
greater light to usher in the day, and the lesser light to usher in the*

night." Therefore, as the vernal equinox was first determined by the rising of the sun on its emergence from the midpoint of the east and later, while the sun was setting at evening, the moon, being then full, followed from the midpoint of the east, so every year the same first month of the moon must be observed in the same order, so that the full moon must not fall before the equinox, but either on the day of the equinox itself, as it was in the beginning, or else after it. And if the full moon falls so much as one day before the time of the equinox, the above reason shows that it may not be assigned to the first month of the new year, but to the last of the preceding year, and is therefore not eligible for the observance of the Easter Festival.

'If it pleases you to know also the symbolic reason in this matter, we are directed to keep Easter in the first month of the year, which is also known as the month of New Fruit, because we should celebrate the mysteries of our Lord's Resurrection and our own deliverance with our minds refreshed to love of heavenly things. We are bidden to keep it in the third week of the month, because Christ, who had been promised before the Law and under the Law, came with Grace in the third age of the world to be sacrificed as our Passover; because he also rose from the dead on the third day after the offering of His Passion, and wished this to be known as the Lord's Day and kept annually as the Easter feast; and because we only observe this rite truly, that is, His passing out of this world to the Father, if we are careful to do so with Him in faith, hope, and love. We are commanded to keep the full moon of the Paschal month after the equinox, so that first the sun may make day longer than night and then the moon may show the whole of her light face to the world, because first "*the Sun of Righteousness with healing in His wings*", that is the Lord Jesus, overcame all the darkness of death by the triumph of His Resurrection and then, having ascended into heaven, sent down the Spirit from on high and so filled His Church, which is often symbolically described as the moon, with the light of inward grace. This was the plan of our salvation which the prophet had in mind when he said: "*The sun was exalted, and the moon stood still in her habitation.*"

'Whoever argues, therefore, that the Paschal full moon can occur before the equinox, disagrees in the observance of our highest mysteries with the teaching of the scriptures, and allies himself with those who believe that they can be saved without the assistance of Christ's grace. Such people presume to assert that they could have attained to perfect goodness even if the true Light had not overcome this world's darkness by His Death and Resurrection. So after the rising of the equinoctial sun, and after the ensuing full moon of the first month, that is, after the close of the fourteenth day of that month – all of which we have received as necessary observances under the Law – we still wait until the Lord's Day in the third week as the Gospel directs. Then at length we keep our proper feast of Easter, to show that we do not, like the ancients, celebrate the breaking of the Egyptian yoke of slavery, but that we venerate with faith and devotion the Redemption of the whole world, which was foreshadowed in the liberation of God's ancient people and completed at Christ's Resurrection. In this way we show that we rejoice in the most certain hope of our own resurrection, which we believe will take place on the Lord's Day.

'This calculation of Easter which I have explained to you depends on a cycle of nineteen years, which began to be observed by the Church long ago in the time of the Apostles, especially in Rome and Egypt, as I mentioned earlier. But through the industry of Eusebius, who took his surname from the blessed martyr Pamphylus, it was reduced to a clearer system, so that whereas notification was formerly sent each year to all the churches by the Patriarch of Alexandria, thenceforward it could be easily understood by everyone, because the fourteenth day of the moon fell in a regular sequence. Theophilus, Patriarch of Alexandria, drew up an Easter table for the ensuing hundred years for the benefit of the Emperor Theodosius; similarly, his successor Cyril drew up a table for ninety-five years in five cycles of nineteen years. After him, Dionysius Exiguus added others in the same way, which extend down to

our own day. This table will soon expire; but today there are so
many people able to calculate that even in our own Church in
Britain there are many who understand the ancient rules of the
Egyptians, and can readily compute the cycles of these paschal
times for an indefinite number of years, even for five hundred
and thirty-two years ahead if they so desire. After this period,
all that concerns the sequences of sun and moon, month and
week, recurs in the same order as before. But I do not propose
to send you these cycles of times to come, because you only
asked to be informed about the reasons for the time of Easter
and said that you were provided with Catholic Easter tables.

'Having written about Easter as you requested, albeit curso-
rily and briefly, I also urge you to make sure that the tonsure,
about which you also asked me to write, is worn in accordance
with Christian ecclesiastical practice. We know that the Apostles
were not all tonsured in the same manner and, although the
Catholic Church is united in one faith, hope, and love in God,
it has not adopted one unvarying form of tonsure throughout
the whole world. On a wider view, looking back to the earlier
days of the patriarchs, we find that Job, the pattern of patience,
shaved his head in time of trouble, which shows that in times of
prosperity he allowed his hair to grow. But Joseph, remarkable
for his practice and teaching of chastity, humility, piety, and
other virtues, shaved his head when about to be freed from
slavery, which shows that, while he was living in prison as a
slave, he did not cut his hair. But notice how each of these men
of God, while differing in their outward appearance, are alike in
cherishing grace and virtue in their inmost hearts. So we may
frankly admit that a variety in tonsure does no harm to those
who have a pure faith in God and sincere charity towards their
neighbour, especially since we do not read that there was ever
any controversy among the catholic fathers about differences of
tonsure such as there has been about diversity in Easter observance or in matters of doctrine. Nevertheless, of all the tonsures
to be found either in the Church or among the races of mankind,
I consider none more worthy of being imitated and adopted
than that worn on the head of the disciple to whose confession

our Lord replied: "*Thou art Peter, and upon this rock I will build my church, and the gates of hell shall not prevail against it: and I will give unto thee the keys of the kingdom of heaven*" Nor do I consider any to be more abhorrent and detestable to all the faithful than that worn by the man to whom, when he wished to purchase the gift of the Holy Spirit, Peter said: "*Thy money perish with thee, because thou hast thought that the gift of God may be purchased with money. Thou hast neither part nor lot in this matter.*"* But we are not shaven in the form of a crown solely because Peter was shorn in this way, but because Peter was shorn in this way in memory of our Lord's Passion. Therefore we who desire to be saved by Christ's Passion like Peter wear this sign of the Passion on the crown of the head, which is the highest part of the body. For, as the whole Church came into being through the Death of Him who gave it life, so each member of it bears the sign of the Holy Cross on his forehead, so that this emblem may afford constant protection against the assaults of wicked spirits and serve as a continual reminder that he must crucify the flesh with all its vices and evil desires. Similarly, those who have taken monastic vows or are in Holy Orders should bind themselves to stricter self-discipline for our Lord's sake, and wear their heads tonsured in the form of the crown of thorns which Christ wore on His head in His Passion, so that He might bear the thorns and briars of our sins and thus bear them away from us. In this way their own appearance will be a reminder to them to be willing and ready to suffer ridicule and disgrace for His sake, and a sign that they are always hoping to receive "*the crown of everlasting life which the Lord hath promised to those that love Him*", and in order to win this crown regard both adversity and prosperity as of equal insignificance. As for the tonsure that Simon the magician is said to have worn, I ask what faithful Christian will not instantly detest it, like magic itself, with the scorn it deserves. On the forehead it has indeed a superficial resemblance to a crown; but when you look at the neck, you will find the apparent crown cut short, so that you may fairly regard this fashion as characteristic of simoniacs and not of Christians. For in this life deluded people thought such men worthy of a lasting crown of glory; but in the life to come they are not only deprived of all hope of a crown but condemned to eternal punishment.

'Do not think that I have spoken in this way about those who wear this tonsure as though they are damned even if they maintain Catholic unity in belief and practice. On the contrary, I am sure that many of them were holy men and pleasing to God. Among them is Adamnan, a renowned priest and abbot of the Columbans, who when he was sent on an embassy from his nation to King Aldfrid and chose to visit our monastery, displayed remarkable wisdom, humility, and devotion in his ways and conversation. I said to him in the course of discussion: "Holy brother, you believe that you are on the right road to receive the crown of life that knows no term. Why then, I beseech you, do you wear on your head the image of a crown which, in a fashion that belies your faith, is terminated? And if you seek the society of blessed Peter, why do you imitate the tonsure of the man whom Peter cursed? Why do you not do everything in this life to show that you love to imitate him with whom you desire to live in blessedness for ever?" He replied: "My dear brother, rest assured that, although I wear Simon's tonsure after the custom of my country, I wholeheartedly abominate and reject all simoniacal wickedness. So far as my frailty permits, I wish to follow in the footsteps of the most blessed Prince of the Apostles." I then said: "I am sure that this is so. Nevertheless, you should give some indication of your inward esteem for whatever derives from the Apostle Peter by displaying openly whatever you know to be his. For I think that your wisdom clearly appreciates that it would be better for you, who are vowed to God, to alter your outward appearance from any resemblance to a man whom you wholeheartedly detest, and whose hideous face you would loathe to see. On the other hand, since you wish to follow the example and teachings of Peter, it would be fitting for you to conform to the outward appearance of him whom you desire to have as your advocate in the presence of God."

'Such, then, were my words to Adamnan, who showed how

greatly he had profited by seeing the observances of our Church; for after he had returned to Scotland, he won over large numbers to the Catholic observance of Easter by his preaching But although he was their lawfully constituted head, he was unable to persuade the monks of Iona to adopt a better rule of life. Had his authority been sufficiently great, he would surely have taken care to correct the tonsure also.

'I now beg Your Majesty in your wisdom, together with the nation over which the King of kings and Lord of lords has placed you, to set yourself to follow all that fosters the unity of the Catholic and Apostolic Church. In so doing, when the might of your earthly kingdom has passed away, the most blessed Prince of the Apostles will gladly open the gate of the heavenly kingdom to you and yours and admit you to the company of God's elect.

'Most dearly beloved son in Christ, may the grace of God the everlasting King keep you in safety to reign many years, and preserve us all in peace.'

When this letter had been read in the presence of King Nechtan and many of his more learned men, and carefully translated into their own tongue by those who could understand it, he is said to have been so grateful for its guidance that he rose among his assembled chieftains and fell on his knees, thanking God that he had been accounted worthy to receive such a gift from England. 'I already knew that this was the true observance of Easter; but I now understand the reasons for it so clearly that my previous knowledge of it now seems to me to have been very slight. I therefore publicly proclaim in the presence of you all that I intend to observe this time of Easter with all my people for ever. And I decree that all the clergy of my kingdom shall adopt the tonsure of which we have now heard the full explanation.' The king at once enforced his statement with his royal authority. The nineteen-year cycles were immediately sent out under a public order to all the provinces of the Picts to be copied, learned, and adopted, and the erroneous eighty-four year cycles were universally abolished. All the ministers of the altar and monks adopted the circular tonsure, and the reformed nation was glad to be placed under the direction of Peter, the most blessed Prince of the Apostles, and secure under his protection.

CHAPTER 22: *The monks of Iona and the monasteries under its jurisdiction begin to adopt the canonical Easter at the preaching of Egbert* [A.D. 716]

NOT long afterwards, the monks of the Irish nation who lived in the Isle of Iona, together with the monasteries under their jurisdiction, were led to God's providence to adopt the Canonical rite of Easter and style of tonsure. For in the year 716, during which King Osred was killed and Coenred succeeded to the government of the Northumbrian kingdom, Egbert the beloved of God – a father and bishop to be mentioned with high respect, of whom I have already spoken more than once – came to them from Ireland and was welcomed with honour and great joy. Being a most persuasive teacher who most faithfully practised all that he taught, he was given a ready hearing by everyone, and by his constant devout exhortations he weaned them from the obsolete traditions of their ancestors, to whom the Apostle's description is applicable: '*they had a zeal of God, but not according to knowledge.*' As I have said, he taught them to observe our chief solemnity in the Catholic and Apostolic manner and to wear the symbol of an unbroken crown. This seemed to happen by a wonderful dispensation of God's grace, in order that the nation which had willingly and ungrudgingly laboured to communicate its own knowledge of God to the English nation might later, through the same English nation, arrive at a perfect way of life which they had not hitherto possessed. In contrast the Britons, who had refused to share their own knowledge of the Christian Faith with the English, continue even now, when the English nation believes rightly, and is fully instructed in the doctrines of the Catholic Faith, to be obdurate and crippled by their errors, going about with their

heads improperly tonsured, and keeping Christ's solemnity
without fellowship with the Christian Church.

Through Egbert's teaching, the monks of Iona under Abbot
Duunchad adopted Catholic ways of life about eighty years after
they had sent Aidan to preach to the English nation.* God's
servant Egbert remained thirteen years on the island, where he
restored the gracious light of unity and peace to the Church and
consecrated the island anew to Christ. In the year of our Lord
729, during which our Lord's Easter was kept on the twenty-
fourth of April, Egbert celebrated the solemnity of the Mass in
honour of our Lord's Resurrection and departed to him the
same day. So he began his enjoyment of the greatest of all
festivals with the brethren whom he had won to the grace of
unity, and ended it with our Lord, the Apostles, and all the
citizens of heaven, where he now enjoys it for ever. And by a
wonderful dispensation of divine providence, the venerable
Egbert passed from this world to the Father not only on Easter
Day, but when Easter was being kept on a day when it had
never been kept before in those parts. So the brethren had the
joy of a sure and Catholic knowledge of the time of Easter, and
rejoiced in the protection of their father departed to our Lord,
by whom they had been converted. Egbert himself showed
great joy that he had been permitted to live until he saw his
disciples accept and keep with him the Easter day that they had
previously always rejected. So the most reverend father was
assured of their conversion. *He rejoiced to see the Lord's Day: he
saw it, and was glad.*

CHAPTER 23: *The present state of the English nation and the rest of
Britain* [A.D. 725–31]

IN the year of our Lord 725, which was the seventh year of
King Osric of Northumbria the successor of Coenred,
Wictred son of King Egbert of Kent died on the twenty-third of
April, leaving the kingdom that he had ruled for thirty-four and
a half years to be inherited by his sons Ethelbert, Eadbert, and

Alric. In the following year Bishop Tobias of Rochester died. He was a very learned man, as I said earlier, and had been a disciple of Archbishop Theodore and Abbot Hadrian of blessed memory. Consequently, in addition to his knowledge of ecclesiastical and general literature, he understood the Greek and Latin languages so thoroughly that they were as familiar to him as his own native tongue. He was buried in the chapel of Saint Peter the Apostle, which he had built within the church of Saint Andrew for his own burial place. He was succeeded as bishop by Aldwulf, who was consecrated by Archbishop Bertwald.

In the year of our Lord 729, two comets appeared around the sun, striking terror into all who saw them. One comet rose early and preceded the sun, while the other followed the setting sun at evening, seeming to portend awful calamity to east and west alike. Or else, since one comet was the precursor of day and the other of night, they indicated that mankind was menaced by evils at both times. They appeared in the month of January, and remained visible for about a fortnight, pointing their fiery torches northward as though to set the welkin aflame. At this time, a swarm of Saracens* ravaged Gaul with horrible slaughter; but after a brief interval in that country they paid the penalty of their wickedness. During this year the man of God Egbert departed to our Lord on Easter Day as I have mentioned, and immediately after Easter, on the ninth of May, King Osric of Northumbria departed this life after a reign of eleven years, having appointed Ceolwulf, brother of his predecessor Coenred, to follow him. Both the outset and course of Ceolwulf's reign were filled by so many grave disturbances that it is quite impossible to know what to write about them or what the outcome will be.

On the ninth of January in the year of our Lord 731, Archbishop Bertwald died of old age, having held the see for thirty-seven years, six months, and fourteen days. In the same year Tatwin, from the province of Mercia, who had been a priest in the monastery of Bredon, was made archbishop in his place. He was consecrated in the city of Canterbury on Sunday the tenth of June by the venerable Bishops Daniel of Winchester,

Ingwald of London, Aldwin of Lichfield, and Aldwulf of
Rochester. Tatwin was a man distinguished for his religion and
wisdom, and extremely learned in holy Scripture.

At the present day Tatwin and Aldwulf preside over the
Churches of Kent; Ingwald is Bishop of the East Saxons;
Aldbert and Hadulac are Bishops of the East Angles; Daniel and
Forthere are Bishops of the West Saxons; and Aldwin is Bishop
of the Mercians. Walchstod is Bishop of the folk who live in the
west, beyond the river Severn; Wilfrid is Bishop of the Hwiccas;
Cynibert is Bishop of the province of Lindsey. The bishopric of
the Isle of Wight belongs to Daniel, Bishop of Winchester. The
province of the South Saxons has now been without a bishop
for some years, and seeks the offices of a bishop from the prelate
of the West Saxons. All these provinces, together with the
others south of the river Humber and their kings, are subject to
Ethelbald, King of the Mercians.

In the province of the Northumbrians, ruled by Ceolwulf,
four bishops hold office: Wilfrid in the church of York, Ethelwald at Lindisfarne, Acca at Hexham, and Pecthelm in the see
known as The White House,* where the number of believers
has so increased that it has recently become an episcopal see
with Pecthelm as its first bishop.

At the present time, the Picts have a treaty of peace with the
English, and are glad to be united in Catholic peace and truth to
the universal Church. The Irish who are living in Britain are
content with their own territories, and do not contemplate any
raids or stratagems against the English. The Britons for the
most part have a national hatred for the English, and uphold
their own bad customs against the true Easter of the Catholic
Church; however, they are opposed by the power of God and
man alike, and are powerless to obtain what they want. For,
although in part they are independent, they have been brought
in part under subjection to the English.

As such peace and prosperity prevail in these days, many of
the Northumbrians, both noble and simple, together with their
children, have laid aside their weapons, preferring to receive the

tonsure and take monastic vows rather than study the arts of war. What the result of this will be the future will show.*

This, then, is the present state of all Britain, about two hundred and eighty-five years after the coming of the English to Britain, but seven hundred and thirty-one years since our Lord's Incarnation. May the world rejoice under his eternal rule, and Britain glory in his Faith! *Let the multitude of isles be glad thereof, and give thanks at the remembrance of his holiness!*

CHAPTER 24: *A chronological summary of the whole book, and a personal note on the author*

As an aid to memory, I have thought it helpful to make a concise summary of events already dealt with at greater length.

In the sixtieth year before the Incarnation of our Lord, Gaius Julius Caesar was the first of the Romans to make war on Britain and was victorious, but was unable to hold the kingdom.

In the year of our Lord 46, Claudius was the second of the Romans to come to Britain and received the surrender of the greater part of the island. He also added the Isles of Orkney to the Roman Empire.

In the year of our Lord 167, Eleutherus became Bishop of Rome, and ruled the Church most gloriously for fifteen years. Lucius, a king of Britain, sent him a letter asking to be made a Christian, and obtained his request.

In the year of our Lord 189, Severus became Emperor and reigned seventeen years. He fortified Britain with an earthwork stretching from sea to sea.

In the year 381, Maximus became Emperor while in Britain. He crossed into Gaul and killed Gratian.

In the year 409, Rome was taken by the Goths, and thenceforward Roman rule came to an end in Britain.

In the year 430, Pope Celestine sent Palladius to be the first bishop to the Christian Irish.

In the year 449, Marcian became co-Emperor with Valentinian. He reigned seven years, during which time the English came to Britain at the invitation of the Britons.

In the year 538, an eclipse of the sun occurred on the sixteenth of February, lasting from Prime to Terce.

In the year 540, an eclipse of the sun occurred on the twentieth of June, and the stars appeared for nearly half an hour after the hour of Terce.

In the year 547, Ida began his reign, which lasted for twelve years. From him the royal family of the Northumbrians derives its origin.

In the year 565, the priest Columba came into Britain from the land of the Irish to teach the Picts, and built a monastery on the Isle of Iona.

In the year 596, Pope Gregory sent Augustine and his monks to Britain to preach the word of God to the English people.

In the year 597, these teachers arrived in Britain. This was about one hundred and fifty years after the coming of the English to Britain.

In the year 601, Pope Gregory sent the *pallium* to Britain for Augustine, who had already been made a bishop. He also sent several ministers of the word, including Paulinus.

In the year 603, the Battle of Degsastan was fought.

In the year 604, the East Saxons under King Sabert received the Faith of Christ through Archbishop Mellitus.

In the year 605, Pope Gregory died.

In the year 606, King Ethelbert of Kent died.

In the year 625, Archbishop Justus consecrated Paulinus as Bishop of the Northumbrians.

In the year 626, Eanfled, daughter of King Edwin, was baptized on Whit Saturday with twelve others.

In the year 627, King Edwin and his people were baptized on Easter Day.

In the year 633, King Edwin was killed, and Paulinus retired to Kent.

In the year 640, King Eadbald of Kent died.

In the year 642, King Oswald was killed.

In the year 644, Paulinus, first Bishop of York and later Bishop of Rochester, departed to our Lord.

In the year 651, King Oswin was killed, and Bishop Aidan died.

In the year 653, the Middle Angles under Peada their prince accepted the mysteries of the Faith.

In the year 655, Penda was slain, and the Mercians became Christians.

In the year 664 an eclipse occurred. King Earconbert of Kent died, and Bishop Colman returned to his own land with the Irish. A plague came. Chad and Wilfrid were consecrated Bishops of the Northumbrians.

In the year 668, Theodore was consecrated bishop.

In the year 670, King Oswy of the Northumbrians died.

In the year 673, King Egbert of Kent died. A synod was held at Hertford in the presence of King Egfrid under the presidency of Archbishop Theodore. It was valuable, and enacted ten canons.

In the year 675, Wulfhere, King of the Mercians, died after a reign of seventeen years, and left the throne to his brother Ethelred.

In the year 676, Ethelred ravaged Kent.

In the year 678, a comet appeared. Bishop Wilfrid was expelled from his see by King Egfrid: Bosa, Eata, and Eadhaed were consecrated bishops in his place.

In the year 679, Elfwin was killed.

In the year 680, a synod was held in the plain of Hatfield under the presidency of Archbishop Theodore to affirm the Catholic Faith: John, an abbot from Rome, attended. Abbess Hilda died at Streanaeshalch.

In the year 685, Egfrid, King of the Northumbrians, was killed. King Hlothere of Kent died.

In the year 688, Cadwalla, King of the West Saxons, left Britain for Rome.

In the year 690, Archibishop Theodore died.

In the year 697, Queen Osthryd was killed by her own people, the Mercian chieftains.

In the year 698, Bertred, the royal commander of the Northumbrians, was killed by the Picts.

In the year 704, Ethelred became a monk after ruling the Mercians for thirty years, and resigned the kingdom to Coenred.

In the year 705, King Aldfrid of the Northumbrians died.

In the year 709, Coenred, King of the Mercians, after a reign of five years, went to Rome.

In the year 711, the ealdorman Bertfrid fought against the Picts.

In the year 716, Osred, King of the Northumbrians, was killed, and Ceolred, King of the Mercians, died. The man of God Egbert converted the monks of Iona to the Catholic Easter and the canonical tonsure.

In the year 725, King Wictred of Kent died.

In the year 729, comets appeared: the holy Egbert departed this life: Osric died.

In the year 731, Archbishop Bertwald died. In the same year, the fifteenth of the reign of King Ethelbald of the Mercians, Tatwin was consecrated ninth Archbishop of Canterbury.

*

WITH God's help, I, Bede, the servant of Christ and priest of the monastery of the blessed apostles Peter and Paul at Wearmouth and Jarrow, have assembled these facts about the history of the Church in Britain, and of the Church of the English in particular, so far as I have been able to ascertain them from ancient writings, from the traditions of our forebears, and from my own personal knowledge.

I was born on the lands of this monastery, and on reaching seven years of age, I was entrusted by my family first to the most reverend Abbot Benedict and later to Abbot Ceolfrid for my education. I have spent all the remainder of my life in this monastery and devoted myself entirely to the study of the Scriptures. And while I have observed the regular discipline and sung the choir offices daily in church, my chief delight has always been in study, teaching, and writing.

I was ordained deacon in my nineteenth year, and priest in my thirtieth, receiving both these orders at the hands of the most reverend Bishop John at the direction of Abbot Ceolfrid. From the time of my receiving the priesthood until my fifty-ninth year, I have worked, both for my own benefit and that of my brethren, to compile short extracts from the works of the venerable Fathers on Holy Scripture and to comment on their meaning and interpretation. These books are as follows:

The beginning of Genesis, up to the birth of Isaac and Ishmael's rejection: four Books.

The Tabernacle: its vessels and priestly vestments: three Books.

The First Part of Samuel, up to the death of Saul: three Books.

On the Building of the Temple: an allegorical interpretation like the others: two Books.

Thirty Questions on the Books of Kings.

On the Proverbs of Solomon: three Books.

On the Song of Songs: seven Books.

On Isaiah, Daniel, The Twelve Prophets, and part of Jeremiah, with chapter headings taken from blessed Jerome's Treatise.

On Ezra and Nehemiah: three Books.

On the Song of Habakkuk: one Book.

On the Book of the blessed father Tobias: an allegorical interpretation on Christ and the Church: one Book.

Chapters of Readings on the Pentateuch of Moses, Joshua, and Judges; on the Books of Kings and Chronicles; on the Book of the blessed father Job; on Proverbs, Ecclesiastes, and the Song of Songs; on the Prophets Isaiah, Ezra, and Nehemiah.

On the Gospel of Mark: four Books.

On the Gospel of Luke: six Books.

Homilies on the Gospel: two Books.

On the Apostle [Paul]: in which I have carefully transcribed in order whatever I have found on the subject in the works of Saint Augustine.

On the Acts of the Apostles: two Books.

On the Seven Catholic Epistles: one Book on each.

On the Apocalypse of Saint John: three Books.

Also, *Chapters of Readings* from all the new Testament except the Gospel.

Also, a book of *Letters* to various persons, including one on the six ages of the world; on the dwellings of the children of Israel; on Isaiah's saying, '*And they shall be shut up in the prison, and after many days shall they be visited*': on the reason for the leap year; and on Anatolius' explanation of the equinox.

Also, *The Histories of the Saints*. I have translated Paulinus' metrical work on the *Life and Sufferings of the confessor Saint Felix* into prose. And I have corrected, to the best of my ability, the sense of a book on *The Life and Sufferings of Saint Anastasius*, which had been badly translated from the Greek, and worse amended by some unskilful person. I have also written the *Life* of our father, the holy monk and Bishop Cuthbert, first in heroic verse and later in prose.

I have written in two books *The History of the Abbots Benedict, Ceolfrid, and Hwaetbert*, rulers of this monastery in which I delight to serve the Divine Goodness.

The Ecclesiastical History of our island and people: in five Books.

A Martyrology of the feast-days of the holy martyrs: in which I have carefully tried to record everything I could learn not only on what date, but also by what kind of combat and under what judge they overcame the world.

A Book of Hymns in various metres or rhythms.

A Book of Epigrams in heroic or elegiac verse.

On the Nature of Things, and *On Times:* a book on each, and one larger book *On Times*.

A Book on *Orthography*, arranged in alphabetical order.

A Book on *The Art of Poetry*, with a small work appended *On Tropes and Figures*; that is, the figures and manners of speech found in holy scripture.

*

I PRAY YOU, noble Jesu, that as You have graciously granted me joyfully to imbibe the words of Your knowledge, so You will also of Your bounty grant me to come at length to Yourself,
> the Fount of all wisdom,
> And to dwell in Your presence
> for ever.

BEDE'S LETTER
TO
EGBERT

✤

INTRODUCTORY NOTE

✤

THIS letter was written a few months before Bede's death. It was completed on 5 November 734; Bede died on 26 May 735. Its style is more rhetorical than that of most of the *History* and more closely resembles that of Bede's sermons and exegetical works. Long sentences abound, there are frequent biblical quotations, and the main inspiration in its sentence structure, its parallelisms and chiasmus, is biblical. In this way its structure has some resemblance to certain 'set pieces' of the *History*, like the stories of Coifi and of Caedmon, and to the *Death of Bede*.

The letter is an example of a private exhortation to a prelate by an author who will probably never become one. It is a rare example of a letter concerning pastoral care in early Anglo-Saxon England. While it is in some ways an artificial exercise, its special interest lies in its variety of information about the good and bad state of the Church in Northumbria: it is a witness to Bede's realism and concern. Here we can read about episcopal government, about the use of the vernacular, about abuses in monasteries and the virtue of the laity. It is a useful check on the picture of Northumbrian Christianity presented in Bede's *History*. The failings of the prelates in 734 help us to understand the stress laid on the simplicity and poverty of Aidan, Colman and Cuthbert as depicted (perhaps too idealistically) in the *History*. The heart of the letter, both in material and style, is the passage on the false monasteries, which were particularly detestable to Bede, a true monk.

His conclusion attributes the decline to riches and avarice. It seems certain that there was much wealth in the Northumbrian Church by this time. Alcuin attributed to Oswald endowments of silver, gold and jewels; tapestries, chandeliers and lanterns are also mentioned (*The Bishops, Kings and Saints of York*, ed. P. Godman, (Oxford 1982), lines 276 ff.). The same author praised Wilfrid II's gifts of silver to York (ibid, lines 1222 ff.) as well as those of Egbert himself. Cuthbert's superb gold and jewelled pectoral cross, as well as the magnificent *Lindisfarne Gospels*, reveal wealth of which Alcuin approved, while Bede perhaps did not: his silences on these matters (like his selective silence on St Wilfrid) are surely indicative of his values.

What effect did Bede's letter have? It must be said that in spite of his exhortations, the Northumbrian dioceses were not divided further, nor were the early medieval laity encouraged to receive the Eucharist as frequently as Bede desired. On the other hand the Council of Clovesho of 747, whether or not attended by Egbert, contains in its Canons passages which were surely inspired by this letter. These include Canon 1 on the quality of the bishops' life styles; Canon 3 on visiting their dioceses every year; Canons 4 and 5 on their duty to sustain the observance of monasteries, even when these are owned by laypeople who cannot be expelled; Canon 9 that no fees should be charged for baptisms; Canon 10 that they learn and teach the Lord's Prayer and the Creed in English.

This translation has been made from the Latin text edited by C. Plummer (*Baedae Opera Historica* (Oxford 1896), I, 405–23), based on but two Latin manuscripts; his numbering of paragraphs has been retained for ease of reference. Some use has been made of the translation by Dorothy Whitelock in *EHD* I (1968), 735–45.

BEDE'S LETTER TO EGBERT

✤

1. BEDE, the servant of Christ, sends greetings to the most beloved and reverend Bishop Egbert.*

Last year when I spent some days with you in your monastery for the sake of study, I remember you said you would like to talk to me again about our common interests in learning. If by God's will it had been possible for me to achieve this, there would have been no need to send you this letter, because then I would have more easily suggested in private talk whatever I wished, or whatever I thought necessary. But since the state of my health, as you know, has prevented this, I have tried to do what I could, through love and brotherly devotion sending by letter what I was unable to say in person. I ask you in God's name not to consider my words to be proud and arrogant but rather the expression of humble duty, which they are.

2. THEREFORE, most beloved bishop in Christ, I exhort you carefully to strengthen with good works and sound teaching that sacred dignity which God, who has given both authority and spiritual grace, has generously entrusted to you. For neither gift can be complete without the other if one who lives a good life neglects the duty of preaching, or if a bishop who teaches correctly neglects to practise right actions. But he who truly accomplishes both is a servant who surely awaits the coming of his Lord and hopes soon to hear the words: 'Well done, good and faithful servant; because you have been faithful over a few things, I will set you over many; enter into the joy of your Lord.'* If however, which God forbids, one who has received the dignity of a bishop takes no pains either to restrain himself

from evil actions by virtuous living or to correct and admonish the people subject to him, then the Gospel clearly indicates what shall happen to him in its sentence on the unworthy servant: 'Cast him out into the exterior darkness, where there will be weeping and gnashing of teeth.'*

3. ABOVE all I would like to persuade you, holy father, to restrain yourself as a worthy bishop from idle conversation, disparaging remarks and other pollutions of an undisciplined tongue, and to devote your mind and your speech to the word of God and meditation on the Scriptures, reading specially the letters of Paul the Apostle to Timothy and Titus, as well as to the words of the holy Pope Gregory as amply expressed in the book of Pastoral Care and in his Homilies on the Gospels.* Thus your speech will always be seasoned with the salt of wisdom and will shine forth as more elevated than common talk and more worthy of God's attention. For just as it is a desecration if the sacred vessels of the altar are profaned for secular use and base purposes, so also is it altogether improper and deplorable if a man who was ordained to consecrate the Lord's sacrament at the altar shall at one moment stand ready to serve God by performing the sacraments, and at the next leave the church to speak trivial irrelevances or to perform evil acts with the very same lips and hands which just before had handled the sacred mysteries.

4. IN order to preserve purity in word and work, the company of men who serve God with faithful devotion, as well as sacred study, are together an immense help. If at any time my tongue begins to speak impurely or evil acts creep in, I can avoid a fall by the help of devout companions. As it is very useful for all servants of God to provide for themselves in this way, how much more is this so for those in holy orders, who have to care not only about their own salvation but also devote themselves to the salvation of the church committed to their care? This is in accordance with Paul's words: 'Besides those things that are without, there is that which presses upon me daily, anxiety for

all the churches. Who is weak and I am not weak? Who is made to stumble and I am not on fire?*

I am not speaking in this way as if I knew that you do the contrary, but because it is rumoured that certain bishops serve Christ in such a way that they have no men of religion or continence with them, but rather those who are given to laughter, jokes, idle tales, feasting and drunkenness and other attractions of a loose way of life. Daily they feed the stomach on rich food rather than the soul on heavenly sacrifice. If you find such people anywhere, I would like you to correct them by your sacred authority and exhort them to have companions of their daily and nightly actions who are able to benefit the people by actions worthy of God and by suitable exhortation: thus are they competent to help forward the spiritual work of the bishops. Read the Acts of the Apostles and you will see, as Luke tells us, what kind of companions Paul and Barnabas had, and what sort of actions they accomplished wherever they went. As soon as they entered towns or synagogues, they took care to preach the word of God and to spread it everywhere.* I desire that you too, my beloved father, should do the same wherever you can. You were chosen by God for this office, you were ordained for this purpose: to preach God's word with great strength, helped by the king of virtues, our Lord Jesus Christ. This you will duly achieve if wherever you go, you promptly assemble the inhabitants and show them this by words of exhortation and the example of good living by your companions as well as yourself: so you will be seen to be like the leader of a heavenly army.

5. BECAUSE the distances between the places which belong to your diocese are too great for you alone to suffice for visiting them all and preaching the word of God in its many hamlets and homesteads within the span of a year, you should certainly appoint several helpers for yourself in this holy work, that is, by ordaining priests and appointing teachers who will zealously preach in each hamlet the word of God and offer the heavenly mysteries and above all perform the sacrament of baptism

whenever the opportunity arises. In preaching to the people, this message more than any other should be proclaimed: that the Catholic faith, as contained in the Apostles' Creed and the Lord's Prayer which the reading of the Gospel teaches us, should be deeply memorized by all who are under your rule. All who have already learnt the Latin tongue by constant reading have quite certainly learnt these texts as well; but as for the unlearned, that is, those who know their own language only, make these learn the texts in their own tongue and accurately sing them. This should be done not only by the laity still settled in secular life but also by clerics and monks who are already expert in the Latin language. For thus it will come about that the whole congregation of believers learns how to be full of faith and how it must protect and arm itself against the attacks of unclean spirits by firm belief: thus it comes about that the whole chorus of those who are praying to God learns what should be specially sought from God's mercy. That is why I have frequently offered translations of both the Creed and the Lord's Prayer into English to many unlearned priests. For St Ambrose the Bishop, speaking of faith, admonishes believers to sing the words of the creed each morning: thus they fortify themselves with a spiritual antidote against the devil's poison, which he can wickedly instil by day and by night. Moreover the custom of repeated prayer and genuflexions has taught us to sing the Lord's Prayer more often.*

6. IF in ruling and feeding Christ's flock your pastoral authority achieves this, no one can say how much heavenly reward you will have earned in the future from the Shepherd of shepherds. In proportion to the rare examples of this holy task being achieved by the bishops of our nation, you will be rewarded all the higher for your singular merit. Thus you will be enkindled, fired by fatherly kindness and solicitude, to lead the people of God through frequent recitation of the Creed and the Lord's Prayer to the goal of understanding and love, hope and faith and the pursuit of those realities which are prayed for. On the contrary, if you accomplish the charge entrusted to you by the

Lord less diligently, you will receive your future portion along with the wicked and lazy servant who kept back his talent,* especially if you presume to demand and receive temporal dues from those to whom you give back no gifts of spiritual benefit. When the Lord, sending his disciples to preach the gospel, said: 'And preach as you go, saying "the kingdom of heaven is at hand", he added, just after: 'freely you have received, freely give; do not possess gold or silver.'* If then he ordered them to preach the gospel without charge, allowing them to receive neither gold nor silver nor any temporal riches from those to whom they preached; what danger, I ask, threatens those who do the contrary?

7. PAY heed then to how serious a sin is committed by those who most diligently demand earthly rewards from their hearers but take no trouble at all with preaching, exhorting or reproving* for their eternal salvation. Ponder this anxiously, beloved Bishop, and give it careful attention. For we have heard, and it is well known, that many farms and small villages of our people are situated in remote hills and dense forests, where for many years on end no bishop has been seen providing any ministry of heavenly grace, but where nobody is exempt from paying dues to this same bishop. Nor do these places lack only a bishop to confirm the baptized by the laying on of hands: there is not even a teacher of any kind to instruct them on the truth of the faith and the differences between good and evil. Thus it comes about that some bishops fail to preach the gospel or lay their hands on believers without reward, but even, which is worse, accept money from their flock which the Lord forbade, yet neglect to perform the ministry which the Lord ordered. Samuel however, God's high priest, acted very differently, we read, through the witness of the whole people: 'Having then lived among you, he said, from my youth until this day, behold I am ready: speak of me before the Lord and before his anointed whether I have taken any man's ox or ass, if I have wronged any man, if I have oppressed any man, if I have taken a bribe at any man's hand, and I will despise it this day and will restore it to you.'* And

they said: 'You have not wronged us or oppressed us or taken anything at any man's hand.'* By the merit of his innocence and justice he deserved to be numbered among the foremost leaders and priests of the people of God and to be worthy to be heard in his prayers by God and to talk with him, as the psalmist says: 'Moses and Aaron among his priests and Samuel among those that call upon his name: these called on the Lord and he heard them. He spoke to them in the pillar of the cloud.'*

8. IF we believe and proclaim that an advantage is conferred on believers by the laying on of hands through which the Holy Spirit is received, then it follows that those who have not received this rite lack this same advantage. On whom does their deprivation reflect but on those bishops who promise to be their protectors, but who are either unable or unwilling to exercise this office of spiritual guardian?* There is no greater cause of this sin than avarice. Against this the Apostle, in whom Christ was speaking, said: 'The root of all evils is the desire for money.' And again: 'The covetous, he said, will not inherit the kingdom of God.'* When indeed a bishop, at the dictate of love of money, in the name of his office takes on a greater population than he can possibly visit and preach to in the course of a year, this evidently results in danger both to himself and to those over whom he is promoted, because he is falsely called their protector.

9. IN making these few suggestions, beloved bishop, about the misfortunes which our nation endures, I earnestly entreat you to try as best you can to correct by a right rule of life those actions which you can see have been done amiss. For you have, I believe, a very energetic helper in this just task, namely King Ceolwulf,* who through his innate love of religion will take care constantly and firmly to help forward whatever belongs to the rule of justice; as you are his closest and dearest kinsman, he will specially help you to perfect the good enterprises you begin. Therefore I would like you to admonish him prudently that you should both take care to restore the ecclesiastical state of our

nation into a better condition than it has been recently. This, I
believe, cannot be accomplished except by consecrating more
bishops for our people, following the example of the lawgiver
who, when he could not sustain the burdens and disputes of the
people of Israel, chose and consecrated, helped by God's counsel, seventy elders with whose careful help he could more easily
carry the burden placed upon him.* For who does not see how
much better it is to divide such a great weight of church
government among several who can easily bear their share
rather than to overburden one man with a load he cannot carry?
For holy Pope Gregory, when he wrote in a letter sent to the
blessed Archbishop Augustine about the faith of our people,
still in the future and needing to be nurtured in Christ, decreed
that twelve bishops were to be consecrated after the faith had
been accepted, among whom the Bishop of York should receive
the *pallium* from the Holy See as a Metropolitan.* I would like
you, my lord, to try now to complete the full complement of
bishops with the help and protection of this king, beloved of
God, so that by abundant bishops the Church of Christ may be
more perfectly developed in the practice of holy religion. But
through the carelessness of earlier kings and very foolish dona-
tions, as we well know, it is not now easy to find a vacant place
where a new episcopal see could be established.

10. THEREFORE I would consider it expedient that with the
consent of a great council, by royal as well as ecclesiastical
decree, the site of one among the monasteries be found where
an Episcopal See can be located. Lest by chance the abbot and
monks oppose and resist this decree, let them be authorized to
choose one of their own community to be ordained as bishop
and then let him rule both the monastery and the adjacent
territory of the diocese.* But if nobody in the monastery can be
found who should be chosen as bishop, then let them search
out, according to canonical statute, one who should be ordained
bishop of the diocese. If with God's help you accomplish what
we suggest, you will very easily obtain also, we believe, that

the church of York receive a metropolitan archbishop in accordance with the decrees of the Apostolic See. If it seems necessary for such a monastery receiving a bishopric that its endowment of lands and possessions be increased, then there are many places, as we all know, given the name of monasteries by a very foolish way of speaking, yet have none of the reality of a monastic way of life. Some of these I would like to be transformed by synodal authority from impurity to chastity, from vanity to truth, from intemperance and greed to continence and holiness of heart, and to be taken over to help the new episcopal see which should be set up.

11. BECAUSE there are many large places of this kind which, as is commonly said, are useful neither to God nor man, because they neither keep the life of the rule according to God's will nor are they owned by thegns or gesiths of the secular power who defend our people against the barbarians, then if anyone establishes an Episcopal See in one of these places because of the needs of the times, he will clearly incur no guilt of deviation from duty but rather will have clearly accomplished a work of piety.* How can it be considered a sin when unjust judgements of princes are corrected by the just decisions of better rulers and the deceitful compositions of wicked scribes are deleted and made void by the discerning judgement of prudent priests? This is in accordance with the example of sacred history which describes the times of the kings of Judah from David and Solomon to the last of the line, Hezekiah, and shows that some of them were religious but more of them were wicked: in turn the wicked rejected the deeds of their virtuous predecessors and then again the just corrected with all urgency the misdeeds of the wicked through the help of the Spirit of God acting through holy prophets and priests: – all this was in agreement with the word of holy Isaiah, commanding and saying: 'Loose the bands of false covenants. Let them that are broken go free and break every unjust document.'*

With this example your holiness, with the devout king of our people, should eliminate the unjust actions and writings of our predecessors, and provide for the sacred and secular good of our province, lest in our time either religion should cease and the love and fear of God who sees our hearts perish, or else by the reduction in numbers of the secular army there should not be enough men to defend our boundaries from barbarian invasion. It is indeed shameful to say how many places called 'monasteries' these men who are entirley ignorant of monastic life have taken under their control, as you yourself well know, so that there is no place left where sons of nobles or veteran soldiers can receive an estate. Thus unoccupied and unmarried, when the time of puberty is over, they live with no purpose of continence: because of this they either cross the seas and leave the country for which they should have fought, or else with even greater guilt and shamelessness, as they have no commitment to chastity, they serve impurity and fornication, not even abstaining from virgins consecrated to God.

12. OTHERS even more disgracefully, since they are laymen with no experience or love of life under a rule, give money to kings and buy for themselves, under the pretext of building monasteries, estates in which they freely indulge their lust: they have these ascribed to them in hereditary right by royal charters which are confirmed by the written assent of bishops, abbots and secular magnates as though they were truly worthy of God. Having thus usurped for themselves small or large estates, free from both human and divine service, they serve in reality only their own desires as laymen in charge of monks. Moreover they do not assemble real monks there, but rather wanderers who have been expelled from genuine monasteries for the sin of disobedience, or whoever they may have enticed out of them, or any of their own followers whom they can persuade to receive the tonsure and promise monastic obedience to themselves.* They thus fill the 'monasteries' they have built with groups of these deformed people and – a very ugly and unprecedented spectacle – the very same men are now occupied with wives and procreating children and now rise from their beds and accomplish assiduously whatever needs to be done

inside the monastic precincts. Moreover they obtain with similar audacity places for their wives, as they say, to build 'monasteries'. as these are laywomen they authorise themselves to be rulers of the handmaids of Christ. To all these people the popular proverb applies: 'Wasps can indeed make honeycomb, but they fill it with poison, not honey.'

13. THUS for about thirty years since the death of Aldfrith our province has been so demented with error that almost all the local rulers have procured for themselves a 'monastery' of this kind and involved their wives in similar guilt for a wicked transaction; as this evil custom has spread, the king's ministers and household have done the same. Thus by a perverse state of affairs many are found who call themselves 'abbots' and at the same time rulers and ministers or servants of the king: although as laymen they could have learnt something about monastic life by hearsay if not by experience, yet they are complete strangers to the character and profession which should teach it. Indeed these people suddenly, as you know, receive the tonsure at their own pleasure and by their own judgement instantly become not monks but abbots. Because they clearly have neither the knowledge of nor the zeal for monastic virtues, what can be more appropriate to them than the curse of the gospel where it is said: 'If the blind lead the blind, both will fall into the pit'?* This blindness could be ended sometime, restrained by regular discipline and expelled far from all the land of holy church by episcopal and synodal authority if the bishops themselves did not help forward and pledge themselves to evil practices of this kind: they not only fail to oppose unjust decrees with just ones but rather take care to confirm them (as we said) with their official approval. In this they are driven by the very same love of money, giving their written approval to these wicked charters, as were the purchasers who obtained 'monasteries' of this kind. *

I would indeed tell you plenty more by letter about such matters and similar abuses with which our province is miserably afflicted, if I did not know that you yourself are well aware of these matters. I have written in this way not as if I were teaching you anything you did not already know, but rather to warn you by friendly admonition to correct with urgent diligence, as far as you can, those situations which you know very well are irregular.

14. AT this present time I earnestly ask and entreat you in the Lord to protect assiduously the flock committed to your care against the persistence of ravening wolves, and to recall that you have been appointed to be not a hireling but a shepherd, who shows his love for the supreme Shepherd by carefully feeding his sheep and by being ready, if necessary, with the blessed prince of the apostles, to lay down his life for these same sheep. I pray that you carefully take heed lest when this same prince of the apostles and other leaders of the flocks of the faithful on the Day of Judgement offer the supreme fruits of their pastoral care, any part of your flock be separated among the goats at the Judge's left hand and deservedly depart with a curse to eternal fire; but rather may you deserve to be counted among the number of those whom Isaiah describes: 'The least shall become a thousand and the little one among the strongest nation.'*

It is your duty to enquire diligently into what is done well and what is done badly in the monasteries of your diocese: taking care lest an abbot is ignorant or a despiser of the rule,* or an unworthy abbess is set up over a community of Christ's servants and handmaids, or on the other hand a contemptuous and undisciplined group of disciples rebels against the rule of their spiritual masters, particularly since, as is often reported, your bishops say that what is done in particular monasteries belongs not to the care of kings or secular magnates, but only to the investigation and judgement of the bishops alone, unless someone in the monasteries has offended against the secular rulers. It is your duty, I say, to prevent the devil from usurping a kingdom for himself in places consecrated to God, lest discord take the place of peace, quarrels that of piety, drunkenness that of sobriety, fornication and homicide that of charity and chastity, lest some should be found among you of whom just complaint may be made in these words: 'I saw the wicked buried who, when they were yet living, were in the holy place and were praised in the city as men of just works'.＊

15. YOU should also care solicitously for those still in secular life so that, as we advised at the beginning of this letter, you remember to provide sufficient teachers of the life of salvation, and that you make your flock learn among other things by what works they may chiefly please God, from what sins they should consequently abstain, with what sincerity of heart they should believe in God, with what devotion they should pray, asking for the mercy of God; how they need with frequent diligence to fortify themselves with the sign of our Lord's cross against the ceaseless snares of unclean spirits and learn how salutary it is for every kind of Christian to receive daily the body and blood of our Lord, as you know is widely practised by the church of Christ throughout Italy, Gaul, Africa, Greece and the whole of the East. This kind of observance and devout consecration to God has been so long absent from and almost foreign to most laymen of our province through the neglect of preachers, that those of them who are considered more devout do not presume to receive communion except at Christmas, the Epiphany and Easter, although there are countless boys and girls, young men and virgins, old men and women, all of chaste life, who could without any shadow of doubt receive communion every Sunday and on feasts of the holy apostles and martyrs, as you yourself have seen done in the holy Roman and Apostolic Church. Married people also, if each shows a measure of continence and professes the virtue of chastity, may lawfully and gladly do the same.＊

16. I HAVE taken care, most holy bishop, to write down these ideas briefly for you, both out of consideration for your love and out of esteem for the common good, deeply desiring and frequently exhorting you to take care to rescue our people from former errors and bring them back to a surer and more direct way of life. If some people of whatever rank or order try to

hold back or hinder your good beginnings, do you for your part, mindful of heavenly reward, strive to bring to a firm conclusion your purposeful and holy policy. I realize that some people will vigorously oppose our exhortation, especially those who feel themselves involved in the sinful practices from which we restrain you; but it is appropriate for you to remember the apostle's answer: 'We must obey God rather than men.'* God's command is: 'Sell what you possess and give alms' and 'unless a man renounces all he possesses, he cannot be my disciple.'* But the recent tradition of some people who claim to be servants of God is rather not to sell what they possess, but even to acquire what they do not yet own. How does anyone dare to approach the service of God, either keeping what he had in secular life or, under the pretext of a better life, amassing riches which he did not have? Even the apostles' censure on Ananias and Saphira trying to do this very thing was not one of penance, nor of compensation, but rather a punishment by condemnation to an instant avenging death. Indeed they had not even chosen to amass others' goods, but only deceitfully to retain their own. Hence it is quite clear how far removed were the minds of the apostles from receiving payments of money, for they served God fittingly under the rule: 'Blessed are the poor, for yours is the kingdom of God;'* and on the other hand they were likewise taught by the contrary example: 'Woe to you that are rich, for you have your consolation.'* Or should we think that the apostle Paul was in error or wrote a lie when he admonished us, saying: 'Brethren, do not err'* and immediately afterwards added: 'Neither the covetous nor drunkards nor exortioners shall possess the kingdom of God.'?* And again: 'Know this, that no fornicator nor unclean, covetous or rapacious man, which is the serving of idols, will have inheritance in the kingdom of Christ and of God.'* Since the apostle clearly calls avarice and rapacity idolatry, how can we suppose those have erred who have either withdrawn from witnessing avaricious deals although the king ordered them, or else have set their hands to rooting out evil documents and their witness-lists?

17. WE should indeed marvel at the temerity of the foolish or rather weep over the misery of the blind who, without any regard for the fear of God, clearly, everywhere and every day are proved to reject and hold of no account what the apostles and prophets have written, inspired as they were by the Holy Spirit. Yet on the contrary they fear to erase and amend what they themselves or others, inspired by avarice or impurity, have written as though it were holy and protected by God, in the manner (if I am not mistaken) of the pagans who despise the cult of the true God yet venerate, fear, worship, adore and invoke as gods the things which they have formed and made in their own hearts, fully deserving that rebuke of our Lord who denounced the Pharisees who preferred their secondary traditions to God's laws in these words: 'Why do you also transgress the commandment of God for the sake of your tradition?'★ Even if they produce charters drawn up in defence of their covetous actions, confirmed by the witness-lists of noble men, then never forget, I beg of you, the judgement of our Lord when he said: 'Every plant which my heavenly Father has not planted shall be rooted up.'★

Indeed I would like to learn from you, beloved bishop, seeing that the Lord testifies, saying: 'Wide is the gate and broad is the way which leads to destruction and many are those who enter it: how narrow is the gate and straight is the way which leads to life and few are those who find it',★ what you believe about the life and eternal destiny of those who are known to go by the wide gate and the broad way for their whole lives, and do not trouble to withstand or resist even in the smallest matters their pleasures and desires of body and soul for the sake of heavenly reward. Or should we believe that they can be absolved from guilt by alms which they were seen to give to the poor amid their everyday greed and pleasures, when the very hand as well as the conscience which would offer a gift to God ought to be clean and absolved from sin? Or should we hope that when they are dead, they can be redeemed by the mystery of the holy Mass, of which they were unworthy while they lived?★

Does the sin of greed seem small to them? I will treat this

matter a little more fully. It caused Balaam, a man full of the spirit of prophecy, to be deprived of the lot of the saints; it defiled and destroyed Achan, son of Charmi, through his share in the accursed thing; it stripped Saul of his insignia of kingship; it deprived Gehazi of the merit of prophecy and contaminated him and his seed with the chronic disease of leprosy; it deposed Judas Iscariot from the glory of the apostolate; it injured with physical death Ananias and Saphira, whom we mentioned above as unworthy of the company of monks and, to come to higher matters, this cast out the angels from heaven and expelled our first ancestors from a paradise of perpetual delight.

If you wish to know, this is the three-headed dog of Hell, to whom the poets gave the name of Cerberus, from whose savage teeth John the Apostle would keep us safe, saying: 'Beloved, love not the world nor the things that are in the world. If anyone loves the world, the love of the Father is not in him. For all that is in the world is the lust of the flesh and the lust of the eyes and the pride of life, which is not of the Father, but is of the world.'*

These things I have spoken briefly against the poison of avarice. For the rest, if we wished to deal on a similar scale with drunkenness, gluttony, impurity and other plagues of this kind, the length of this letter would be inordinately extended.

May the grace of the supreme Shepherd keep you safe, most beloved bishop in Christ, for the salutary feeding of his sheep. Written on the Fifth of November, in the third indiction.

CUTHBERT'S LETTER
ON THE
ILLNESS AND DEATH OF THE
VENERABLE
BEDE, THE PRIEST

✤

INTRODUCTORY NOTE

✤

THIS admirable letter was written by Cuthbert, monk, and later Abbot of Jarrow, who confirmed and supplemented its contents in a letter to Lul nearly thirty years later (see note 1). An eye-witness account, it seems to date from soon after 735: it reveals deep admiration for Bede himself, but also a desire to write for posterity in a style close to Bede's own. This makes it a most fitting memorial to Bede as an effective teacher and as a model monk.

The deathbed of a saint is a literary genre of which there are many examples, for instance Martin of Tours, Columba of Iona, Ailred of Rievaulx and Hugh of Lincoln. Cuthbert's letter stands comparison with all these: its disciplined structure and controlled emotion make it especially moving. It adds to our knowledge of Bede and his community while being entirely consonant with what Bede tells us about himself in the last chapter of his *History* and about his community in his *Lives of the Abbots*. Recent archaeological discoveries at Jarrow by Professor Rosemary Cramp add to this knowledge, enabling us to envisage Bede's cell as small and about ten feet square, with a low wooden screen separating, what is thought to be the prayer-area, from the rest.

Stylistically the *Death of Bede* is a superbly worked mosaic of quotations from, and allusions to, New Testament texts describing the death of Christ and the death of Paul, patristic and liturgical elements and Bede's own preface to his *Life of St Cuthbert*, the whole arranged in a complex biblical structure. With Cuthbert's other letter, it is good evidence for the early cult of Bede as a saint.

It soon enjoyed a wide circulation, as is clear from the survival to our own day of sixty-five medieval manuscripts with early examples from both England and the Continent. It has often been translated before, notably by John Henry Newman, Charles Plummer and by Colgrave and Mynors who took the Latin text from the Hague manuscript (see E. van K. Dobbie, *Cedmon's Hymn and Bede's Death Song*, New York 1937, and N. R. Ker, *Medium Aevum* viii (1939), 40–44). More recently Dr David Howlett has convincingly identified it as an example of biblical style, abounding in parallelisms and chiasmus and very precisely composed (see his 'Biblical Style in early insular Latin' in *Sources of Anglo-Saxon Culture*, eds. P. E. Szarmach and V. D. Oggins, Kalamazoo 1986, pp. 127–47). There seems no doubt that Cuthbert learnt this skill from Bede himself, who practised it in the *History* (ii. 13 and iv. 24). This translation owes much to this article, based on the Bamberg MS Staatsbibliothek A.I.47, the most accurate transcript of the Continental recension; but for this edition it has not been possible to reproduce all the nuances of the biblical style.

CUTHBERT'S LETTER ON THE
ILLNESS AND DEATH OF
THE VENERABLE BEDE,
THE PRIEST

✤

To his most beloved fellow-teacher in Christ Cuthwin, Cuthbert his fellow-disciple wishes eternal salvation in God.★

The little present which you sent me I received with much gratitude, and with much pleasure I read your devoutly learned letter; from these I found out what I specially desired to know, that you are lovingly offering masses and fervent prayers for our father and master Bede, beloved of God.

Therefore, through love of him rather than through confidence in my own ability, I am delighted to tell you in these few words how he passed from this world, since I understand that this is what you desired, this is what you requested.

He was indeed troubled by illness and especially frequent breathlessness, yet he was almost without pain before the day of the Lord's Resurrection, that is for almost two weeks; after Easter he continued in the same state, cheerful and joyful, and giving thanks to Almighty God every day and every night and indeed every hour until the day of the Lord's Ascension, which was the 26th of May.★

Every day he gave lessons to us, his students; for the rest of the day he was busy singing the psalms as best he could. He would spend the whole night in prayer and thanksgiving to God unless a short sleep prevented him. When he woke again, he immediately meditated on the accustomed chants from Scripture, not forgetting to give thanks to God with hands outstretched.

In all truth I can say that I never saw nor heard any other man so diligent in giving thanks to the living God. 'O truly blessed man.'* He often sang the sentence of St Paul the Apostle, saying: 'It is a fearful thing to fall into the hands of the living God'* as well as many other words of Scripture, with which he admonished us from the slumber of the soul by thinking in good time about our last hours.* And in our own language (as he knew our poems well) he would say:

> Before that enforced journey no one becomes
> Wiser in thought than he may need be,
> For considering before his going hence
> What for his spirit of good or evil
> After his death day might be judged.*

He would also sing antiphons for our consolation and his, of which this is one:

> O king of glory, lord of Might,
> Who rose today in victory above all the heavens,
> Do not leave us orphans,
> But send us the Father's promised Spirit of Truth,
> Alleluia.*

When he came to the words 'Do not leave us orphans', he burst into tears and wept copiously. After an hour he would repeat what he had left unfinished and thus he continued the whole day. And when we heard this, we shared his sorrow and wept; we wept and cried in turn; indeed we wept as we studied. In this kind of joy we passed Paschaltide until the same Ascension Day.

And he rejoiced exceedingly and gave God thanks because he had deserved to suffer in this way, and he would often say: 'God chastises every son whom he receives'* as well as the words of Ambrose: 'I have not lived in such a way that I am ashamed to continue life among you, but I do not fear to die, because we have a uniquely good God.'*

In these days, besides our lessons and the chanting of psalms, he was much busied with two short works which are specially worthy of memory: the translation into our own language for the Church's benefit of the Gospel of St John from the beginning until the passage where it says: 'But what are these among so many?',* and also certain excerpts from the Book of Cycles by Bishop Isidore, about which he said: 'I do not wish my students to read lies, or to work at this task in vain after my death.'*

When the Tuesday before the Lord's Ascension came, his breathing became much worse and a small swelling appeared in his feet.

None the less he continued his teaching all that day and dictated cheerfully; among other things he said several times: 'Learn quickly now, for I do not know how long I shall live, nor whether after a short time my Maker will take me.' But he seemed to us to know very well when his end would come. And so he spent all that night awake in thanksgiving.

At daybreak on Wednesday he told us to finish the writing which we had begun. We did this until the third hour. From then onwards we processed with the relics of the saints, as the custom of that day required.*

There was one of us with him who said: 'Beloved master, there is still one chapter missing from the book you were dictating, but it seems to me difficult to ask you for more.' But he answered: 'It is easy. Take your pen and prepare it and write quickly.' And this he did.

At the ninth hour he said to me: 'I have a few treasures in my little box: pepper, handkerchiefs and incense.* Run quickly and fetch the priests of our monastery to me, so that I can distribute to them these little gifts which God has given me.' This I did with some trembling. When they came he spoke to them, urgently asking each of them to say masses and prayers for him with diligence; this they gladly promised.* But they were all very sad and they all wept, especially because he had said that they would not see his face much longer in this world.*

But they rejoiced about one thing he had said: 'It is time, if it so please my Maker, that I should be released from the body and come now to Him who formed me from nothing when I did not exist. I have lived a long time and the Holy Judge has provided well for me during my whole life. The time of my release is near;* indeed my soul longs to see Christ my king in all his beauty.'* This and many other admirable words he spoke in joy for our great profit until he came to his last day at vespertime.

Then the boy of whom I spoke, Wilbur by name, said again: 'Beloved master, there is still one sentence left, not yet written down.' He answered: 'Write it then.' After a short time the boy said: 'Now it is written.' And he replied: 'Good. It is finished.* You have spoken the truth.* Take my head in your hands,* for it pleases me very much to sit opposite my holy place where I used to pray, so that as I sit there I may call upon my Father.' And thus, on the floor of his cell singing: 'Glory be to the Father and to the Son and to the Holy Spirit' and the rest, he breathed out his spirit from his body. And it should be believed without doubt that, because he had always worked hard in the praise of God, his soul was carried by angels to the joy of Heaven which he desired. All who heard or saw the death of our blessed father Bede said that they had never seen anyone else end his days with such great devotion and peace. For as you have heard, as long as his soul remained in his body he sang: 'Glory be to the Father' and other words to the glory of God and with hands outstretched did not cease to give thanks to God.

I would like you to know also that much more could be spoken or written about him, but now my ignorant tongue cuts short my words. Nevertheless I intend with God's help to write more fully later what I myself have seen and heard about him.*

Here ends the letter of Cuthbert on the death of the venerable Bede, the priest.

NOTES

✦

BEDE'S ECCLESIASTICAL HISTORY

P. 41 Ceolwulf became king of Northumbria in 729. In 731 he was forcibly tonsured and abdicated. In the same year however he returned as king. He became a monk at Lindisfarne in 737; he died in 764.

P. 42 Albinus was abbot of the monastery of SS. Peter and Paul (later called St Augustine's) Canterbury, 709–32. Bede says (v.20) that he knew Greek well, and was virtually bilingual in Latin and English.

P. 42 Nothelm visited Rome during Gregory II's pontificate (715–31); Gregory was formerly librarian of the Roman church. Nothelm became Archbishop of Canterbury in 735; he died in 739.

P. 43 For this translation see R. Ray, 'Bede's vera lex historiae', *Speculum* lv (1980), 1–21. Bede regarded it as the historian's duty to report 'common belief' at least of a level generally acceptable to an educated community. This included reports of miracle stories, but also wider folk traditions such as elements in ii. 2.

P. 44 In these early chapters Bede quotes extensively from Orosius, Pliny, Solinus and Gildas. He skilfully assembles these elements into a lively and readable narrative. The reference to 28 cities is from Gildas, that to jet from Solinus. For Bede's weaknesses in his account of later Roman Britain, see D. N. Dumville, 'Sub-Roman Britain: History and Legend' in *History* lxii (1977), 173–92.

P. 45 Basil, *Hexameron*, Latin translation, *PL*, iii, 908

P. 45 Bede's word *Scotti* is translated 'Irish' throughout. Irish settlers had come to Argyll and the western Islands: this colony came to be known, like its founding kingdom in north-east Ireland, as Dalriada.

Five languages in Britain and five books of God's Law (the Pentateuch) so there will be five books of the *Ecclesiastical History*.

P. 46 H. Mayr-Harting, *The Coming of Christianity*, p. 50, plausibly suggests that this is a witty parody by Bede of pseudo-scientific contemporary writing. Bede certainly had a sense of humour and sometimes wrote with tongue in cheek.

P. 47 The true dates are years of Rome 699 and 700, i.e. 55 and 54 B.C. Orosius is the main source for this chapter and the next.

P. 48 This should be the year of Rome 796 or A.D. 43.

P. 49 This story is borrowed from the *Liber Pontificalis*, but it really refers to Lucius, King of Edessa and to one of his castles called Britium. But this legend had a very long life; see ODCC, s.v.

P. 50 In reality Hadrian built the Roman Wall from *c.* 122, but it was rebuilt by Severus in 205–08. It has a stone wall and deep ditch on its northern side; forts, castles and turrets at intervals, as well as an earthwork. The whole was 80 Roman miles long, extending from Wallsend to the Solway Firth. Bede's account is a bookish one; it owes more to Vegetius and Orosius than to his own observation.

P. 50 This sixth chapter is largely borrowed from Orosius, *Historia adversum paganos*, vii, 25. Diocletian reigned 284–305; the persecution lasted 303–05. It was probably the most painful ever experienced by the Christian Church in the Roman Empire, although it varied in severity in different areas. Bede leads up to the martyrdom of St Alban, which for him was a welcome link between the Church of the patristic age and the Anglo-Saxons, some of whom benefited from Alban's miracles. Verulamium and its Chiltern area may well have been conquered by Anglo-Saxons only in *c.* 570. Some recent scholars date Alban's martyrdom however to one or other of the earlier persecutions: see ODS, s.v.

P. 51 Venantius Fortunatus, *Carmina* viii, iii (*MGH Auct. Ant.* IV, 1, 185). Bede's account of Alban comes from the third version of his Passion. The existence of the martyrdom church is inferred from Gildas, but seems likely enough.

P. 55 Arianism was the most fundamental heresy in Christian history: it denied the divinity and eternity of the Son of God and therefore of Christ. Arius was condemned at the council of Nicea (325), which also formulated the Nicene Creed. Nevertheless it revived later and several barbarian peoples accepted it. Like other Christian Fathers Bede thought of all heresies, wherever they occurred, as threats to orthodoxy. Arianism in Britain may not have been so widespread as Bede seemed to think, but different varieties of paganism certainly flourished.

P. 56 Pelagius, usually described as a Briton, taught mainly in Rome and Africa, though some trace of his teaching survived in Ireland. He exaggerated the unaided power of the human will to do good, minimizing the need for divine grace and the effects of Original Sin. The Church in Britain was labelled 'Pelagian' by foreign churchmen, but Gildas said nothing about it. Bede however wrote the preface to his Song of Songs commentary against the Pelagian Julian of Eclanum. The verse at the end of this chapter was quoted several times by Bede: it is attributed to Prosper of Aquitaine (P.L. li, 149–52).

P. 58 Bede's next four chapters are inevitably based mainly on Gildas: the substance of the account has some validity, but much detail is disputed; see Dumville as in note to p. 44.

P. 60 Bede, following Prosper of Aquitaine, sees Palladius rather than the more important and British Patrick as main apostle of Ireland. For recent Patrician controversy see *ODCC* and *ODS*, s.v.

P. 62 This famous chapter begins with an approximate date: elsewhere Bede dates the tribes' arrival to 445/7. The Roman troops had left in 407 and the native rulers were unable to sustain permanent control. Bede's account is selective but substantially accurate, the last paragraph, dramatically rhetorical, is from Gildas and cannot have been of universal application.

The key to understanding the passage on Angles, Saxons and Jutes is that it attempts to explain the political realities of 731. Archaeologists have discovered overwhelming evidence from cremation urns and their patterns that in many parts of England, Angles and Saxons settled side by side rather than in different parts of the country. The Jutes have been much disputed, but they had admitted archaeological links with Kent. The area of *Angulus* was indeed deserted as Bede says; a rise in water-level could well have contributed to the departure of its people. Angles and Saxons formed the bulk of the settlers, but Frisians and Franks from the Ruhr such as *Boructuari* and *Rugini* were also among them (v. 9). Frisians are mentioned as merchants in London (see iv, 22), but they did not form independent political units. Hengist and Horsa are semi-mythical characters, probably conflated in some details from different traditions by Bede's Canterbury source.

P. 64 The battle of Badon Hill (*Mons Badonicus*) was an important defeat for the Anglo-Saxons, some of whom returned to the Continent, but it did not in the long run hinder their steady advance. Its date was *c.* 495: its place has been variously conjectured as Bath, Badbury Hill (nr. Swindon) or somewhere in Dorset.

P. 65 Germanus died *c.* 440 and his Life by Constantius (*c.* 475), the basis of Bede's ch. 17–24, though Gaulish in viewpoint, testifies to serious contact between the churches of Gaul and Britain. Germanus' intervention, important for Britain, was less so for the general history of the heresy. Although British Pelagians seem to have had status and wealth, it is improbable that they were a serious threat in Gaul and Britain. See E. A. Thompson, *St Germanus of Auxerre and the end of Roman Britain* (1984).

P. 68 Germanus' visit to Alban's shrine is important evidence for the continuity of the cult as well as to the use of relics in the fifth century. Both the exchange of relics and the use of earth soaked in the martyr's blood are well known elsewhere.

P. 69 Bede was less interested in the military and political aspects of this battle (whose place and exact date are unknown) than in its illustration of how a man of God could also be an effective man of action.

P. 72 In this chapter Bede falls back on Gildas as a source, but emphasizes the refusal of the British (Welsh) to preach the Gospel to the Anglo-Saxons.

Moreover the Roman Empire had no further part to play in Bede's story. During this chronological gap of about 150 years the Anglo-Saxons consolidated their settlements and kingdoms. The contrast between the energetic preachers from Ireland and Rome and the non-cooperative Welsh is fundamental for the whole book.

P. 72 Although earlier chapters provide the general context, this one marks the 'real subject' (Plummer) of Bede's work. Its Kentish inspiration is certain. Some or all of the letters of Gregory used by Bede were inserted at a late stage; but it should be noted that Bede did not use or did not have access to *all* of Gregory's letters which relate to England. These still provide a useful check on, and supplement to Bede: their author died over a century before Bede wrote.

P. 73 Gregory here clarifies Augustine's authority as of an abbot over his monks. Bede did not know of Gregory's letter to Eulogius referring to the consecration of Augustine as bishop in Germania before he reached England. Instead (i. 27) he deduced wrongly that Augustine returned to Arles for consecration.

P. 73 Indictions were cycles of fifteen years used by Roman and papal administrations in reckoning dates. Bede says elsewhere of this system: 'If you wish to find the indiction, take the year of Our Lord, add three and divide by fifteen; the remainder gives you the indiction for the current year.' (L.S.P.)

P. 75 The Anglo-Saxon hide was the amount of land necessary to support a family. It had no uniform measurement because the quality of land differed so much. Maitland estimated it at 150 acres.

P. 76 Chapters 25, 26 and 33 represent the Kentish account of the mission as current about 100 years after Augustine's death.

P. 77 The authenticity of these replies has been much controverted, but current opinion generally favours authenticity except for V (on marriage concessions). They reveal some of the problems of the Church at Canterbury, as well as Augustine's inexperience and Gregory's wisdom. Detailed commentary would be out of place here, but overall the first four are the most important. For further study see P. Meyvaert, 'Bede's Text of the *Libellus Responsionum*' in P. Clemoes and K. Hughes, *England before the Conquest* (Cambridge 1971). It is important to realize that these questions and answers circulated in manuscripts well before Bede was writing, but they provided welcome (if disproportionate) extra material.

P. 79 WH pp. 217–18: reading 'like herbs in a pot' as an alternative.

P. 79 Note here the contradiction between Gregory's pastoral guidance and the Laws of Ethelbert which decree a ten-fold compensation for stealing church property, a strong deterrent against violence towards a vulnerable yet royally protected group.

P. 90 The year 601 was decisive in the progress and consolidation of the Augustinian mission. The increase of equipment and personnel, the embryo organization of the Church in England, the papal letters of congratulation for Ethelbert and gentle reproof for Bertha (this one apparently unknown to Bede) all point to Ethelbert's recent conversion to Christianity. The waiting period of about four years should not surprise anyone who realizes how important it was for the King to obtain his aristocracy's support before abandoning traditional pagan belief. The grant of the pallium to Augustine indicates stability in the present and confidence in the future. A band of white wool worn by popes and archbishops over their sacerdotal vestments, it was eventually a sign of jurisdiction and of communion with the papacy. Gregory intended Augustine to have metropolitan authority over all bishops in the southern province, including the Welsh. Gregory used old records to choose London as Augustine's see; he seemed unaware of the political reality of his day in England. Canterbury, not London, was Ethelbert's principal town: his power as overlord king extended very much further than the small area of his direct rule in Kent. Gregory's plan of metropolitan rank for York was permanently realized only from 735, and it has endured to this day.

P. 92 This letter, which should follow and not precede that to Ethelbert (i, 31), contains directives important in missionary history. The principle of gradual conversion and of the implicit toleration of neutral and harmless pagan customs enabled Christianity to co-exist with, and eventually absorb, native art-forms and outlooks. Mention of the temples by Gregory indicates familiarity with these Roman buildings, but it is by no means certain that Anglo-Saxon paganism had buildings of this kind. Shrines were made of wood, in the open air (see ii. 13).

P. 96 This chapter forms a natural sequel to i. 26; it is likely that Bede inserted i. 27–32 at a late stage. The Canterbury church dedications resemble those of Rome. Christ Church was the equivalent of the old Roman cathedral of St Saviour (later called St John Lateran); the single monastery just outside the walls was dedicated to the two patrons of the Roman monasteries. This last was intended to be a mausoleum for kings who would be protected from evil spirits by the prayers of the monks and the adjacent shrines of archbishops.

P. 97 The awkward position of this chapter partly depends on the date of the battle it describes: it also introduces the reader to the founder of Northumbrian political power.

P. 98 For Bede Gregory was contemplative monk, teacher and pastor, as well as 'apostle of the English', a title accorded him also by the Whitby Life of Gregory and by Aldhelm. His pastoral ideals were variously realized by Augustine, Theodore, Aidan and Cuthbert. After including Gregory's epitaph Bede recounts the famous and not necessarily fictitious story of the English slaves in the Roman market: its place, out of chronological sequence, reveals a different source, probably both oral and Northumbrian.

P. 104 British Christianity, which had once produced saints like Patrick and Gildas, now revealed insular resentment which Bede found it hard to forgive. The meeting place was probably in Gloucestershire.

P. 106 For Bede the refusal to accept the usual Easter date was a sign of disunity and schism. The subsequent battle of Chester is dated *c.* 615

P. 108 Bede gives the day of the month, but not the year of Augustine's death, which was between 604 and 609.

P. 111 These are the kings who are called Bretwaldas (i.e. Overlord kings) by the Anglo-Saxon Chronicle. Although they held this title in turn, the reality of their developing overlordship varied greatly. Originally the title indicated a southern pre-eminence, but the powerful Northumbrian kings later gave it a more extensive geographical reality in accordance with its meaning of 'Britain-ruler', originally a flattering name based on poetic terminology.

P. 114 The initial refusal of Eadbald to accept Christianity is an indication that conversion had not been forced on the magnates. On the other hand the pagan reaction in Kent and Essex demonstrates the underlying persistence of these beliefs. In several kingdoms the pattern was first, conversion of king and magnates, more or less shared by the rest of society, followed by apostasy and revival of paganism, and finally by a reconversion which proved permanent.

P. 115 The Four Crowned Martyrs are usually identified as Persian stonemasons who were martyred in the early fourth century. The Canterbury dedication could be due to relics of them coming from Rome (see i. 29), where they were venerated in a fine basilica on the Celian Hill, close to Augustine's monastery. See *ODS*, s.v.

P. 118 Irish evidence suggests that about this time Man was considered Irish; Welsh annals confirm Bede's account that Anglesey (including Puffin Island) was occupied by Edwin.

P. 119 A thegn was a noble man by birth and usually in the military service of the king. See WH, p. 223.

P. 129 This famous account, a rhetorical set-piece, shows the council or witan in action. The arrangement of the hall has been strikingly confirmed by the excavations of the royal palace at Yeavering, Northumberland, where a large hall and open-air assembly place have been identified. There was also a Christian church, where Aidan later preached. The speeches in this account were probably retouched by Bede: the deeply poetic and religious character of the second one are striking. The assembly probably took place at York.

P. 131 Native buildings at this period were of wood or wattle: stone ones were due to Italian or Gaulish influence.

P. 133 Redwald was the most famous, but probably not the only king whose commitment to Christianity was fatally flawed: he wanted to worship God simply as a more important spirit (daemonium) among a number of others who included the pagan gods. The Christian Church rightly rejected such syncretism. Redwald is nowadays generally believed to have been the king whose burial ship at Sutton Hoo (the grave-goods are now at the British Museum) has revolutionized our knowledge of the material culture of a provincial royal court. The weaponry, the jewellery and the everyday objects reflect a civilized way of life which can be glimpsed also in the pages of *Beowulf*. The baptismal spoons (with *Saulos* and *Paulos* inscribed) and some motifs on silver bowls are Christian in character, but the overall impression is not specifically Christian. This accords well with one who first accepted, but later rejected Christian belief. Bede's mention of Wuffings suggests a connexion between East Anglia and Sweden: the Sutton Hoo burial mounds are similar to those at Old Uppsala, while the helmet reveals Swedish workmanship.

P. 134 This was Littleborough. The fine pen-portrait of Paulinus is unique and convincing.

P. 135 The *Tufa* was covered with feathers or foliage and was the standard of the Bretwalda. A large, wrought iron object among the Sutton Hoo treasures may well be its framework.

P. 138 These have been identified respectively as the bishops of Armagh, Clonard, Nendrum, Connor and Bangor. The remainder (from Cronan onwards) are abbots of Moville, Tory Island, Leighlin, Inis Celtra and Iona. Saran Ua Critair died in 661, the others sooner.

P. 140 Cadwalla (Cadwallon), son of Cadfan was king of Gwynedd. There is some Welsh evidence to suppose that Edwin, when an exile at Cadfan's court, had been his companion, but none the less had conquered Anglesey and Man (Bede, ii. 9). In his attempt to throw off Northumbrian domination, he appealed to the most obvious neighbouring ally.

P. 143 The kingdom of Northumbria formed a union (more or less precarious) between several tribes and two dynasties. Bernicia (Bernice) extended from Durham and Northumberland northwards as far as the Firth of Forth (at its greatest expansion), while Deira (Dere) was approximately all Yorkshire, with Lindsey (Lincolnshire) a province claimed by both Northumbria and Mercia. First Bernicia was dominant under Ethelfrith, then Deira under Edwin, then Bernicia again under Oswald and Oswy. These dynastic struggles with exiles, violence and assassination, of which Oswin (ii. 14) was an unfortunate casualty, formed the political background to the growth of the Church. No ecclesiastical historian could possibly ignore them.

P. 147 The island monastery of Iona was founded by Columba (c. 521-97), from which he and his followers spread the Gospel in Dalriada and the western islands. The churches subject to Iona included Durrow and Derry in Ireland, and initially Lindisfarne.

P. 148 Ninian (5th century), founder of Whithorn and apostle of the surrounding area, was a scholar, a traveller and an admirer of St Martin of Tours

(d. 397), some of whose relics he may have brought to Scotland. The identity of the southern Picts and the extent of his apostolate are disputed (see *ODS*, s.v.), Whithorn became a bishopric in *c* 731.

P. 148 The charismatic Columba, a characteristic example of Irish 'pilgrimage for Christ', was best known to the Middle Ages through the Life by Adomnan (abbot of Iona 679–704) which records mainly his prophecies, miracles and visions; but Bede did not know this work. The extent of Columba's apostolate has often been exaggerated; he should be considered the most important figure of the Irish in Scotland rather than as the apostle of Scotland in any widespread sense. According to Adomnan there were some Anglo-Saxon monks at Iona in Columba's day before 597, (see *ODS*, s.v.).

P. 149 Bede was describing Iona custom, not the prevalent practice in Ireland as a whole. Evidence for this reveals a reality which was not uniform. Overall the bishops did not lose either their sacramental or their pastoral roles, but were subject to some temporal control by abbots, especially where these acted as major secular rulers. See R. Sharpe, in *Peritia* iii (1984), 230–70.

P. 150 What made Lindisfarne different from Iona was that its ruler from the beginning was a bishop. It seems that an abbot or prior was the internal ruler of the monks, subordinate to the bishop (iv. 26). The choice of Lindisfarne as the Northumbrian See appears most unsuitable for accessibility and location, but intelligible because of its closeness to the royal palace at Bamburgh. Bede's lyrical and idealized portrait of Aidan is best understood if full weight is given to its contrast to 'the apathy of our times'. His followers lived presumably very close to Lindisfarne if they had really adopted the Latin psalter and the monastic fasts. Not much is heard of Aidan in southern Northumbria. Bede's sources were part monastic (Lindisfarne?) and part royal (Yeavering?).

P. 153 Birinus (like Augustine and Paulinus) was consecrated bishop before starting his apostolate. He too preached primarily to the king. Oswald's role in the gift of Dorchester is one of confirmation by a bretwalda looking for an ally against powerful Mercia. Dorchester had been a small Roman town and was in an area of dense and early Anglo-Saxon settlement. Its vulnerability to Mercia as a border town together with the consolidation of the Wessex monarchy at Winchester soon led to its losing its pre-eminence. It was however revived as the bishopric of the East Midlands in the early tenth century.

P. 154 Agilbert, bishop of Dorchester 650–60, took part in the synod of Whitby (664) and was bishop of Paris 668–90. He died and was buried at Jouarre, where his fine tomb survives. See *ODS*, s.v.

P. 155 Faremoûtier-en-Brie was founded by St Fara *c*. 617.

P. 155 Bede surely intended this statement to apply specially to monasteries for women, as several had been founded for men. Anglo-Saxon nunneries however generally developed as 'double' monastieres like Whitby, Ely, Wimborne Minster and others, where there were separate enclosures for men and women. The monks exercised priestly and educational functions besides providing protection.

P. 157 Ethelburga, Fursey (iii. 19), Etheldreda (iv. 19) and Cuthbert (iv. 30) are four saints whose bodies Bede claimed were incorrupt. Cuthbert's is by far the best documented: see *AB*, pp. 20–21; *ODS*, s.v.

P. 161 Virgil: *Aeneid* ii. I.

P. 163 Acca, disciple and successor of Wilfrid as Bishop of Hexham, (709–31, d. 737), was Bede's diocesan bishop, to whom he dedicated some exegetical works.

P. 164 The spread of Oswald's cult was caused partly by the very brutality of his killing and dismemberment, a sign of his sacrificial killing to pagan gods. His head went to Cuthbert's shrine at Lindisfarne, part of the body to Bardney (later to Gloucester) and part was taken by Willibrord to Frisia. This in turn led to churches being dedicated to him in Holland, France, Switzerland, Germany and North Italy.

P. 168 Penda's attack on Bamburgh would have been unknown but for this passage describing Aidan's saintly powers. He mounted at least one more invasion before his disastrous confrontation with Oswy at Winwaed (iii. 24). Aidan seems to have been the first to use the island of the Inner Farne as a hermitage, but he was followed by Cuthbert (iv. 28), Ethelwald (v. 1) Felgild (*AB* 100–01) and subsequently by several monks from Durham.

P. 171 The East Anglian kings' reigns are now dated as follows: Redwald (ii. 15) d. *c.* 620; Earpwald, *c.* 620–27, who was possibly succeeded by an unknown pagan king; then Sigbert, 630–*c*.650 who shared the rule with Egric for a part or the whole of his reign; Egric died with him. Anna succeeded at an unknown date and died in 654: his daughters Etheldreda and Sexburga (iv. 19) were abbesses of Ely, Ethelburga (q.v.) was Abbess of Faremoûtier, Withburga of Dereham was a recluse (not mentioned by Bede) see *ODS*, s.v.

P. 173 The monastery founded by Sigbert and Fursey was probably at Burgh Castle, near Yarmouth, but in *c.* 651 it was deserted by the Irish: after that date Irish influence in East Anglia ceased.

P. 176 This was Lagny on the river Marne. Fursey's cult was based on Péronne in Picardy, long called *Perrona Scottorum*. There were other Irish monasteries in France and Switzerland, some of them founded by Columbanus, for whom see *ODS*, s.v.

P. 176 Felix died in 647; Thomas in 652; Bertgils in 669. The Gyrwas' province included parts of Northants, Hunts, Lincs and Cambs.

P. 177 The conversion of the Middle Angles (a sub-kingdom of Mercia in Leics and Northants) was an important development prepared (as in Kent and Northumbria) by a royal marriage. The place of Peada's baptism was

Walbottle (Northumb.). Bishop Dimma (Diuma) of the Middle Angles was buried and venerated at Charlbury (Oxon). Cedd moved on to Essex *c.* 653–64, when he took part in the Synod of Whitby (iii. 22 and 25).

P. 179 This is Bradwell-on-Sea (Essex), where Cedd's church, built in Kentish style, survives modified but recognizable. His community presumably formed a minster church, whose priests lived under an appropriate, non-monastic rule.

P. 182 Hereditary succession to monasteries as family property was a deeply rooted custom, sometimes protected by law, in both Germanic and Irish society. It was not universal but it long remained in England and elsewhere. Bede's letter to Egbert (see below) presupposed it, but reformers like Wilfrid and Benedict Biscop opposed it, as did Ethelwald and others in the tenth century. See *EHD* I, 864–49.

P. 184 Described in biblical terms by Bede, this battle of the Winwaed was decisive for the time in ending the Mercian military threat to Northumbria. Followed by the inappropriate rule of Mercia by Oswy and the assassination of Peada, it is a reminder of the real violence of contemporary life.

P. 184 Whitby, a double monastery for nuns and monks ruled by an abbess, was intended to be the burial place for the Northumbrian royal family. Eanfled, Oswy's widow, became Abbess until she was succeeded by her daughter Aelffled, the friend of both Cuthbert and Wilfrid.

P. 186 Interesting architectural details about the church at Lindisfarne precede the long account of the Synod of Whitby. The fact that Rome's most intransigent supporter was the Irishman Ronan shows that the line-up was not simply 'Irish versus Roman' but rather 'Western Europe and Southern Ireland versus Iona and its Irish satellites'.

P. 187 The confusion between Dalfinus, count of Lyons and his brother Annemundus, Archbishop of Lyons occurs in Eddius' Life of Wilfrid, from which Bede almost certainly copied it.

P. 187 Streanaeshalch was the Old English name for the place renamed Whitby after the Viking invasion and settlement there. Although always called the synod of Whitby, it would be more accurately named the synod of Streanaeshalch.

P. 189 A similar argument had been used by the Irish controversialist Cummian, when he wrote to Segene, Abbot of Iona in *c.* 634: 'Rome is mistaken; Jerusalem is mistaken; Antioch is mistaken; the whole world is mistaken; the Britons and the Irish alone hold the truth.' *Epistola de controversia paschali* (*PL* lxxxvii, 974). Bede's account of this synod should be compared with Eddius' shorter but similar one in his Life of Wilfrid (*AB*, pp. 14–16).

P. 192 This is not so much an appeal to the historical Peter or to his relics, but rather to the belief that Peter's decisions were best known in current controversies through the decisions of his successors, supported by the whole Church, especially in the Councils. With the Petrine primacy went Petrine approval of the 'Roman' Easter. The decision taken at Whitby would bind all Northumbrians and subsequently through the council of Hertford the whole Church of Anglo-Saxon England.

P. 192 Differing styles of tonsure, itself a sign of dedication to God, became concrete symbols of party loyalties. Roman clergy shaved the crown of the head but left a circle of hair all round the head above the temples, in memory of Christ's crown of thorns. The Celtic clergy however shaved the front of the head, but allowed the hair to grow in flowing locks behind. Allegiance could be discerned at a glance. In the language of controversy the first was attributed to St Peter, the second to Simon Magus. Both claims are quite unhistorical. See also E. James, 'Bede and the Tonsure Question', *Peritia* iii (1984), 85–98.

P. 194 Bede contrasted this with later practice in the Letter to Egbert, p. 344. It seems that he rhetorically exaggerated some aspects of the poverty of Lindisfarne: only a wealthy monastery could have produced the Lindisfarne Gospels thirty-five years later. Its wooden buildings could have been rich and extensive.

P. 195 Egbert was the future reformer and monk of Iona; see v, 22.

P. 196 This was Chlotar III, son of Clovis II, both of whom were concerned with building and reforming monasteries.

P. 197 This is usually interpreted as joint action by the bretwalda Oswy in association with the local king of Kent. More subtle suggestions make Bede read back from the papal letter to formulate his original statement.

P. 200 Wulfhere, son of Penda, ruled Mercia 659–74. Bede does not mention him among the bretwaldas (ii. 5), but his attack on Egfrith was at the head of a joint southern army (Eddius, c. 20, *AB*, pp. 126–7).

P. 205 Theodore and his immediate successors exercised more authority than later archbishops of Canterbury, especially in the north. Bede presents Theodore's episcopate as ideal because the Church was united under firm government, learning flourished, dioceses were multiplied and two councils were held. Bede's account of Theodore is the only extended near-contemporary one extant, but compare Eddius' remarks in his Life of Wilfrid (*AB*, pp. 150–52).

P. 212 Mayo was subsequently known as Mayo of the Saxons, whose monks were praised by Alcuin as specially learned. After Colman's death they converted to Roman usage and their bishop claimed close association with York.

P. 213 The exclusively ecclesiastical Council of Hertford was the first of its kind in England. It promulgated canons which were first approved by the Council of Chalcedon and subsequently adopted in the West. There was nothing original in them but they were amazingly appropriate to the needs of the Church in England in 673. Nine out of the ten canons concerned the clergy, who were to be united in their celebration of Easter (ch. 1, extending Whitby's decision nationwide), and to be just in respecting the rights of both bishops and monasteries (chs. 2–6); synods should be held regularly at Clovesho and the number of dioceses increased. The tenth canon on marriage reaffirms traditional belief and practice, and gives no support to seeming laxity in the so-called *Penitential of Theodore*.

P. 225 Theodore divided bishoprics in the same kingdom and took good care to avoid their having territory in more than one. He also made each diocese territorial with a town as its centre rather than a kingdom: in this way he made the new dioceses conform to the pattern of the older ones, Canterbury and Rochester, and to that of the Western Church as a whole.

P. 236 Etheldreda (Audrey) was one of the most famous saints of Anglo-Saxon England. Bede's account, which came partly from Wilfrid, should be compared with that of Eddius in his life of Wilfrid (*AB*, pp. 125–8). Bede's interest in her was strong enough to be expressed in a poem in her honour (iv. 20).

P. 237 Sexburg had founded the nunnery of Minster-in-Sheppey. The sarcophagus mentioned was Roman and came from Cambridge.

P. 239 The following version reproduces the alphabetic acrostic with which Bede adorns his tale, including his spelling of Christ with initial X (the Greek letter chi) as in the familiar abbreviation Xmas. It does not attempt to imitate his elaborate device of repetitive half-lines, which makes the hymn remarkable rather for ingenuity than poetic excellence.

P. 240 Theodore is here shown as a political mediator and also as an ecclesiastic proposing, like others since, the compensation of *wergild* instead of bloodshed.

P. 243 This chapter is of special interest because it tells us what could happen to the wounded in battle; it reveals how hard it was for a nobleman to hide his class; it relates to an incident probably inspired by Gregory's *Dialogues* (iv. 59) but which would have appealed to believers in magic, whereby physical bonds were loosened whenever spiritual powers came into play; it reveals the existence of Frisian merchants in London and shows Bede including a miracle story at one remove from the reality.

P. 243 As in the cases of Aidan, Theodore, Caedmon and others, Bede's account of Hilda represents virtually all we can know about her.

P. 250 The special importance Bede attached to this topic is shown by the elaborate biblical structure of the account. Both the skill and the wide range of Caedmon's poems made them a powerful aid to preaching; their impact could be continuous through learning by heart, while their appeal to a race familiar with poetry and music transcended all classes. Caedmon adapted ancient themes and formulas to the revolutionary new ideas of

Christianity. The disappointment for us is that none of Caedmon's poems have survived, but from the age of Bede we have the unique poem *The Dream of the Rood* (ed. M. Swanton, 1970): this enables us to glimpse what has been lost.

P. 254 Ps. 65 (66), 5.

P. 254 This was at Nechtansmere (Donnichen, Forfar) in 685. Although Egfrid's attack on the Irish was unprovoked, that on the Picts was not. The victor Bridei had expanded his power to the Orkneys and had refused to pay tribute. Egfrid had already lost a battle to the Mercians in 679 which had resulted in the loss of Lindsey. Cuthbert rightly warned him about the power of the Picts: Bede correctly regarded this battle as the end of Northumbrian supremacy. Aldfrid, a well educated but illegitimate son of Oswy by an Irish princess, revived Northumbrian fortunes in a smaller and more realistic territory. After the Forth was recognized as the most viable frontier, relations between Picts and Northumbrians were good (v. 21). Egfrid and Aldfrid were both benefactors to Wearmouth and Jarrow (*AB*, pp. 194 and 201); both quarrelled with Wilfrid (*AB* pp. 151–53 and 170–73).

P. 254 Virgil; *Aeneid* II, 169.

P. 256 The last six chapters of this book are devoted to Cuthbert, the most characteristic saint of Bede's Northumbria; they also occur in manuscripts of Bede's *Life of Cuthbert* (*AB*, pp. 41–102). The incorruption of Cuthbert's body (iv. 30) led to the spread of his cult, a process increased by the several translations of his relics 875–1104. See *ODS*, s.v.

P. 267 John of Beverley, Bishop of Hexham from 687, Bishop of York 705–21, ordained Bede deacon and priest. His miracles were recorded by Alcuin as well as by Bede. Their varied character and frequent direct speech give them special interest.

P. 276 Ine (Ini) was powerful and important. His law code (*EHD I*, 364–72) reveals a Christian society so well established that some breaches of Church law met secular punishment; there are also passages which reveal the existence of high-status Britons under Saxon rule. As a pilgrim to Rome at the end of his life he was in the company of several other Anglo-Saxon kings. He ruled from 688 to 726.

P. 278 Chapters 9–11 are devoted to the work of Anglo-Saxon missionaries preaching among the Germanic tribes whence they had come: this longer list should be compared with i. 15. Egbert's plans seem to have veered between an Irish 'pilgrimage for Christ' in voluntary exile and a more direct pilgrimage to Rome. In fact he achieved neither and was diverted to Iona.

P. 280 Willibrord (658–739), a Yorkshireman who was educated by Wilfrid at Ripon, went into voluntary exile on his departure, in Ireland for twelve years. There he joined Egbert and Wigbert. His consecration as Bishop at Rome is recorded in his own hand in the *Calendar of St Willibrord*. He worked long and hard with varying success at the mission entrusted to him by the papacy: he set up a Metropolitan See at Utrecht (Holland) and founded a monastery at Thhtrmach (Turrmlburg), where he died in 739 and was buried. See Levison, pp. 53–69 and *ODS*, s.v.

P. 281 Apostles to the Anglo-Saxons in England counted no martyrs among their number, but the Hewalds were the first martyrs among the Anglo-Saxon missionaries on the Continent. The principal reason for their different fates was the attitude of the secular rulers: in England initially reserved, then supportive but in Frisia initially hostile from the natives but later protective from the Emperors Pippin and Carloman.

P. 284 Chapters 12–14 contain a series of visions concerning the after-life. The first is the most famous, the last provides the important conclusion that these stories should rouse people to penance. Such stories have a long history. Pagan prototypes led to Christian versions: first in Ireland, then in England (both Boniface and Bede provide examples); later they flourish again in the twelfth century until the culmination is reached in Dante's long masterpiece.

P. 286 Virgil: *Aeneid* VI, 268.

P. 293 Adamnan, Abbot of Iona 679–704, wrote the famous *Life of Columba*. Bede, who did not know this work, concentrated on the description of Jerusalem, thus introducing his readers to the historical geography of early Christianity. Bede clearly approved of pilgrimage, whether to local shrines or to Rome or to distant Jerusalem.

P. 298 Daniel is mentioned in Bede's Preface; he also corresponded with Boniface, surprisingly never mentioned by Bede. Aldhelm (639–709) is treated briefly as monastic founder (of Malmesbury, Frome and Bradford on Avon) and Bishop of Sherborne from 705. His works in prose and verse can now be read in modern editions (ed. M. Lapidge). Bede's tribute to Aldhelm's style seems ironical to anyone who has studied both writers; there can however be no doubt of Aldhelm's learning, mainly acquired at the Canterbury schools of Theodore and Hadrian.

P. 300 Bede's extended obituary of Wilfrid depends partly on the Life of Eddius, partly on other sources. Bede omitted much: the Synod of Austerfield, several papal letters and most of Wilfrid's European involvement, for which see *AB*, pp. 132–35 and 153–57. The epitaph however mentions summarily Wilfrid's importance as builder and art-patron. It has often been said that Bede's account lacks warmth: twenty years after Wilfrid's death Northumbria's need was for the healing of his controversies. It may be that this detached account contributed to a view accepted by all parties and the emergence in Alcuin's writings of both Cuthbert and Wilfrid as official Northumbrian saints. See also D. P. Kirby, *St Wilfrid at Hexham* (1974) and 'Bede, Eddius Stephanus and the Life of Wilfrid,' *EHR* lxxxxviii (1983), 101–14.

P. 301 Actually Archbishop Annemund, brother of Dalfin Count of Lyons.

P. 307   See M. Lapidge, 'The School of Theodore and Hadrian,' *ASE* xv (1986), 45–72.

P. 309   This chapter emphasizes Jarrow influence in Pictland in matters both computistical and architectural. Although the letter is often believed to be Bede's, there seems no need to exclude the possibility of Ceolfrith, Bede's early teacher, writing it himself or through another.

P. 309   Plato, *The Republic* 473D.

P. 318   Acts viii, 20–21; where Peter rebukes Simon Magus.

P. 322   Aidan had arrived in Northumbria in 635; it was now 716. The reconciliation of Iona and the death of Egbert suitably concluded the story of growth from diversity to unity.

P. 323   This is often believed to refer to the defeat of the Arabs at Tours by Charles Martel in 732, a date which would make it a later addition; Wallace-Hadrill however suggests it records the victory of Odo of Aquitaine in 721. Both victories seem to accord badly with the comet of 729.

P. 324   This is Candida Casa or Whithorn in Galloway.

P. 325   This cryptic remark, unexpected from a monk, is best explained by reference to the Letter to Egbert; see below, pp. 343–47.

BEDE'S LETTER TO EGBERT

P. 337   Egbert succeeded Wilfrid II as Bishop of York in 732; he became archbishop (as Bede forecasted) in 735, and died in 766. He was praised by Alcuin, who was one of his pupils, for outstanding rule and teaching, for generosity to the poor and to the church of York. Egbert was fortunate in his successor Ethelbert, whose educational achievements surpassed his own. Egbert was of royal birth, being the relative of one king and the brother of another.

P. 337   Matt. xxv, 21–23.

P. 338   Matt. xxv, 30.

P. 338   Gregory's *Pastoral Care* was the standard medieval textbook for the training of the clergy; his *Homilies on the Gospels* inspired many sermons.

P. 339   2 Cor. xi, 28–29.

P. 339   cf. Acts xiii, 2–42. In the next sentence Bede's word caput (= head) is translated as father.

P. 340   Ambrose, *De Virginibus* iii, 4, 20. The repeated genuflexions associated with particular prayers were an Irish custom. Bede's translations of the Creed and the Lord's Prayer have not survived, but their existence is significant evidence of the interest of this cloistered monk in pastoral needs. Other Old English translations of these prayers are extant, but none are in the Northumbrian dialect.

P. 341   cf. Matt. xxv, 18.

P. 341 Matt x, 7–9.

P. 341 cf. 2 Tim. iv, 2.

P. 341 1 Sam, xii, 3.

P. 341 ibid, xii, 4.

P. 342 Psalm xcviii, 7–8.

P. 342 In this paragraph *praesul* is translated in its first meaning 'protector' rather than the more usual 'prelate.'

P. 342 1 Tim. vi, 10.

P. 342 1 Cor. vi, 9–10.

P. 342 Ceolwulf, Egbert's cousin, became King of Northumbria in 729; he was deposed and restored in 731, the year when Bede dedicated his *History* to him. He resigned the throne in 737 and became a monk at Lindisfarne; he died in 760.

P. 343 cf. Num. xi, 16.

P. 343 See above, pp. 90–91.

P. 343 Unlike many medieval monks, Bede actively supported the concept of monasteries becoming dioceses. There is no firm evidence that Wearmouth or Jarrow was ever considered as the site of a diocese.

P. 344 Bede shows a sensitivity to the needs of the State as well as of the Church not always manifest in monastic writings.

P. 344 Is. lvii, 6.

P. 345 This passage is partly inspired by St Benedict's description of false monks in the first chapter of his Rule.

P. 346 Matt. xv, 14.

P. 346 Unless Bede is indulging in rhetoric, he here criticizes Northumbrian bishops of the previous thirty years, who included Acca of Hexham, Oethilwald of Lindisfarne, John and Wilfrid II of York.

P. 347 Is. lx, 22.

P. 347 cf. *Rule of St Benedict*. ch. 65.

P. 348 Eccl. viii, 10.

P. 348 This precious evidence on this topic is extremely rare. It seems however that this recommendation of frequent communion by the laity was generally disregarded by the Church until the twentieth century. Similarly Gregory's and Bede's plans for York to have twelve suffragan bishops were not realized throughout the Middle Ages, partly because the Scottish bishoprics rejected the hegemony of York.

P. 349 Acts v, 29.

P. 349 Lk. xii, 33; xiv, 33.

P. 349 Lk. vi, 20.

P. 349 Lk. vi, 24.

P. 349 1 Cor. vi, 9.

P. 349 1 Cor. vi, 10.

P. 349 Eph. v, 5.

P. 350 Matt. xv, 3.

P. 350 Matt. xv, 13.
P. 350 Matt. vii, 13–14.
P. 350 See above, pp. 241–3, 359 for further evidence of this belief.
P. 351 I Jn. ii, 15–16.

CUTHBERT'S LETTER ON THE ILLNESS AND DEATH OF THE VENERABLE BEDE THE PRIEST

P. 357 Cuthbert later became Abbot of Wearmouth and Jarrow. Some letters of his addressed to Lul, Archbishop of Mainz, survive in the correspondence of St Boniface (ed. M. Tangl, MGH, nos. 116, 126, 127). The first of these, dated 764, gratefully acknowledges the gift of a silk robe 'for the relics of Bede, our master of blessed memory.' Cuthbert continued: 'It seems right to me that the whole race of the English in all provinces wherever they are found, should give thanks to God that he has granted to them so wonderful a man in their nation.' Hence his importance was not regional, but national.

P. 357 It is agreed that Ascension Day fell in 735 on 26 May.

P. 358 This phrase and some others seem inspired by the Office of St Martin of Tours, based on the letter by Sulpicius Severus on his death.

P. 358 Heb. x, 31.

P. 358 cf. *Rule of St Benedict*, ch. 4: a monk should 'keep death daily before one's eyes.'

P. 358 This poem is not found elsewhere, but it occurs in both Northumbrian and Wessex dialects in the continental and insular manuscripts respectively of this Letter. Bede was its probable author.

P. 358 Antiphon for Magnificat from Vespers of Ascension Day. This quotation contains the same number of words as the Old English poem above.

P. 358 Heb. xii, 6.

P. 358 cf. Paulinus, *Vita Ambrosii*, ch. 45 (PL xiv, 43).

P. 359 The passage translated by Bede was probably the whole of the first six chapters. Verse 9 is mentioned here, but it seems likely that Bede finished the chapter, (see below) at verse 70 in modern versions, the first climax of the Fourth Gospel. See Howlett, p. 145.

P. 359 C. W. Jones and P. Meyvaert have both emphasized Bede's academic distrust of Isidore's work. By making excerpts from his *De natura rerum* (here and often called *Libri Rotarum*) Bede removed the erroneous elements, so saving his students much frustrating work. Meyvaert (*Famulus Christi* p. 59) here reads *exceptiones* instead of *excerptiones* and translates it as 'corrections.'

P. 359 This refers to the Rogation processions at which the Litany of Saints is sung and their relics carried.

P. 359 Pepper presumably for flavouring the frequently dull monastic food,

incense as a perfume in monastery or church and handkerchiefs as a
welcome personal accessory. Gregory's *Dialogues* (ii. 19) mention nuns
giving presents of handkerchiefs to one of Benedict's monks.

P. 359 See above pp. 241–3 for passages attesting to the current belief in the
value of posthumous masses and prayers.

P. 360 cf. Acts xx, 38.

P. 360 2 Tim. iv, 6.

P. 360 Isaiah xxxiii, 17.

P. 360 John xix, 30.

P. 360 cf. Mark xii, 32. Wilbur is Bede's scribe.

P. 360 cf. Luke xxiii, 46. By changing his position Bede could see his place of
prayer.

P. 360 If it were ever written, this Life has not survived. See above, note 1.

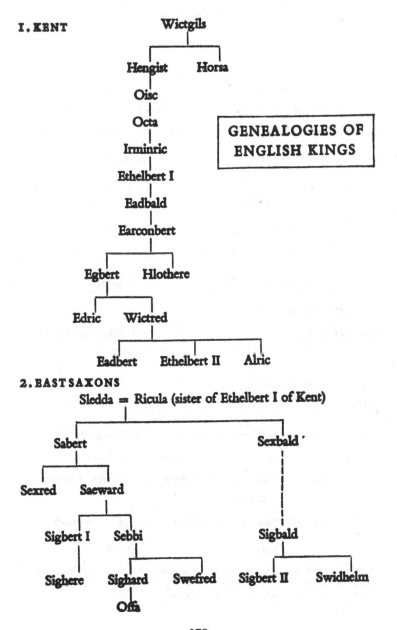

1. KENT

Wictgils
├── Hengist
│   └── Oisc
│   └── Octa
│   └── Irminric
│   └── Ethelbert I
│   └── Eadbald
│   └── Earconbert
│   ├── Egbert
│   │   └── Edric
│   └── Hlothere
│   └── Wictred
│   ├── Eadbert
│   ├── Ethelbert II
│   └── Alric
└── Horsa

GENEALOGIES OF
ENGLISH KINGS

2. EAST SAXONS

Sledda = Ricula (sister of Ethelbert I of Kent)
├── Sabert
│   ├── Sexred
│   └── Saeward
│   ├── Sigbert I
│   │   └── Sighere
│   └── Sebbi
│   ├── Sighard
│   │   └── Offa
│   └── Swefred
└── Sexbald
    ┊
    └── Sigbald
        ├── Sigbert II
        └── Swidhelm

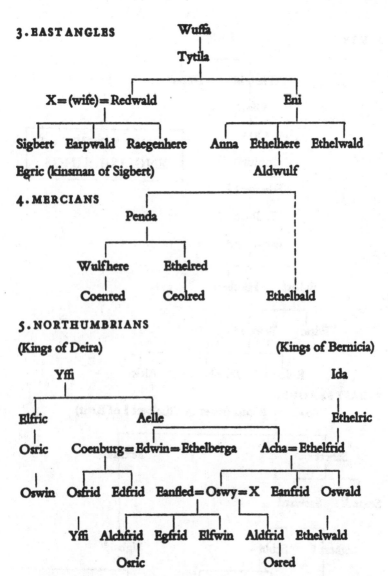

3. EAST ANGLES

Wuffa

Tytila

X = (wife) = Redwald

Eni

Sigbert   Earpwald   Raegenhere

Anna   Ethelhere   Ethelwald

Egric (kinsman of Sigbert)

Aldwulf

4. MERCIANS

Penda

Wulfhere   Ethelred

Coenred   Ceolred   Ethelbald

5. NORTHUMBRIANS

(Kings of Deira)   (Kings of Bernicia)

Yffi   Ida

Elfric   Aelle   Ethelric

Osric   Coenburg = Edwin = Ethelberga   Acha = Ethelfrid

Oswin   Osfrid   Edfrid   Eanfled = Oswy = X   Eanfrid   Oswald

Yffi   Alchfrid   Egfrid   Elfwin   Aldfrid   Ethelwald

Osric   Osred

Note that Edwin's first wife Coenburg was daughter of a Mercian king Cearl, whose connexion with the preceding genealogy is not clear; his second wife Ethelberga was daughter of Ethelbert I of Kent.

6. WEST SAXONS

The genealogy of these kings, mainly derived from sources other than Bede, is too complicated to justify its inclusion here.

FOR FURTHER READING

✤

P. H. Blair, *The World of Bede* (1970)

J. Backhouse, *The Lindisfarne Gospels* (1981)

G. Bonner, ed., *Famulus Christi* (1976)

G. Bonner, D. Rollason, C. Stancliffe, eds., *St Cuthbert: his cult and his community* (Woodbridge 1989)

J. Campbell, ed., *The Anglo-Saxons* (1982), *Essays in Anglo-Saxon History* (1986)

B. Colgrave and R. A. B. Mynors, *Bede's Ecclesiastical History* (Oxford 1969): J. M. Wallace-Hadrill, *Bede's Ecclesiastical History: a Historical Commentary* (Oxford 1988)

A. C. Evans, *The Sutton Hoo Ship Burial* (1986)

D. H. Farmer, *The Oxford Dictionary of Saints* (1987)

R. Gardner, *Healing Miracles* (1987)

D. P. Kirby, *St Wilfrid at Hexham* (Newcastle 1974)

M. Lapidge, *Aldhelm: the Prose Works* (Woodbridge 1979)

H. Mayr-Harting, *The Coming of Christianity to Anglo-Saxon England* (2nd ed. 1990)

J. N. L. Myres, *The English Settlements* (Oxford 1986)

T. Reuter, *The Greatest Englishman* (1980)

M. Swanton, *The Dream of the Rood* (Manchester 1970)

J. F. Webb and D. H. Farmer, *The Age of Bede* (Penguin Classics 1988)

D. M. Wilson, *The Archaeology of Anglo-Saxon England* (Cambridge 1976)

P. Wormald and others (eds.), *Ideal and Reality in Frankish and Anglo-Saxon Society* (Oxford 1983)

The following older books are still very useful:

C. F. Battiscombe, *The Relics of St Cuthbert* (Oxford 1956)

W. Levison, *England and the Continent in the Eighth Century* (Oxford 1956)

F. M. Stenton, *Anglo-Saxon England* (Oxford 1965)

C. Plummer, *Bedae Opera Historica* (Oxford 1956)

The
BRITISH ISLES
at the time of
BEDE

PICTS

Iona

Dumbarton
Pennelaun
Abercorn
Melrose
Hexham
Gateshead
Carlisle
Whithorn
Derwentwater
I. of Man

Armagh

Durrow

Anglesey
Bangor
Oswestry
Chester

Caerleon
Malmesbury
Bredon
HWICCAS
Dorchester
Reading

WEST
SAXONS
Winchester
Stoneham
Meon
Redbridge
Bosham
Selsey
Solent
I. of Wight

Inchkeith
Coldingham
Lindisfarne
Bamburgh
Yeavering

Jarrow
Monkwearmouth
Hartlepool
Whitby
Catterick   Lastingham
DEIRA
Ripon
York   Goodmanham
Beverley
Leeds   Barrow
Hatfield   LINDSEY
Littleborough   Bardney
Lincoln   Partney

MERCIANS
Lichfield   Stamford   GYRWAS   Burgh
MIDDLE   Peterborough   EAST   Castle
ANGLES   Oundle   Ely   ANGLES   Dunwich

EAST   Rendlesham
Hertford   SAXONS
St Albans   Hatfield   Ythancaestir
London   Barking
Chertsey   Rochester   Reculver   Thanet
Canterbury   Richborough
SOUTH   KENT
SAXONS
Ambleteuse
Boulogne
Etaples

BERNICIA
NORTHUMBRIANS
BRITONS

SCOTS

0   50   100   150
Miles

ARMORICA

GAUL

Paris →

W. Bromage

York

ANGELN

London
Canterbury
EAST FRISIA
WEST FRISIA
Utrecht
Etaples
Boulogne
Péronne
Echternach
Cologne
Fulda
Andelys
Compiègne
Trier
Mainz
Paris
Lagny
Metz
Chelles
Troyes
R. Loire
Langres
Strasbourg
Tours
Brie
Lyons
Vienne
Milan
Pavia
R. Po
Arles
Is. of Lerins
Rome
R. Seine
R. Moselle
Rhine
R. Rhône

0   100   200   300 miles

Western Europe at
the time of Bede

INDEX

The following abbreviations are used: ab. abbot; archb. archbishop; b. bishop; br. brother; d. daughter; E. East; k. king; M. Middle; N. North; n. note; q. queen; S. South; s. son; W. West.

THE STORY OF PENGUIN CLASSICS

Before 1946 ... 'Classics' are mainly the domain of academics and students; readable editions for everyone else are almost unheard of. This all changes when a little-known classicist, E. V. Rieu, presents Penguin founder Allen Lane with the translation of Homer's *Odyssey* that he has been working on in his spare time.

1946 Penguin Classics debuts with *The Odyssey*, which promptly sells three million copies. Suddenly, classics are no longer for the privileged few.

1950s Rieu, now series editor, turns to professional writers for the best modern, readable translations, including Dorothy L. Sayers's *Inferno* and Robert Graves's unexpurgated *Twelve Caesars*.

1960s The Classics are given the distinctive black covers that have remained a constant throughout the life of the series. Rieu retires in 1964, hailing the Penguin Classics list as 'the greatest educative force of the twentieth century.'

1970s A new generation of translators swells the Penguin Classics ranks, introducing readers of English to classics of world literature from more than twenty languages. The list grows to encompass more history, philosophy, science, religion and politics.

1980s The Penguin American Library launches with titles such as *Uncle Tom's Cabin*, and joins forces with Penguin Classics to provide the most comprehensive library of world literature available from any paperback publisher.

1990s The launch of Penguin Audiobooks brings the classics to a listening audience for the first time, and in 1999 the worldwide launch of the Penguin Classics website extends their reach to the global online community.

The 21st Century Penguin Classics are completely redesigned for the first time in nearly twenty years. This world-famous series now consists of more than 1300 titles, making the widest range of the best books ever written available to millions – and constantly redefining what makes a 'classic'.

The Odyssey continues ...

The best books ever written

PENGUIN (◉) CLASSICS

SINCE 1946

Find out more at www.penguinclassics.com